THE SECRET SIX

The Secret Six: Cases & Events

1930	
Philip Meagher Shot	February 5, 1930
The Secret Six Founded	February 7, 1930
Kopelman Kidnapped	February 28, 1930
Congressman DePriest Extorted	September 8, 1930
Lincoln National Bank Robbery	September 17, 1930
Alexander Jamie Hired	October 31, 1930
Marion Wright Extorted	November 22, 1930
William Kuhn Detained	December 6, 1930
1931	
Police Shakedown of Verner Daniels	January 5, 1931
Shirley Kub Flees Grand Jury	January 21, 1931
William Kuhn Nolle Prossed	January 21, 1931
Plumbers Union Raid	January 22, 1931
Shirley Kub Gets Four Months	March 13, 1931
Shirley Kub Testifies Again	March 21, 1931
Serritella and the Short-Weights	April 1, 1931
Clark Gable Stars in *The Secret Six*	April 17, 1931
Edward Andell Embezzlement	August 11, 1931
First National Kidnapping Co. Report	September 14, 1931
First National Bank Robbing Co. Report	September 15, 1931
"Branches in All Cities"	September 15, 1931
Edgar Dudley Does Los Angeles	September 24, 1931
Godman Shoe Theft	October 5, 1931
Al Capone Goes to Prison	October 24, 1931

Lawrence Stern Jewelry Heist	November 4, 1931
Second National Bank Robbing Co. Report	November 10, 1931
Shirley Kub Gets Thirty Days	December 30, 1931
1932	
Return of the Lincoln Bank Bonds	January 5, 1932
Third National Bank Robbing Co. Report	January 7, 1932
Call for a National Secret Six	February 4, 1932
Indian Ghost Gas Station Bombing	February 7, 1932
Third National Kidnapping Co. Report	March 5, 1932
Milk Charity Conviction	March 11, 1932
Dr. James Parker Kidnapped	March 14, 1932
Fourth National Bank Robbing Co. Report	March 22, 1932
Col. Randolph Calls for Torture	August 7, 1932
John Swanson Wiretaps Secret Six	September 1, 1932
Secret Six Accuses John Swanson	October 24, 1932
John Swanson Strikes Back	October 26, 1932
The Secret Six Grand Jury Fiasco	October 28, 1932
First Smith Extortion Bombing	November 09, 1932
Kuhn Verdict	December 02, 1932
Second Smith Extortion Bombing	December 31, 1932
1933	
Shirley Kub Visits the Jeffery Tavern	January 16, 1933
The End of the Secret Six	January 18, 1933

THE SECRET SIX

THE RISE AND FALL OF CHICAGO'S GREATEST VIGILANTES

KEVIN E. MEREDITH

RED LIGHTNING BOOKS

THIS BOOK IS A PUBLICATION OF

Red Lightning Books
1320 East 10th Street
Bloomington, Indiana 47405 USA

iupress.org

First Printing 2026

For customers in the European Union with safety or GPSR concerns, please contact Mare Nostrum Group B.V., Mauritskade 21D, 1091 GC Amsterdam, The Netherlands. Email: gpsr@mare-nostrum.co.uk

Cataloging information is available from the Library of Congress.
ISBN 978-1-68435-239-5 (hardback)
ISBN 978-1-68435-240-1 (ebook)

To Amelia, Jodie, and Connie.
May you one day find
your grandfather's books interesting.

CONTENTS

THE SECRET SIX

Introduction

ALMOST A CENTURY after his reign of terror ended, Alphonse "Al" Capone remains America's most famous gangster, a Chicago crime kingpin who dispensed illegal liquor and gangland murder with the same ruthless efficiency.

The only serious crime that was ever pinned on him, however, was tax evasion. In summer 1931, a few months before he was sentenced to eleven years in federal prison for that crime, Capone said something peculiar.

"The secret six has licked the rackets," he mourned. "They've licked me. They've made it so there's no money in the game any more."[1]

The secret six.

Often it was capitalized: The Secret Six.

And in some of the tens of thousands of newspaper articles written about the shadowy Chicago crime fighters in the early 1930s, they put quotation marks around the name, as if they weren't quite sure what to make of them: "secret six" or "Secret Six."

Who were the Secret Six?

By any objective measure, they were the greatest vigilantes in American history, or quite possibly human history.

Besides getting credit from Capone himself for their work destroying his vice empire, the Secret Six—founded in Chicago in February 1930—can claim a stunning sweep of accomplishments: They solved dozens of major cases, pioneered the use of groundbreaking new crime fighting technologies, and played a leading role in the launch of the Untouchables made famous by G-Man Eliot Ness. They were summoned before Congress, emulated by other cities across America, and repeatedly cited in newspapers nationwide as experts on crime and punishment.

And then, amid the promise, the success, the hype, and viable plans for launching a nationwide network of vigilante groups, the Secret Six vanished. On January 18, 1933—one month shy of their third birthday—the nation's greatest vigilantes limped into history's dustbin.

There would be no more Secret Sixes. Mysterious, well-funded men (and women) would never again battle crime in Chicago, or in any other American city. Crime victims from that day forward would turn consistently to public authorities.

Between February 1930 and January 1933, the Secret Six reigned, its fame and prowess driving America into a new model of crime and punishment and, arguably, into a new way of life. And then, something happened that ended it all; the nation turned away from the experiment and, for the most part, never spoke of it again. Why?

This is the book about what happened, about the rise of the Secret Six and what ended them, a first and essential accounting of a grand, messy and at times hilarious story, a story intrinsic to America's gangster era, to the downfall of its most famous crime lord, and to the nation's general history as well. This isn't the first book that mentions the Secret Six, and the plaudits still roll in, praise for the intrepid crime fighters in books about Capone, early 1930s Chicago gangsterdom, prohibition, and the Chicago World's Fair of 1933 and 1934. Until the story is told completely, however, it really hasn't been told at all.

Behind the heroics, the legends, and the claims of greatness that persist even today, there was the true story, as remarkable, shocking, and downright laughable as any other in the nation's history. It was a story of violence, sex, hubris, torture, bigamy, cynical public relations, and consistent lying. There were deals with the devil, feral recklessness, and a breathtaking betrayal. And in the end, a self-immolating madness.

America rarely does things by half measures, and when its second largest city decided to go into vigilantism, it went all in. And when the Secret Six fell, they fell hard.

PART I

DAMSEL IN A BURNING CITY

But if the worst comes to the worst, we cannot do better than emulate our ancestors.

—**Col. Robert Isham Randolph, February 10, 1930**

1

The Case of the Extorted Debutante

THE FIRST LETTER arrived on November 22, 1930.

It was addressed to eighteen-year-old Marion Wright, at her family's grand Chicago apartment at 49 East Cedar Street. Marion, the daughter of wealthy steel executive William Van Doren Wright, was just weeks away from her debut at the exclusive Casino Club. But first she'd have to deal with something less pleasant.

The typewritten letter, postmarked at Chicago's Loop post office the previous evening, read (Letters and newspaper extracts appear as written, including errors.):

> Dear Miss Wright: In this present business depression many organizations are being authorized to relieve the unemployed. Working on this plan, I am authorized by my council to force a person or persons by extortion to donate their share.
>
> My associates have perfected a wonderful but deadly dart. With the use of powerful but silent springs this weapon is capable of striking an object at 3,000 feet. Imagine this dart dipped in a very deadly poison. Now, with this knowledge, I am positive you will comply with our wishes and place at my disposal a small sum of $25,000.* The account must be in denominations of $20.
>
> Of course, I will expect you to withhold all the transactions from the police. But then, if you fail, which I hope you will not, then I will be forced to do something rash. It will be necessary for you to advertise in the Chicago

* Almost $500,000 in 2024 dollars.

Renowned Chicago architect Benjamin Marshall designed and lived in the elegant apartment building at 49 East Cedar Street, where eighteen-year-old Marion Wright received increasingly creepy extortion letters from "Lester McKay." / Kevin Meredith

Tribune personal column the following words: "McKay, everything done as per instruction."

The amount must be sent in a plain, sealed package to "Mr. Lester McKay, care General Delivery, Chicago."

Otherwise, the date for our showdown will be set for November 30, 1930.

Honestly, Miss Wright, I hope it won't be my choice to commit the deed, because, darn it, I fell in love with your photo, which shows the power of your personality.[1]

More typewritten letters followed in the coming days. The writer's skin-crawling creepiness grew, along with, by the end, his greed and unhinged malevolence. The second letter, postmarked at the Wicker Park postal substation on November 26, 1930, read:

> As a rule we will warn you three times. This being the second time, you will have the pleasure of reading a third and last letter. The 30th day of this month is almost here and I am certain that the counting of seconds, as you must be doing, is not such a pleasant reaction.
>
> We shall use every method to get the desired part of our demands. Kidnapping is crude and there is no thrill to that. So we have a wonderful way of changing our victim's mind.
>
> May I again state our demands? If so, then follow our words of demand closely.
>
> You must place in a plain sealed package 1,250 of the $20 currency bills. The total amount will be $25,000. The package must be addressed as following:
>
> Mr. Lester McKay, General Delivery, Chicago. This done, you must place in the Chicago Tribune the following advertisement (in the personal column): "McKay, everything done as per instruction."
>
> Have seen you in person last night, and may I compliment you on your good looks?[2]

The third letter was also sent from Wicker Park on November 26, this one postmarked at 10:30 that night and apparently provoked by Miss Wright's failure to place the personal ad in the *Chicago Tribune*:

> Dear Miss Wright:
>
> It will soon be necessary for me to throw caution to the winds and from sheer desperation expose myself to the danger of committing the crime you have been warned of.
>
> Allow me to say a few words of heed. I wonder if you realize that at the present time that a life is held very cheaply. If you value the life if your father, or maybe your own, highly, the small sum of $25,000 ought not to stand in your way.
>
> Some time ago I would myself laugh at any person who would send me a letter of threat, but now, knowing the inside force of an extortioner has changed my mind. May I advise you to do something and fulfill the part of the demands as required? Being nonchalant, I would even walk into any trap that you can conceive. This is my last warning, Marion. Pardon me, but may I call you by that name?
>
> Yours for a long life
>
> Mr. Lester M'Kay[3]

tracted for by any one but myself after this date JOE W. KOWALSKI. :

M. D. P.: PLEASE COMMUNICATE WITH me. M. R.

McKAY: EVERYTHING DONE AS PER instruction. M. S. W.

BUSINESS PERSONALS.

Marion Wright's message to her extortionist, from the personals section of the November 27, 1930, *Chicago Tribune*. / Chicago Tribune/TCA

The next day, the first part of the extortionist's instructions were carried out. In the personals section on page 43 of the November 27, 1930, *Chicago Tribune*, this two-line notice appeared: "McKAY: EVERYTHING DONE AS PER instruction. M. S. W."

"McKay" spotted the notice. His bizarre fourth letter, postmarked December 1 and sent again from Wicker Park, read:

> Dear Miss Wright:
>
> On my arrival from New York this evening I have discovered that my organization has blundered something terribly. It is one curse of employing drug addicts.
>
> I have noticed from reviewing the back issues, or rather copies, of the Tribune that your response has been very gratifying and will extend the final day for December 5 of this month coming.
>
> To you this may look impossible, as the date of the previous letters point to the fact that I must have resided in this city at that time. I have written the letters in advance, and these I mailed when demanded.
>
> I am going to send an unknown person for this package, and any means on your part to trace him or otherwise arrest him will mean the death of some one in your household. May I depend on the love that you have toward your parents as means for the safety of the delivery of the amount demanded?
>
> My best regards to you, Miss Wright. As ever.
>
> Mr. Lester McKay.[4]

Although the requested ad had been published, the money was apparently never delivered. A fifth letter was sent around December 3, 1930, one week before Marion's social debut: "I find I must make an example of this household, especially your father. The police promise protection, but the real protection is from the underworld. The package now must contain $50,000 in the denominations I suggested. Remember the police have no use for dead bodies."[5]

Extortion, like kidnapping, was big business during the Great Depression, and for good reason. Grab someone from a wealthy family, hold on to them for a few days, and reap a fortune in cash. Or skip the snatching and just send letters, as our friend Lester McKay did, and if the mark came through, enjoy the ill-gotten gains.

Many extortion missives were sent by cranks with no ability to follow through. There was thirteen-year-old Parker Kaehler, for example, who in November 1932 sent an anonymous letter to his neighbor in Evanston, Illinois, demanding that he leave $100 under some bushes. If the neighbor failed to follow through, young Kaehler warned, "You have the choice of having your home bombed, or probably a few kids killed."[6]

When the boy went to collect the fruits of his scheme, he found not cash but six cops waiting for him, guns drawn. According to the news article, "Police sent him home after an appropriate lecture."

But sometimes, the extortionists were deadly serious.

When Samuel A. Cowan, a real estate broker of some means in Cleveland, Ohio, didn't pay the $5,000 demanded of him, they came to his house in the dark of night and set off a bomb that "wrecked the porch of the house, damaged the front and showered plaster and wreckage through some of the front rooms."[7]

No one was hurt in the blast, but according to press reports, "the detonation was heard for miles around and hundreds of spectators gathered at the house."[8]

A wealthy bank president was bombed *before* he'd received a demand for cash. The explosive went off in the hands of his wife, who was not hurt. A note included with the bomb advised its recipients to await further instructions, which came a few weeks later. The price for peace? A sum of $4,000, or about $75,000 in 2024 dollars.[9]

Which extortionist letters were backed up, and which were sent by cranks? One couldn't tell. So Marion Wright's father, understandably, was frightened enough by the letters that he hired a bodyguard for her.[10]

A decade after the extortionist reached out to her, Marion would join the US Army, and her husband would throw himself off the tallest building in Hollywood. But in late 1930, the letters were her biggest concern. "I had a gentleman with me as a guard," she recalled. "He went everywhere with me. I was extremely nervous."[11]

In addition to hiring protection for his daughter, Mr. Wright called the authorities. He did not get in touch with the Chicago Police Department, however. In what most likely qualified as one of the worst decisions he ever made, Wright called in the Secret Six. The Secret Six sprang into action, and the Windy City vigilantes quickly launched another of their signature debacles.

2

A City on Fire

BY 1930, VARIOUS ORGANIZATIONS IN CHICAGO were keeping a tally of bombings in the city. The numbers were impressive, according to a December 28, 1930, story in the *Chicago Tribune*. "Officials of the Employers' association announced that there had been 71 bombings in 1930," the *Tribune* reported. "While the number was below that for preceding years, the damage was far greater—$508,450,* as compared to $197,109 in 116 bombings in 1929. Three persons have been killed and a score injured."

The story, which reported 116 bombings each in 1928 and 1929, had been prompted by a particularly active month of explosions: "The Carson-Pirie bombing was the fourth in a series of explosions which have shaken the walls of large business concerns since Dec. 7. On that day the main plant of Sears, Roebuck & Co. was bombed; two days later a charge of dynamite wrecked the entrance and shattered windows on the north end of the Furniture Mart, and on Christmas eve the largest building in the world—the Merchandise Mart—was damaged by a bomb."

Officials speculated that many of the bombings had resulted from labor disputes, for example, as retribution for the use of nonunion truck drivers at the businesses that had been attacked. Other bombings were blamed on "bootlegger wrangles," disputes over who was buying booze from whom, such as the December 26 explosion that "shook a Chinese restaurant and an adjacent night club." Another theory about those behind the bombings

---

* About $10 million in 2024 dollars.

was put forth by acting Police Chief John Alcock, who guessed that someone wanted to make Chicago's finest look bad. Gordon Hostetter, executive director of the Employers Association, suspected a Soviet plot intended to disrupt the 1933 World's Fair and its celebration of free-market innovation.[†]

Whatever the causes, more than once a week in 1930, something in Chicago was getting blown up.

The Great Depression, whose start is usually dated to October 29, 1929, and which is generally credited for more than a decade of financial upheaval and rampant crime in the nation, can't be blamed for all the mayhem in Chicago. In fact, the Windy City had been suffering from chaos and corruption for years. In 1926, no less than Vice President Charles Dawes, a Nobel Peace Prize recipient and longtime resident of the city, went to the US Senate to ask for a federal intervention.

Dawes spoke of a "reign of lawlessness and terror" in Chicago, whose start he dated to 1922. Chicago's criminal element, Dawes claimed, "have formed a super-government of their own . . . who levy tribute upon citizens and enforce collection by terrorizing, kidnapping and assassinations." Chicago's crime lords, Dawes continued, "have become fabulously rich as rum-runners and bootleggers, working in collusion with police . . . politicians and public officials." Although the making and selling of liquor had been outlawed by the US under Prohibition in 1920, Dawes charged that five breweries were selling beer "openly and under police protection." He added, "evidence multiplies daily that many public officials are in secret alliance with underworld assassins, gunmen, rum-runners, bootleggers, thugs, ballot-box stuffers, and repeaters.[‡]"[1]

Dawes cast his aspersions widely, pointing to "the attendance of judges, city and county officials, and politicians as mourners at the funerals of hoodlums slain by gangland's guns."[2]

The federal government declined to offer any help to Chicago, and others accused Dawes of exaggerating the city's distress to make his political rivals look bad. But there was ample room for concern. In 1931, the city of 3.5 million people suffered 344 murders, or almost one per day.[3]

---

† The plot, if there was one, failed. The World's Fair was held in Chicago as scheduled and was a rousing success.

‡ A repeater is someone who keeps getting caught breaking the same law.

Prohibition had been a gift to Chicago's gangsters. What should one expect when something everyone wants is available from only the crooks? According to one study, American alcohol consumption dropped significantly in 1920, the first year of Prohibition, but began rebounding the next year, quickly reaching about 70 percent of pre-Prohibition consumption.[4]

Once booze had been outlawed, pimps, petty thieves, and backroom bookmakers found a new market ripe for the taking, and some of them became fabulously wealthy businessmen, protecting their markets with murder and extortion, finding new lines of commerce to invest in, and infiltrating local governments and police stations.

Sitting atop Chicago's vice rackets was Al Capone, who remains to this day America's best-known gangster, a man whose rumored fortunes made him one of the richest people in history. The truth of Capone's wealth and criminal reach can be hard to establish; search his name on the internet and you'll find consistent but unsourced assertions that his net worth reached $100 million at his financial peak, and he paid himself a salary of $3 million[§] per year.[5]

Capone operated massive distilleries and thousands of speakeasies in Chicago, and allegedly, to keep things running smoothly, he paid out half a million dollars in bribes to the police monthly.[6]

Capone also contributed an alleged $50,000 to the mayoral campaign of William Thompson in 1927. When Thompson won, according to allegations published in the *New York Times* and elsewhere, he held up his end of the bargain, granting Capone "the undisputed right to run gambling houses, operate slot machines and control the sale of beer and liquor in the area south of Madison Street."[7]

When bribes and political contributions didn't work, Capone was equally comfortable with murder. "Scarface Al," as he was sometimes called, is widely blamed for the 1929 St. Valentine's Day Massacre, in which seven associates of the rival North Side Gang, run by George "Bugs" Moran, were lined up against a wall and murdered in cold blood by four well-armed assailants. "Two of the executioners were in police uniform, and the seven men thought they were facing only arrest," reported the *Chicago Tribune*.[8]

[§] Roughly $2 billion and $60 million, respectively, in 2024 dollars.

We may assume that William Van Doren Wright, executive of the Edgewater Steel Company, was well aware of all this, of the crime and chaos that gripped the city, of the hint of police involvement in mass murder, and of the fact that no one was ever convicted for that Valentine's Day bloodshed.

So in late 1930, when Wright's daughter started getting those extortion letters, it's perhaps understandable that his first call wasn't to the police, but to the Secret Six.

3

The Tenth Man

THE HORRIFIC STATE CHICAGO had been reduced to by early February, 1930, was neatly summed up in an article appearing on page three of the *Miami Herald*. "Tenth Man Is Shot in Chicago Streets," the headline blared, a second headline announcing a "13th Bomb Explosion." The story's first paragraphs read like the opening lines of a superhero comic book, except that most reputable comic book publishers would have toned it down a little:

> Murderers, bombers and bank robbers terrorized bankrupt* Chicago today in what police called one of the worst crime waves in the city's history. The tenth man to be shot in the streets here in six days fell critically wounded on the staid University of Chicago campus. . . . Seven of the others, mowed down with a machine gun or revolver fire, have died. The thirteenth explosion since the first of the year . . . wrecked two stores, sent dry good and shoes sailing through the streets. . . . The second bank robbery of the new year terrified a dozen employees and customers. Two robbers fired shotguns in [the] bank. . . . The epidemic of holdups, apartment house robberies and sluggings continued unabated. There has been an average of 20 such crimes here nightly for the last week.[1]

The "tenth man to be shot" was of particular note at the time, his murder carried on the wires and mentioned in newspapers across America. While

* Adding insult to injury, Chicago was in the midst of a budget dispute, unable to pay its police, firefighters, or teachers. See, for example: "Controller Calls for 41% Police Slash; 32% Reduction for Firemen in Schmidt's Plan; Teachers Payless as Vacation Begins," *Chicago Tribune*, December 21, 1929, 1.

The Secret Six was launched in the wake of the shooting of Philip Meagher, who was supervising the construction of a hospital, shown here, that still stands on the University of Chicago campus. / Kevin Meredith

most of the killings during that era were gang versus gang violence, the tenth victim was no criminal. He was Philip Meagher, construction superintendent for the H. B. Barnard company, and at the time of his shooting, he was managing the construction of a new hospital on the University of Chicago campus, at the intersection of Fifty-Ninth Street and Maryland Avenue. Meagher was said in the press to be twenty-five, married, and the father of two children.

The *Chicago Tribune* offered the most detailed account of the attack, which took place on Wednesday afternoon, February 5, 1930. According to the paper, two men showed up at the construction site to ask about Meagher, and afterward they headed back to their car and parked a block away. Soon after, Meagher emerged from a construction shed to walk with carpenter foreman Andrew Ebert to Drexel Avenue, a few blocks away. The two men pulled up behind him in their car, "alighted from it and commenced firing at Meagher's back from a distance of eight or ten feet. The first bullet punctured a kidney and narrowly missed severing Meagher's spinal column. Meagher turned and the gunmen ran back to their machine, firing three more shots as they reached it."[2]

Meagher was taken to the hospital and lingered at least four more days, or maybe much longer,[†] telling the police "I have no enemies" and speculating that labor troubles were to blame. As the *Chicago Tribune* noted in its coverage of the crime, Meagher had been permitted by court decree to hire nonunion workers to build the hospital (a beautiful stone structure that now houses the University of Chicago's Student Wellness Center), but someone wasn't happy about it.

Regardless of the reason, this was the shooting that got under Chicago's collective skin. Meagher was young, respected, a Chicago stalwart who should have given decades more service to his city. If he could be attacked, anyone could. Something had to be done, and if the police wouldn't do it, the people would.

Just a day after the shooting, when it looked as though Meagher might recover, an article in the *Chicago Tribune* about the crime included this portentous sentence: "Col. Robert Isham Randolph, president of the Chicago Association of Commerce, also took cognizance of the Meagher shooting and said he would call it up for discussion when the executive committee of the association meets tomorrow."

[†] There is some question concerning whether Meagher died as a result of the shooting, for which no one was ever convicted. Quite possibly, he wanted the gangsters to think he was dead so they wouldn't come after him again, and the press cooperated. Multiple press outlets, in fact, beginning on February 10, 1930, referred to Meagher's death or murder, not just his wounding (see, for example, the phrase "Philip H. Meagher's Death" in "Direct Action" on page 6 of the February 10 *Decatur (Illinois) Herald*), but an official death announcement or obituary didn't appear in the indexed press at that time (or on any later discoverable date). Furthermore, the 1940 US Census reports a Phillip Meagher at 9618 S. Prospect Avenue in Chicago, with an occupation listed as superintendent for the building construction industry. Contrary to newspaper reports at the time of his shooting, however, the Phillip Meagher in the Census spelled his first name with two *l*'s, had just one child, seventeen-year-old Wayne, living at the home, and was born in 1896, making him about thirty-four at the time he was shot.

This was no mere citizens' meeting, it should be noted. The Association of Commerce represented Chicago's top business concerns, and its members were among the city's wealthiest and most powerful. These were people who could add or take away hundreds of jobs with the stroke of a pen and who decided what got built where, a group whose political endorsements carried considerable weight. In an interview he gave to the *Saturday Evening Post* later that year, Randolph summed up the Association of Commerce as comprising "fourteen well-organized departments, 91 employees, 6,948 members."[3]

Randolph, elected president of the Association just two months before, was confronted the morning after Meagher's shooting and "asked very pointedly what we were going to do about it," he told the *Evening Post*.

In the next two days, the Association of Commerce moved with such speed that one must wonder if Randolph had already worked out his plan and was simply waiting for an excuse to hatch it.

On Friday, February 7, the Association's top leaders convened at the Hotel LaSalle, summoning Chicago's two top law enforcement officials—Chicago Police Chief William Russell and John Swanson, the state's attorney for Chicago and Cook County.

"We plan a frank talk," Randolph told the *Chicago Daily News* prior to the meeting. "We are asking Russell and Swanson to lay their cards on the table. This meeting is the first step in a war on crime which will continue as long as I am president of the Association of Commerce."[4]

Randolph then went on to say two very different things to the *Daily News*: "We are going into the situation with open minds, without any preconceived notions," he said first. And then he gave away the game: "I believe that we will form a small committee, made up of representatives of the community at large, to work with the police and prosecutor. I believe the police department is undermanned and we may take steps to remedy that situation."

So, while Meagher was still fighting for his life, Russell and Swanson met with the executive committee of the Association of Commerce in a futile bid to explain themselves. Russell complained that his department was "undermanned," asserting, "We have enough policemen to . . . fight criminals after the crimes are committed, but we have not nearly enough men effectively to prevent crime." Swanson's contributions to the proceedings were less definitive, dismissed in a *Chicago Tribune* article as "a somewhat extended speech" which "some of the business men after the meeting declared they were unable to remember."[5]

In a statement issued prior to the meeting, Swanson was more direct, and perhaps more memorable: "I am only the state's attorney, and I can only prosecute such matters as are placed before me by the constituted authorities. If the people want me to step out of my official job and clean up this situation they must provide me with the money and the authority. Then I will find the men and go to work."[6]

Swanson also offered an interesting take on criminology, proposing that recent crackdowns on lesser crimes had led to greater ones. "The bloody conflict now in progress," he told the *Chicago Herald and Examiner* in a February 7 story, "is due at least in part to the suppression of the gambling, liquor and vice interests, cutting off the rich revenues previously obtained by less violent methods, and driving the hoodlums into the 'business' of assassination."

Neither Russell's nor Swanson's entreaties before the Association of Commerce could stop what happened next. By the end of the meeting—and clearly a foregone conclusion all along—a bold new plan was launched by the Association of Commerce and reported nationwide: "The time has come," the group asserted ominously in a written statement, announcing the "Appointment of a 'committee of citizens of known courage and action [who] represent sufficient resources and influence," and which would be "authorized to study the situation and prepare a definite plan of action."[7]

The preamble to this declaration of vigilantism, if such it can be called, read as follows:

> Hundreds of indictments without subsequent convictions, countless felonies where no arrests have followed, the almost total failure of the responsible agencies to halt bombing and other criminal attacks upon legitimate business, and the attempt during the past few days of paid killers to murder Philip H. Meagher, a Chicago builder of unquestionable reputation and long service to the community, indicate conclusively that the time has arrived when the legally responsible authorities must be called upon either to show why they cannot carry out their oath of office, or for the citizens of the city to take steps to assure the maintenance of justice and a definite curtailment of crime.[8]

"The problem of law enforcement in Chicago," the statement continued, "has reached a stage where representative citizens and business organizations must take personal and direct action."

In fewer words: The cops and the courts have failed us. Now it's our turn. The time for vigilantism has arrived.

Chief Russell and State's Attorney Swanson could have protested, could have called for cooler heads, might have offered a plan of their own to get things under control. They did no such thing, however, both offering meek non-endorsements of the Association's declaration.

"Prosecutor Swanson, after reading the business men's statement, said the criticism of himself and his office was not justified," read the *Chicago Tribune.* "Commissioner Russell would not comment on the business men's meeting. Nor would he discuss the subsequent statement."[9]

Russell and his supporters weren't going down without a fight, however. The Citizens' Police Committee, formed the previous year and working with Russell to reorganize his department, issued a "statement of confidence" in the chief, blaming the city's current crime crisis on an underfunded force, and Prohibition.

"Prohibition has given the gangs and the gunmen great resources. All the gangsters are organized," Police Committee member Col. Albert A. Sprague told the *Chicago Tribune,* adding hopefully (and quite erroneously, as it turned out), "Anyway, it's pretty ridiculous for any group to say it is going to take over the duties of a police chief or force and I know our business men have no such ideas."[10]

That Friday night, in a bid to let his actions do the talking where words no longer mattered, Russell ordered a major crime offensive, what the *Chicago Tribune* called "a departmental policy of harassing all persons with unsavory records."[11]

The chief, "smarting under the critical utterances of the Association of Commerce," ordered his forces to "bring in the fellows who are really bad," announced a frontpage article in the *Minneapolis Tribune.* "I want every known gangster in Chicago hunted down tonight and brought to the bureau."[12]

The names, addresses and haunts that made up Chicago's criminal underbelly were well enough known that at least one newspaper, the *Chicago Daily News,* published a front-page list of them on February 7. The list, praised by Col. Randolph himself and other business leaders as an essential "crime-war guide," also offered a compendium of the very public shenanigans of local gangsters:[13] "Beer and alky are being made and delivered as usual.

The racketeers can be found riding elevators to their Loop offices. Some hotel lobbies are still cluttered with their presence. Tailor shops see them in lengthy conference as to pockets that will hold a pistol without spoiling the sartorial effect. The hoodlums can be seen waving forks in downtown tea-rooms and restaurants by day and night, making whoopee in the brightest of the city's oases for playboys."[14]

The syndicate led by Al Capone, Chicago's top mobster, conducted a "gangland court" daily in one of the city's hotels, the *Chicago Daily News* claimed, where a man identified only as "the Enforcer" (probably Frank Nitti) held decision-making authority over everything from violence among outlaws to routine police assignments: "Not a 'pineapple' (hand grenade) can be tossed at a recalcitrant saloon-keeper, not a blackjack nor pistol butt can go klunk on a foe's head, not a 'nosey' or 'hungry' policeman can be transferred, not a rival beer truck hijacked, nor an enemy of the syndicate be sent on a one-way ride until 'the Enforcer' has given the word."

In the face of such brazenness, Russell's troops were as eager to prove themselves as he. "Spurred by talk that 'the police have failed us' in the last fortnight of homicide and thuggery," read the *Minneapolis Tribune,* "155 detective squads dashed through Chicago last night and put on the most extensive rodeo or roundup in the history of Midwest crime detection."

"Although the police force has not had a pay day since before Christmas, every man was eager to do more than his part," reported the *Chicago Tribune.* "They were working extra hours and with days off canceled, and those working all night were ready for a long day in court today."[15]

The Minneapolis paper claimed that after the first night of the raid, "915 prisoners packed every precinct station in the town to the bursting point."

The count more than doubled in the next two days. "Police Seize 2,101 in 3 Day Crime Drive," declared the *Chicago Tribune* in a front-page headline February 12.

The picking up of thousands of Chicago toughs should not be expected to proceed without drama, and there was no shortage of it during the raids, the *Tribune* reported in a front-page story February 10. Detective Frank Vitek noticed a car parked in an alley near Ogden and Kirkland Avenues and headed toward it. "When he was within a few feet of the car the men in it started shooting at him," claimed the article. One of the bullets hit his thumb, which had to be amputated. Another shootout occurred when

Abraham Rudsky robbed Michael Calurs, a butcher, of $50.‡ "As soon as he had the chance Calurs armed himself and ran after Rudsky, firing at him and being fired upon in return. Sergt. (Lawrence) Cooney and his men heard the shots and took Rudsky into custody after a struggle." Several more arrestees were caught in the middle of stickups.

A major element of the drive was the "showup," managed by Lieutenant John Sullivan. According to the *Chicago Tribune,* "nine prisoners at a time were paraded and made to talk before a room in which 500 citizens were watching to identify men they had seen engaged in crimes."[16]

The *Minneapolis Tribune* added further details to the showup, claiming that 451 suspects "were paraded at police headquarters before an almost equal number of persons who had been robbed, slugged, shot, kidnaped, or bombed, and under a blinding glare of electric lights 28 were picked out by the victims."[17]

The count of Chicagoans wanting justice eventually reached one thousand people, the *Minneapolis Tribune* reported. "So great was the crowd of victims in the corridors that more than 500 were turned away." To limit the press of humanity, those clamoring for a look at the suspects "had to be issued tickets at the district stations."[18]

This was a new broom, Russell made clear, and not just a one-time purge inspired by talk of vigilantism. "Every gangster found out of jail at any time must be brought in at once," the article quoted him as saying. "I have given you orders that apply not only for today. Those same orders must be followed, tomorrow, day after, next week, next month."

Where does one go to find the bad guys in 1930 Chicago? A boxing match, for one. Russell and Chief of Detectives John Egan brought forty men to a boxing event at the Coliseum, twenty-five plainclothes cops mingling with the attendees from seats scattered about the hall, fifteen more watching the exits. With police funds running dry, the plan ran into a minor fiscal crisis, according to the *Chicago Tribune,* with Chief Russell paying for the tickets out of his own pocket. In the end, forty cops and the department's top brass caught just seven men, two named colorfully: "Cockeyed Mulligan" and John "Dingbat" Oberta. Only two were kept in jail overnight, while the other

‡ Worth almost $2,000 in 2024 dollars.

five were released with a warning from Chief Egan that "his department would permit no more congregating by hoodlums at prize fights, no more swaggering in loop hotels and restaurants. Every racketeer is subject to arrest on sight," so "to avoid future discomfiture they had best leave town."[19]

Illegal gun possession was a special focus of the raids, a charge leveled against thirty-three of those arrested. Was it working? Had the mere talk of vigilantism spurred Chicago's cops to new heights in the war on crime? Yes, at least temporarily.

"Before the arrests began, stickups averaged over 50 each night for the preceding week, with a record of sixty-one last Friday night," the *Chicago Tribune* reported. On the first night of the campaign, robberies had been cut by almost half, to twenty-six, and robberies fell by half again, to thirteen, for each of the next two nights.[20]

"Thus far 65 gunmen have been swept off the streets," reported the *Reading (Pennsylvania) Times*, "reducing murder and robberies with a gun to (the) smallest figures in a decade."[21] Predictably, amidst the criticism from the Association of Commerce, Russell and his top detective, Egan, crowed of their successes in near-epic terms in that *Chicago Tribune* article. "Chicago policemen place their lives second to the performance of duty," Russell boasted, adding, "The police will not relax and the department is going to kill these hoodlums, put them in prison, or drive them out of the city."

"It's a quiet night; we have broken the criminal back," Egan said a little after midnight Monday morning, three days into the campaign. "They're on the run. Most of them were from out of town, anyway, and they've gone to wherever they believe they will get a better reception."

Egan's claim received a solid—albeit unenthusiastic—endorsement from those other places. The *Minneapolis Tribune* reported a week after the crackdown began that its effects were being felt in two Illinois towns and as far away as Missouri. "Quincy, Peoria and St. Louis are complaining that Chicago is driving criminals into their territory. Scores of fugitives from the (Chicago) police here have been taken in these cities."[22]

"From St. Louis," reported the Associated Press, "a sudden increase in crime brought a police order to watch for transient Chicago criminals."[23] Even the oft-cynical *Chicago Tribune* praised the efforts, noting that "police kept up such an offensive against the criminal element that Chicago might soon come to be known as the gunless city."

Col. Randolph, however, was not impressed. The *Baltimore Sun* said the weekend campaign "means nothing to Mr. Randolph. . . . He declared the department would get plenty of time to bring in people who mean something in gangland and that the gesture of the last two days meant nothing at all."

And there were still doubters among the Fourth Estate as well. The *Minneapolis Tribune,* for example, noted that "when the blotters had been filled, there was a notable lack of such names as Moran, Capone, Guzick, Aiello. . . . The gentlemen who, under the spotlight of publicity, have built up Chicago's red record had somehow eluded the police net."[24]

"Not a single real-size gunman, gangster or racketeer has been apprehended," agreed the *Baltimore Sun,* which dismissed the raids as "theatrical" in a front-page headline. Chicago's kings of crime, the article alleged, "apparently have been tipped off and are laying low."[25]

Nevertheless, the campaign was so successful that it had to be paused after a week for one impressive reason, according to Pennsylvania's *Reading Times*: Police "ceased raiding the haunts of crime this morning largely because all cell room in the city was occupied."[26]

However, effective as it was in bagging the crooks and bringing down, at least temporarily, Chicago's crime numbers, Russell's gambit to restore his force's relevance was too little too late, and the citizens of America's second largest city (only New York was bigger) were going to take things from here, thank you very much. In the end, the top cops all but stood aside.

It's quite likely this was a singularity in American history, law enforcement in a major city (or in any village, town or borough, for that matter) tolerating a crimefighting plan hatched by someone other than themselves.

The national press took note. "Chicago Citizens Open War on Crime," announced the *New York Times* headline on February 8. "Business Group Assails Officials and Begins Drive to End Reign of Violence."[27]

Other reports struck a distinctly cautionary note, however, as they compared this vigilante effort to the Wild West, and to the gangsters themselves. "Businessmen feel they should organize among the same line as the gangsters if they expect to clean up city," declared a story in the *Richmond (Indiana) Item* February 11. "Just as existing 'enforcing committees' of gangland now mete out their type of justice in the underworld," read the piece, "so this committee of . . . business and civic leaders devise ways to make these outlaws observe society's laws."[28]

The *Herald and Review* of Decatur, Illinois, voiced its misgivings this way: "One wonders what the citizens can do when the police and prosecutors fail. Will they organize vigilante associations or hire armed guards, reproducing the crude forms of justice of the frontier or the mining camp?"[29]

But maybe something had to be done, to save face if for no other reason. "The name of Chicago," Col. Randolph mourned, has become "a scandal in other cities. For the last month our members have been coming back to Chicago from New York and Baltimore and other cities and telling us we must do something."[30]

In line with the colonel's complaint, the *New York Times* story about the new initiative ended with these words: "While the business leaders were in session the march of crime went on. Four gunmen, immaculate and sleek as gangsters these days are, drove a high-powered automobile into an alley after a tarpaulin-covered truck, which they mistook for a beer truck. When they discovered their mistake they figuratively said, 'O, well,' kidnapped the driver and stole the truck, goods and all."

How many leaders were going to drive this effort? The *Times* said the Chicago Association of Commerce executive committee comprised thirty-three members, but that *Richmond Item* article referenced just "six business and civic leaders" as directors. According to the *Chicago Tribune,* Col. Randolph promised on the day the effort was launched that he would reveal the six members the next day. But then he changed his mind.

"Their names will not be given out," he told the *Chicago Evening Post.* "We can work more effectively if the membership of the body is not known."[31] With that decision, the name of the group became all but inevitable. "Mr. Randolph has selected his leaders," reported a front-page story in the *Baltimore Sun* on February 8, "but nobody knows who they are and, what's more, nobody is going to know. There will be six of these men and under each of them will be a group of fearless fellows sworn to last-ditch action in the elimination of gangsters. The sextet of leaders have already been christened 'the secret six.'"[32]

And so the Secret Six was born—two days after the Meagher shooting, and nine months before William Wright would call on them to find out who'd been extorting his daughter.[§]

[§] The group had an official name, sometimes mentioned in the press of the day, but it was a mystique-less mouthful: The Association of Commerce Committee for the Prevention and Punishment of Crime.

In one peculiar side note to the story, the Association of Commerce already had a group in place, its Crime Commission, focused on fighting crime in Chicago. The Commission was led by a highly respected professional, but the Secret Six decided not to bother them. The new group, according to the *Chicago Tribune*, "has not invited Frank J. Loesch, veteran crime fighter, who is president of the crime commission, as well as a member of President Hoover's crime commission."[33] Asserted the *Kansas City American*, "The plan to ignore its own creation—the crime commission—caused a good deal of talk among attaches of the commission."[34]

No, the Secret Six was going to be a fresh start, untainted by even the whiff of failure from any preceding effort—including its own. "The trouble with impressive committees against crime," Randolph explained to the *Chicago Evening Post*, "is that they too frequently have turned into town meetings which talked on and on and forgot to do anything."[35]

Randolph, solely responsible for selecting the members of the Secret Six, drew upon his military background to complete the team. "I don't know what the political affiliations are of any of the six men on the committee," he said. "I don't care. That doesn't make any difference. I do know they are men I can trust. I'm picking them out the same way I would if I were conducting a campaign on the field of battle."[36]

Before we look at all the organization accomplished, the war on crime it waged and the way it ultimately went down in flames, a question must be asked: Was the Secret Six really necessary? Was Chicago uniquely infested with criminals, so crime-ridden the normal forces of authority were helpless against it, or was there a lot of crime in Chicago simply because, at almost 3.4 million souls and counting, there were a lot of people in Chicago?

Possibly the latter. The Association of Commerce themselves acknowledged as much in another passage from their vigilantism manifesto: "It is true that statistics compiled by the prominent casualty companies and other unbiased authorities outside Chicago show that, compared on a per capita basis with other large American cities, Chicago is far down on the list of serious felonies, and . . . the city continues to advance in commercial and cultural undertakings."

Nevertheless, the Association continued, "the facts remain that the recent failures of law enforcement . . . can no longer be countenanced."[37] In an interview with the *Chicago Daily News* two days after the Meagher shooting,

Randolph admitted it wasn't so much the quantity of crime as its quality that had spurred them to action. "Chicago isn't ridden more by the criminal element than any other large city," he said, "but there is the spectacular fashion in which murders are committed here. This must be stopped."[38]

So maybe Chicago was as safe, statistically, or even safer than other big American cities. Indeed, the Chicago Police Department had shown that—undermanned and unpaid as they were—they could haul in more than two thousand undesirables in a three-day sweep, in the process reducing crime by 75 percent, at least temporarily.

But an innocent man, whose employer was a member of the Association of Commerce, and with a lifetime of good works before him, had been shot down in cold blood, and the rich, powerful men of Chicago couldn't just stand by.

Was the Secret Six project just an elaborate but ultimately irrational outpouring of raw, moneyed emotion? It didn't matter. For whatever reason, American vigilantism had come into its own. And Chicago's wild ride was about to get a lot wilder.

4

A Burning City Sparks a Nation's Hope

IF THE FIRST objective of Chicago's Secret Six was winning the nation's attention, it must be said they succeeded grandly, and secrecy could hang. In February 1930 alone, hundreds of articles appeared in newspapers across America, often on the front page, about the group's founding, its initial operations, and its future plans. It didn't hurt that Robert Isham Randolph, the leader of the effort, possessed a flair for the dramatic, a knack for sloganeering, and a dark side.

Randolph, a Chicago native born in 1883, was an engineer by trade, following in the footsteps of his father, Isham Randolph. In the first two decades of the twentieth century, he focused on public works, serving the Chicago Sanitary District, the Illinois Improvement Commission, and the state's Rivers and Lakes Commission. He partnered with his father from 1914 to 1920 and started his own consulting firm when his father died in 1920. At the time of the Secret Six's founding, he was a senior partner in the Randolph-Perkins engineering firm. Often called Colonel Randolph, he earned his military title with the National Guard, which sent him to the Mexican border in 1914 during minor hostilities with that nation, and then to Europe during World War I, where he reached the rank of colonel and commanded the 535th Engineers Corp.[1]

Randolph studied at the Virginia Military Institute, Chicago's Armour Institute (now the Illinois Institute of Technology), and Cornell University. He married Martha Maclean in 1912.[2]

Robert Randolph, from a 1920 Sanitary District campaign flyer. / Courtesy of Chicago History Museum, Robert I. Randolph scrapbooks [microform], 1921–1944.

According to a 1920 campaign flyer, which Randolph circulated in an unsuccessful bid for a trustee role on Chicago's Sanitary District Board, he supervised construction of the Twenty-Second Street and Dearborn Street bridges over the Chicago River. While in wartime France, the flyer stated, he had helped build a railroad in the St. Mihiel area.

The *Chicago Daily News* elaborated on Randolph's World War I service: "His job in France was to set up lines of communication, rail and other, and keep them open."[3] "We were never under rifle fire," Randolph recalled for the story, "but we worked in artillery range most of the time."

On the weekend of the Secret Six's formation, the *Baltimore Sun* sat down with Randolph, declaring him worthy of the new role: "If one were to set out on a country-wide search for a man who typified the vigilante of pioneer days and ran immediately into Mr. Randolph, the hunt would end," the *Sun* opined, describing him as a "slim, tall, well-built man in his middle forties, keen grey eyes that never leave a questioner's face; a veteran of two wars . . . whose father saw to it that he got his education at the Virginia Military Institute; a pithy commentator whose language is colorful."[4]

The *Chicago Herald and Examiner* also found Randolph qualified to take on Chicago's crime—almost mystically so: "Here is no blue-nosed St. George shaking a wooden sword at the dragon of crime," the *Herald and Examiner* declared. "Here no fanatic, apoplectic with indignation; here no tinpot messiah with a dozen schemes to bring in the millennium before the month is up. But here is a native Chicagoan, born in Englewood—61st and Stewart, to be exact—who sees that his city is in a bad way."[5]

"Personally, I'm all for the hoodlums killing each other off," Randolph told the *Baltimore Sun*. And if that didn't do the trick, Randolph added, "Somebody will get rid of these people or else—" The piece noted that "Mr. Randolph left the end of the promise to imagination."

The interview continued with the *Sun's* reporter asking, "Will you supersede the law if the law does not act?"

"Things will be done in the name of the law if it is possible to do them that way," was Randolph's noncommittal answer, although he expressed the hope that the state of Illinois, or even the federal government, might step in.

"And if all these things should fail?" the reporter persisted.

"But if the worst comes to the worst," Randolph replied, his next words harking back to something old and vaguely menacing, "we cannot do better than emulate our ancestors."

So what was the plan, exactly? In the weeks following the formation of the Secret Six, Randolph created a secret document that was promptly leaked to the press. Each resulting story focused on whatever details most interested that reporter. The *Journal and Courier* of Lafayette, Indiana, was one of the first to reveal its findings, publishing a real page-turner on February 20, 1930. The article described the Association of Commerce's plan as a "gigantic desperate drive against crime, with unlimited financial backing, by a system of secret investigation."[6] The effort, headed up by the Secret Six, would feature "a tremendous secret system of espionage," with the goals of "ridding Chicago of crime and gangsters and the breaking up of political alliances with the underworld."

The *Journal and Courier* said (quite wrongly, as it turned out) that the Secret Six's investigators would be "employed in much the same manner as in army espionage work, with no investigator knowing any of his fellows and with the investigator's work being investigated before any final action is taken." Keeping each Secret Six detective in the dark about the work of the other detectives would prevent the leaks that often hobbled official police work, the plan asserted. Too often, a crook who feared he was being sniffed out could employ bribes or threats to get the facts from an amoral cop. But the Secret Six would offer no such opportunity, they claimed. "Usual tactics of gangsters, murderers, bombers and other criminals in following the progress of investigations will be of no avail."

The *Baltimore Sun*, which also received an early draft, reported that "Three sets of investigators will work on every phase of the inquiry and the results of their investigations [will be] compared; this to protect the association from being sold out by any of its operatives."[7]

Before they could start putting Chicago's criminals behind bars, however, the Secret Six would have to gather information, and there was no shortage of it waiting for them, in the form of "data compiled by the Employers association on rackets, bombing, and the activities of union labor officials who sponsor violence, extortion, intimidation or other forms of criminality" as well as "the files of the citizens' Committee to Enforce the Landis Award, and the records of the Chicago Crime Commission."[8]

But the announcement of a new, secret campaign against the gangsters opened the floodgates. "Information is pouring into the offices of the association," announced the *Baltimore Sun*. "Gunmen, racketeers and murderers who have roamed the streets by day and sat at night club front tables during the small hours are being listed as to the matter of their homes and hangouts and the times where they can be located in either."[9]

The *Sun*, which took a consistently favorable view of the vigilantes' cause while it denigrated the police department wherever it could, added, "This information is being passed on to the police, who always have professed ignorance of this vital information."

The information was coming not just to the Association of Commerce, according to the *Sun*, but to Col. Randolph personally: "Since the inauguration of the Secret Six and consequent announcement in the press that the

Association of Commerce, which lists on its books every man of prominence in the city's industrial life, had informed the peace-enforcement organization that if they did not get busy the association would take matters into its own hands, Mr. Randolph's office has been inundated with letters, telephones calls, telegrams and personal visits—all testifying to the grip that the gangster has obtained upon this city."[10]

Within a week, the *Sun* reported on February 21, this information dump was being measured in agricultural terms: "Already in the Association of Commerce offices there are three bushels of anonymous letters telling of crime conditions in certain sections of the city and county," the *Baltimore Sun* declared. "Every one of these letters will be thoroughly investigated."[11] A central complaint of the messages, the *Sun* reported, was that business owners were being extorted not just for cash, but to steer their businesses to certain firms. And failure to contract with the preferred entities would mean a reduction in business from the city itself, indicating official collusion.

How much was this extortion costing Chicago? Staggering sums, according to articles that circulated in papers across the nation: "Randolph said his investigators and accountants had figured the annual toll Chicago pays to racketeers at $145,000,000.* At that rate, every man, woman and child in the city pays something like $45 a year toward defraying the cost of illegal activities. Almost every business in Chicago, Randolph continued, pays tribute to the organizers of bogus trade unions, fake banquets, racketeering employers' associations and all the other similar organizations which have given Chicago the appellation of 'the racketeering capitol of the universe.'"[12]

Ironically, the proven ability of Chicago commerce to pay off the crooks meant that the resources were already there for prosecuting those same people, with just a minor diversion of cash flow. Randolph, who did considerable work in the engineering of water flow and redirection, may even have seen the problems as comparable, the simple shutting off of one valve and the opening of another. And so it was that one of the Secret Six's first slogans, carried on the front pages of hundreds of newspapers across the nation on February 21, 1930, summed up the plan neatly: "Millions for Prosecution; Not One Cent for Tribute."[13]

---

* Worth almost $27 billion in 2024 dollars.

"The first thing to be accomplished," announced the *Minneapolis Tribune* in a story about the Secret Six's plans, "is to induce all businessmen to cease paying tribute to racketeers and pay a part of the blackmail into the coffers of the association for the prosecution of all racketeers and other criminals."[14] Money was one of numerous ways the Secret Six departed from the traditional notion of an American vigilante. These were not lone gunslingers wandering the wilderness. They were rich businessmen who knew other rich businesspeople in a city of considerable wealth. So, a central focus of the group's beginnings was its budget—at least a million dollars.

To put that number in perspective, the entire Chicago city budget of 1929 was $60.3 million, with more than a quarter of that money, some $16 million, going to the police department. In 1930, the force employed 6,719 people, including 5,443 patrolmen and 30 policewomen, according to that year's official police report.[15] The average annual salary of a police patrolman in 1930 was estimated by the *Chicago Tribune* at about $2,414, meaning that every million dollars raised by the Secret Six could pay the salaries of 414 officers for a year.[16]

But would the businesspeople of Chicago agree that this was a good use of their money? And were they saying as much to Randolph? Yes and yes, apparently. As the *Knoxville (Kentucky) Journal* reported, "Business men have assured him, Col. Randolph declared, that they would willingly contribute toward rigid law enforcement. Using the funds that ordinarily went to the gangster chieftains for 'protection,' the moneys would be used to employ expert investigators."[17]

According to a story in the *Omaha World-Herald*, Randolph claimed that "The 'secret six' has already received assurances that make the collection of ample funds certain. One man agreed to subscribe 10 per cent of any fund raised up to a million dollars."[18]

"Anything from $1,000,000 to $3,000,000[†] will be available for operations," added the *Baltimore Sun*. "In other words, the tribute payers, emboldened by the Vigilante program, will give their cash to the latter to finance a short, quick war against having to pay it for all time to the gangster."[19] As these plans were detailed in that last week of February 1930, the gulf

---

[†] From nearly $20 million to more than $50 million in 2024 dollars.

between the frontier vigilante and the Secret Six continued to grow. Along with the fortunes at play was the issue of how the money would be used.

The cash wasn't going to pay for gunslingers or the guns they would sling. There would be no budget for hanging rope or torches needed to burn down scofflaw homes and hideouts. Instead, according to the *Minneapolis Tribune* and many other newspapers, the Secret Six fund "would be used to obtain evidence that would stand up in court."[20] An Associated Press story carried in many papers that week put the total anticipated Secret Six budget at up to $5 million, almost a third of Chicago's annual police department expenditures in 1930.

Where would the money go? Secret Six planned to employ "legal counsel, special investigators, under cover men, special prosecutors, guards and such other assistance as it may from time to time require," reported the *Chicago Tribune*.[21]

Who would handle all that cash? Randolph would soon appoint one hundred men to the Secret Six's oversight committee, as well as "twelve men who are to form a committee to collect and disburse the funds necessary to the association's fight against racketeering and other crime. . . . Col. Randolph said most of the dozen had been chosen and had agreed to act."[22]

The objective of the Secret Six, the *Chicago Tribune* reported, was less focused on stamping out "holdups, burglaries and attacks on women" and more on "crimes involving restraint of business," with an aim to "ferret out those, no matter what their station in society may be, who profit by the criminal acts of others or by political influence."

In another departure from the classic model of frontier vigilantism, the Secret Six would not create their own system of justice but would instead "cooperate with the established agencies," "supplement the work of the constituted authorities," and "assume some of the duties of the county officials," reported the *Tribune*, adding that the group planned to "form an organization of investigators and lawyers which will oversee and augment the staff of State's Attorney Swanson." To that end, the "protection of witnesses" would also be a part of the group's mandate.

In the report outlining its formation and goals, the *Chicago Tribune* noted, the Secret Six "commended both the police department and the state's attorney because of the recent cleanup by the police department." The new group was, however, keeping local authorities at arm's length for the time being: "Police Commissioner Russell said the Association of Commerce members have offered him no assistance, either in men, money or advice. State's Attorney Swanson was not consulted by Col. Randolph's committeemen."

Those doing the work of the Secret Six would remain secret, as would what they were up to, at least for the short term, Randolph told the *Tribune*: "The lawyers whose services would be used would not become known until they have to appear in court. . . . The public will learn of the accomplishments of the secret committee and its staff only when its evidence is presented to the grand jury."

Among the most ambitious of the Secret Six's goals was the time allotted to the project: half a year. The vigilantes even had another slogan to go along with their promise. "Crimeless Chicago in six months," announced headlines and stories in more than one hundred newspapers across the nation in late February and early March of 1930. Col. Randolph, according to the Associated Press story, had promised "that the anti-crime drive will be unremitting and said the six months estimate was based upon the least length of time in which gangland facts could be obtained, indictments returned and convictions obtained."[23]

The Secret Six couldn't do it on their own, however, Randolph admitted, declaring "a clean-up of the city can be made in six months if all law enforcement agencies co-operate."[24]

The *Chicago Tribune* tended toward the least sensational coverage of the Secret Six, and true to form, they offered another caveat to Randolph's promise. "We are going into this thing with determination," Col. Randolph told the paper. "We do not expect to make a clean sweep of everything that is wrong in Chicago in six months, but we do expect to convict so considerable a number of the racketeers that now infest the city that the rest will respect and fear us."[25]

Meanwhile, the Chicago Police Department kept up their anticrime crusade. "Unpaid police still continued their drives on the criminals and close to 800 were arrested in the 16 hour period ending last midnight," the Associated Press reported nationally on February 21.[26] The force, which appeared particularly concerned about the way they were being portrayed in the press, was making adjustments on the fly.

"On the orders of Commissioner William Russell, Chicago police continued today their hunt for 'higher-ups' and temporarily abandoned their attack on the small fry," reported the *Baltimore Sun*. "Added to the roster of important gunmen placed under arrest since the crime drive began a fortnight ago was the name of Frankie Foster, one of George ('Bugs') Moran's retinue, who returned this morning from the South."[27] The Associated Press story offered some additional insights: "Foster told police he had just returned from Florida and 'thought the drive was over.'" Other relatively bigger fish picked up in the drive's second week, reported the *Chicago Tribune*, were "Albert Van Pelt, 50 years old, of 5916 South La Salle Street, believed to be head of a south side safe cracking clique, his brother, Earl, and his wife, Nellie."[28]

Around the same time, the police effort produced its first conviction: "While police continued their roundup of criminal suspects and gun-toters today, George Mootz, 21, one of the first seized in raids which have netted 7,000 persons, was sentenced to serve nine months in jail for carrying a concealed weapon."[29]

Along with the successes came more of Randolph's mixed drumbeat of praise and denigration. While he "commended the recent police drive which resulted in arrests of more than 3,000 criminal suspects in little more than a week," according to a United Press wire story, Randolph followed up with a harsher-than-usual dismissal of Chief Russell's efforts, calling them "temporary measures such as are adopted by popular clamor, aroused by some particularly atrocious crime, and just as frequently relaxed when the public excitement is abated."[30]

Slogans and Hope

A decade after Prohibition gifted America's criminals with a vast and profitable new market, protected with a murderous ruthlessness that was now creeping inexorably into the homes and businesses of the law-abiding—and three months after the October 1929 beginning of the decade-long Great Depression—the nation's citizens were ready for something hopeful, something interesting. In the dead of winter in 1930, the Secret Six delivered, churning out bold promises backed up by at least three slogans: "Crimeless Chicago in six months," they declared. "Millions for prosecution; not one cent for tribute," they implored. They branded their effort the "million dollar drive on undesirables."[31]

The marketing worked. "Hundreds of offers of aid from all parts of the country have poured into Col. Randolph's office," read an Associated Press story that ran in more than one hundred newspapers in late February and early March of 1930. "Many of these, he said, were from Canadian mounted police, college students, Texas Rangers and former sailors, marines and soldiers."[32]

Two men, dismissed as "drug store cowboys down Cincinnati way," by the *Chicago American* on February 27, set their fees precisely in a letter to Randolph. "For the sum of $25 a week, just enough to buy near beer[†] with, we will guarantee to get rid of Al Capone . . . Joe Saltis and all the rest of your so-called hard guys."

The Association of Commerce itself marveled at the publicity it had generated, declaring in a headline in its weekly newsletter, "Thousands of Items Printed Throughout Country Telling of Association Stand for Clearing Out Gangsters." Announced the Association, "The crime campaign is receiving big headlines all over the country" although "still but a few days old." Crowed the group, the drive "has sent a spark flying around the nation in the interest it has aroused in other cities. Newspaper clippings by thousands from all over the United States, letters from associations and individuals from Chicago and a wide area around it, and telegrams and telephone calls have poured into the Association offices, all of them of a commendatory nature."[33]

The Chicago Museum of History, which holds a large volume of Col. Randolph's records, files, letters, and newspaper clippings on a single, thick reel of microfilm, does not have a record of every commendatory thing that landed on Randolph's desk, but someone—probably Randolph himself—set aside a March 31, 1930, letter for safekeeping from Datus M. Hervey of San Diego, California. "Sir:" began the letter from the fifty-year-old Hervey, a chief pharmacist for the US Navy, "The very favorable reports that are being circulated via newspapers throughout the United States in regard to your ability in handling the Chicago situation, are being received with a great deal of enthusiasm by the American people."

[†] Near beer was beer with an alcohol content low enough to keep it legal under Prohibition rules.

It was the letter's second paragraph that, presumably, earned it a permanent place in the Randolph files: "I have talked with quite a number of people on this coast regarding you and asked what they thought the consensus of opinion would be if you should 'throw your hat in the ring' for President of the United States. Each and every one expressed the opinion that you would be an excellent choice for that position. . . . Please give this your earnest consideration—for the benefit of the Country."

The Editorialists Have Their Say

After the reports of the Secret Six had been distributed nationwide, it was time for the newspaper editorialists and analysts to have their say, and by early March 1930, a good deal of ink was being devoted to opinion and speculation about the Secret Six.

"Citizens, the underworld, and the world at large," declared Pierre John Huss in a widely distributed piece, "are awaiting with keen interest the effects of a much heralded million-dollar onslaught on crime here by business and industrial leaders headed by the 'Secret Six.'"[34]

Huss, who would go on to win fame as a World War II correspondent, and who interviewed Adolf Hitler multiple times, continued hopefully:

> The steam-rolling method has been left to the police, who have resorted to it widely in the last few weeks with the expected results—a "showup" parade of 5,000 suspicious persons and the clogging of courts with cases of minor police characters. The "Secret Six," however, intends to divide the city in its "badland" sections, place an investigating committee in charge of each district and secure information not only on criminals in that section, but also of the status and character of policemen, politicians, judges, lawyers and "moneyed" powers. On the basis of this data, it hopes to sweep into the hands of the law not only the current criminals and gangsters, but also the "big shots."

While most commentary on the Secret Six took a wait-and-see perspective, the *Chicago Herald and Examiner* was firmly in the vigilantes' corner. "Carrying concealed weapons and indiscriminate shootings have disgraced Chicago before the world," the paper proclaimed. "This is no pioneer town. But when criminal gangsters indulge in the bravado and violence of border outlaws the people of this city who represent the energy of its business, law and order should apply promptly and vigorously the effective methods of old-time vigilantes."[35]

Other editorials expressed concerns for the safety of the nascent group. "The members of the 'Secret Six' who are directing and financing the war on crime are not known to the underworld," noted one commentary carried on the wires. "However, it is highly probable that gangsters' spies are endeavoring to find out who their enemies are and who is trying to separate them from the illegal privileges they have enjoyed so long. These 'six' may yet be found victims of the machine gun terrorists as the crusade progresses."[36]

Another widely distributed editorial noted that going after crime, even armed with $1 million, would not be easy. "The task is a particularly tough one," the writer opined. "Chicago gangland itself can probably raise a campaign fund of more than $1,000,000 with less effort than the business men put forth."[37] And then there was this response, which appeared without a headline in the papers that carried it, reading in its entirety, "The 'Secret Six' Committee of Chicago says that the city will be without crime in six months. This is probably the premier fish story of the season."[38]

The most strident criticism of the Secret Six was voiced in California where, from the suburbs of Los Angeles, the *Anaheim Bulletin* called the formation of the vigilante group "perhaps the nearest approach to civil war that this nation has experienced since the slavery question was settled." The paper described developments in Chicago as "a plan to abolish government," declaring that "it is the law-abiding pitted against the criminal, and the former in taking the law in its own hands becomes criminal."[39]

All the attention garnered by the group produced concern along with derision, and in the first week of March 1930, Col. Randolph found himself needing to clarify things. "Head of 'Secret Six' Denies Vigilante Aim," read a typical headline over an Associated Press story that ran in dozens of newspapers: "Chicago's secret six committee of six will not employ 'vigilante methods' and 'is not going to fight booze,' Col. Robert Isham Randolph, president of the Association of Commerce, said last night.

'The secret six,' Colonel Randolph enlightened Chicagoans, will aim at the hoodlum element, which 'has profited so greatly through sinister operations and which has given Chicago a bad name. It is not necessary to employ vigilante methods,' he said, 'for after all, Chicago is not a Sodom or a Gomorrah. It is not ruled by corruption and crime.'"[40]

Would there be the violence one typically associates with vigilantism? Randolph was asked. No, he replied, the Secret Six was not going to hurt anyone. It wasn't a lie, most likely, because Randolph couldn't see into the future. But he was wrong. There would be violence. Worse, Randolph himself would offer a formal justification for that specialized form of violence called torture. But Randolph's protestations may have been sincere at the time they were first issued.

With or without promises of vigilantic excess, the Secret Six—in the era before television—were providing near-daily entertainment of the highest order. On February 28 and March 1 alone, more than one hundred papers in thirty-five states reported on the Secret Six's new anticrime drive, according to the newspapers.com database. Among those papers were six in California, including the *Los Angeles Times,* which ran a story on the fifth page of its March 1 edition under a stack of dramatic headlines:

Chicago Wipes Criminal Slate

Secret Committee of Six to Carry Out Slogan[§]

Group May Use $1,000,000 in Driving Out Crooks

The *Los Angeles Times* was one of the papers they read in Hollywood, of course, to keep up with the local and national news but also, surely, to get ideas for new movies, new storylines that captured the heroic national spirit at a time when things were looking bleak. We must imagine more than one producer or movie mogul clipping the *Times* story, bringing it into the office, and asking for script ideas. Or maybe an established scriptwriter might have seen one of the many stories being published about the group in some respected national journal and put her own screenplay together. These would be highly speculative scripts, however, given that the Secret Six was in its infancy, with no achievements to boast of yet. The absence of facts has never bothered Hollywood, though; it has always been able to make up for a lack of reality with a rich imagination.

But rest assured, the Secret Six were on their way to accomplishing things. Later in 1930, the father of an eighteen-year-old debutante named Marion Wright would come to them for help with an extortion problem of equal parts malevolence and creepiness.

The case of the extorted society girl was still nine months away, however, while within the first ten days of March 1930—a scant four weeks

[§] The slogan cited in this story was "Crimeless Chicago in six months."

since the Secret Six had been created in response to the shooting of Philip Meagher—the wealthiest and best-known vigilantes in America's long history had cracked their first case.

The Case of the Home-Wrecking Kidnappers

It all started when Theodore Kopelman, a wealthy insurance company vice president in Chicago, married badly. He and Myrtle Kopelman (originally Thoren) quickly divorced, but Myrtle wasn't quite done with him. She joined up with a kidnapping ring and allegedly suggested they snatch her ex and get a $25,000 ransom from him.

"She told the gang he would be 'easy picking,'" the *Chicago Herald and Examiner* reported. "'Didn't I get twenty-five grand out of him myself in alimony?' she boasted."[41]

So that's what they did, picking up Kopelman near his home at 548 Surf Street on February 28, 1930, and imprisoning him for sixty hours in a cottage at Camp Lake, Wisconsin. Pay up, they told him, backing up their demands with the threat of torture with a red-hot poker.[42]

With the help of friends, Kopelman came up with the first installment of $4,000 in the first days of March, and the gang let him go with his promise that the rest would soon be forthcoming.[43] But he didn't just hand over the remaining cash and keep the story to himself, as other victims of the cabal had done. On March 6, he went to Col. Randolph and the Secret Six, who pulled in Chicago lawyer Walter Walker. Walker passed on his information to Patrick Roche, chief investigator for the Illinois Attorney's office, and the wheels started turning. "Working anonymously," reported the United Press in one version of the story, "the six millionaires aided police in staging the trap."

As instructed by the police and the Secret Six, Kopelman told the kidnappers to come to his sister's "exclusive Michigan avenue gown shop" to collect the next installment of the ransom, but instead of money, the gang found the cops waiting for them.[44] When Myrtle and five male members of the gang were apprehended and charged with kidnapping, the Secret Six got the credit, nationwide.

"Chicago's 'Secret Six' Breaks Up Kidnap Ring," announced a typical headline, on page three in the *Idaho Statesman* on March 11, 1930.

"Members of Alleged Torture-Extortion Ring Face Death if Convicted," declared the frontpage headline in the *Minneapolis Tribune* on the same date. "Business Men's 'Secret Six' Credited With Bringing Gang to Justice."

Some versions of the story alleged that the gang comprised seventeen members and had won a quarter million dollars in ransom and extortion money in the previous two months.[45]

A highlight of many of the versions of the story was the lovers' triangle involving Myrtle, suspected gang member Norman Resnick, and Norman's wife, Helyn: "Last April Norman and I were married," Helyn told the *Chicago Daily News*. "After a while he began staying out nights. At first, we were happy. Then he got out of work—but he had money. At one time I found two checks in his pocket, payable to him and signed with this Myrtle's name. He wouldn't tell me who Myrtle was—only said, 'Honey, I'm in bad company. You'd better leave me!' I decided I'd better do no such thing so I got out and started a hunt for this Myrtle."[46]

Helyn found Myrtle and presented her with a marriage certificate, but to no avail. "My dear," Helyn said the twenty-six-year-old Myrtle had told her, "that boy of yours is madly in love with me. It amuses me. I'm tired of old men who shower money on me. He's young and clever and I can use him."[47]

When twenty-one-year-old Helyn threatened to sue Myrtle for alienation of affection, Myrtle—who on occasion claimed to be the widow of St. Valentine's Day Massacre victim Peter Gusenberg—warned, "If you cross me, you'll find yourself at the side of the road in a ditch. I'm not looking for publicity and I won't have it."

Following the trap laid by Roche and the Secret Six, the women had what was presumably their final showdown, a meeting described dramatically in the *Chicago Tribune*. Myrtle, pretty and blonde and now in custody, was brought into Roche's office, hiding her face with the collar of her fur coat. The red-haired Helyn was waiting for her. "You should hide your face, even if it is beautiful!" Helyn cried. "You should be ashamed of yourself—a woman of your age, roping in young boys."[48]

Roche wasn't just trying to help the newspapers sell copies by bringing the two together, suggested the *Chicago Herald and Examiner*. He was using a "time-honored and always effective method—invoking the hatred of another woman, an injured woman, bringing the two together and letting the laws of psychology do the rest."

The scheme worked, the article suggested: "In addition to the one kidnaping on which the indictments were based, the blonde 'revealed certain details of two others in which the victims were a real estate man and a broker who gave up $28,000 in payment for their release. She is expected to make many more revelations, equally important, before she stops talking. What the blonde's own punishment will be, for she, too, is under indictment, may depend upon her service as a state's witness.'"

Helyn's love for her husband persisted even after he'd "twisted her arms and struck her and compelled her to sign" a letter admitting she was only Norman's sister. But now that he'd been arrested, Helyn was at last done with him, telling the *Chicago Tribune* "she hoped her husband would get a heavy penalty, and that if justice deserved it, the death penalty. He has to learn his lesson some time."

It should be noted that the kidnapping case wasn't cracked because of the Secret Six's investigative prowess, its underworld contacts, or its army of private detectives. Kopelman called them on the strength of publicity alone, which is all they had going for themselves in their first month of existence.

After his kidnappers released him with the expectation that he'd hand over another $21,000 for the privilege of not being burned with hot pokers, Theodore Kopelman could have gone straight to the Chicago Police or to State's Attorney Chief Investigator Patrick Roche, with quite possibly the same outcome. But where the established law enforcement institutions were sullied by the foibles and failures inevitable in any human undertaking, the Secret Six were spotless in the winter of 1930—the subject of glowing headlines coast to coast (and in several Canadian papers as well), and without a failure yet to their secret names.

No wonder Theodore Kopelman called the Secret Six. No wonder William Wright, nine months later, would call the same outfit to attend to that annoying matter of his daughter's extortion. The Secret Six might prove to be as human as any other Chicago crime busters. Indeed, they might prove to be far more human than their tax-funded public counterparts—more bumbling, more reckless, and more given to dark impulses. But the power of public relations when an organization is new and there hasn't been the time or opportunity for stumbles cannot be discounted. Publicity alone won their first case for the Secret Six, and it was publicity alone, in late March 1930, that had Chicago's criminal element spooked.

PART II

FIRST CASES OF THE SECRET SIX

All the resources of science and extra-legal expedients such as listening in on telephone conversations, are at the disposal of operatives of Chicago's 'Secret Six.' . . . No one knows who our operatives are and the operators themselves do not know each other.

—Col. Robert Randolph, October 15, 1931

5

Early Impact (and a Little Lying)

A SCANT SIX weeks after their formation, the Secret Six was forcing Chicago's crime element to recalibrate. The *Chicago Herald and Examiner* was the first to get the story, with hundreds of papers nationwide republishing the article in the last week of March 1930.

"Gangland," began the lede, "was gathering a vast defense fund to combat the anti-crime drive of the 'secret six.'"[1] While the Secret Six planned a far-reaching enterprise, the defense fund set up by the bad guys had a very specific purpose: "to be used the first time in the trial of five alleged extortionists indicted for kidnapping Theodore Kopelman."

The Kopelman case, presented in the previous chapter, was the Secret Six's first big win. Kopelman had called the Secret Six as soon as he'd been set free to collect the ransom his abductors demanded. The Secret Six had called the cops, and both forces were waiting when the crooks came to pick up their money. Col. Randolph, predictably, took the criminal fund drive in stride. "If they can raise a million dollars," he promised, "we can raise two or three million."

The first effort of the gangsters was, it must be said, a failure—and not just because Randolph declared it one. The trial was held late that spring for the three men who'd snatched Kopelman as he was on his way to work—Samuel Gold, twenty-four, unfaithful husband Norman Resnick, twenty-three, and Seymour Pellar, twenty-two. The jury took just an hour to render their verdicts, on June 5, 1930.

As Judge Harry Miller peered at the decisions, "all three defendants stood facing the court," reported the *Chicago Herald and Examiner.* Pellar's verdict was the first to be read. "His face turned gray as the word 'guilty' was spoken. And when the clause fixing the punishment at twenty years was read his knees gave way and he fell forward, sprawling over a table. His co-defendants on either side caught him by the elbows and prevented him from dropping to the floor."[2] Despite the trio's claim that "Kopelman plotted his own kidnapping in order to obtain money from his sister," Resnick and Gold got the same judgments.[3]

Charges were dropped against the three other suspects in the kidnapping—Charles Hadesman, home wrecker Myrtle Thoren (Kopelman's ex and, later, the married Resnick's girlfriend), and Irving Sandler, owner of the cottage in Camp Lake, Wisconsin, where Kopelman was imprisoned for two and a half days. The first three convictions were enough, though, for the upstart crimefighters.

"The 'Secret Six' . . . were also vitally interested in the Kopelman case, and highly pleased with its outcome," reported the *Herald and Examiner,* "regarding it . . . as the first big test of their power." The convictions were handed down in June 1930. But strangely, two months earlier, in April 1930, Col. Randolph was already pointing to another "test of their power" that the Secret Six had passed with flying colors.

The Case of the Seven Bombers

For a story published on April 10, 1930, Col. Randolph told reporter C. Roy Greenaway of the *Toronto Star* that "So far the Secret Six have sent seven men to the penitentiary for bombing. These represent four separate cases."[4]

It was a peculiar claim. In fact, as one digs through the newspapers from those heady first weeks of Secret Six operations, one finds not corroboration for the claim, but something else entirely: Col. Robert Isham Randolph, World War I veteran, Chicago business stalwart, and esteemed leader of America's greatest band of vigilantes, seems to have been *lying.*

This is important, because Randolph's lack of a solid partnership with the truth—and by extension the Secret Six's lack of the same thing—was going to be central to the group's story in the coming months and years.

While the *Chicago Tribune* and other papers offered extensive reportage of the Secret Six's role in the Kopelman kidnapping case, nothing showed up in the *Tribune* or any other readily-available source about bombers put away by the Secret Six in the first two months of their existence. There was no shortage of *Chicago Tribune* stories about bomber arrests and convictions in early 1930, of course. Bombing, like kidnapping, was a big deal in Depression-era Chicago, and the three most prominent cases prosecuted in winter 1930 appeared regularly on the *Tribune's* front page, under headlines like "Convict Two Butchers as 'Bomb Trust'" (February 26), "Melrose Park 'Bomb Farm' Raided; Nab 11" (March 8), and "Two Bombers Found Guilty on Third Trial" (March 22). But none of these stories, or any others published in those months about bombings in the *Chicago Tribune,* mentioned the Secret Six. Nor does the timing work—in not one of the three bombing cases referenced was there both arrest and conviction within the brief existence of the Secret Six. And really, no matter how determined or well-funded they were, the Secret Six simply could not have investigated four separate bombings, gotten the perpetrators arrested and put on trial, and produced seven guilty verdicts in two months. That's not how the wheels of justice turn. But, for the sake of argument, let's say the Secret Six had somehow performed four separate miracles of jurisprudence in their first eight weeks of existence. If that had happened, surely the publicity-driven Col. Randolph would have succeeded in getting that claim published somewhere other than in Canada.

Was it just a case of one reporter getting the story wrong? Possibly. But Randolph had a lot to say about bombing in the early days of the Secret Six, and his claims showed a lot of what we might politely call *creativity.*

For example, while Randolph gave the Secret Six full credit for the seven bomber convictions in the *Toronto Star* on April 10, closer to home and two weeks earlier, on March 27, he was giving all the credit to other organizations, as suggested by the following passage from a nationally-distributed wire story: "Colonel Randolph pointed out that . . . States Attorney Swanson has obtained convictions against seven bombers—the first of this class of criminals to land in cells."[5]

A few days later, on April 2, Randolph and Assistant State's Attorney C. Wayland Brooks delivered a joint address to the Chicago Association of Commerce on the topic of "how its 'Secret Six,' appointed by President Randolph two months ago to clean up bombing and racketeering in the city, was functioning."[6]

Brooks mentioned two March 1930 bomber convictions, but he didn't point to the Secret Six, instead praising the investigative work of Joseph

Altmeier, a former butcher with no published Secret Six affiliation, who'd gone undercover to gather evidence against a large bombing ring.

Content to accept credit by association in that instance, apparently, Randolph didn't correct Brooks about who really collared those bombers, instead taking credit for a different set of remarkable feats: "President Randolph stated that the 'Secret Six' had encountered a hundred rackets. They had quietly driven many racketeers out of the city with the assistance of the police, inspired business men not to submit to blackmail and killed off a score of promising rackets by backing up resistance to threats."

All in less than two months, mind you.

The willy-nilly distribution of accolades continued well into the year. Four months after the birth of the Secret Six, in mid-June 1930, another reporter was letting the Secret Six take full credit for an eighth bomber conviction. The story, by Edwin Balmer, received national distribution and declared, "In a case of terrorism by bomb the 'Secret Six' caught the bomber on a Sunday, and on Friday of the same week he was starting a twenty-year sentence."[7]

Like many of the other claims of successful Secret Six antibomb ventures, no name or date was provided, but this must have been a reference to Frank R. Phillips, an ex-convict from Canada who learned to work with explosives in France in World War I and came to Chicago to perfect his craft. If the price was right, he'd blow up anything for you. A new speakeasy that was refusing to buy your liquor, say, or a shop that wouldn't pay for protection.

Phillips was arrested May 18, 1930, in the act of planting a bomb at the back door of a coffee shop at 507 North Clark Street, the *Chicago Tribune* reported.[8] Who led the seven Chicago cops who made the bust? Not the Secret Six, according to the *Tribune,* but Patrick Roche, chief investigator for the Illinois State's Attorney's office.

Who broke the case? Roche again, at least according to the *Tribune.* There'd been a bombing on Kinzie Street a few weeks earlier, the paper reported, and that got Roche's office involved. "In investigating this bombing," the *Tribune* reported, "Roche came upon information which led him to the belief that Phillips was guilty and that he planned another bombing soon. The investigator was intent upon getting actual evidence of the bombing and he decided to attempt to catch the bomber in the act of placing the bomb."

Upon his capture, Phillips immediately confessed to several bombings, and Roche's team found "large quantities of detonator caps, fuses and electric wires" at his home in the basement of the Regal Hotel. Given the strength of the case against him, and Phillips' apparent eagerness to atone for his sins, he pled guilty four days after his arrest, receiving a sentence of "one to twenty years" at Joliet Penitentiary in what the *Chicago Tribune* described as "one of the speediest trials recorded in the Criminal courts."[9]

At no point in any of those stories was the Secret Six mentioned as contributing to the case. Maybe Roche had been tipped off by the Secret Six or helped in some other way, but if so, why wasn't that said? Why was the press crediting the Secret Six for convicting nameless bombers in unspecified cases, while the detailed accounts of the actual cases made no mention of the publicity-hungry vigilantes?

The Secret Six wasn't the only group taking credit for putting away seven bombers in 1930, incidentally. By the end of that year, in a *Chicago Tribune* article about a new wave of business bombings, the Chicago Employers' Association was also reaching for the same limelight, with a slightly more modest claim. "The association has aided materially in the conviction of seven bombers in 1930," declared Gordon Hostetter, Association executive director.[10]

"Aided materially," is one thing. Singlehandedly sending "seven men to the penitentiary for bombing," as Randolph had told the *Toronto Star* in April 1930, is another thing altogether. And saying you put an unnamed bomber away for twenty years when all the work was done by the state's attorney is a lie, plain and simple.

As the twig is bent, so grows the tree, and by the first week of April 1930, the growing Secret Six was bending in a number of peculiar ways: "It has become fashionable in Chicago to treat the criminal with refreshing roughness," read a story that went over the national wires on April 4. The article focused on the new cooperation among Chicago's law enforcement bodies and didn't offer any specifics on how that "roughness" was being carried out, but the policy nonetheless received a ringing endorsement from Randolph, who "today advised that only by those methods can the city clear itself of the present bad reputation it enjoys the world over."[11]

Randolph, whose tough-on-crime philosophy would eventually extend to torture, was also toying with the idea of dabbling in Chicago governance within a month of the Secret Six's founding. A wire story that made the rounds in late March 1930 included this note from an interview with

Randolph: "The secret committee, its head explained, may be forced to go into politics in special instances where information warrants, but so far as possible this field will be avoided."[12]

In that article, which offered up Randolph as Chicago's leading voice on crime and punishment, he blamed illegal alcohol sales as the root of the city's crime problem and said his group was focused on combatting "the leeches who have attached themselves to business through rackets of all sorts." He departed from standard practices by praising Chief Russell's gangster crackdown and offered a few kind words as well for State's Attorney Swanson's prosecution of bombers, but implied that the formation of the Secret Six had inspired both men to boost their efforts. "Just the threat of action," he declared, "has served to cause officials to change their attitude."

The officials might beg to differ, at least if one believes Canada's overwrought take on the Secret Six.

6

The Truth of the Secret Six

IN THE SAME April 10 *Toronto Star* article where Randolph took credit for seven bomber convictions, reporter C. Roy Greenaway asked Chicago Police Chief William Russell about the Secret Six. He recorded the chief's response this way: "'That Secret Committee of Six is all a myth,' he roared, with terrific he-man volume. 'That Committee of Six is all d—d [Russell presumably said "damned"] newspaper bologna. There isn't any Committee of Six.'"[1] Greenaway asked the same question of Commissioner of Detectives John Stege. "We have never heard a thing about it," Stege told him. "We don't know what it is all about." But when Greenaway caught up with Randolph himself, the man was glad to establish the existence of the Secret Six and to demonstrate his bona fides as Chicago's newest but instantly most authoritative voice on the prosecution of crime. "Ours is a strictly military intelligence system," Randolph said. "We employ our own agents. They work singly. One does not even know the other." Randolph continued with a statement that would end up not being true in the years to come, but perhaps he believed it at the time: "Mind you, we have no idea of adopting any extra-legal methods. . . . What we are aiming to do is simply to provide a real intelligence system."

Randolph also took aim at Chicago Mayor Bill "Big Bill" Thompson, widely viewed as a corrupt crony of Al Capone: "We still have the rottenest city administration we ever had," Randolph told the paper. "Under Big Bill Thompson. But he's through."

Thompson probably saw the article, but he waited eight months before serving a little cold vengeance, suing Randolph for $1 million on a defamation complaint. Randolph had alleged publicly that a prize drawing set up by Thompson and promoted over the radio sounded a lot like an illegal lottery, and the event was cancelled. Asked about Thompson's suit, Randolph expressed no concern, and indeed nothing came of the matter.[2]

Randolph enjoyed his interview with the *Toronto Star*, in particular when told of his dismissal by Chicago Police officials, and his smile took on mystical significance in the most histrionic passage of Greenaway's florid piece:

> Col. Randolph's smile is exactly the kind that "Bugs" Moran and "Scarface Al" see in a nightmare. It is the smile of something that you fill full of lead and yet keeps coming on. . . . Across their path is a foreboding shadow, cast by a secret organization in the interest of law and order. And behind that secret organization is the cryptic, deranging smile of Col. Robert Isham Randolph. You imagine again the colonel waiting behind a line of machine guns for the one annihilating moment. You feel for certain that he will give the order at that devastating second. The result is exactly what the colonel planned it should be. And after it is all over, the colonel is still smiling.

The myth was already strong in early spring of 1930, but that's all they had in those heady first days, myth and promise. Soon, however, the Secret Six would add tangible results to their portfolio, fulfilling their expectations beyond, most likely, even Col. Randolph's imaginings.

Sometimes, the Secret Six took a case from start to finish. They would get the first call from the victim, or the victim's relatives, and they would investigate, interrogate, deliver the suspects and the incriminating evidence to the authorities, and only then stand back while the wheels of conventional justice turned. Powerful and rich as they were, the Secret Six could not try or convict; neither could they imprison for more than a few days.

Often, their involvement in a case was less comprehensive. They might pass on a tip to the regular cops or assist an investigation that the cops directed. Sometimes, they caused things to happen by their mere existence: Cops worked harder knowing their competition was looking for headlines; criminals got wind of Secret Six involvement and abandoned crimes.

Edwin Balmer, a Chicago native, reporter, and successful novelist, wrote a six-article series about Chicago crime in mid-1930, and he asked fellow journalists what they thought of the Secret Six. "Competent newspaper men have told me that they class the six with Santa Claus," Balmer wrote, "in other words, it is a pleasing name for processes which would have happened anyway."[3] Chicago police officials were as reticent about the Secret Six with Balmer as they had been with C. Roy Greenaway a few months before: "Police Commissioner Russell and Commissioner of Detectives Stege would not discuss the matter with me at all," Balmer reported. "They would neither deny nor confirm the useful existence of the 'Secret Six.'"

But make no mistake, the Secret Six got things done. Had they never existed, crimes would have gone unpunished, ransoms would have been paid and then spent on new kidnappings, and extortionists would have grown rich. Much of this book will present the Secret Six's positive impact and best work, something for the reader to keep in mind as we delve into the group's disastrous final acts. But first, so the reader doesn't start suspecting that I made all this up, here are a few words about how this book was researched.

Regarding My Methodology

My principal source was newspapers.com, a searchable, indexed database of thousands of newspapers from the last three centuries, most but not all in the United States. As of early 2024, newspapers.com had scanned nearly a billion pages into their database, using a system that was able to read, store, and make searchable almost every word on each of those pages.

It is a remarkable—and at times overwhelming—resource. A search of the term "secret six" from 1930 through 2023 turned up more than sixty-two thousand stories, any one of which might contain some vital scrap of Secret Six history. And although a machine can find those stories, only a human (so far) can understand their meaning and decide what part, if any, they should play in a book about the Secret Six.

I did not read all sixty-two thousand stories for this book, nor did I need to, because most of them were duplicates. When the Secret Six made news, the story would go out on the wires and hundreds of newspapers would pick it up. Fortunately, newspapers.com search results are presented as a series of pictures from the place on the page where "secret six" appeared, meaning I could very quickly identify redundancies and skip over them.

Many of those sixty-two thousand stories, further, were not about the Chicago vigilantes. Thousands of them concerned a 1931 movie, *The Secret Six* (yes, inspired by the vigilantes—more on that in the coming chapters). And if someone kept a "secret six months," for example, a pair of young lovers in Battle Creek, Michigan, who got engaged in summer 1929 but didn't tell anyone for half a year, the newspapers.com database would pull up that story too.

Because the same stories about the Secret Six ran in papers across America within days of their distribution over the wires, I found I could narrow my search to a half dozen of the most populous states—Illinois, of course, along with New York, California, Pennsylvania, and a few others—and still find the same stories repeated ad nauseam. I estimate that I looked at upward of ten thousand articles in the researching of this book, including every article written about the Secret Six published in the *Chicago Tribune*, whose coverage of the vigilantes was unparalleled for its thoroughness, insight, and, occasionally, snark. About a third (my own rough estimate, based on references to the *Tribune* in endnotes) of the Secret Six story could have been told by reading the *Tribune* alone, while the hundreds of other papers I consulted served often simply to back up or embellish what was reported in the *Tribune*.

When necessary, however, I dug deeper. When a Secret Six story emerged about a particular person, for example, or in a place other than Chicago, I would search that as well. Many heroes and villains (mostly villains) who made news in Florida, Nebraska, California, and so forth, were the subject of separate name and place searches.

My methods were not foolproof. Not every newspaper has yet been scanned into the newspapers.com database, not even every newspaper in Chicago. The scanning technologies used by newspapers.com don't catch everything; there are instances where they missed "secret six" and other search terms. Thus, something noteworthy about the Secret Six—an amusing anecdote, an interesting case, some profound error of judgment—might not have made it into these pages. But what is here will, I hope, meet two objectives. First, I mean it to be a fascinating account, and the first full account, of America's best-funded, most determined, and most successful foray into vigilantism. But second, and equally as important, I want this book to stand up to historical scrutiny, for both the facts presented and the conclusions drawn.

Was every word printed by the 1930s press about the Secret Six true? No, and where the lies, errors, and overstatements are obvious, I'll point them out, as I already have. But there is much truth to be found in the old newspapers, I believe, particularly when multiple reporters and newspapers covered an event in similar ways and with similar facts, presenting narratives consistent with other Secret Six exploits before and after.

When quoting a newspaper directly, I almost always honored the way things were written in those old newspapers, even when they might look like typos to modern readers. "Someone" was written as "some one" back then, with a space; the *s* in "street" wasn't capitalized when referring to street addresses (e.g. "Clark street"); and "kidnaping" and "kidnapers" were spelled with one *p*, whereas two are preferred today. Many newspaper headlines were written in all caps, regardless of the story's importance, and that's one place where I rejected an exact transcription, just to make the text easier to read.

I feel a particular burden to explain my methodology because of the subject matter: 1930s Chicago gangsters. It is a cohort and an era of special, even obsessive, interest for many, and it is thus rife with legend, embellishment, and rumor. I have stumbled across my share of tales unsupported by any source, after which I embarked on further research and discovered that the original story was simply wrong or, at best, not something I could verify.

For example, what of the Garage Café? The illegal, alcohol-dispensing speakeasy, a consistent element of Secret Six lore, was allegedly created by the vigilantes as a place where Chicago's gangsters could feel comfortable while undercover Secret Six operatives plied them for data.

Col. Randolph boasted of the establishment in a March 1934 interview with the English-language *Japan Advertiser*, conducted while he was in Tokyo to visit his grandson.[4] "The Secret Six opened up a speakeasy of its own to 'play' with the gang bootleggers in Cicero," the *Advertiser* shared. "The premises were fitted up like a real joint at a cost of $12,900."* A story in the *Memphis (Tennessee) Press-Scimitar* repeated the claim, saying the Secret Six "got information thru stool pigeons and for six months even ran a speakeasy to obtain information."[5]

While tales of the Garage Café are standard fare in Secret Six histories, just two articles about the business are discoverable in the indexed press, both in the *Chicago Tribune*. But neither story mentions the Secret Six, and the address in both instances is 60 East Thirtieth Street—a church stands there now—which is not in Cicero but about six miles east of that Windy City suburb.[6]

---

* Worth more than a quarter million dollars in 2024.

Truth is essential to understanding the American spirit, and the American spirit as it expressed itself in the Great Depression– and Prohibition-eras possesses a singular and universal significance, a story vital not just to American history but to all of human history as well.

To that end, no claim about the Secret Six will go uncited, and the references—to the newspaper, the date, the page number, the headline, and the author, where available—will be included as endnotes so that the readers can verify things for themselves. Where the content of a newspaper article requires several successive paragraphs to relate, I will footnote it just once, but will strive to make clear in adjoining paragraphs where the details came from.

Newspapers.com was important, but not the only resource used for this book. *The New York Times* keeps its own indexed set of papers, and I referred to it now and then. Anyone who wants to write about the Secret Six must make a pilgrimage to the Chicago History Museum, which keeps on a single roll of microfilm the scanned images of Col. Randolph' selected papers, clippings, letters, and more, including much about the vigilante group he led for three years. While no book has focused primarily on the Secret Six, a number of recent publications have touched on them, and I went through a half dozen of these. I might have sometimes spent a day typing names and search terms into Google and other more obscure databases, occasionally culminating in an email to someone who might have a little more information about something. And then, there is the vast trove of FBI reports and documents compiled as part of the investigation of the Edward Bremer kidnapping in January 1934. And when I say vast, I mean tens of thousands of pages, sometimes unreadable or barely readable, some handwritten, and some violently redacted. None of it was organized except generally by chronology; none of it was indexed in any way, electronically or otherwise, and thus too often neglected by historians. But I found some interesting Secret Six information there, which will be discussed in future chapters.

So now, let us press forward with a gaggle of shot-up gangsters.

7

Shooting in the Dark

ON THE EVENING of May 31, 1930, three killers gathered outside a Chicago poolroom at 857 North Clark Street, waiting. And when Samuel "Moonshine Sam" Monistero, Joseph Ferrari, and Tony Tornatore stepped out, according to the *Chicago Tribune*, the hired guns went to work.[1]

"Three men ran screaming late Saturday night into the calm of Washington Square," the United Press reported in a nationally distributed story. "Behind them were three pursuers whose revolvers barked a tattoo of lead. When the three in front fell dead or dying on the grass, the murderers ran to a waiting automobile and escaped."[2]

The *Chicago Tribune* offered a less dramatic but presumably more accurate account of the victims' fates. Monistero "had a bullet wound in the abdomen which physicians said might prove fatal." Ferrari was also still alive but suffering from "four bullet wounds in his body." Tornatore was hospitalized with merely "a bullet wound in the arm." Why were the three marked for death? They were described by the United Press as "terrorist members of the notorious Joe Aiello gang," which was engaged in a new war with Al Capone's gang.

Within hours, Aiello's crew reportedly responded to the outrage with their own bullets, the United Press story revealed, traveling to the Manning Hotel in the village of Fox Lake, some fifty miles northwest of Chicago. Four men and a woman were "eating, drinking, and making merry" in an enclosed porch at the hotel, which stood on the shore of Pistakee Lake, the *Chicago Tribune* reported. The shooting started at 1:40 a.m. and,

"Within a few seconds a hundred bullets crashed through the panes of glass enclosing the porch. . . . There was no warning, no opportunity to flee or fight back. No one was able to see the slayers, who were clothed in the darkness of the night as they emptied machine guns and automatic pistols. The assassins' excited escape was heard, but none of them was seen except as shadows."[3]

The *Chicago Tribune* listed the dead as Sam Pellar, believed to be a member of Al Capone's gang, Michael Quirk of the Klondike–O'Donnell gang, and Joseph Bertsche, "safe blower and notorious crook with a police record of 30 years."

Some of the three mortally wounded men proved surprisingly animated in their final moments, according to hotel bartender Louis Capella: "Pellar ran upstairs to the kitchen before he fell dead, Bertsche ran up the other stairs into one of the bedrooms, where he fell."

Wounded were beer baron, George Druggan, and Vivian Ponic McGinnis. Druggan was given "a 50–50 chance to live" by his surgeons. McGinnis, wife of Chicago attorney Arthur McGinnis, was "shot four times in the abdomen," the *Tribune* reported. "I went to her and started to help her up," Capella told the *Tribune* the morning after what came to be known as the "Fox Lake Massacre," "but she screamed at me to go away."

Despite the severity of their injuries, Druggan and McGinnis survived the shooting and were close to recovery a month later, the *New York Times* reported.[4] And, in a peculiar twist, Vivian divorced her husband, married Druggan three years later, and went on to live another sixty years, dying in 1993 at age ninety.[5]

While police told the *Tribune* the Fox Lake killings were part of a war for new beer territories beyond Chicago's city limits, the United Press claimed the shootings represented a fight for survival by gangs whose profits were getting choked in the Windy City, thanks in part to its new vigilantes. "[Behind] the war of extermination between Capone and Aiello was seen the hand of the Chicago Crime Commission, the 'secret six' of the Association of Commerce and the Police Department," read the United Press story. "All three organizations have been struggling for six months to make gangsterism unprofitable. They shut gambling houses, closed dog race tracks and raided breweries so frequently that all of Chicago's gangsters could not exist on the business available."

Public Enemies

The Chicago Crime Commission, also a creation of the Association of Commerce, was mentioned earlier in this book as having been snubbed by the Association when it formed the Secret Six. Although the press of the day sometimes lumped the Crime Commission and the Secret Six together or used their names interchangeably, the bodies were distinct; when he was founding the Secret Six, Randolph requested no help from either the Crime Commission or its president, Frank Loesch, a nationally recognized figure on crime and punishment who also served on President Herbert Hoover's national crime commission.

Although the Chicago Crime Commission, unlike its secretive upstart little brother, never employed private detectives, went undercover, worked on individual cases, or tortured anyone, it was an important player in Chicago law enforcement and did its part to reduce gangland operations. One of its most famous acts was distributing a "public enemies" list of twenty-eight of Chicago's most notorious gangsters, together with a list of how authorities should make their lives unpleasant. (It was published in April 1930, two months after the formation of the Secret Six, and quite possibly inspired by them.) The list included Al Capone, his brother Ralph, Capone liquor rivals Joe Aiello and George "Bugs" Moran, and several men who belonged on the list on the strength of nickname alone, particularly Edward "Spike" O'Donnell, Tony "Mops" Volpe, and William "Three Finger Jack" White.[6]

Loesch urged "vigilant watchfulness and arrests" against the twenty-eight, as well as "deportation of criminal aliens. Raids on disorderly houses controlled by them. Raids on gambling houses, night clubs, dog tracks, etc., in which they are interested or which they frequent, . . . Publication of business and residence addresses, business affiliations."

The formation of the Secret Six in February 1930 seemed to propel Chicago toward far more aggressive policing, but so too did the Crime Commission's April 1930 list. In fact, Police Chief Russell, list in hand, swore to "cooperate in harassing the 'public enemies' in every way possible," including by forming a "hoodlum squad" which would be tasked with "hunting these 28 men and arresting them whenever they appear on the streets."[7]

Not to be outdone by the Crime Commission and its list, the Secret Six was also playing a leading role in gathering information on crime that year.

In September 1930 alone, the group was mentioned at least three times as a key player in major criminal investigations:

- The Secret Six, the Chicago Crime Commission, and the Employers' Association united to gather data listing the tributes paid to Chicago's mobsters, with the ultimate objective to "break the grip of the racket bosses," the *Daily News* of New York City reported on September 1. Not even miniature golf courses were spared the gangsters' grip, the groups had learned. Each of Chicago's two hundred courses had to pay $35 upon incorporation and another $5 monthly to the crooks, for a total first year outlay in 2024 dollars of close to $2,000 (worth almost $40,000 in 2024 dollars). The crooks were also preparing to demand union dues from all miniature golf employees, the *Daily News* reported.[8]
- The Association of Commerce hired Attorney Marshall Solberg, also employed as assistant prosecutor in John Swanson's State's Attorney's office, to help the Secret Six gather evidence against racketeers in the city.[9]
- When John P. McGoorty, chief justice of Chicago's Criminal Court, issued a call for a prosecutorial war on the city's racketeers, State's Attorney Swanson pledged his support and said he expected the Secret Six "to supply considerable evidence" in the drive.[10]

The Secret Six did more than merely gather information, however. In late 1930, a Black Congressman was in danger, and the Secret Six was on the case.

8

The Case of the Extorted Congressman

OSCAR STANTON DE PRIEST was born to former slaves in Florence, Alabama, in 1871. Like many Black and mixed-race people in the decades after the Civil War, his parents fled Southern oppression, first heading to Salina, Kansas, in 1878, where the young man made money as a painter and decorator. In 1889, when he was eighteen, his parents moved farther north, to Chicago, where, De Priest went into real estate, a field in which he excelled.[1]

He was elected to the Cook County Board of Commissioners in 1904, and in 1915 became the first African American elected to the Chicago City Council, representing the Second Ward.[2] Thirteen years later, in 1928, the pioneering De Priest achieved another historic milestone, becoming the first African American congressman elected to the House of Representatives from a northern state.[3]

Chosen to represent the First District of Illinois, he was also the first Black Congressman from any state since 1901.[4] De Priest's arrival in Congress was not without controversy. Congress's Southern segregationists, appalled that a Black man would soon be serving equally beside them, tried in vain to block the swearing in of all of the Illinois delegation, and when First Lady Lou Henry Hoover invited De Priest's wife, Jessie, to a tea on June 12, 1929 (as she did for the spouses of all Congresspeople), the White House was inundated with hostile telegrams.[5]

On September 8, 1930, animosity toward De Priest took on a much more personal tone, when he received a letter at his Chicago office at 3439 South

State Street. "You are not wanted in Washington," declared the letter, described by the *Chicago Tribune* as "crudely printed on cheap paper."[6]

"Hon. Oscar De Priest:" the letter began, "We come to Chicago with the avowed purpose of assassinating you. We have been well paid for this mission. However, having no personal grievance against you, we have decided to play the middle against both ends. We are to receive $5,000 at the conclusion of the job. In exchange for your life and documentary and other evidence against certain high officials in Washington and Alabama, we demand from you ten thousand dollars;* now we know you have it and we demand it without fail."

The letter, signed the "Brooklyn Rats," promised that if they didn't get their money, or if De Priest notified anyone, "it will only react as a steam shovel for your grave," adding "nothing on earth will save you no matter how much wealth or influence you may have."

On the advice of John Hawkins, De Priest's bodyguard and a former policeman, De Priest went to the Secret Six, not the Chicago police. He took the letter to Col. Randolph the day after its arrival, and Randolph encouraged him to go, again, not to the police but to Secret Six lawyer Walter Walker. It was Walker who worked with the Illinois State's Attorney's office to develop a plan to catch the extortionists.

In the following days, in twists and turns worthy of a spy novel, De Priest was instructed to run a personal ad in the *Chicago Daily News*, reading "I agree to your proposition, O. D. P." De Priest ran the ad on Thursday and Friday, September 11 and 12, and on that Friday, the extortionists told him to "have ready for instant delivery a package containing ten thousand dollars in five, ten and twenty dollar denominations." As instructed, De Priest headed out that evening with bodyguard Hawkins and a Black plainclothes policeman, their destination the restroom of the Douglas Park elevated line, where they found, as the *Chicago Tribune* described it, "a match box, within which were further directions on a wadded sheet of paper."

The instructions on the wadded sheet told De Priest to go "three blocks west to a ramp at 17th and Wood streets, leading to the elevated tracks of the Baltimore and Ohio." Once there, the *Tribune* reported, Hawkins and the plainclothes officer hid in a box car, and "De Priest, carrying a cigar box containing $200 [note, not $10,000] in marked money, proceeded alone. In

---

* Worth almost $200,000 in 2024 dollars.

accordance with the match box directions, he found a shanty on which a huge X was chalked. The shanty was locked, but an aperture had been sawed in the door and there De Priest dropped the cigar box."

Now it was time to launch the stakeout hatched by Secret Six attorney Walker and the State's Attorney's office. Walker, Lt. Andrew Barry, and Barry's squad of Chicago cops waited overnight, watching the shanty. At 10:00 a.m. the next morning, a milk truck belonging to Capital Dairy pulled up to the shanty; the driver got out, unlocked the building, retrieved the cigar box, and returned to his vehicle.

Barry and his squad followed at a judicious distance, watching when a sedan pulled up to the milk truck. The truck driver, the *Chicago Tribune* reported, "alighted from the truck, conferred a moment with three occupants of the sedan, and drove on." Barry's team noted the sedan's license plate and raced back to headquarters to look it up. Turns out the owner of the car was one Julius J. Link, described in the *Tribune* as twenty-eight years old and "a minor political figure in De Priest's district." The cops got a search warrant and raided Link's home before noon that day, where they arrested Link and seized "a quantity of liquor, two sawed off shotguns and a pistol."

The milk truck driver, twenty-five-year-old Solly Lason, was picked up when he arrived at the milk depot, the *Tribune* reported. And although Link refused to talk, Lason confessed to everything, claiming that Link—a longtime acquaintance—had proposed the plot to him. A man Lason identified as Joseph Gladstone was also in on the plot, he told authorities, who quickly concluded that Gladstone was most likely "racketeer" Joseph Goldstein, and they began the hunt for him and his regular partner in crime, "notorious forger" Aaron Moshiek. "The Police suspect Moshiek may have organized the plot," the *Chicago Tribune* reported the day after Link and Lason were arrested.[7]

Observing one of the more peculiar law enforcement conventions of the era, the Chicago Police assembled all available parties to the crime in one place and invited the newspapers to come and snap a few pictures. So here we see, on page two of the September 14, 1930, *Chicago Tribune*, arrestees Solly Lason and Julius Link sitting together with a handful of law enforcement officials, including Chicago Police Lt. Andrew Barry and Secret Six lawyer Walter Walker. And in the middle of the portrait sits Congressman De Priest, who appears to be inspecting a pipe or a very long, homemade gun. Lason looks on from De Priest's immediate right, a shotgun and a belt

The main players in the Oscar De Priest extortion case. Left to right, seated: Suspect Solly Lason, Congressman Oscar De Priest, suspect Julius Link, and Secret Six attorney Walter Walker. Left to right, standing: Police Captain Paul Wheeler, Assistant State's Attorney C. Wayland Brooks, and Police Lieutenant Andrew Barry. The guns in the picture were seized from Link's home. / Chicago Tribune/TCA

or vest lined with shotgun shells draped across his lap. Link, looking dapper in a suit and tie, appears to be unarmed, his eyes on something in the middle distance.

The Chicago police also invited both De Priest and, apparently, the *Tribune* into at least part of the interrogation of Link. Link, who had run unsuccessfully for a seat in the Illinois legislature "on the anti-De Priest ticket at the last election," whirled on the congressman as Barry was questioning him and shouted, "You've got all the patronage in the district. I'm broke. I've been starving to death down there."[8]

Link went on to plead guilty to the crime and, in June 1931, was sentenced to six months in jail. De Priest, who fought for racial equality and anti-lynching laws in Congress, "appeared in court," according to newspaper wire stories, "and agreed to reduction of the charge against Link from a felony, under which he would have been liable to several years' imprisonment, to a misdemeanor."[9]

Solly Lason's trial was scheduled to begin a few days after Link's sentencing, but no more appears in the searchable press about him in any context. We might guess the trial never occurred, the forgiving De Priest wishing to be done with the matter and believing the humble milk truck driver had been duped into his role as an extorter. Joseph Goldstein was never caught, and Moshiek was dropped as a suspect.[10]

A year later, in October 1931, Secret Six chief Robert Randolph gave his group credit for solving the De Priest case and knocked the Chicago police in the process. Randolph, after twenty months as head of the Secret Six, had come to Rochester, New York, to speak to the Chamber of Commerce there. He was by then renowned nationwide as one of America's most respected crimefighters and feted frequently by social and business groups around the country eager to hear his thoughts on crime and punishment.

"All the resources of science and extra-legal expedients such as listening in on telephone conversations, are at the disposal of operatives of Chicago's 'Secret Six,'" reported the *Rochester Democrat and Chronicle,* which quoted Randolph as boasting (quite inaccurately) that "No one knows who our operatives are and the operators themselves do not know each other."[11] In running down a list of Secret Six accomplishments, the *Democrat and Chronicle* reported, Randolph spoke of "how an attempt to extort $10,000 from Oscar De Priest, colored representative in Congress, was broken up" by the Secret Six. "It was not very clever detective work," he said of the De Priest case. "Most anyone could have detected it, even a policeman."

De Priest was elected twice more to Congress, serving a total of six years before he lost in 1934. He ran again and lost again in 1936, after which he returned to real estate and local politics. He was a delegate to the Republican National Convention in 1936 and served another term on the Chicago City Council, from 1943 to 1947. And, despite all the death threats and at least one instance of extortion, he died of natural causes in 1951.[12]

The De Priest incident of September 1930 was one of three major extortion cases the Secret Six worked that autumn, two where they followed the same playbook, and a third, involving a debutante named Marion Wright, where they went off script with catastrophic results.

In October, Dr. Lewis K. Eastman, head of the Keystone Hospital, started getting letters. "Pay us $5,000 or we'll kidnap your three children," read the first. Follow-up letters demanded that the money be paid in certain denominations, including "seven hundreds, ten fifties."[13] The final letter instructed Eastman to package up the money and give it to a Western Union messenger, reported the *Chicago Herald and Examiner.* The messenger was to be instructed to wait with the package "on the northeast corner of Kostner and Madison sts. at 4 o'clock" on the afternoon of October 23, 1930. When someone approached the messenger and asked for "the package for Tony," the messenger was to hand it over.

As Rep. Oscar De Priest had done the previous month, and as steel magnate William Van Doren Wright would do the next month, Dr. Lewis Eastman went not to the police but to the Secret Six, and together they set a trap: "A uniformed messenger with a package was sent to the spot. Detectives in a car a block away were watching. A 12-year-old boy called for the package, got it, and boarded a street car. The police trailed the car until the boy alighted at Cicero av. and Madison st." There, the boy handed over the package to John Dalton, and the Secret Six swooped in and arrested Dalton, twenty-one, whose brother Willie, according to the *Herald and Examiner,* "in 1921 stole $750,000 in securities from the Northern Trust Company."

Once in custody, Dalton named Thomas Hughes, nineteen, as his accomplice. The twelve-year-old boy, identified only as "Harold" by the *Herald and Examiner,* "had no knowledge of the plot" and performed his unwitting role in the scheme for $1.50.

The Secret Six brought Assistant State's Attorney C. Wayland Brooks in once the perpetrators were arrested, and he received the following confession from Dalton: "We've been planning this job about a week. First we thought we'd pick a man from the telephone book to get the money from, but we wanted to be sure we got a rich one, and Hughes said Dr. Eastman must be rich because he drove a Rolls Royce. We typed out letters on a machine at the Austin night school and mailed the last one from Cicero, so Dr. Eastman would think it came from Capone or somebody like that."

The Secret Six protected congressman and wealthy doctors alike at the end of their first year in existence, and a few weeks later they would turn their attention to the extortion letters being sent to the daughter of a wealthy steel magnate, committing the earliest of a series of epic stumbles. But in late fall of 1930, the press was glowing and the vigilantes were riding high.

9

The New Top Cop, and the Case of the Pinochle Shootout

BY THE END of their first year, news on several scores compounded the historic preeminence of the Secret Six:

- In November 1930, the Secret Six announced that a staggering $5 million, worth almost $100 million in 2024 dollars, had been raised in cash and pledges to help the group fight crime over the next five years. Given that a Chicago cop's average annual salary was $2,414, the money was enough to assemble and field a police force of over four hundred officers for a year.[1]
- At the end of October, the Secret Six brought on federal prohibition agent Alexander Jamie as chief investigator. "In his prohibition job," the *Chicago Tribune* reported, "he was known to have refused huge bribes, and government officials speak of him as a man of high intelligence and integrity."[2]
- Jamie, representing the Secret Six, spoke at an unusual Chicago-region crime initiative directed by police administration professor August Vollmer. Launched November 20, 1930, at the University of Chicago, the 115 attendees included judges, police chiefs, and J. Edgar Hoover, head of the Federal Bureau of Investigation.[3]

The hiring of Jamie, universally considered incorruptible, was major news, with papers across the nation announcing both his appointment by the

Secret Six and the immense power he would wield. He had not left his job with the feds—he simply had been granted a leave of absence, meaning he remained a G-man as well as the top cop for the Secret Six, which, at the time, was still being afforded a remarkable degree of both respect and authority by public law enforcement agencies in Chicago. The United Press summed up Jamie's role this way:

> Jamie . . . will be given triple powers in his offensive against gang machine gunners and racketeers. He retains his federal powers by virtue of his furlough and will be given state and city police powers to such an extent that he probably will become a sort of law enforcement dictator, wielding powers, both legal and extra-legal, that will transcend those of the commissioner of police and the state's attorney . . . Commissioner John H. Alcock,* State's Attorney (John) Swanson and his investigator, Pat Roche, will be carrying out Jamie's orders in the greatest crime drive in the history of Chicago.[4]

In a profile of Jamie published by the *Rock Island (Illinois) Argus* a year after his appointment, he was described as "a quiet, shy man, who always catches the 5:15 to Beverly, his suburban home. . . . He is six feet tall, slender and quiet as a mill pond. His wife is principal of one of the Chicago schools."[5] Jamie was born and raised in Pullman, a suburb of Chicago, the *Argus* wrote. "He had been in law enforcement all his adult life and knew the ways of the wayward thereabouts. At Washington, he was first deputy commissioner under E. C. Yellowley and then chief of the special intelligence unit."

Weeks after joining the Secret Six, Jamie was still making news for his federal work. On December 12, 1930, Jamie and his undercover team were credited for the investigative effort that led to the indictment of eighteen suspected prohibition violators, including Al Capone's brother Ralph. Ralph was described in news reports as "the principal owner" of two illegal speakeasies, the Cotton Club and a second establishment known variously as the Mont Marte or Greyhound Grill.[6]

Interviewed the day after his appointment to the Secret Six by the International News Service, Jamie suggested that it was time for the Secret Six to "sink out of sight" after nine months in the eager pursuit of headlines.

---

* Chicago's embattled police chief, William Russell, was replaced by Acting Chief John Alcock in June 1930.

"In the past the law enforcement agencies have been hindered by too much publicity," Jamie said. "Gangsters were given advance notice that the police were looking for them. From now on there will be a lid on this sort of thing, as far as possible."[7]

"We will work through the regularly established agencies, supplemented by a staff of our own investigators for special work," promised Jamie, who was described in the article as both "field marshal" and "commander-in-chief" in the "war against the underworld." Added Jamie, "You won't hear about us until the results are turned up in the courts." Jamie's pledge of secrecy was almost immediately violated, as it would be repeatedly in the years to come. There was, for example, a pinochle game that turned bloody within a month of Jamie's hiring.

The Case of the Pinochle Shootout

Every Saturday night about 6:00 p.m. in the early 1930s, business owners in what is known today as the West Loop of Chicago would gather at a café on 818 West Randolph Street to play pinochle.

The merchants brought plenty of cash to the weekly competition, and five members of the underworld took note and began planning their own visit to the event. The indiscreet hoods spoke openly of their plans to raid the games on November 29, 1930, and were overheard by "stool pigeons," who passed on the word to others who eventually relayed them to the Secret Six.[8] The Secret Six, in turn, notified Chicago Police Chief of Detectives John Norton,[†] providing Norton with what the *Chicago Tribune* described as "detailed and exact reports of the intended robbery hours before its execution."[9]

Two police sergeants, Daniel Healy and Edward Tyrrell, assembled a team of eight plainclothes cops, and at 5:00 p.m., they set up a stakeout in a building across the street from the café. "At 5:55 a black sedan pulled to the curb," the *Chicago Tribune* reported. "Two men emerged from the sedan, peered through the restaurant window, and beckoned towards the car. Another pair got out, leaving one man at the wheel, and all four entered the restaurant. . . . Twenty players were at the restaurant tables when the robbers entered. Obeying sharp commands they had crowded to the wall with hands upraised." Tragically, the police had apparently decided to let

[†] Norton replaced John Stege as chief of detectives in June 1930.

the robbery get going before they intervened, stepping in from the restaurant's vestibule and announcing themselves only after the thugs began rifling through the victim's pockets.

Out on the street, meanwhile, Sergeant Healy confronted the getaway driver, shoving his shotgun through the sedan window and telling the man to surrender. Instead, the driver put the car in gear and it "leaped forward, the fender brushing the sergeant. He fired three shots, the last of which apparently took effect, for the wrecked car was bloodstained when found ten minutes later." After the car crashed into a building at 733 West Randolph, four hundred feet from the café, the driver fled. The police speculated he was Sam Battaglia, "recently acquitted of a charge of robbing Mayor Thompson's wife."

Inside the café, where the cops initially had the upper hand, the gunfire on the street was clearly audible, and it led to disaster. "Sergt Healy unwittingly precipitated the gun play" within the restaurant. "Startled by Sergt. Healy's shots in the street," the *Chicago Tribune* reported, (suspected robber Dan) Clementi wheeled and found himself facing the muzzle of Sergt. Tyrrell's gun. He dropped his pistol and raised his hands." However, the gunfire from the street prompted another of the crooks to start shooting, and "Clementi retrieved his weapon and ran toward the kitchen."

At this point, it was bedlam, the cops and the crooks trading gunfire in the crowded café, with a fifty-eight-year-old egg wholesaler named Leonard S. Sanor caught in the middle. "As shots whizzed from both sides, the terrified Sanor arose and started across the room. He fell, a pistol bullet in the back of his head."

Two of the four robbers, Joseph "Little Katzie" Catrino and Joseph Pupelli, attempted to exit the restaurant and were arrested by the waiting cops without further ado. The other two crooks, Clemente and Philip Epstein, headed for the basement. Three weeks after the shootout, the *Chicago Tribune* revealed what happened next. As Sanor lay dying:

> (Officer) Tyrrell plunged after them nevertheless, his shotgun roaring, and they ran down the basement stairs, still armed, and protected by the dark of their hiding places. Tyrrell dashed headlong to the stair well.
>
> "Come out of there, you," he shouted down. "I'll blow your heads off if you don't."
>
> "Stick your head down here and you'll get it blowed off yourself!" a voice screamed from the pit of blackness.

> "I will, will I?" shouted Tyrrell, and he stumbled down toward the voice. "Throw those guns away and come over here," he ordered. Presently two forms slunk to his side and he herded them back into the restaurant.[10]

For his courage, Tyrrell won a $100 award from the *Chicago Tribune*. And the Secret Six, whose tip was mentioned once again in the *Tribune's* story about the award, got another feather in its cap—if by feather one means credit for a stakeout so poorly conducted by the cops they're lucky only one innocent man died.

But why did the Secret Six get mentioned at all? On the day he was hired, October 31, 1930, Alexander Jamie promised that "You won't hear about us until the results are turned up in the courts." But a month later, articles in at least two newspapers identified the Secret Six as the tipsters in the pinochle raid. And three weeks after that, the Secret Six was still getting the credit. Normally, because police informants turn up dead often enough, they are never identified. Unless they want to be. Either Jamie wasn't really trying to reduce the publicity given to his new employers, or someone else was working against him.

At the end of 1930, however, Jamie had a bigger problem on his hands, because he didn't quash the Secret Six investigation into Marion Wright's extortion.

10

The Case of the Queer Actor

BETWEEN NOVEMBER 22 and December 3, 1930, eighteen-year-old Marion Wright received five increasingly bizarre extortion letters. As described in detail in the first chapter of this book, the letters demanded first $25,000 in cash, then $50,000, the latter sum worth almost $1 million in 2024. If she didn't pay up, she was warned, "a wonderful but deadly dart" with a range of three thousand feet would be "dipped in a very deadly poison" before it was aimed her way.

The letter writer, who identified himself as "Lester McKay," admitted he employed "drug addicts," and ended his second letter with a confession: "Have seen you in person last night, and may I compliment you on your good looks?"

In one letter, received a week before the young socialite's debut at the exclusive Casino Club, he threatened to kill Marion's father, wealthy steel magnate William Van Doren Wright. "I was truly alarmed when I received the letters," Mr. Wright testified in court two years later. "In fact, I went armed for a while. As the letters continued to come in, I notified the Secret Six and asked for a guard."[1]

Secret Six detective Edgar Dudley, a former Prohibition agent, was assigned to the Wright case. "Dudley came to my house and discussed the letters with Marian* and myself," Mr. Wright testified. "He went over all her list of acquaintances and her actions for weeks past."[2]

---

* The correct spelling of Miss Wright's first name was *Marion*, but its frequent misspelling as *Marian* by the press is maintained here for the sake of historical accuracy.

The letters kept arriving, Mr. Wright said, prompting him to send Marion to St. Louis for her own safety. Before she left, however, she told Dudley she could think of just one acquaintance who might, possibly, fit the profile of the extortionist: William Speer Kuhn Jr. As Mr. Wright described it later in court, "the only person she could think of who had acted queer was Kuhn. She mentioned him."

Mr. Wright did not go to the police, and the Secret Six, now under the guidance of former Prohibition agent Alexander Jamie, did not go to the police either. Instead, they decided to work the case themselves. As in the extortion cases of Congressman De Priest and Dr. Eastman, the Secret Six at first advised compliance with the extortionist's demands. Donald L. Kooken, Jamie's assistant, placed an ad in the *Chicago Tribune* as demanded. It appeared on page forty-three of the November 27, 1930, paper. "McKAY:" it read. "EVERYTHING DONE AS PER instruction M. S. W."[3]

Along with placing the ad, the Secret Six began looking into William Kuhn. Kuhn, square-jawed, handsome and, like Marion, from a wealthy family, was a strange lad. He had a drinking problem. He might also be called, in modern parlance, a sexual predator, although that's not what anyone would have called him back then. And he was not particularly lucky.

According to newspaper reports, William Kuhn first met Marion Wright at Chicago's exclusive Casino Club in mid-November 1930.[4] The two hit it off at first. The eighteen-year-old Marion, who had recently returned to Chicago after attending high school in France,[†] went on several dates with twenty-three-year-old William, who worked with his older brother as an investment clerk.[5]

The worldly Kuhn, eager to show Marion the adult playgrounds where Chicagoans could buy and drink illegal liquor, "escorted her on several occasions to night clubs and once to a speakeasy."[6] On their first date, Kuhn admitted in court to drinking "two or three" highballs. Their last date was to a speakeasy on Chicago's north side, the first such establishment Marion had ever visited, according to her 1932 testimony.[7]

[†] Marion attended Mlle. Le Boucher's school in Paris, according to a note in the social pages of the May 4, 1930, *Chicago Tribune*, but she probably didn't graduate. The 1940 Census lists her as having just three years of high school education.

As was their habit, they started their time together that night at the Casino Club, but Kuhn proposed they go to Bal Tabarin in Chicago's Loop to meet some friends. They took a taxi together, but they ended up not at Bal Tabarin but at 69 East Walton Street. In court testimony two years later, Marion recalled the conversation this way, according to the *Chicago Tribune:*[8]

"Where are we?" she asked.

"This is a speakeasy," Kuhn told her.

"I'm not supposed to go into speakeasies."

"Aw, come on," Kuhn retorted, winning over the girl, who was often described as "pretty" in the stories about her.

Marion claimed in her testimony that Kuhn drank "at least two highballs" at the speakeasy and also got hold of a pint of gin at some point, which he finished up at their next stop, the College Inn. After that, they got into a cab for the drive back to the Wright home.

"What was his condition on the way home?" Marion was asked during a trial in 1932.

"He was extremely drunk—incoherent," Marion answered. "I thought he was out of his head."[9]

The *Chicago Tribune* reported the rest of Marion's witness stand testimony this way:

"Did he attempt to kiss you in the taxicab?

The witness flushed and replied briefly[,] "Yes."

"Did you permit it?"

"No."

"Was he insistent?"

"Yes."

"What happened when you got home?"

"I told my father I thought he was not all there—that he was a queer actor and that I would never go out with him again."

Kuhn himself remembered the incident similarly. The *Chicago Tribune* recorded his testimony in court as follows:

"In the cab on the way home did you try to kiss her?"

"Yes."

"Did you throw your arms around her?"

"Yes."

"What did she say?"

"I don't remember anything she said except 'No.'"[10]

Drunk and rejected, Kuhn grew angry, according to news reports: "As they parted after the quarrel, Miss Wright admitted to police, Kuhn remarked that he would 'get even.'"[11]

It was Edgar Dudley's first case with the Secret Six, and it was an easy one. A suspect with a drinking problem, a predatory streak, and a motive. But Dudley kept digging. Kuhn's drinking behavior was particularly disturbing. Dudley discovered that alcohol had cost the young man at least one clerking job at a brokerage house.[12]

While Kuhn was described in one newspaper story as "The son of a wealthy retired California broker and a resident of the exclusive Ambassador East Hotel," who was "well known in Chicago society," Dudley learned that Kuhn was also known well by the speakeasies.[13]

As he researched Kuhn's behavior at the speakeasies, Dudley kept Mr. Wright abreast of his growing concerns. Wright remembered the gist of one of those conversations during his 1932 testimony: "[Dudley] told me he didn't know whether he had the right man, but that we certainly had a queer actor. He had gone to some speakeasies where Kuhn was well known and had been told in one that he had been barred from there because of his actions, and at another they said he would buy a highball and sit for half an hour and talk to it as though it were a person."[14]

Dudley, his investigation into Kuhn gaining steam, got access to the room at the Ambassador Hotel that William Kuhn shared with his brother Wendell. There, Dudley testified in 1932, he "found lurid detective stories."[15]

Unbeknownst to either William or Wendell, Dudley and other detectives were methodically closing the net around the younger brother, as recounted in a wire story that made the rounds in December 1930: "Learning of the 'get even' remark which [Marion] said Kuhn had made, Detectives William Knowles and Leo Carr of the 'Secret Six' visited the investment house where Wendell Kuhn is an executive and where William is employed as a clerk. Samples were taken from seven typewriters in the business house."[16]

The detectives brought the typed samples and the original extortion letters to no less than Dr. Ferdinand Watzek, an esteemed Viennese criminologist who was working with the crime detection laboratory at Northwestern University. After reviewing the documents, Dr. Watzek "submitted an opinion that samples of typewriting from machines available to Kuhn in the brokerage office where he worked were identical with that in the extortion missives."[17]

One of the typewriters was impounded, but the thoroughgoing Dudley wasn't done yet. Did William ever work late, alone? Is that when he might have typed the five extortion letters to Marion? Yes, on both counts.[18]

The proof was overwhelming that William Kuhn was the imaginative extortionist, the inventor of the (most likely fictitious) "wonderful but deadly dart." He had the means, motive, and disposition to have written those five letters, which weren't just skin-crawlingly creepy but also full of explicit threats to kill Marion and her father. This was a serious crime. Recall that the man who extorted Congressman De Priest with threats of death got sentenced to six months, but could have served years for the plot.

The crime was also part of a growing and terrifying trend among Chicago's upper crust, ensuring its aggressive prosecution by law enforcement, official or otherwise. As the *Chicago Tribune* reported in December 1930, "So serious has the extortion racket become that several families, it is said, have sent their debutante daughters to winter homes while others have employed private detectives to protect them."[19]

Unfortunately, William was out of town when the Secret Six decided it was time to bring him to justice; he was visiting his sister in Boston. So Edgar Dudley and Alexander Jamie visited his brother, Wendell, while he was at work at Winthrop, Mitchel & Co., a brokerage firm.[20]

Dudley and Jamie started off by reading some of the extortion letters to Wendell. Wendell, asked to summarize his reaction two years later in court, said he told the detectives, "Those are malicious letters," adding, "I told them that my brother had never done a malicious thing in his life. I said that I couldn't see how he could have had anything to do with the notes."

Dudley, Wendell recalled, "told me he had been investigating my brother and his activities. During the investigation, he told me, he had entered our rooms at the Ambassador hotel seeking a typewriter from which the typewritten notes might have been made."

While Dudley admitted to Wendell he'd found no such machine in the brothers' rooms (he probably didn't mention the typewriter they'd found at the brokerage office, but that's not clear), he mentioned the "two volumes of detective stories," and "said he believed my brother got the idea for writing the letters from reading these tales." To that assertion, Wendell remembered, "Of course, I just laughed at him, but he was serious. He wanted to know what my brother habitually read."

Wendell told Dudley and Jamie that his brother read the *Saturday Evening Post* and *Time* magazine, and claimed that the two detective novels were gifts from friends, and were among "thirty or forty other books there." The titles of the two books were not revealed in the press, but the *Cincinnati Enquirer* hinted at least one of them might have been a Sherlock Holmes book, suggesting the extortionist "stole Conan Doyle's stuff with poison darts as the lethal weapons, for the famous English writer had his dacoits (meaning villains) . . . use them in his mystery tales. A clever dacoit, however, was doing good if he hurled a dart fifty feet. Miss Wright's enemy claimed 3,000 feet was not too far to deal death."[21]

The Secret Six sleuths next brought up the question of William's drinking. Wendell, clearly trying to protect his brother throughout the interview, recalled the exchange this way when he testified in November 1932:

"Do you know that your brother is well known in speakeasies on the near north side, so well known, in fact, that in two of these places he is called by his first name by the bartenders?"

"I'm not surprised. Many of his friends and my own friends as well as lots of other people go to speakeasies."

"How about his drinking? That's bad, isn't it?"

"My brother, like all other young men of this day, drinks. Sometimes he even drinks too much. But he is not a malicious drinker."

Despite Wendell's brotherly protestations, the detectives grew certain they had their man, and they asked Wendell to implore his brother to come back to Chicago to face the music. Wendell complied, calling his brother to let him know he was a wanted man, and William Kuhn returned to Chicago, showing up voluntarily at the offices of the Secret Six on December 6, 1930.

Determined to tie up all the loose ends, to prove beyond a shadow of a doubt that William was indeed the extortionist, the vigilantes kept Kuhn in their own custody for three days, until December 9.[22]

He was held in the Secret Six's makeshift jail at the St. Clair Hotel, a building that still stands at the corner of North St. Clair and East Ohio streets, its elaborate façade protected by the faces of snarling lions.[‡]

[‡] This author visited the old hotel in 2023 with hopes of uncovering some lingering evidence of the Secret Six's lockup, as it remains an important historic site, perhaps

The St. Clair Hotel, more recently a Chicago migrant shelter, was used by the Secret Six to hold and interrogate suspected criminals. William Kuhn spent several days there answering questions in the Marion Wright extortion case. / Kevin Meredith

---

the only place in America where vigilantes were officially empowered to incarcerate suspects for days without official charges. The building, renamed the Inn of Chicago at some point, served at the time of the author's visit as migrant housing for the City of Chicago. The author's excited queries about a prison operated there ninety years earlier by the Secret Six did not imbue the site's Hispanic managers with similar excitement, as none of them spoke much English. Instead, the author's visit left them confused, if not frightened, and he was politely asked to leave.

Menacing lion's heads still guard the exterior of what was once the St. Clair Hotel, used as a jail by the Secret Six. / Kevin Meredith

While imprisoned there, William was subjected to the full arsenal of investigative procedures perfected by the Secret Six since its founding ten months before. First came the interrogation by Dudley and others, with one newspaper claiming he'd been "mercilessly grilled for thirty-six hours in a hotel room by agents of this extra-legal body."[23] Next, Dudley escorted Kuhn to the Institute for Juvenile Research at 907 South Lincoln, where Kuhn was given a lie detector test by no less than John Larson, the man who'd created the polygraph in 1921.[24]

Testifying during the 1932 trial, Larson presented himself as both the originator of the lie detector test and established his scientific bona fides, citing "a list of subjects taught by himself in various universities, including biology, physiology, pharmacology, and psychiatry," and claiming "he was licensed to practice medicine and surgery in Illinois."

"Kuhn had expressed willingness to take the test," Larson said. The scientist "told of strapping a hollow tube across Kuhn's chest to record changes in breathing and adjusting cuffs on his wrists to show variations in blood pressure under the stress of emotion." Then came the questions:

"Then I asked, 'Have you any guilty knowledge of the extortion in regard to Marian Wright?' He answered, 'No.' I asked, 'Did you write this letter?' (showing him one of them). He said, 'No.' 'Do you know who did?' Again he said, 'No.' I showed him one of his actual letters to his brother and asked, 'Did you write this?' He said 'Yes.' Then I repeated those questions."

Larson's conclusion, as published in the *Chicago Tribune*: "The lie detector showed that Kuhn had guilty knowledge of the extortion letters received by Miss Wright."

Pursuing a confession by the youth, the Secret Six also tried to get him to spill the beans to someone masquerading as a fellow criminal. The entirety of the ruse was summed up in a newspaper wire story from November 1932: "A defense witness, Harry W. Gordon, 'Secret Six' investigator, testified that he, posing as a confidence man, was locked up in a hotel room with Kuhn and that the latter admitted his guilt to him."[25]

Finally, given the way the Secret Six worked several other cases, it seems likely they also tried to get William to confess to his own flesh and blood. While William was a prisoner of the Secret Six, the group allowed Wendell to visit him, most likely in a room at the St. Clair Hotel set up so they could eavesdrop on the brothers, possibly through an electronic bugging device, maybe through a hole in the wall (they used both in other cases, as will be described in the coming chapters).

All the Secret Six got from the meeting, however, was Wendell telling William "not to confess to anything."[26] But even without a brother-to-brother confession, the Secret Six had all they needed to get William Kuhn charged, tried, and convicted, and on December 9, 1930, after keeping the lad for three days, they went to the authorities.

Transitioning Kuhn from their custody to formal charges in an official court was no small undertaking, however. But before we delve into that process, the peculiar powers granted the Secret Six must be acknowledged. Not only were they the first and only law enforcement body summoned when a number of serious crimes were committed in Chicago, they also employed impressive powers of investigation, arrest,

Extortion suspect William Speer Kuhn Jr. / Chicago Tribune/TCA

and incarceration, all with little or no oversight from the Chicago Police or any other official body.

In fact, as stories through the years revealed, a number of police officers on the Chicago Police Department payroll were assigned exclusively to the Secret Six, taking orders from Alexander Jamie while working for the city. Two of them were named in the press as having participated in the Kuhn case, Sgt. William Knowles and Lt. Leo Carr, although Carr would later try to blur his involvement with the vigilantes. Other stories suggested that as many as five Chicago cops were at times assigned to the Secret Six.

Having city cops on your private police force meant you could do things private detectives typically couldn't. Recall that it was Knowles and Carr who got into Kuhn's place of work to check out the typewriters. How exactly they got permission to poke around at the private firm wasn't mentioned in the press, but one might guess some showing of police badges was involved. They may have gotten access to the Kuhn brothers' hotel room the same way.

Give the Secret Six credit though, and kudos to Edgar Dudley in particular, for quickly identifying Kuhn as the chief suspect, for darkening the doors of speakeasies and doing the other background work necessary to establishing the young man's character flaws, for successfully bringing him into custody, holding him for three days, locking him up with a plant, turning loose the inventor of the lie detector on him.

Now all they had to do was hand the boy and the evidence over to the authorities, and let the wheels of justice turn.

Case closed.

11

The Passion of William Speer Kuhn Jr.

NOW THAT THE SECRET SIX were done with William Kuhn, formal charges were required. The task was handled by Leo Carr and William Knowles, lieutenant and sergeant, respectively, for the Chicago police, but both on loan to the Secret Six.

The handoff from private to public institutions was not without its hiccups, however, as was revealed in court two years later. Although Carr didn't have a formal warrant charging Kuhn with extortion, "he believed he was in possession of sufficient evidence to connect Kuhn with the felony," he testified in November 1932.[1] The actual complaint against Kuhn, for attempted extortion, was signed by Knowles and presented to Municipal Judge John Lyle.

But there was a problem. Carr admitted to Lyle that neither Marion Wright nor her father wanted to prosecute young Kuhn. The newspaper articles about the crime don't say why the Wrights were hesitant, but we might guess they were reluctant to launch a felony case against someone in response to some, ultimately, silly letters. If the Wrights weren't going to press charges or participate in the prosecution of Kuhn, Lyle presumably recognized, a lot of time would have been wasted on a case that was about to fall apart. So Judge Lyle spoke bluntly to Lt. Carr, as Lyle testified in 1932: "I told the lieutenant that I didn't believe the police department should be responsible. I then insisted that either the girl or her parents should sign the complaint."[2]

Surely, the judge's decision created a minor panic. These blasted extortion letters were dropping all over Chicago's finest neighborhoods, the grandees going armed, their debutante daughters going about with bodyguards or fleeing to other towns. The threats alone were bad enough, but sometimes the letters were accompanied by actual bombs. The letters were nearly impossible to trace and the prosecutions rare, but now they'd caught someone red-handed, a talented, articulate, and especially creepy practitioner of the dark and growing art. Turn him loose, and he was sure to strike again. Just as bad, perhaps, abandon the case and lose a powerful example of the value of Chicago's new experiment in vigilantism.

So the Secret Six got Assistant State's Attorney C. Wayland Brooks involved. Brooks had been working closely with the Secret Six since their founding. As mentioned previously, he had been brought into other cases once the vigilantes were done working them, and in April 1930, two months after the Secret Six was established, he and Secret Six chief Robert Randolph stood together to present an update of Secret Six progress to the Chicago Association of Commerce. When Brooks ran for Illinois State Treasurer in 1932, he proudly listed his work with the vigilantes among his qualifications. "Appointed as assistant state's attorney of Cook county," read one campaign ad, "prosecuting many famous cases, especially for Chicago's 'Secret Six.'"[3]

So Brooks was happy to assist the Secret Six with the dilemma. If Knowles's signature wasn't good enough, he'd get the girl to sign. On December 8, 1930, while Kuhn was still in Secret Six custody, Secret Six Detective Edgar Dudley called William and Marion Wright to the Felony Court.[4] Brooks wanted to hear from the victim herself about Kuhn and why he was a suspect. Testifying in court two years later, she said she passed on what the Secret Six had revealed to her about her erstwhile gentleman caller: "I told him that Dudley and others said that Kuhn was barred from two speakeasies because he was a person who talked to his highball glass. And that the lie detector had proved him guilty."[5]

Brooks then drew forth the extortion complaint against Kuhn, crossed out Knowles's signature and told Marion to sign next to it.[6] "I said I didn't want to sign it," Marion recalled, "and father said he didn't want me to sign."

Another crisis. With Judge Lyle waiting for a complaint he could act on, and the Secret Six desperate to close another case and bring an extorter to justice, the victim wasn't cooperating. Brooks saved the day, assuring Mr. Wright and his daughter that nothing bad would happen if she signed. (Brooks, as it turned out, was disastrously wrong.) As Marion recalled, "Mr. Brooks said we wouldn't be responsible, so I did sign."

Left to right: William Van Doren Wright, his daughter Marion Wright, and Assistant State's Attorney C. Wayland Brooks, during a meeting on the day Marion signed a complaint against Kuhn. / Chicago Tribune/TCA

Brooks, asked at the same trial two years later about that moment, admitted that "Miss Wright signed the complaint without reading it."[7] Marion herself corroborated Brooks's testimony, calling herself an "unsophisticated debutante" at the time and saying of the complaint, "I hadn't the slightest idea what it was."[8]

With the complaint against William Kuhn officially filed, he could be officially arrested, his bond amount could be set, and the press could be notified. And this was big news. On December 10, 1930, the second biggest headline on the front page of the *Chicago Tribune* trumpeted Kuhn's arrest. "Seize Youth in Society Extortion Plot," the headline began. "Death Threats to Debutante Ask $25,000."

The story started with the villain's name and followed with his age, residence and parentage. "William Kuhn, 23 years old, living at the Ambassador East hotel, said to be the son of a retired California broker, was booked last night at the detective bureau on a charge of extortion in connection with an alleged $25,000 blackmail plot against Miss Marian Wright, 18 years old." Judge Lyle set bond at $7,500, the *Chicago Tribune* reported, an amount worth over $100,000 in 2024. Bond was posted by Kuhn's brother Wendell "a few minutes after the charge had been formally recorded."

The *Tribune* noted that Kuhn had been "seized" several days before by the Secret Six, and that his arrest was "based on four letters (the fifth letter hadn't been revealed by authorities yet) which threatened death to Miss Wright or her father." The *Tribune* added that the letters "were well written" and the first letter "described poisonous darts which could be dispatched noiselessly 3,000 feet."

Kuhn, spotted in court by the *Tribune* on December 10, was described as "nattily dressed," but the paper said he "appeared ill at ease before the judge. He toyed with his hat as the court was told that he was arrested Monday night after Mr. Wright had appealed to the 'secret six.'" Kuhn had lawyers by now, including John P. McGoorty Jr., son of the chief justice of the Criminal Court.[9]

Kuhn, according to the *Tribune,* "denied knowledge of the letters. He declared that any suspicion against him was ridiculous." Wendell Kuhn called the arrest "a mistake." According to one version of the story that went out on the wire, William called the charges "absurd."[10]

The brothers could protest all they wanted. Justice, in the form of a most toxic publicity, was about to be served, nationwide. Search "William Kuhn" from December 10, 1930, to January 20, 1931, in the newspapers.com database, and one will find stories about the boy and pictures of his handsome face in hundreds of newspapers across the nation (as well as two Canadian provinces). In the forty-eight contiguous states, the database indicates, newspapers in only four states did not mention Kuhn and his threats in the forty days after his arrest. Marion was called a "society girl" in some stories, her role in "Junior League theatrics" also noted, the fact that she was just eighteen years old—little more than a child—was almost always cited. Many papers (including in the January 9 edition of the *Fairbanks Daily News-Miner* in Alaska, not yet a US state), ran a small Associated Press piece featuring two pictures, one of Marion and William Wright, the other of William Kuhn, with a brief summary of the case, including the fact Kuhn had tried "to make the girl the victim of an extortion plot" and was "the son of a wealthy retired broker, living in California."[11]

Some articles mentioned the role of the Secret Six in the case, but many did not. But it hardly mattered to the cause of justice. A budding Chicago extortionist had been exposed. Surely he would never work in Chicago again. Or anywhere else, for that matter, doing anything. Who would want their groceries bagged, their shoes shined, their hedges trimmed by the likes of William Speer Kuhn Jr.?

Still, convicted by just the Secret Six and public opinion so far, Kuhn needed his day in court, where the kind of conviction that led to months or years in jail could be meted out. And here, the wheels of justice met another of the kind of snag common among criminal cases. Judge Lyle wanted to hold his first hearing on the charges against Kuhn on December 11, 1930. However, Marion's debut at the Casino Club—the very place where she'd met William a few weeks before—was scheduled for the evening of December 10, and she told the judge "she was to make her debut to society that night and would be too tired to appear in court the next morning." So the first hearing of the case was set back more than a month, to January 14, 1931.[12]

While William Kuhn, presumably, spent the evening of December 10 simultaneously mapping out his defense and surveying the tatters of his shredded reputation, Marion was having fun. The *Cincinnati Enquirer* offered this portrait of the girl on the night she was introduced to Chicago society:

> Guarded from threatened poison darts by a detail of private detectives, lovely Marian Wright, who made her bow to Chicago society last night in the exclusive Casino Club, today voiced her determination to unmask the extortionist plot against her.
>
> Gold Coast elegantes, giggling "debbies" and stately dowagers attended her coming-out party, while in the background lurked the operatives who had been retained to protect her.
>
> Somehow the stag line refused to view the letters seriously, and the smiling Marian was frequently referred to as the "darting debbie."

> But to the girls—ah, she was a heroine to them and they looked at her with awed faces as she recounted her reactions to the notes she had received from the extortionist with a flair for Casanovan adventure.[13]

The romance of the crime did not escape the notice of the press, and they can be forgiven for reducing the case to, as one wire story put it, an "oriental mystery thriller."[14]

But the extortion of Marion Wright was first and foremost a criminal matter, and further investigation was required by more official bodies. Like any such case, not all of the details fit neatly into the prevailing, nationally distributed narrative.

12

Nolle Prossed

WILLIAM KUHN PASSED through the holidays of 1930 with two dark clouds over his head, one criminal and one reputational. The reputational disaster might never be fixed, but maybe there was some hope for his criminal reckoning, set for January 14, 1931, when Municipal Judge John Lyle had decided his trial should begin.

Though Lyle had been described as the scourge of Chicago's criminal element in the press of the day, the intervening month and the spirit of the season had apparently softened the judge's heart where young Kuhn was concerned. The humiliating story of Lyle's opinion was distributed in mid-January 1931 by the Associated Press and ran in papers large and small, including the *Los Angeles Times*. It read in its entirety: "William Kuhn, 23-year-old son of a retired California broker, is no extortionist but a 'young kid with love fancies,' Judge Lyle said today. He postponed consideration of extortion charges against the youth and instructed his attorneys to have a conference with the parents of Miss Marian Wright, society debutante, to whom Kuhn wrote threatening letters. The letters were traced to him by examination of the typewriter he used."[1]

Note that the story assumed Kuhn's guilt and left only his motivation subject to question. Here was a youth—a young man, really, at the start of a career in finance—so emotionally immature he could find no other way to express his love for an attractive debutante than by threatening to kill her and her father.

Although extortionists often went to prison when they were caught, Judge Lyle proposed probation for Kuhn, if things could be worked out with Marion's parents.[2]

Meanwhile, the investigation continued. Someone, possibly one of Kuhn's attorneys, brought in a second forensic expert to take another look at those extortion letters. The man they found, Albert S. Osborne, was described in the *Chicago Tribune* as a "New York handwriting expert" who was "considered the foremost man in in his field." Osborne's startling conclusion, reported in the *Tribune's* January 22 edition: "The letters were not written on the typewriter in the brokerage office."[3]

Assistant State's Attorney C. Wayland Brooks, the Secret Six advocate who'd convinced Marion to sign that complaint against William the previous month, acknowledged in Superior Court on January 21, 1931, not only that the letters weren't written on the machine from William's brokerage, but that one of the extortion letters "was mailed from Chicago while Kuhn was in Boston." Brooks also admitted, vaguely, that "letters similar to those sent Miss Wright had been received after Kuhn's arrest." Brooks had no choice but to drop the case, to "nolle prosse" it, in legal terms.[4]

The first five letters sent to Marion Wright were well-documented in the press, their content and postmark date recorded for posterity. But Marion also received a sixth letter, the *Tribune* reported, postmarked in Chicago on December 9, 1930, while William Kuhn was in the custody of the Secret Six.

And then, after Kuhn's arrest was announced in the press, the enterprising "Lester McKay" started writing to Kuhn. "The same person who had threatened Miss Wright wrote a series of . . . letters to William Kuhn after his arrest became publicly known," the *Chicago Tribune* reported. "The writer demanded $25,000 and agreed to produce proof that Kuhn was not involved in the extortion demands."[5]

The new letters, dated December 11 and 13, helped exonerate William Kuhn themselves, however, no payment necessary. They were "obviously written on the same typewriter" used in the extortion of Marion Wright, Fred Burnham, Kuhn's attorney, told the *Chicago Tribune.*

William Kuhn, after more than a month of pillory and abuse, his name and picture splashed on newspapers coast to coast, had been found innocent before his trial even got underway. So he did what any young man from a wealthy family would do after suffering the nationwide destruction of his persona. He sued.

He sued Marion Wright. He sued her father, William Wright. He sued Secret Six detectives Alexander Jamie and Edgar Dudley. He sued respected criminologist Ferdinand Watzek, who had mistakenly reported a match between the typewriters used by "Lester McKay" and those available at Kuhn's brokerage. Kuhn sued in Superior Court for false arrest and malicious prosecution. He demanded $100,000, worth about $1.85 million in 2024.[6]

He didn't sue the Secret Six directly only because the group, "having no corporate existence," the *Chicago Tribune* explained, "could not be named a party to the suit in its own name."[7]

Fred Burnham, whose client had suffered national humiliation, turned the tables on the Secret Six, pulling no punches as he lambasted the group in stories that would also appear nationwide: "Attorney Burnham said the prosecution in the case was so bungled that his client felt that those responsible for keeping him under a cloud of suspicion for nearly two months should be made to pay. The attorney said it should have been obvious from the outset that his client was unjustly accused. 'When I first looked at the original letters and a specimen from the suspected typewriter I knew that a mistake had been made,' Burnham said. 'It did not take an expert to tell that they were not written on the same machine.'"[8]

Burnham, working to clear his client's name immediately after Kuhn had been charged the previous month, complained of a runaround by Chicago's police and prosecution, claiming that he'd "asked permission at that time to have J. Fordyce Wood, a handwriting expert of standing in Chicago, examine the documents, but was shunted from one official to another without any satisfaction."

Burnham noted that the Secret Six had simply ignored important exonerating evidence, particularly the arrival of more extortion letters while Kuhn was in Secret Six custody, and evidence the letters had been typed on the same typewriter as previous missives, even though the machine from Kuhn's workplace had been impounded.

Among those covering the fiasco was W. A. S. Douglas, writing for the Chicago bureau of the *Baltimore Sun,* who had offered articles of support and encouragement when the Secret Six was founded eleven months before. In that early coverage, he praised Col. Robert Randolph as "a man who typified the vigilante of pioneer days" and promised that, operating under each of the six men of the Secret Six, would "be a group of fearless fellows sworn to last-ditch action in the elimination of gangsters."

Douglas's latest report took on a decidedly different tone.

"The Secret Six," he began in a frontpage story, "may or may not be making a good job of their plan to rid the city of Al Capone and his like. However, one thing seems certain. In the realms of private probing they have come such a cropper that their leader Alexander Jamie, former prohibition agent, and two other 'Secret Sixers' are being sued for $100,000 for false arrest."[9]

The irony of Kuhn's lawsuit must be noted: Wrongly accused of trying to extort $25,000 from Marion Wright, he was now—thanks to Secret Six bungling—demanding that she, her dad, and the bunglers themselves cough up four times the original ask. The negative national press continued for weeks for the Chicago vigilantes. One of the most scathing pieces appeared in the February 7 *San Francisco Examiner,* which summarized Kuhn's ordeal this way: "Arrested by Chicago's famed and powerful 'Secret Six,' as the alleged author of the 'poison dart' letters that threatened the life of a popular debutante. Mercilessly grilled for thirty-six hours in a hotel room by agents of this extra-legal body of the Chicago Association of Commerce. Held for two months in jail in spite of the fact that the 'death' letters kept coming to the girl. And finally, discredited in Chicago, compelled to return to California."[10]

Kuhn was certainly not held for two months, but that wasn't the point. With its reference to a sinister "extra-legal body" refusing to admit exonerating evidence even when someone's livelihood was at stake, the message was clear: America's new experiment in well-funded vigilantism had taken a dark turn.

The *San Mateo Times,* the California paper serving the town where Kuhn's parents lived, and where Kuhn fled after he filed his lawsuit, spun the story in David and Goliath terms with its page one headline: "S. M. Boy Fights Chicago Big 6."[11]

Kuhn would have to wait twenty-two months for his showdown with the Secret Six, twenty-two months before a jury of Kuhn's peers would render a verdict after hearing the full story of what the vigilantes did and didn't do. But in the meantime, for the Secret Six, it was full speed ahead. There were more criminals to catch, more devils to deal with, and, now and then, other opportunities to really screw things up.

And then, there was Al Capone. The Secret Six had set their sights on the mobster since the moment of their founding. In 1931, they would get their man. Or so the legend goes.

PART III

THE SECRET SIX VS. AL CAPONE

Alphonse Capone: Colonel, what are you trying to do to me?
Col. Randolph: Put you out of business.
Alphonse Capone: Why do you want to do that?

—From a meeting between Al Capone and Col. Robert Randolph, as recalled by Randolph in November 1932

13

Al Capone Comes Home

BORN IN NEW YORK CITY in 1899, Al Capone moved to Chicago twenty years later to pursue a career in lawbreaking, climbing the ranks quickly until, by the late 1920s, he had achieved the dual feat of remaining out of prison while enjoying nationwide criminal notoriety. It wasn't until May 1929 that his luck ran out, in Philadelphia, where he was arrested for carrying a gun. He was sentenced quickly to a year in prison, and he was still incarcerated in Pennsylvania ten months later when the Secret Six was born.

As his mid-March 1930, release date neared, the papers started talking. "Capone Faces New Troubles upon Release," warned a prominent headline in the *Pittsburgh Press*. "'Secret Six' Will Watch Every Move."[1]

"The 'Secret Six,'" read the United Press story, carried by dozens of papers across the nation, "which has as its aim the riddance in Chicago of gangsters, will keep a close watch on Capone, it was learned. All movements of the six so far have been under cover but it is known they have investigators in the field and are planning a wide crime offensive in the future."

Capone was freed, with time off for good behavior, on Monday, March 17, 1930, and he headed immediately to Chicago, arriving the next day. The city's cops were still conducting their Secret Six–inspired sweep and they were waiting for him. "Capt. Patrick McCauley of the Grand Crossing station posted police squads near the Capone home at 7244 Prairie avenue," reported the *Chicago Tribune*. "Fifteen policemen were also stationed at the municipal airport. Should Capone or his guards appear armed, the police plan to jail them."[2]

Capone took to the tracks instead of the skies, however, the *Tribune* describing him as "speeding westward toward Chicago . . . in accustomed gangster style aboard the Broadway Limited, the most luxurious train of the Pennsylvania system." He further eluded authorities by keeping away from his Prairie Avenue property, a surprisingly modest brick structure that still stands.*

It wasn't until that Friday morning, three days after his arrival in Chicago, that Capone turned himself in voluntarily. That evening, after several tense meetings with Chicago police and other authorities, Capone returned to what the *Tribune* called his "secluded suite at the Lexington hotel on South Michigan Avenue."[3]

The suite, which the police apparently didn't know about until after Capone had planted himself there, seemed to serve as a second home and office for the kingpin, complete with rooms for his mother, wife, and sister, and a buzzer to summon staff, set into "a large mahogany desk, with pictures of George Washington and (Chicago Mayor) Big Bill Thompson smiling down on the gold encrusted inkstand."

He rented the twelve-room suite by the year at the Lexington, according to a United Press wire story. "To reach his luxurious office," the story revealed, "the visitor must pass through 11 rooms, each of which contains two or more 'pistol secretaries' whose glances are keen and memories long."[4]

A few days after his return to town, Capone would leave this refuge for a reckoning of sorts with local authorities, but on that same date, when Genevieve Forbes Herrick of the *Chicago Tribune* gave him a chance to tell his side of the story, he invited her to the Lexington.

"All I ever did was supply a demand that was pretty popular," Capone insisted, describing his trade as "selling beer and whisky to the best people." He went on to allege that "some of our best judges use the stuff."

His reputation as the king of the gangsters was undeserved, he insisted. "Say, I'm only 31, and I've been blamed for crimes that happened as far back as the Chicago fire," he complained, citing the 1871 disaster that took place twenty-eight years before his birth.

"All he ever did, he reiterates, was to ply his trade," Herrick wrote. "And if his trade was so popular that it brought him a home in Miami Beach and

---

* Zillow, consulted in late 2024, set the 1905 dwelling's size at about 2,800 square feet and its value at $367,000.

a reputation for giving one hundred dollar tips, that's the fault, he claims, of the customer, not of the dealer."

Quite possibly because a female was doing the interview, the *Tribune*'s subscribers were treated to this passage:

> The door at the far end of the large room opens and a young but competent gentleman comes in.
>
> "Please ask my wife and sister to come here," commands Capone.
>
> Presently the door opens again. Two women enter. One is rather tall and slim—that is Mrs. Capone. The other is shorter, plumper—she is Mafalda, his sister. The introductions over, they chat in subdued pleasantries and retire with swirls of blue chiffon.
>
> "Did you notice my wife's hair?" asks Al Capone.
>
> We had. It was lustrous and fluffy.
>
> "No, I mean the streak of gray," he adds. "She's only 28, and she's got gray hair, just worrying over things here in Chicago."

Capone repeatedly protested his innocence during the interview, insisting that it wasn't criminal behavior but his undeserved reputation alone that was getting him into trouble. His ten-month stint in the Pennsylvania prison, he said, was "not for carrying a gun, but because my name is Capone. I'd never been indicted before. Why should I be?"

Chicago seems to have disagreed, lumping him in with the rest of the city's undesirables, according to a second story about Capone published in that day's *Tribune*. "You're no better than any other hoodlum and you are going to be arrested on sight," Capone was warned in person by by John Stege, chief of Chicago detectives. "You don't belong here and we don't intend to let you live here. You'll be arrested as often as you show yourself to any of our detectives."[5]

After Stege issued his warning, he had Capone escorted to Chicago's federal building to see if officials there wanted to charge him yet with evading income taxes, but that well-publicized investigation was still ongoing. Police got a similar response from John Swanson with the state prosecutor's office.

"No one at the offices of either the government or state prosecutor wished to take charge of Capone," the befuddled *Chicago Tribune* mused, "though for years the gang leader has been reputed the head of the largest bootleg, gambling, and vice syndicate in Chicago and many killings have been attributed to his gang by the police."

Although he remained free that day, Capone wasn't out of trouble. As the article noted, he'd been "brought into the federal court more than a year ago charged with failure to pay the government's tax on his 1928 and previous incomes." A trial loomed, and the only thing that stood between the mobster and another stint in prison, authorities believed, was his ability to discreetly dispose of the witnesses.

Capone, according to the article, told the Chicago police that "all I want is not to be arrested if I come downtown," to which Stege replied, "You're out of luck. Your day is done."

Toward the end of his visit with local authorities, Capone was forced to meet with Assistant State's Attorney Harry S. Ditchburne. Ditchburne didn't have a new indictment for the gangster, but he at least had hard questions, according to the *Chicago Tribune*:

"What do you know about the Valentine day massacre of the seven Moran fellows?" Ditchburne asked.

"I was in Florida then," Capone replied.

"Yes, and you were in Florida, too, when Frank Yale was murdered in New York," Ditchburne said.

Since Ditchburne's words weren't in the form of a question, Capone had no response.

"Your name was prominently connected with the massacre and the Yale murder," Ditchburne noted.

Frankie Yale, a Brooklyn mobster, had been a close associate of Capone's, supplying him with much of the liquor Capone's gang sold in Chicago before their relationship soured in 1927. Yale was shot to death while driving home on July 1, 1928, when four men in a car pulled alongside Yale's Lincoln coupe and, after a brief pursuit, slew him with shotgun and submachinegun fire. Capone was suspected of having arranged the hit, but no one was ever charged for the crime, and Capone always denied involvement.

"I get blamed for everything that goes on here," Capone protested, "but I had nothing to do with any of the things you talk about."

"Your name is synonymous with a large gang," Ditchburne shot back. "Perhaps you personally don't commit the murders, but we assume that your gang is in control . . . and we are not far wrong in assuming your gang is responsible for many of those murders."

"I'm not responsible for what others do," was Capone's response.

Ditchburne, who was perhaps hoping for actionable intelligence, if not an outright confession from the crime lord, had reached the end of his patience. "You're not a good citizen," he declared. "We have to protect the public, and such fellows as you must go."

Capone, possibly trying to offer an olive branch, told the cops he'd be leaving for his home in Miami in a week, the *Chicago Tribune* reported. Later that day, he shared a different departure date with the *Tribune*: "All I want to do is to mind my own business, wind up my affairs here, and leave for my home in Miami in about three weeks."

The Secret Six probably viewed Capone's plans with mixed feelings. Getting people like him out of Chicago was the whole point of their campaign. But if he found a refuge that put him beyond local police persecution while he continued to run Chicago crime from a headquarters with better weather, justice had once again been foiled.

Other articles made clear that the Miami jaunt was only temporary, however. Capone, according to a Universal Service wire story, "reiterated today his intention of making Chicago his permanent home in spite of the threat of the authorities to arrest him every time he appears on the streets."[6]

"I need the sunshine for a month or two," Capone told the Service. "I shall take a little trip to Maimi, Fla., after I get things straightened out here. You see I haven't had much sunshine for the last 10 months. But after that I'm coming back to Chicago and stay here. I don't see how anyone can stop me."

Capone, however, wasn't going to find his welcome to Miami any warmer than in Chicago. They sometimes referred to his cold greeting in the Sunshine State as the "Chicago Plan."

14

Al Capone Goes South

THEY'D NEVER WANTED Al Capone in Florida. In fact, the cry went up as soon as word got out that Capone had bought a house on Miami Beach's fashionable Palm Isle. "'Oust Capone!' Beach Citizens Tell Officials," read the front-page headline in the May 25, 1928, *Miami News*. "Delegation Calls on Law Enforcement Agencies Friday." Miami Beach city officials, the article declared, had received "hundreds of complaints from members of the exclusive winter colony."

Neighborly contempt notwithstanding, one could do worse than Palm Isle as a place to hole up, if one had some holing up to do. Capone's home, at 93 Palm Avenue, was listed for sale on Zillow in late 2023 for a staggering $31 million. Built in 1922 by real estate developer Clarence Busch (no relation to the beer brewing Busch family), the structures comprised almost 5,800 square feet, according to the listing, with nine bedrooms and six bathrooms, a pool, guesthouse, and one hundred feet of access to a short canal that led to Biscayne Bay. The listing, posted in July 2023, described the home as "the ultimate waterfront paradise" but made no mention of its gangster-era occupant. Unfortunately, no buyer surfaced and, a month after the listing was placed, in mid-August of 2023, the property was demolished.[1]

Ninety-five years before its destruction, soon after rumors began circulating of the property's acquisition by Capone, a reporter for the *Miami News* dropped by the place, noting that "a high stone barricade had been erected around the residence and remodeling had been started."

Capone would go on to spend at least $100,000—almost $2 million in 2024 dollars—to add a gatehouse, searchlights, a large swimming pool, and a coral rock grotto.[2] Capone, concerned about attacks from the water, had a cabana built near the canal and posted guards on its second floor, according to some legends.[3]

Despite his neighbors' protestations and official attempts to convince him to leave, Capone kept the home ready for his return while he was imprisoned in Pennsylvania. But as soon as he announced plans to head to Miami—and well before he actually arrived—the absence of Southern hospitality must have been obvious to the mobster.

On Thursday night, March 20—three days after Capone left Pennsylvania—the Miami Beach Police and the Dade County Sheriff's Office paid a visit to Capone's waterfront home, the *Miami Herald* reported, looking for booze, and probably for Capone himself.[4] "The search for liquor was rewarded by the discovery of 10 sacks and three bottles in a bathroom on the second floor of the residence and connected with what was pointed out as Alphonse Capone's suite," the *Herald* article stated. The police also found "an iced bottle of champagne in the refrigerator and several other bottles in a closet off the kitchen."

Police didn't find the head mobster. He was still in Chicago, getting interviewed that day by the police and the *Chicago Tribune*. But the cops did stumble across some lesser Capones, namely "John and Albert Capone, said to be brothers of Alphonse (Scarface Al) Capone."

At least one of the two alleged brothers must have been lying about his name, or about his relationship with Al Capone; or maybe the cops or the *Herald* got it wrong. Al Capone is known to have had three brothers, Ralph, Frank, and James. While Ralph and Frank joined their brother in hoodlumery, James went straight, changing his name to Richard James Hart and working in law enforcement. So he wouldn't have been lurking around the Capone mansion. And Frank had been dead for six years, shot in a Chicago election melee in 1924. There was no John or Albert, although there was an Albert Driginano, whose name showed up in other Capone-related arrests that year.[5] And there was an eleven-year-old son, also named Albert—Albert Francis Capone, specifically—who was mentioned in a *Miami Herald* story as a resident of the Capone property at the time of the liquor bust.[6]

Whoever they were, the two would-be Capones and four more were arrested in the raid and "spent more than four hours in the county jail and when released were prevented from returning to the Capone home by deputies who guarded the gates of the estate with orders to arrest any person who attempted to enter."

While in custody, the Capones were asked about Al's whereabouts by D. C. Coleman, Dade County chief deputy sheriff. They replied, in classic mobster fashion, that "he was not here, but would be here in time."

Official hostility to Capone was, in fact, statewide. Within days of the gangster's release, Florida Governor Doyle E. Carlton "issued explicit instructions to all sheriffs of Florida to arrest Capone on sight and escort him to the state line."[7]

However, the Chicago-inspired campaign of harassment against a private citizen—no matter how unsavory his reputation—was quickly quashed on US Constitutional grounds by Federal District Court Judge Halsted Ritter. "No lawful cause or reason whatever exists for the banishment or expulsion of the plaintiff from the state of Florida, or for the deprivation of his constitutional rights," Ritter's March 22, 1930, order read. The order, issued to sheriffs in the twenty counties along Capone's expected highway route, forbade "seizing, arresting, kidnaping or abducting the plaintiff, Alphonse Capone, without warrant or authority of law." Ritter's order further enjoined the sheriffs from "molesting, annoying or interfering with the said plaintiff in entering the state of Florida, and proceeding to his home in Dade County." According to the *Maimi Herald*, the order had been prompted by complaints from Capone attorneys J. F. Gordon and Vincent Giblin, who said their client was expected to head to Miami March 24 or 25.[8]

Capone foiled whatever reception awaited him—regardless what Judge Ritter had ruled—by postponing the arrival to his southern home until a month later, Easter Sunday morning, April 20, 1930. Capone's move-in was so quiet it might have surprised even him. The initial silence was deceptive, though. The kingpin was walking into a buzzsaw.

What he was leaving behind in Chicago wasn't much better, however.

"All for Al"

"'Secret Six' Vows War to Death on Capone Alliance," announced the *Chicago Herald and Examiner* in a front-page story April 17, 1930. Published three days before Capone reached his Miami mansion, we might imagine him putting that article at the top of his road trip reading materials.

The story was a follow-up to an exclusive story in the previous day's paper, in which the *Herald and Examiner* announced "the amalgamation of all

Chicago's gangland factions under the leadership of Al Capone, with the rallying cry, 'All for Al and Al for All.'"

As soon as he'd returned from prison in Pennsylvania, apparently, Capone had been busy shoring up support and building alliances, and after a month's work, everything was in place. Ten months in stir hadn't killed the crime lord; it had made him stronger.

For Col. Randolph and the Chicago Association of Commerce, the timing of Capone's alleged ascension to even greater power proved embarrassing. In the week that story broke, Randolph and thirty-four other Chicago business leaders were in Houston, visiting the city as "goodwill ambassadors." The Chicagoans had likely come to the Texas city hoping to make a good impression, talk up the virtues of their town, and build a business link or two. But their hometown hoodlums had other ideas.

The *Herald and Examiner* story about Capone's latest empire building foray had been carried on the national wires, and had in due course landed on the front pages of the Houston papers—just as the Windy City contingent was getting to town. The Capone story, the *Herald and Examiner* reported, "was the first news from Chicago to meet the Association of Commerce's thirty-four goodwill ambassadors upon their arrival."

Surely the ambassadors wanted to talk about anything else but Chicago's most infamous citizen. During their visit, they boarded yachts to look at a new canal linking Houston to the Gulf of Mexico; they toured historic battlegrounds; and they enjoyed a dinner hosted by the Houston Chamber of Commerce.

But Capone couldn't be ignored. "The alliance exposed through The Chicago Herald and Examiner became the chief topic among the Chicagoans and the theme of Col. Randolph's address before a Rotary Club luncheon," the paper declared.

Herald and Examiner reporter Victor Rubin had accompanied the ambassadors to Chicago, and he was taking notes as Col. Randolph played offense. Randolph described the Capone gang as "organized enemies of society" and declared them "no more formidable as a single unit than as scattered outlaw bands."

In fact, Randolph said, "the new alliance may make them a simpler object of attack," continuing, "Chicago's crime situation has been due to the battling of bootleg gangs against rivals encroaching on their territory. . . . Each of the gang killings has been a benefit to us in ridding us of one more undesirable citizen. Evidently the gangs have now become tired of decimating each other and decided it was better to call a truce. We must now devote all our energy to getting rid of them instead of letting them get rid of themselves."

In Chicago, the respected head of a new vigilante group was openly celebrating the death of Capone's employees and plotting the collapse of his vast enterprise. And Capone was about to experience a very frosty reception in the Sunshine State as well.

15

Al Capone, Miami, and the "Chicago Plan"

TO FLORIDA AND MIAMI in the spring of 1930, Al Capone's arrival was not just embarrassing or inconvenient. The gangster's decision to move south represented a threat to a way of life to many there, and the furious response galvanized against him—some of it the direct result of the Secret Six's birth—is best understood as a people caught in an existential crisis.

"Bloodshed and crime or peace and order," declared a front-page editorial in the *Miami News* on April 27, 1930. "This is the choice presented to Dade County citizens in the case of 'Scarface' Al Capone . . . now seeking to establish headquarters in Miami for himself and his gang of Chicago gunmen."

Noting that Miami's fight against Capone had attracted "nation-wide attention," the editorial continued by describing what was about to be lost: "the future of Miami as a resort city and a home for the better element of America's population who come here for recreation."

The editorial hinted that Capone represented something vaguely un-American, both in how he looked and the way he got around—more like a foreign potentate than the rest of Miami's visitors, who were merely wealthy: "All the glitter and display of a pirate chief of old attends this swarthy aristocrat of modern crime when he travels abroad. Bullet-proof automobiles, a body guard and luxurious pullman cars cater to his whims."

Capone wasn't just Miami's problem, however, the editorial concluded, "it is the problem of the nation at large, and upon the answer given in Miami courts depends the nation's answer to the challenge of crime—now seeking to become 'respectable.'"

To understand the visceral horror Capone created wherever he went, one might turn to pages four and five of the May 19, 1930, *Miami News*, a piece consistent with other contemporary coverage of the outlaw. "Statistics chronicle that he has assassinated hundreds of men in his time," the article declared, continuing that, Capone

> owns dozens of (brothel) houses in Chicago, and all through the country go his white slavers, enticing girls from small country towns and from farms, picturing to them an easy life in Chicago, at good pay, as actresses or cashiers or salesgirls in big stores. They come to Chicago, they disappear. The great maw of Capone's vice machine has swallowed them and they never return. A newspaper reporter in Chicago estimated recently that in Capone's brothels, in the last 10 years, more than 100 girls had committed suicide . . . but no one can ever even surmise how many thousands of girls he has murdered in his brothels . . . who have as truly died at his hands untimely deaths from the life led there.

A threefold strategy of harassment quickly emerged in Miami to deal with the Capone problem: 1) Go after his property; 2) Go after the people around him; 3) Implement the "Chicago plan," that February 1930 program of gangster arrests inspired by the formation of the Secret Six.

So comprehensive was the assault on all things Capone that by early April 1930, the *Miami News* described the mobster as "fast becoming a king without a country." The article noted the "extreme measures . . . being taken to eliminate (Chicago) organized crime and praised the example set by the Secret Six, which was 'stacking its thousands in equal donations' and 'bringing results.'"[1]

"Gangsters' Retreat"

The attacks on Capone's Palm Isle home began the moment word got out in 1928 that he had bought the place, but when he announced plans to return to it after his Pennsylvania prison stint in 1930, efforts picked up in earnest, with raids beginning in early March 1930, the cops pounding the doors in a fruitless search for murder suspect Roy "Crane Neck" Nugent.[2]

A month later, on April 22—two days after Capone arrived in Miami—a petition was filed to have the Capone mansion padlocked as a public nuisance. Vernon Hawthorne, Florida state's attorney for Dade County, complained in the petition that Capone's estate was "a place frequented by common gamblers, keepers of gambling places, habitual loafers, idle and disorderly persons, persons engaged in the illegal use, sale and exchange of spirituous wines, malts and liquors."[3] And all that commotion, Hawthorne continued with a tone of indignation bordering on the Biblical, "tends to annoy and does grievously annoy the community, and has become manifestly injurious to the morals and members of the people of said community."

The petition said the home had been purchased on July 18, 1928, by Mae Capone, Capone's wife, but Mr. Capone was clearly in charge, and Mr. Capone was clearly a bad guy, "generally referred to by such titles as the 'Master Mind of Crimedom,' 'King of the Racketeers,' 'Commander-in-Chief of America's Underworld,' and other and various titles of similar venomous and criminal significance that strike horror and terror to the minds of all law-abiding, decent and self-respecting citizens."

With such a persona in charge of the property, the outcome was inevitable, the petition asserted. The home was "frequently designated as [a] Gangsters' Retreat," popular with people of "unsavory type, character and reputation" who "congregate in said premises for the purpose of revelry and drinking," and whose "goings in and out of said premises at all hours of the night evidencing evil and debaucherous conduct greatly frighten and terrorize the citizens of said neighborhood." Hawthorne's petition was to receive its first consideration before Circuit Court Judge Paul Barns the following Saturday morning.

Meanwhile, the debauchery would continue, but among a dwindling number of Capone associates, because—thanks to a second strategy of attack launched by local officials under the Secret Six–inspired Chicago effort—being seen with Capone in South Florida, working for Capone in South Florida, or being burdened with the last name *Capone* in South Florida, had become a significant inconvenience.

There was Jack McGurn, for example, "Al Capone's right hand man," who was arrested on a fugitive-from-justice charge at a Miami Beach golf course on March 31, 1930. Also picked up was Tony McGurn, Jack's brother, and an unnamed "pretty blonde woman," who was let go after being questioned.[4]

Others who suffered because of their Capone connections:

- Albert Capone, identified as Al's brother in newspaper reports at the time, who was arrested repeatedly on vagrancy charges. On

April 12, the cops picked him up on the fourteenth hole of a Miami Beach golf course.[5]

- Frankie Newton, caretaker of Capone's Palm Island mansion, who was convicted in late April of being caught with liquor at the home and given the choice of paying $500 or spending six months in jail.[6]
- Frank "Soldier" Leavitt, a 275-pound member of the Miami police force, who was fired for "conduct unbecoming an officer" after he made three visits to the Capone home. Leavitt, a former wrestler who conducted publicity tours for the city, said he was just stopping by to chat with a Chicago friend (not Al Capone), but he lost his job all the same.[7]
- Frank Gallat, a Miami property owner whose more than thirty-year residence in the city qualified him as a respected Miami "pioneer." Gallat had done some work at the Capone mansion the previous year, and that got him "arrested by Miami police . . . while eating dinner with Mrs. Gallat" on May 9 and "held in the city jail for about two hours on a charge of 'investigation.'"[8]

In the third prong of the local assault on Al Capone, the gangster himself was the target of a Miami Beach version of the anticrime initiative launched in Chicago that winter. Miami officials called it the "Chicago Plan" or the "Chicago Policy," an arguably unconstitutional program of harassment against anyone generally suspected of being an outlaw, regardless of the existence of a conviction, or even an indictment.

"Mayor (C. H.) Reeder declared Miami police would arrest Capone every time he appeared in the city," reported the *Miami News* in early May 1930.[9] The order was carried out immediately, repeatedly, and ruthlessly.

The first arrest of Capone took place about 2:30 p.m. on May 8, 1930, at the intersection of Biscayne Blvd. and N. E. Thirteenth Street. Detectives G. S. Wilkinson and H. G. Howard were waiting for him, apparently, stopping him once he'd arrived in Miami proper, just a block from the County Causeway bridge (now the MacArthur Causeway).[10]

"Miami has adopted the tactics of Chicago," announced Mayor Reeder, who'd hurried to the police station in the wake of the arrest. "We are out to get all the crooks, big and small, and run them out of Miami."

Picked up with Capone were John Capone, twenty-six, Albert Drignano, thirty-eight, and Nick Circulla, thirty-one, all of whom gave Capone's mansion as their address. No guns were found on the men or in their car, "although it was subjected to a minute search," the *Miami Herald* reported. But the cops found an impressive $1,161 in cash in the kingpin's pocketbook, worth a little over $21,000 in 2024 dollars.

Incensed Capone attorneys Vincent Giblin and J. F. Gordon stormed the police station as soon as they'd gotten word of the arrests, according to the *Herald*. "We want to see these men and we will see them, and we are going to see them this afternoon," Gordon barked at S. C. McCreary, Miami's director of public safety. "On what authority are you keeping me from seeing them?"

"On my own," was McCreary's terse reply. "They are going to be held until we can fingerprint them and question them."

"I am going to sue for a writ of habeas corpus," Gordon thundered. "Just because you have a job you have become chesty. It has gone to your head."

His patience running thin, McCreary turned to Capt. V. H. Mathis, who'd been standing with him behind the counter in the police station's reception area.

"Captain," McCreary said, "search him."

The following scene ensued:

> "You are not going to search me," Gordon replied, backing from the counter. The police captain and others came from behind the counter and approached Gordon. "Take your hands off of me," he said, as one officer grabbed at the attorney's wrists.
>
> Gordon backed slowly to the door, with the half circle of police officers following and grabbing at his wrists. On the sidewalk, after a short scuffle, he broke free and half ran toward the corner of W. Flagler street.
>
> "Catch him!" police officers shouted, and Gordon was stopped by a police officer who was coming around the corner at the time. The attorney was led back to the police station, where he submitted to the search.*

After that fracas, Gordon and Giblin got in to see their client, and by 4:30 that afternoon—two hours after their arrest—Capone and his three henchmen were in circuit court before Judge Uly O. Thompson.

McCreary, first to speak before the judge, claimed to have received nearly one thousand complaints about Capone, in person and by letter, "from

---

*Nothing incriminating was found among Gordon's things, the article indicated.

people here who are afraid for their property and life. I consider Capone and his associates a public menace, particularly to children."

Countered Giblin, "The officers arresting Capone expected to find guns, but didn't. They expected resistance. It didn't develop . . . If this is the kind of government we must have then we might just as well tear up the constitution and let anarchy reign."

Judge Thompson agreed.

"The prisoners are ordered to be discharged," he said. "I find that no charges are pending against them and I don't think that they are legally held."

As the men cleared the court, Mayor Reeder declared that Miami had made its point. "They know now that we don't want them in Miami."

With Judge Thompson's decree, it seemed the campaign of arresting Capone on sight was over. "'Chicago Policy' Toward Capone is Ended Here," announced a headline on the front page of the May 11 *Miami News*. The article indicated some confusion among city officials, however, and Capone and various associates were picked up several more times in May 1930.[11]

Throughout it all, Capone was doing his best to lead the respectable life of a rich man in a beautiful Florida city.

Al Capone, "Genial Host"

In early May 1930, some of the classmates of Capone's eleven-year-old son, Albert Francis "Sonny" Capone, worked up the nerve to ask if they could swim in his dad's pool. Perhaps out of fatherly love, perhaps in a bid for some shred of respectability, Capone agreed, and "the group grew from a small number to 50," the *Miami Herald* reported, mostly boys but with "a scattering of girls," all of whom arrived on Saturday, May 17, "with the written consent of their parents."[12]

"While the boys and girls were swimming a long table was placed on the lawn as a surprise," the *Herald* said, "and servants piled the table with chicken and soft drinks, and three large cakes. Balloons and noise-making devices were scattered along the table by Capone and the servants . . . and each boy and girl was presented with a box of candy by Capone's son as a parting gift."

Following up on his children's party, Capone a few weeks later threw a "good will" banquet for more than fifty adult Miamians, including his lawyers, a "publisher of small weeklies," and "representatives of two Miami undertaking establishments," the *Miami News* reported. "Playing the genial host earnestly, Capone urged his guests to take off their coats and neckties, making themselves 'perfectly at home,' and waited on tables himself." Capone's mother made an appearance, telling guests she "didn't raise her boy to be a gangster."[13]

But all good things must come to an end, and by July 1930, Capone was planning his return to Chicago, for reasons both personal and professional. While his lawyers had eventually put a stop to his being arrested on sight, and the attempt to padlock his mansion also failed, things were spinning out of control for the man they called Scarface, a growing vortex of chaos best handled with a trip back to the Windy City. The temporary peace among the gangs had been broken with a fresh spate of violent deaths, and Capone's liquor empire in the city was crumbling.

And Secret Six chief Col. Randolph, through a comprehensive study of the kingpin, and a secret meeting with him, was refusing to let up.

16

Col. Randolph Meets the Kingpin

ALTHOUGH AL CAPONE'S spring 1930 return from a year in a Pennsylvania prison seemed to have resulted in new unity among Chicago gangsters, and unprecedented powers for the crime lord, it would all prove illusory.

"Police are convinced the gangs of Scarface Al Capone and George (Bugs) Moran are back at each other's throats," read a June 1930 wire story by the Consolidated Press. "War and more of it is in prospect, inspired by double-crossing, greed and hard times."[1]

Despite the fact "a merger was negotiated to take effect when Alphonse Capone left his Philadelphia jail," the article said, "now this is upset by the slaying of a whole batch of Capone adherents, presumably by Moran followers." The article referenced "the apparent epidemic of slayings recently in various cities," mostly aimed at Sicilians with gang ties, including seven shot in Chicago in the past week, seven more in Detroit, and five in Boston.

But Capone seemed to get a modicum of revenge for the murders on the day he returned to Chicago from Miami, August 2, 1930. After he celebrated his arrival with a party for one hundred guests, the United Press reported, word arrived in town that Jack Zuta, "one of Capone's most militant enemies" and "business manager of the Moran-Aiello gang," had just been shot to death in the resort village of Delafield, Wisconsin.[2]

"The Wisconsin murder was executed with the same confident skill that have marked numerous other crimes which the police have credited to Capone gunmen," the United Press declared.

Capone could still kill with impunity, but the walls were closing in on the gangster. Federal Prohibition agents who couldn't be bribed were conducting devastating raids on his distilleries. In June 1930, Alexander Jamie (a few months before he was hired by the Secret Six) was credited with leading a "raid on a mammoth brewery" in which "one of the largest sources of Chicago's beer supply was shut off."[3]

Seized in the raid, which followed "weeks of undercover investigation," was "50,000 gallons of barreled beer, 75 half barrels and 150,000 gallons of beer in process of manufacture."

A week later, the papers were reporting another two dozen raids of Capone alcohol facilities in Chicago's Cicero district. Attacked were distilleries and breweries which produced an estimated two thousand gallons per day and "turned in a clear profit of between $15,000 and $20,000 weekly."[4]

Losing somewhere between $1.3 million and $2 million a month (in 2024 dollars) must have stung, but ultimately more devastating to the criminals was the decision to go after the crooks for not paying federal income taxes. Ralph Capone, Al Capone's brother, got three years in prison for the crime in June 1930 (a verdict announced at the top of the *Miami News* front page and surely seen by the gangster as he made his rounds in the city that day).[5]

A similar fate was suffered by three members of the same family. Jack Guzik, described by the Associated Press as "business manager for the Capone liquor and vice syndicate," was sentenced in December 1930 to five years in prison for income tax evasion.[6] Jack Guzik's brothers, Harry and Sam Guzik, said to be "aligned with Jack in his activities as business manager of the Capone beer and liquor interests," were picked up on the same charges in September 1930.[7]

And then there was Frank Nitti, one of the biggest fish in Capone's circle, a man whose capture was so important the Secret Six kept taking credit for it.

Who Caught Frank Nitti?

In early October 1930, the federal government launched, according to a United Press wire story, a "countrywide search for Frank Nitti, said to be business manager for Scarface Al Capone."[8]

The *Chicago Tribune* said Nitti, also called Capone's treasurer or enforcer in some reports, was "wanted on charges of evading some $277,000 in income taxes," but had "eluded authorities since his indictment by the federal grand jury last March." In furtherance of the manhunt, the feds had "printed 150,000 posters bearing the Capone gangster's photograph and details of the $1,000 reward offered for information leading to his capture."[9]

The *Tribune* noted that some ten thousand of the posters were to be handed out in Chicago, with every cop, federal marshal and deputy sheriff getting one. The rest would be "distributed among postoffices, jails, and police stations throughout the country."

The effort paid off on October 31, 1930, when Nitti, believed by some to have fled to Italy on a forged passport, was caught at what the *Chicago Tribune* described as his "richly furnished apartment" in Berwyn, Illinois, a little over ten miles west of downtown Chicago.[10]

"The arrest," the *Tribune* reported, "was made by detectives and federal agents led by Patrick Roche, chief investigator for the state's attorney's office."

A day after his capture, the *Chicago Tribune* offered more detail on how Nitti was rounded up. "Nels E. Tessem of the intelligence unit, internal revenue department, had trailed him to his apartment at 3201 Clinton street, Berwyn. Tessem learned the allusive Nitti's whereabouts by following the movements of Louis Greenberg, head of the Roosevelt Finance company, 3159 West Roosevelt road, described by federal authorities as a loan shark and banker for the Capone mob. Greenberg was questioned several times by A. P. Madden, chief of the intelligence unit, and although he denied dealing with the Capone gang, he visited Nitti in his apartment."[11]

Despite that precise account of how Nitti was tracked down by the feds, Secret Six head Col. Randolph insisted it was his vigilantes who'd captured the gangster, making the claim publicly at least twice.

"We turned up Jack Netti," Randolph told a reporter for the *Buffalo Times* four months after the capture. Either Randolph or the reporter got both the first and last name of the gangster wrong, but he was obviously talking about Frank Nitti in the interview, which was given prior to his address before the Buffalo Chamber of Commerce. "The police couldn't find him," Randolph declared, going on to contradict the *Chicago Tribune* account regarding both Nitti's home and who nabbed him. "We offered a $1000 reward for information leading to his apprehension, and had him within a week. One of the jackals told us he was living in a suburban bungalow. We found him there.

The cash reward turned the trick."[12] Randolph repeated the claim in a late 1931 summary of Secret Six successes, telling of "how spending $1000 for information, the operatives of the secret six located Frank Nitti, notorious Capone gang leader, now serving time at Leavenworth."[13]

Regardless who really caught Nitti, his decision to plead guilty to income tax evasion two months after his apprehension resulted in an eighteen-month prison sentence, and was considered another piece of bad news for Capone.[14]

The Secret Six and the Anti-Capone Crusade

Many forces were gunning for the gangster, but the Secret Six had at least created the impression they were leading the charge. Col. Randolph's ability to speak authoritatively about Capone and his operations enhanced that image. In an announcement to the press in March 1931 about their findings, Col. Randolph declared:

> Our investigation shows that it costs Capone $1.80 a barrel to brew beer and that other manufacturing charges, such as cooperage, bring the total to no more than $3. The standard normal price to speakeasies is $55, leaving a gross profit of $52. The least of the expenses of distribution is trucking. The highest item is protection. The armed guards who accompany the trucks and gunmen hoodlums who collect from the speakeasies can be had by Capone for $100 to $150 a week. Higher-salaried gangsters are needed to fix the police and still more intelligent operators are used to see the right politicians. The closest estimate we can make on Capone's payroll is 2000, counting brewers, truckmen, armed guards, collectors, fixers and custodians of brothels, gambling houses and handbooks, which his syndicate directly owns.[15]

When Randolph insisted he knew how to shut down the gangster, he was given a national platform, the popular *Collier's* magazine. In the March 7, 1931, edition of the publication, under the title "How to Wreck Capone's Gang," he proposed ending prohibition as a primary part of the plan.

The Secret Six were also working to pin a particular murder on the kingpin, of the many he is believed to have orchestrated. Joe Howard, a beer-running "minor gangster," was shot to death at a Chicago saloon on May 8, 1924, quite possibly by Capone himself after Howard had run afoul of the crook. "The 'secret six' public safety committee," newspapers reported in February 1931, "is understood to have spent thousands of dollars delving into the murder in an attempt to convict Capone."[16]

Al Capone, from a 1929 mugshot. / Public Domain

So in the early 1930s, when Capone felt the walls closing in, his cries for mercy went not to the federal government, Chicago police or Illinois authorities, but to Col. Randolph of the Secret Six.

After Capone was sentenced to eleven years at the federal penitentiary at Leavenworth for income tax fraud in October 1931, both men spoke of their encounters, Capone sharing his memories in a May 1932 prison interview with the *Chicago Tribune.*

> The gangster said Robert Isham Randolph, organizer of the Secret Six, came to him in Florida and appealed for aid in the efforts to stop industrial and commercial bombings. He told of a proposition he said he made to Mr. Randolph and he couldn't understand why it was not accepted. All Capone wanted was a free hand in the booze business and he would cooperate with the Secret Six in stopping bombings. He'd run down the bombers and put them to work in his booze organization.
>
> "I laid my cards on the table and asked him to lay his," said Capone. "Well? What do you think I got?" he shrugged his shoulders and turned to the window with a gesture of futility.[17]

In a November 1932 interview with the *St. Louis Times Star*, Randolph spoke similarly of the meeting with Capone, but he said it happened at the Lexington Hotel in Chicago, in February 1931, and constituted his "most interesting experience as chairman of the 'Secret Six' to date."

Randolph said he was driven to the hotel by Capone henchman Jake [Jack] Guzik, they entered through a back door and took a freight elevator up to Capone's floor.[18] "After going through many doors, and passing numerous thugs and gunmen I finally was taken into a suite occupied by Capone, who was seated at a desk, with his back to the wall. There were slots in the doors. . . . A rifle barrel could be thrust through each slot."

But the meeting was oddly cordial.

"He served some good beer," Randolph recalled, "sent a man out to buy me a package of cigarets and then asked, 'Colonel, what are you trying to do to me?'"

"Put you out of business," Randolph said he replied.

"Why do you want to do that?"

"We want to clean up Chicago, put a stop to the killings and gang rule here."

According to Randolph, Capone admitted that the campaign against him was working, a campaign that he seemed to think had been orchestrated entirely by the Secret Six: "Colonel, I don't understand you. You knock over my breweries, bust up my booze rackets, raid my gambling houses and tap my telephone wires. . . . You're putting me out of business. Even with beer selling at $55 a barrel, we didn't make a nickel last week."

Randolph shouldn't be so quick to celebrate, Capone warned him: "Do you know what will happen if you put me out of business? . . . I have 185 men on my personal payroll. . . . They're all ex-convicts—gunmen. . . . What will happen if you put me out of business? I'll tell you, you'll turn every one of those 185 respectable ex-convicts loose on Chicago."

And then Capone, still operating under the illusion of Secret Six power, offered a bargain: "If the Secret Six will lay off of my beer, booze and gambling rackets I'll police this town for you. I'll clean it up. There won't be a stickup, a murder nor a (pocketbook) grabbed in Cook County."

Randolph would not give in to the gangster, of course (because he couldn't), and Capone would go on to blame the colonel's intransigence for his business failure. But he didn't appear to be bitter toward anyone. In a July 1931 interview Capone granted to Ted Tod of the *Chicago Herald and Examiner*—when he was still free but had pled guilty and was awaiting sentencing—Capone began with a message of contrition. "For the months that he will spend in prison will, he feels, recompense society and the government in full for his sins against them," Tod wrote, and "will make it possible for him to return to Chicago and establish a legitimate business."

"I have a wife and a 12-year-old son to think of," Capone told Tod, "and as fine a mother as any man on earth. The time that I will be away will cause them some suffering, but in the end they'll benefit through my going to prison, because they will have a father, husband, son who never again can be looked upon as a law violator. I have pled guilty and I am going to accept whatever punishment is given without contesting the government's charges."

Capone also had a message for the people of Chicago, what he called a "swan song of a racketeer":

> I am only 32. I want the people to realize that in my few adult years it would have been utterly impossible for me to have done all the things that have been credited to me. . . . I see nothing morally wrong in making a living out of prohibition. And violating the prohibition law and running some gambling places make up the only so-called crimes I ever have committed. The Capone, as portrayed in books, in newspapers and in conversations by people who are supposed to know me well is a person I don't recognize or know. I have always been opposed to violence—to shootings. I have fought, yes, but fought for peace. And I believe I can take credit for the peace that now exists in the racket game in Chicago.

In his interview with Tod, Capone gave the Secret Six all the credit for his downfall. His full lament, which would be picked up by the wires and published nationwide: "The Secret Six has licked the rackets. They've licked me. They've made it so there's no money in the game any more. Most of the fellows who've been working with me realize this as well as I do. That's why I think they'll do the same thing as I'm going to do when I come back from Leavenworth—go into honest business."[19]

Randolph claimed to be "gratified that Capone gives (the Secret Six) so much credit" but, in a departure from standard practice, "declined to accept first credit for ridding Chicago of Capone, passing that honor to United States Attorney George E. Q. Johnson, who prepared the government's cases."[20]

Johnson in turn credited the Secret Six for his successes in a 1932 interview with syndicated journalist Neil Clark. "United States District Attorney

George E. Q. Johnson," Clark wrote, "told me it is a question whether he could have convicted ten of the higher executives in the Capone outfit had it not been for the work of the Secret Six in ferreting out, protecting and producing at the proper time certain key witnesses for whom the machine guns of the gang were spoiling."[21]

Oddly forgotten in the exchange of credit-giving were the G-men, led by federal prohibition agent Eliot Ness.

Whither the Credit?

In his 1957 book *The Untouchables,* a bestseller that spawned television shows, movies, and several more books, Ness described in great detail doing exactly what Capone accused the Secret Six of doing, specifically "knocking over his breweries, tapping his telephone wires and harassing him in various other ways."

When it came to going after Capone's breweries, for example, Ness detailed dozens of raids, some conducted with his own invention, a "powerful, 10-ton truck with a special steel bumper covering the whole radiator" which would be used to "crash through the steel doors which I assumed must be the standard equipment at Capone breweries."[22]

"With the unbeatable tactics we had now developed into a science," Ness wrote at the conclusion of one raid account, "we cost him another two hundred and fifty thousand dollars in beer, equipment and trucks by wiping out two more breweries."[23]

Among the many successes described by Ness, often accomplished at great personal risk, was the capture of a "giant still . . . geared to turn out the almost unbelievable total of twenty-thousand gallons a day." Ness described that capture alone as "another backbreaking blow to the mob's financial situation."[24]

The Secret Six, despite Capone's allegations, wasn't raiding Capone's breweries, because they couldn't. They didn't have the authority to storm private property with the small armies of federal men Ness brought; neither did they have Ness's custom-built truck. And there's not a single account discoverable in the press of the Secret Six attacking a brewery. Maybe they provided a tip here and there, but Ness, who gave the Secret Six credit for creating the Untouchables and putting Ness in charge of them (Ness's older sister was married to Alexander Jamie) never gave them credit for a brewery tip.

But did the Secret Six wiretap Capone, as the gangster claimed (and Randolph didn't dispute)? Probably not. Wiretaps were a key strategy of Ness and his crew, and he went into great detail in his book on both how taps were set up and what Ness learned from them. Wiretap installations were a dicey affair, Ness wrote, conducted by necessity at the tops of telephone poles near gangster headquarters, creating the significant risk of being seen and alerting the thugs to the operation. We may be fairly certain Ness wouldn't have wanted anyone else climbing around Capone's offices to put in their own taps.[25]

Finally, what of Capone's complaints that the Secret Six were "harassing him in various other ways"?

That might have been the Secret Six. Of course, toward the end of his reign, everyone was harassing Capone and his henchmen in "various other ways," including rival crooks, the governor of Florida, and every cop in Chicago and Miami. Maybe Capone was referring to Col. Randolph's regular habit of presenting the details of Capone's business plans with the press.

But here too, Ness stands out for his special powers of harassment. For example, just to infuriate Capone, he staged a parade of the forty-five trucks, tankers, pickups, vans and other vehicles, most of them brand new, that had been confiscated in raids on Capone's empire. Just before the procession reached the Lexington Hotel on Michigan Avenue, where Capone was holed up, Ness called the kingpin. When Capone picked up the phone, Ness recalled addressing him by the name only his closest associated were allowed to use: "Well, Snorkey, I just wanted to tell you that if you look out your front windows down onto Michigan Avenue at exactly eleven o'clock you'll see something that should interest you."[26]

So why did Capone give the Secret Six all the credit for his downfall? Why did he continue to appeal to Col. Randolph for mercy when his real enemy was the feds, wrecking his business infrastructure from one side while they pursued an income tax conviction on the other? Maybe his mind was already addled by stress and the syphilis that would go on to end his life in 1947. Or possibly his perceptions were colored by the steady newspaper drumbeat of Secret Six prowess, of cash raised, of cases solved, of criminals jailed. Maybe he noticed that the aggressive new police campaign against gangsters—the Chicago Plan—had been launched literally the night of the Secret Six's founding.

Capone may even have sensed kindred spirits among the Secret Six. Recall that he described himself as "opposed to violence—to shootings" and claimed he "fought for peace" and could "take credit for the peace that now exists in the racket game in Chicago." Perhaps he was deluded or just trying to clean up his image as he headed to prison, but maybe he believed he was on the same team as Col. Randolph's Secret Six, an unofficial but powerful force determined to pursue his idea of justice.

In fact, on at least one occasion, Capone and the Secret Six worked together.

When sixty-two-year-old Chicago attorney Benjamin McWilliams disappeared in late March 1931, his brother, Chicago Superior Court Judge Paul McWilliams, asked the Secret Six to find him. The Secret Six, coming up empty, turned to Capone for help, and Capone promised, "I'll do what I can" and "ordered several gangsters to find the lawyer."[27]

Unfortunately, this collaboration of the mobster and the vigilantes bore no fruit. McWilliams' body was found a month after he'd disappeared "in the river under the Clark street bridge," newspapers reported. "The body bore no marks of violence, police found, and it was believed the attorney either committed suicide or was drowned accidentally shortly after he disappeared."[28]

While the record indicates a brief and unsuccessful partnership between the Secret Six and Capone, and a minor role as well for the vigilantes in Capone's downfall, Col. Randolph and his band were still getting the lion's share of credit months and even years after Capone headed to prison.

In December 1931, for example, the Republican National Committee announced that they would hold their 1932 convention in Chicago, a decision that indicated for many the rehabilitation of the city. Articles about the city's selection singled out Col. Randolph, "head of the city's famous 'Secret Six' . . . widely credited with causing the arrest and trial of Capone.[29]

The Case of the Cruising Capone Witness

In the few brief Secret Six histories published to date, one story of concrete action against Capone is often told, the Secret Six's protection of a key witness. Because those expected to testify against Capone often ended up dead before they could get to court, the Secret Six went to extreme measures on behalf of one man, Col. Randolph claimed multiple times.

In a widely covered luncheon speech at Northwestern University in September 1931, Randolph said the Secret Six had traced $350,000 in canceled checks to the manager of a gambling syndicate. As luck would have it, the man and a woman he wasn't married to took a weekend jaunt from Illinois to St. Louis, and the man was arrested and jailed in Danville, Illinois, for violating the Mann Act, a federal law which forbade the transporting of women across state lines for purposes which were at the time considered immoral. In order to avoid federal charges, the man agreed to testify against Capone. Keeping him safe until he could take the stand was key to the case.

"That man is taking a South American cruise for his 'health' now," Randolph claimed at the gathering.[30]

Another wire story about the same Northwestern University speech provided additional details. Randolph claimed the Secret Six had forced the man (not named in either article) to testify against Al Capone's brother Ralph at his income tax evasion trial. "The same man," Randolph said to the gathering, "is now taking a South American cruise. . . . He will be brought back and kept 'on ice' in a safe place until he can testify against Al Capone in the latter's income tax trial."[31]

The story was still being told a year later, with additional details, in a glowing Secret Six review written by Neil M. Clark:

> A certain bookkeeper in a Cicero gambling house had a lot of firsthand knowledge of the money transactions of the Capone gang. The first conviction in the series of income-tax prosecutions was won largely through his testimony. He had to be kept alive to testify in later trials. If turned free, it would have been just another case of lilies and slow music, and he knew it. He was hidden in a hotel room so long that he got deathly sick of it. So the Secret Six escorted him to New Orleans, put him aboard a South American freighter in the captain's custody, and he had a gorgeous three months' vacation on the high seas and returned in good health and spirits to aid in the conviction of Al Capone himself. (The) Secret Six did this. The government probably couldn't have saved the life of the bookkeeper.[32]

Was it true? Like a surprising number of other tales told by Randolph, it might not have been. The *Chicago Tribune,* which attended Randolph's speech at Northwestern University, had learned through the years to take the colonel's proclamations with a grain of salt and the pursuit of corroborating witnesses. Their version of the witness-on-a-cruise story concluded with this passage: "At the federal building prosecutors who obtained the convictions against Ralph Capone and Guzik said that they did not recall the details mentioned by Col. Randolph. The only man it was said, who possibly might fit the description was Fred Ries, former cashier in a number of Cicero gambling houses. Ries was a government witness against Jack Guzik, but not against Ralph Capone, and the prosecutors said that they did not believe he had any information that could be used against Al Capone.'"[33]

Rare as criticism was in those days of the Secret Six, it happened. A reporter in Woodland, California, was not impressed by similar content in an October 1931 speech Col. Randolph delivered at the National Theater there. After taking issue with Randolph's pronunciation of Al Capone's last name ("kay-pone"), the reporter continued, "Colonel Randolph was not very convincing in his speech as to the big part the 'secret six' played in pulling 'Kay-pone' into court. Curiously, too, he neglected to refer to the Swedish Mr. (E. Q.) Johnson, who compiled the statistics that convinced a Federal court jury that Capone was short on his income tax returns."[34]

Capone's imprisonment wasn't the only thing the Secret Six had to crow about in 1931, however. Although it began with that unfortunate William Kuhn affair, the year was a good one for the vigilantes, who fought against everyone from embezzlers and crooked cops to national bank robbing and abduction corporations. All their battles were well-publicized, even if, in the latter two cases, their foes were imaginary.

PART IV

THE WAR CONTINUES

"The spy business is a nasty business and
a dangerous business and none of us like it,
but there are times when the only effective way to
fight fire is with fire."

**—Col. Robert Isham Randolph,
November 22, 1931**

17

The Best Cases of 1931

OVERALL, 1931 was a very good year for the Secret Six. The press adulation alone, offered in papers coast to coast in late 1930 and early 1931—less than a year after their founding—would have been enough to make any team of detectives proud:

- A story published in distant California described the Secret Six as one of an "imposing array of forces" poised to drop the noose around Chicago's criminal element and as one that "stands a good chance of strangling its criminal victim." Such an outcome would make Chicago, "once the object of world-wide repute as a crime capital . . . the first big city to free itself of gang influence."[1]
- Randolph's growing fame earned him speaking invitations around the nation. He showed up in January 1931 to make a speech in Buffalo, New York, where the local paper gushed, "As head of the 'secret six' Randolph conducted what is believed to be the most intensive drive on organized crime ever attempted in this country."[2]
- A second *Buffalo Times* article, based on an interview with Randolph a month later, described him as "head of one of the world's most famous detective organizations."[3]
- Coverage of the vigilantes was truly international. Even the press in Australia took note of the group's efforts, describing the Secret Six as "a private professional army" which "set out to fight the gangs with their own weapons, and by their own methods."[4]

In his extensive travels as a respected crime speaker, Col. Randolph also made it to Louisiana in January 1931, where he spoke heroically before the New Orleans Association of Commerce: "They dare not kill me," he said of the criminals his group sought to destroy. "If they would, there would be a few lynchings and they know it."[5]

Unlike standard police forces, the detectives of the Secret Six did not walk a beat. Instead, many of the cases came to them, meaning a varied workload, investigations large and small. Their willingness to work with criminals added to their work.

The Case of the Illegal Still Shakedowns

One such criminal, Verner Daniels, described by the *Chicago Tribune* as a "Negro still owner," complained to Alexander Jamie in January 1931 that Chicago cops were stopping by his operations on a near-daily basis to demand hundreds of dollars in bribes in exchange for not reporting him. The shakedowns, by a total of eight officers arriving at different times, were so onerous at his 4225 St. Lawrence Avenue enterprise that he "dismantled his still and sold it for junk."[6]

Jamie, who used to pursue the purveyors of liquor backed by the full faith and credit of the United States government, proposed helping the hooch peddler with a sting against the cops. Daniels, the *Tribune* reported, "was instructed to give the policeman marked money."

The cops, identified by the *Tribune* as Oliver J. McCormick and Peter J. Lowery, showed up to collect their tribute, but "became suspicious . . . discovered they were being watched and started to drive away but they were arrested." The two "denied that they asked Daniels for bribes, but said they demanded $8 for damage done to an automobile fender in a collision." Nevertheless, they were "charged yesterday in federal warrants and held in bonds of $3,500."

Authorities were also looking for "four motorcycle policemen" who "appeared on the scene of the still and demanded $200," and two other men, also believed to be city cops, "who posed as 'Miller and Burns' of the state's attorney's office," and had extorted $200 from the still operator.

The Secret Six case was an important one, on numerous counts. Verner Daniels probably couldn't call the Chicago Police department, both because he was engaged in a criminal enterprise and because it was the department itself that was extorting him—eight men in three teams. That he was Black would probably have been a third strike against him in an age when racism was still implicit if not overt throughout America. So Daniels called the Secret Six, and the vigilantes came through, arranging a sting and making sure the authorities got wind of it.

The case was, presumably, a new development in a city where police corruption appears to have been common. Maybe your captain wouldn't care if you made a little money on the side shaking down Black still operators, but the Secret Six did. Play it straight or see your name in the *Chicago Tribune,* just another disgraced cop facing federal charges.

This was the Secret Six at their best.

The Case of the Plumber's Union Racketeers

On January 22, 1931, "a raiding squad from the state's attorney's racket bureau" stormed the Plumbers Union, seizing books and records, the *Chicago Tribune* reported. The *Tribune* noted that "the raid was made on information supplied by the secret six committee of the Association of Commerce."[7]

Members had been complaining, presumably to the Secret Six after their protests to other authorities fell on deaf ears, about an unemployed plumbers fund, the *Chicago Tribune* reported. "The members said they have been refused information as to what was being done with the $6 assessment each week against each working member for the aid of the unemployed. The complaining members say they were told it was 'none of their business' when they asked for an accounting."

The raid prompted union members to call several meetings in the next ten days, where disaffected dues payers launched a "protest against racketeering officials." In a front-page story, the *Chicago Tribune* offered up these details from a February 1 gathering, held under police protection at the Majestic Ballroom on West Madison Street: "The discussion throughout the meeting centered on the eleven years of terrorism through which the union members have lived. No election of officers had been held in that time—at least no meeting at which the rank and file were allowed to vote, the dissenters declared. Members have been slugged and intimidated and, according to many, robbed. 'There has not been a legitimate audit of our books in the 11 years of hoodlum rule,' one member declared."[8]

By June of 1931, the 3,700-member Chicago Plumber's Union seems to have cleaned up its act, with the *Chicago Tribune* celebrating the "free election of officers" in unexpectedly peaceful balloting the previous day, after years of rule by the likes of "Skinny" Madden, Big Tim Murphy, Dapper Dan McCarthy, Billygoat Taglia and other "heroes of the underworld who had no regard for labor, for unionism, or anything else but their own profits."[9]

Embezzlers and Jewel Thieves

In August 1931, Edward Jordan Andell, formerly assistant to the vice president at retail firm Montgomery Ward, allegedly embezzled $7,500, worth over $100,000 in 2024. He disappeared on July 1, 1931, but was traced to an efficiency apartment in St. Louis, Missouri, and arrested there. "Andell," reported the newspaper wire story, "was located by detectives of the Chicago Association of Commerce 'Secret Six committee.'"[10]

When $104,000 in gems (worth almost $2 million in 2024) was stolen from Lawrence F. Stern on September 3, 1931, the wealthy Chicagoan called in the Secret Six. After a two-month investigation, Secret Six detectives united with the Pinkerton Detective Agency and police in Gary, Indiana, to corner three men and two women in a luxurious apartment in that city. The actual theft, according to press reports, had been committed by Wilma Harges, a "stunning blonde domestic" from Austria who'd been working for Stern. Intending to turn state's evidence, she helped alert authorities to the ring, claiming she'd taken the jewels after being threatened with deportation. She identified one of the alleged ring members as her boyfriend, claiming she didn't know he was married when he seduced her.[11]

In some news stories about the arrests, Leo Carr was identified as leading the team that made the bust.[12] This was the same Leo Carr, incidentally, routinely identified by the press as both a lieutenant with the Chicago police and a Secret Six investigator, the same Carr who had played an important role in the botched investigation into Marion Wright's extortion.

But toward the end of 1931, despite starting the year with a black eye, the Secret Six was declaring itself victorious.

1931 in Review

"The 'secret six,'" wrote journalist Oliver Sherwood in November 1931, "this week gave an accounting of its two years of activity and found itself assessed as successful."[13]

"Businessmen two years ago were caught with their backs to the wall as a result of racketeering and gang dominance," Sherwood wrote. "Tribute was being exacted from established enterprises, politics was being influenced by hoodlums and the police seemed helpless against a combination of politicians and criminals."

But then the Secret Six arrived, Sherwood wrote, and "as a result of this work, largely spying and coordinating of underworld information on which prosecution could be based, rackets have been put on the run, gangs put on the defensive, with many leading gangsters in prison, and bank robber gangs broken."

Sherwood interviewed Col. Randolph for his article, recording pronouncements from the man worthy of a dime store page-turner. "The antisocial elements fear this mysterious and secret force that is working against them," Randolph said, continuing:

> We gather bits of information here, there and everywhere. We have listening posts all through the underworld and sit at those listening posts night after night and week after week. Our spies work their way into the enemy camp and sometimes we find enemy spies in our camp. We buy information from enemy traitors, stool pigeons, so-called, and we pay for it "on the line," in the language of the hoodlum. Sometimes we buy false information, but we never buy a gold brick twice from the same man. The spy business is a nasty business and a dangerous business and none of us like it, but there are times when the only effective way to fight fire is with fire.

As he often did in interviews with the press, Randolph shared an untruth with Sherwood, claiming that "the 'secret six' has not attempted to usurp any of the functions of the legally constituted authorities, entrusted with crime fighting. Rather, this extra ordinary organization has supplemented that work, bulwarked by the secrecy of its operations."

A year before the story was published, the Secret Six took William Kuhn into custody, holding him prisoner for days in their own makeshift lockup after doing their own investigation. And his was not the only case where the Secret Six certainly did "usurp" the work of other authorities, gathering clues without police knowledge or involvement, arresting, interrogating and sometimes beating suspects.

But with Capone in prison and the rest of Chicago gangdom on the run, the Secret Six's continuing operation wasn't a given. They'd been going at it for almost two years in late 1931, and they had scored enough victories that they might have been justified in calling it quits.

"Chicago Wins War on Crime" announced the *Los Angeles Times* on December 21, 1931. The story below that headline, picked up from the Associated Press wire service by papers across the nation, began with a veritable trumpet of victory for the once-beleaguered Windy City:

> Chicago's anticrime campaigners looked back tonight on a year of work and pronounced themselves confident that organized crime has been crushed.
>
> To the Chicago Crime Commission and the "Secret Six" backed by wealthy and influential citizens was given most of the credit. A vigilant Federal government and a militant press were given as the other factors.
>
> Reorganization of the Chicago police force, the conviction of Al Capone on income tax charges, and enactment of legislation directed against gangsters, said Frank J. Loesch, president of the Crime Commission, have left the criminal begging for quarter.
>
> "Organized law enforcement has fought it out with organized crime," said Loesch, "and we have won. The gangster has been conquered."[14]

Was the Secret Six ready to hang it up? No, it wasn't time yet, said Alexander Jamie, the vigilantes' top investigator. "Al Capone is in jail, his brother Ralph is in jail," Jamie said for the story, "and so are Jack Guzik and others. They were the men most capable of leading, but there are others. We can get those remaining into prisons—and we will."

18

The Best Cases of 1932

THE CONVICTION OF Alphonse Capone was one of many victories ascribed to the Secret Six by the end of 1931, but the vigilantes were eager to keep fighting. In 1932, the Secret Six investigated short weighters, charity cheats, tax fixers, and even a ghost who needed a place to live. And they almost always got their man (or ghost).

The Case of the Fraudulent Scales

Sometime around the start of February 1931, Chicago's Better Business Bureau notified the state's attorney's office that the merchant scales in Chicago might be off, by design.

Keeping the scales accurate was the job of the city sealer, a role held at the time by Daniel Serritella, generally described as good friend of Al Capone and the gangster's eyes and ears in Mayor William "Big Bill" Thompson's Capone-friendly administration.

A scale that overcharged every consumer by a few cents a pound could make good money for its owner, enough that the merchant would be glad to pass some of the ill-gotten profit back to the colluding city officials. Catching a short-weighter is simple enough—select a product, have it weighed on the merchant's scale, pay for it, and then bring it to an accurate scale and see if there's a difference.

Such an investigation isn't cheap, however. The goods must be bought before they can be weighed, and the undercover buyers must be paid for their trouble. So the Illinois State's Attorney's office, headed by John Swanson, brought in the Secret Six, who may have been the only investigative organization in Chicago with the money to go after the short-weighters.[1]

The case was assigned to Secret Six agent Edward G. Wright, and he pulled four other Secret Six operatives onto his team, according to the *Chicago Tribune*. Wright "set up an office in the Transportation building and had hired and sent out women investigators to make purchases in grocery stores and meat markets."

Satisfied after two months of Secret Six efforts that he had enough evidence to move, Swanson ordered a raid on April 1, 1931. "Squads of state's attorney's detectives invaded the city hall shortly after 8 o'clock," the *Chicago Tribune* reported, "and took possession of Serritella's office. They seized all his records and took them to the Criminal Court building for perusal by the grand jury. Nearly thirty employees of Serritella's office were questioned by the grand juries."[2]

The raid was national news, as was the outrage expressed by Chicago's mayor. "Mr. Thompson announced that he would seek a legislative investigation of Mr. Swanson's office," the *New York Times* reported on its front page, "and said that he had instructed Mr. Serritella to go to [Illinois capital] Springfield and ask that such an inquiry be conducted."[3]

Surprisingly, Swanson didn't give credit to the Secret Six for the raid, saying only that after the Better Business Bureau had raised questions about the scales, "his assistants had been working secretly ever since." Possibly, this was one of the rare instances where the Secret Six worked a case the way they said they would. Recall that within two weeks of his founding of the Secret Six, Col. Randolph promised that "the lawyers whose services would be used would not become known until they have to appear in court. . . . The public will learn of the accomplishments of the secret committee and its staff only when its evidence is presented to the grand jury."

The involvement of the Secret Six in the short-weighting case would not be revealed for more than a year, in May 1932, when Serritella and his chief deputy, Harry Hochstein, went to trial on charges of "conspiring to allow merchants to short weight patrons."

Edward Wright, identified then as the Secret Six's investigation head, testified at the trial of Serritella and Hochstein that the women had indeed been overcharged, by amounts ranging "from 2 cents to 25 cents."[4]

Total losses suffered by Chicago shoppers under the "gigantic conspiracy" were estimated at "millions of dollars," the *Chicago Tribune* reported after the trial, with "more than 200 short weight instances in a couple of weeks when the investigation started. Many of them were in chain stores."[5]

Evidence presented at the trial, the *Tribune* reported, proved that Serritella had agreed to "fix short weight tickets in return for contributions," which Serritella insisted were campaign contributions but which, according to the prosecutors, "were for his own enrichment." Trial testimony suggested Serritella also "took foodstuffs from the merchants, whose scales he was to supervise, to feed his constituents and ward heelers." Some of the food bribes taken from the merchants may also have been "sent to Capone's soup kitchen on South State street."

The involvement of the Secret Six in the case drew particular interest from defense attorney Michael Ahern, who wanted to know more about the vigilantes.

"Who are the members of the Secret Six?" Ahern asked Wright.[6]

"I don't know all of them," Wright admitted.

"Well, who do you know?"

"Mr. Jamie is the director," Wright said. "Robert I. Randolph is a member."

"Who are the others?" Ahern demanded.

"I don't know," Wright replied.

"Is the Secret Six sworn to obey the constitution?"

"I don't know," Wright said.

"Are its members elected by the people?" Ahern persisted.

"No, sir."

"As a matter of fact, isn't it a sort of super government—"

The rest of Ahern's question was cut off by an objection from the state's attorney's lawyer, and Wright was allowed to leave the witness stand.

Serritella, described in the *Chicago Tribune* story as "Al Capone's representative in public office," was a state senator at the time of the trial. But with Capone in prison, and ample evidence of Serritella's corruption amassed by the Secret Six and others, he and Hochstein were both convicted, given one-year sentences in the county jail, and fined $2,000 (worth more than $30,000 in 2024 dollars).[7]

"The political leaders," the *Chicago Tribune* reported, "seemed completely crushed by the severe penalty imposed."

The protestations of defense attorney Ahern, who had also represented Al Capone in his income tax trial, were ignored by Judge James J. Kelly. "The defense tried out everything before this jury from the newspapers to the Secret Six," Kelly noted, asserting that the trial had nevertheless been fair.

Serritella and Hochstein were allowed to leave the courtroom and remain free while the case was appealed, the *Tribune* reported. After he was sentenced, Serritella "got to his feet and gave his belt a hitch, grabbed for his hat and started from the courtroom. Some of his swarthy henchmen, who were seated nearby, formed a circle around him and escorted him from the building. The performance was said by some police officers to have been a duplicate of the way Capone was escorted from the courtroom when he was tried."

Prosecutor Harold Keele called the conviction and sentencing "the death blow to the Capone gang."

The *Tribune* speculated that Serritella would likely be impeached as a result of the conviction, and removed from the Illinois senate. More than a year later, however, in November 1933, his and Hochstein's convictions were overturned on appeal on the grounds that the men were asking for favors for many merchants, not just those whose scales they neglected to balance.[8]

Serritella remained active in Chicago politics into the 1940s, departing public life at some point before April 1953, when he was "adjudged mentally ill and committed to the custody of his brother, Vincent" by a judge in what was called "Psychopathic County court."[9]

The Cases of the Stolen Goods

Thefts of things in Chicago might have been a given in Chicago, just a cost of doing business there, but the Secret Six had other ideas, working a number of cases that would likely otherwise have gone unsolved.

On October 5, 1931, 199 cases of shoes were stolen from a truck on its way to Chicago from the H. C. Godman Shoe Company in Columbus, Ohio. The shoes were valued at $9,000.*

A manager with the trucking firm involved in the shipment claimed the cases had been hijacked by gangsters, but the Secret Six smelled a rat. Maybe someone had tipped them off that a ring of eight shoe thieves were involved.[10] "The men were captured by Lieut. James B. Kerr of the Secret Six," the *Chicago Tribune* reported in January 1932.[11]

---

*Worth $180,000 in 2024.

The evidence against the men was strong, apparently. Four pleaded guilty before trial, and the other four, who declined a jury trial, were found guilty by Federal Judge John P. Barnes and sentenced to terms totaling more than 41 years. The stiffest sentence, nine years, was handed down to chief conspirer George Cornett, manager of Central Motor Freight Lines.

The shoe theft was one of several such cases the Secret Six worked in late 1931 and early 1932, and in February 1932 the vigilantes were enjoying another round of public adulation, courtesy of the newspaper wire services: "The "secret six," gang-fighting unit of the association of commerce, was credited today with effective work in a new field—thefts from merchandise trucks. The association's cartage theft committee reported that no trucks had been hi-jacked for six weeks although the racket has been costing Chicago business men $1,000,000 a year."

"Prior to that," he said (the story didn't name the official quoted), "two or three trucks a week, carrying goods worth $20,000, were being robbed. The secret six got evidence on which three gangs were convicted."[12]

The Case of the Homeless Ghosts

Lafayette Hopkins, a wealthy man variously described in the press of the day as either a half-breed Indian or Indian chief, as well as a well-known realtor, asked his wife for one thing as his death approached: Do not sell the family home, the home where both he and his father had lived. "If you do, I'll haunt you and the man who buys it," he'd warned her.[13]

In the United Press version of Hopkins' warning to his wife, he noted that his father had hung himself in the home, explaining, "My father killed himself here. His ghost likes the place. I'm planning to come back here myself and our ghosts will make this our happy hunting grounds. We don't want to be disturbed."[14]

His wife of twenty-five years, Ella Hopkins, agreed to keep the home, but after Mr. Hopkins died at the age of 80 sometime in 1930 or 1931, she came to regret her promise, because "her husband's spirit annoyed her aged mother," who was sharing the home with her. So Ella decided to sell the property.[15]

William Lambert, who owned a gas station at 5765 Higgins Road, across the street from the one-hundred-year-old farmhouse, agreed in 1930 to buy the home for $7,000.[16]

The sale reportedly caused great displeasure to the ghosts of Lafayette Hopkins and his father, also named Lafayette Hopkins, a wealthy Native American who, according to reports at the time, "came to Chicago from New York 100 years ago and purchased much of the land in what is now Jefferson Park."[17]

After she sold the house, Ella moved to Washington, DC, but both ghosts followed her. "During a session of wine drinking," she reported later, "the spirits of her husband and father-in-law began to appear and demand that she 'get back that homestead.'" Thenceforward began a campaign of terror from the persistent apparitions, said Ella, who complained that the ethereal duo "haunted her dreams, and made her life 'a living hell.'"[18]

"I am very uncomfortable with this man Lambert," Ella says her dead husband told her. "I do not like him. The spirit of my father is not so very comfortable either. You had better get (back) that house."[19] According to the United Press, the specter told his wife that selling the house "had made of him and his father just a couple of homeless ghosts wandering around without a roof to cover their heads."[20]

Ella Hopkins moved back to Chicago and, eager to bring the haunting to a close, according to the *Chicago Tribune*, sent a letter to William Lambert, asking if she could buy the house back from him for $9,000, which was $2,000 more than he'd paid. The dwelling "was her husband's ancestral home," she explained in her letter, and it was "designed for his spirit to roam in forever." She sold it, she explained to Lambert, "only because her husband's spirit disturbed her 80 year old mother."[21] (A more corporeal version of the story was making the rounds at the same time, however, where Mrs. Hopkins wanted the home back because it was worth $20,000.[22])

Ghosts or no ghosts, Lambert refused to consider Mrs. Hopkins' offer, so she sent a second, more serious letter, warning that "the curse of a dead man would rest on any stranger who lived within the walls, and would strike death once every year." Still, the *Tribune* reported, Lambert refused to budge.

In the meantime, Mrs. Hopkins took up lodging at 4219 Kenmore Avenue. Did she drive by her old house? Some wag in the photo department at the *Muncie (Indiana) Morning Star* guessed that she did, superimposing the ghostly image of a two-story-tall Indian chief over a picture of the dwelling. "Above is an artist's conception of what Mrs. Hopkins saw each time she passed her old home," the caption declared.[23]

But things got much more serious on February 7, 1932, when Lambert's gas station was bombed. The next day, Mrs. Hopkins sent a letter to Lambert, saying she was "too ashamed to look you in the face," but explaining that she "never had a moment's peace" since she sold the house. "I felt condemned to have caused you all this horrible grief and I am sorry to the bottom of my heart (if I have a heart).... On my bended knees I ask and beg your humble apology [*sic*] for the horrible crime I have committed."[24]

Mrs. Hopkins also claimed in the letter that she'd changed her mind about the attack. "I was just one day too late as I was going to write that doctor a letter and tell him to call it all off."

Lambert, according to the *Tribune,* contacted the Secret Six's Alexander Jamie, and Jamie assigned Lt. Leo Carr and Sgt. William Knowles to the case. Lambert showed the team the letters from Mrs. Hopkins, and the detectives, armed with written evidence of both motive and confession, confronted the widow. She in turn confessed to asking for help from Dr. Leslie Ofner (spelled "Offner" in some press reports).

Both Mrs. Hopkins and Dr. Ofner were picked up by the cops, and in a search of the fifty-year-old woman (some reports put her age at fifty-three), the *Chicago Tribune* reported, "Police matrons found $6,800 in cash sewed into her clothes." Ofner, in speaking to the police, "described himself as a doctor who handled many gangster cases," said he'd known the deceased gangster Jack Zuta, and admitted that "most of his friends are now dead or serving prison terms." Regarding the Lambert gas station bombing, the doctor said he'd first met Mrs. Hopkins when she asked for help getting her home back the first week of February, and he offered a full confession to Assistant State's Attorney Walker Butler and Chicago Chief of Detectives William Shoemaker.

"She wanted Lambert's place bombed," Ofner told the men. "She just wanted the front blown away. I told her the job would cost $1,000, and she gave me $10, and three days later brought me $300. I hired (James) De Milio to bomb the place. After it was bombed, Mrs. Hopkins gave me $50 more. That was all I got." Dr. Ofner told the officers he called in De Milio to do the bombing because he was a good "stickman."

De Milio was also picked up but denied any role in the bombing, claiming that "a man known as Eddie invited him for an automobile ride on the night of Feb. 7." They parked near Lambert's gas station, De Milio recalled, according to the *Tribune*, and Eddie left the car. The story continued, "Later he reappeared, excited. As they drove away a blast was heard. At no time, De Milio asserted, did he know of the bombing."

The *Tribune* reported that Mrs. Hopkins corroborated Dr. Ofner's story, and the two of them, along with De Milio, and Edward Schleickert, who had not yet been arrested, were charged with bombing, conspiracy to bomb, and malicious mischief.[25]

The *Tribune* reported that although Mrs. Hopkins corroborated Dr. Ofner's story at the time of their arrest, the two had since apparently put their heads together, agreeing to tell a different story at their trial a few weeks later. "Mrs. Hopkins wept," the *Chicago Tribune* reported, "as she told of paying Dr. Offner $360 to hire a thug to 'punch Lambert in the nose.'"[26]

When his turn came to testify in his defense, "Dr. Offner also denied any knowledge of a plot to bomb Lambert's filling station. He testified he received $250 from Mrs. Hopkins for the purpose of hiring a thug to punch Lambert's nose."

"James DeMilio was hired to strike Lambert," Offner testified, "but he had no instructions to bomb the place as far as I know."

Dr. J. M. Houston, described by the *Chicago Tribune* as a "surprise witness," was next called. The doctor, "who at one time treated Dr. Offner," referred to "a sheaf of notes" as he testified. The sum of his testimony: "Dr. Houston considered Dr. Offner to be of unsound mind."

After deliberating five hours—and despite those letters the Secret Six collected from the victim, and the other investigative work done by the vigilantes—the jury found both Mrs. Hopkins and Dr. Offner innocent. Charges were presumably dropped against De Milio and Schleickert as well, as no further record of them appears in the searchable press.

The Case of the Milk Fund Cheat

In 1924, two groups, calling themselves the Missouri Veteran's Association and the Disabled Veterans Association, started a telephone fundraising drive. The campaign was a success, reportedly raising as much as $1,000 in a week (some reports said in one day), but the campaign was not authorized by any officially registered veteran's charity group, and campaign publicity materials named officials who were not part of the drive and didn't support it.[27]

Among those crying foul were officials with the Jerome L. Goldman Post of the American Legion in St. Louis, Missouri. They and others pointed to Jacob K. Karchmer, who listed himself as executive director of the Missouri veteran's groups.

Karchmer did not take the accusations lying down. A US Marine veteran and editor of the *Missouri Veteran* newspaper, Karchmer placed advertisements accusing the all-Jewish Goldman Post of being run by "stoolpigeons of the Ku Klux Klan." He also wrote what the *St. Louis Post-Dispatch* described as "scorching letters" to A. E. Goldstein, commander of the Goldman Post, in which he accused Goldstein of "being biased and unfair."[28]

The letters also accused Goldstein of "twiddle and twaddle" in his management of the post, and offered a veiled threat as well, stating that "every time he thought of Goldstein he would 'put on his kid gloves lest he might forget that he was a gentleman.'"

By May of 1924, the post had had enough, scheduling a trial in which they would consider expelling Karchmer from the post for, ironically, "conduct unbecoming a gentleman."

Karchmer, who had served as a clerk during World War I and was never sent overseas, showed up for trial with "a bag of technicalities," including Robert's Rules of Order, the US Constitution, "the by-laws of a church," and his Marine discharge papers.[29]

The trial was an utter disaster for Karchmer, a native of Vilna, Russia, and described by the *St. Louis Post-Dispatch* as "a dapper little man of engaging personality and rapid-fire flow of language." The discharge papers, which Karchmer believed would help his case, listed Karchmer's character as "indifferent" and included the order "that he not be re-enlisted in the marine corps." Also entered into evidence was a "letter from the Adjutant of the Marine Corps at Washington," which "said Karchmer was of radical temperament." And there was a telegram from a man in San Franciso to the American Legion in Missouri stating that Karchmer "was a fraud and had solicited money without authority in the name of disabled veterans."

A letter from Karchmer's commanding general said the man "was under surveillance during the war, and was not to be re-enlisted in the corps because a board of officers had ruled that he was undesirable."

"Other witnesses," the *St. Louis Star and Times* reported, "testified in an effort to prove that Karchmer had misrepresented his connections with the legion in soliciting money for his association."

Karchmer represented himself during the trial and, according to the *St. Louis Post-Dispatch,* "staged a series of lengthy cross-examinations of witnesses that bordered on filibustering, and was frequently accused of attempting to prolong the trial until everyone went home so there would be no one left to vote."

The trial lasted five or six hours and ran until 2:00 a.m., according to the press, at the end of which Karchmer was given ten minutes to present his closing arguments. "I want to talk longer than ten minutes in my own defense," Karchmer protested before he removed his legion button and announced, "I quit."

Karchmer was told he couldn't quit, a vote was taken, and it was unanimous, 51–0, to expel Karchmer from the American Legion post. "You have been expelled from the Jerome L. Goldman Post and the American Legion," he was told after the vote.

That night, after the meeting, Karchmer was asked by a reporter for the *St. Louis Post-Dispatch* why he hadn't prepared a better defense. He explained that "circumstances over which I had no control have recently upset me a little. You see, I am in love with a very fine little girl and this is bound to upset a man on trial for his honor."

Jacob Karchmer's ignominious ouster from the American Legion was covered in at least three Missouri newspapers, but that didn't keep the man from doing the same thing, over and over again for years to come, using his real name.

On July 15, 1925, St. Louis police raided Karchmer's office, arresting him and twenty-one employees, and charging him with obtaining money under false pretenses. Karchmer and his workers had been selling tickets to a play with claims the proceeds would benefit the Rescue Workers of America, but Karchmer had failed to turn the money over to the charity.[30]

Later in July 1925, St. Louis area newspapers noticed that Karchmer was selling tickets for an event on behalf of the United Workers for the Blind in Missouri. Receipts two weeks before the event had climbed to $2,594, but Karchmer was obligated to give the association just $750 of that money, meaning net proceeds to him worth at least $1,845 (almost $30,000 in 2024 dollars).[31]

Nothing, typically, came of the charges against Karchmer, and two years later, in 1927, he was back at it, this time sending packs of neckties around the nation under the names "Necktie Tyler, the Blind Tie Salesman" and "Paunee (sometimes Pawnee) Bill, the Blind Tie Man."† The letters implied that the blind men were trying to make a living despite their disabilities, and asked either that the ties be returned or paid for.[32]

Karchmer's operation employed as many as five hundred workers at its peak and sent 1.3 million packages of ties, reported the *St. Louis Post-Dispatch*, noting that the ties "were obtained wholesale at $1.10 a dozen and then offered to the public at four for $1.25."[33]

It was the sheer bulk of the effort that contributed to its downfall, with newspapers around the country reporting the arrival of ties to their cities and warning their readers of the scam and its connection to Jacob Karchmer. "Newspapers Help Put Fraud out of Business" announced a typical headline, this one appearing in the *Bismarck (North Dakota) Tribune*.[34]

"The flood of neckties which went out of St. Louis under the direction of Jacob L. Karchmer, promoter of things with a charity appeal, has stopped," read the article. "Newspapers aroused by the complaints that were coming into their offices . . . warned their subscribers, outlined plans that would tend to stop the practice and secured a statement from postoffice authorities that persons receiving unordered merchandise through the mails were under no obligations to return the same."

The same year it was begun, Karchmer's venture went bankrupt.[35]

Creating believable, sympathetic fictions to get money from the misled and softhearted was, unfortunately, the only thing Karchmer seemed able to do. By November 1929, he'd moved to Chicago and was arrested there for embezzling $2,600 in tickets to a veterans' charity dance sponsored by the American Legion.[36]

In February 1930, after six years of scandal involving his given name, Jacob Karchmer was finally using an alias, Edward S. Harris. And under that

---

† The two men were real, their pictures featured in the solicitations, but they held no ownership stake in the tie business. According to the *St. Louis Post-Dispatch's* January 10, 1928, report about the business, Karchmer paid the blind men a respectable $50 a week (worth almost $2,000 today) for the use of their names and likenesses. Karchmer's own salary was triple that.

name, officials alleged, he and a fellow fraudster named Morris Rubin were using the names of charitable organizations to sell dance tickets, turning over $5,000 of the proceeds and keeping $50,000[‡] for themselves. The men had named their business Universal Sales and Publicity Bureau and were operating out of a hotel on Cass street when they were arrested by a Chicago postal inspector and charged with using the US mail in their scam.[37]

The arrest of Karchmer and Rubin occurred on Saturday, February 8, 1930, one day after the birth of the Secret Six. Maybe Col. Randolph or one of the other associates of the vigilante group noticed the story in the *Chicago Tribune,* and maybe they followed it to its disappointing conclusion: as was the case repeatedly for Karchmer, nothing came of the charges against him.

But two years later, the Secret Six were watching the affable man who'd started his checkered career in 1924 by scamming Missouri's American Legion. When Karchmer opened up the Chicago Infants Free Milk Depot at 20 East Jackson Boulevard, the Secret Six hired Florence Johnson to spy on the charity's operations. Miss Johnson got a job as a clerk there, and the meticulous notes she kept on the scam's finances were exhibit A when Karchmer was arrested for fraud by federal authorities. And at the man's trial, she was the star witness.

"A girl who masqueraded as office clerk while she took notes for the secret six exposed a charity racket in federal court Thursday," the Associated Press announced in March 1932, continuing: "The jury took her word for it, and convicted Jacob Karchmer of using the mails to defraud those charitably inclined persons who contributed to support his Chicago infants free milk depot." The evidence showed more than 70 per cent of the weekly contributions of $200 and up went to salaries and expenses of Karchmer and assistants. The rest was devoted to the milk depot. "The government witness was Miss Florence Johnson who obtained employment in Karchmer's office and took daily notes which she reported to the secret six and the government."[38]

Another version of the story quoted federal prosecutors as alleging that "Only 10 per cent of Karchmer's receipts went to charity."[39] The article continued, "Karchmer faces a possible sentence of fifteen years' imprisonment. He is said to have conducted other rackers, both here and in St. Louis, under the guise of charity."

---

‡ Worth almost $2 million in 2024 dollars.

Two days after his March 1932 conviction, Karchmer faced what was probably the most severe consequences of nearly a decade of channeling money away from the needy and into his own pockets: A $1,000 fine and two years in federal prison.[40]

He was taken into custody immediately and spent perhaps half a year in prison before his lawyers got him out on appeal in October 1932. The three judges of the United States Circuit Court of Appeals "held that the evidence showed a legitimate scheme rather than a scheme to defraud, and that the case should not have been submitted to the jury."[41] After his release, Karchmer returned to St. Louis, Missouri, and to his preferred calling. He was arrested in August 1933 for selling pictures of President Franklin D. Roosevelt to NRA members, claiming proceeds would benefit an orphans' home.[42]

A year later, in August 1934, Karchmer and two colleagues were arrested for "operation of a business without registering the name of the business with the Secretary of State." The men "made telephone solicitations for donations" for their St. Louis firm, Life-Line Home, "which they represented as being a charitable organization for the care of unemployed girls."[43] Those charges were dropped two months later, when Karchmer convinced a judge he had applied for the required license just before his arrest.[44]

Beyond that brief stint in federal prison, the law was apparently helpless to fix things, but karma got into the act in April 1935, taking a tragic swipe at the serial huckster. Karchmer, his wife Mary, and their three daughters were driving back home from Texas "when their car, driven by Karchmer, was sideswiped on a curve by a machine going in the opposite direction and forced off the road. The other car did not stop."[45]

The accident, which occurred on US Highway 66 near Lebanon, Missouri, was detailed by the *St. Louis Post-Dispatch*, which had chronicled many of Karchmer's charity schemes. "The Karchmer automobile turned over three times and was demolished," the paper reported. "Mrs. Karchmer died of a fractured skull. . . . Evelyn, 10 years old . . . suffered a head injury and face lacerations, Norma (6) a broken arm, leg injuries and scalp lacerations, and Madeline (3) a broken collarbone. Karchmer suffered a wrenched knee and was able to return home with his wife's body."

The wreck did not kill Karchmer, but it might have done something the Secret Six, their "girl undercover operative," half a year in federal prison, and a dozen arrests couldn't. Jacob Karchmer, named by newspapers with stunning regularity between 1925 and 1934 for his charity scams, never again appeared in the searchable press after the accident.

The Case of the Tax Fixers

In autumn 1932, Patrick C. Carey wandered into the Story & Clark Piano Company and sat down with Edward Story Jr., whose family had been running piano and organ companies for more than seventy years. Carey proposed a scheme, clearly illegal, for lowering Story & Clark's 1931 property taxes.[46]

The business's taxes were about $28,000 in 1931 ($533,000 in 2024 dollars), and Story said he felt that amount was appropriate. Carey replied by warning him, "But remember, your taxes will be boosted next year, and you might be interested in holding them down."

Story suggested that Carey share his idea with L. B. Bull, Story & Clark's secretary and treasurer. But before Bull met with Carey, Story warned Bull of what was in the works. In his meeting with Bull, Carey made his criminal intent clear: "I can slip another schedule in the files if you will give me 50 per cent of the tax reduction," Carey proposed. Carey was a registered public accountant with no access to the tax schedules or tax files kept on each business in Chicago, so Carey's offer indicated corruption within the tax assessor's office.

Bull declined Carey's offer, but he left the door open to further negotiations. However, as soon as Carey left Bull's office, Bull called Alexander Jamie with the Secret Six. A few days later, Carey returned with a new offer: instead of paying me half your tax savings after the schedules are swapped out, he told Bull, give me $300 in cash up front and I'll make it worth your while.

Bull said yes, and on October 5, 1932, Carey returned. Bull paid him $300 in marked bills, and Carey delivered in dramatic fashion, the *Chicago Tribune* reported: "To carry out his end of the deal he tore into pieces the 1931 tax schedule of the Story company."

Carey left the Story and Clark building on Michigan Avenue and walked straight into the arms of the Secret Six. Arresting officers were Lt. Leo Carr and Sgt. William Knowles, who worked together on many of the Secret Six's biggest cases. The vigilante cops also picked up as evidence that schedule

Carey had torn up, and then they interrogated Carey, quickly winning both a confession and the name of his inside man, special deputy assessor Art Hollaman. Carr and Knowles promptly went to Hollaman's apartment and nabbed him as well.

At some point in the process, the Secret Six brought in the regular authorities. Assistant State's Attorney Harry S. Ditchburne handled questioning and filed conspiracy charges against Carey and Hollaman. Hollaman, who denied he knew Carey or had played any part in the scheme, was described by the *Chicago Tribune* as "one of six employes in the assessor's office having exclusive access to schedules already filed and approved." The article noted that "there was nothing to prevent him from removing a bona fide schedule and substituting a schedule with reduced valuation."

The day after the two men were arrested, however, county assessor J. L. Jacobs told the *Chicago Tribune* that the alleged scheme to swap out tax schedules would not have worked because the records "are kept in triplicate by different staffs and closely checked to prevent possible fixing."[47] Jacobs also proposed a Depression Era motive for Hollaman's crime: He hadn't been paid in four and a half months due to the local government's insolvency.

No further records appear in the indexed press about the two men and, given their plot was destined to fail, Story & Clark was reportedly the first and only firm they hit up, and neither had any known criminal record, charges might have been quietly dropped or settled with a minor fine.

Or maybe it was something else. By late 1932, the Secret Six's careless investigating habits and spotty record of winning convictions were well-documented, and maybe the real cops and the official courts might have been leery of dragging another Secret Six case through the system.

Other Noteworthy 1932 Cases

Inevitably, if one reads about Chicago crime in early 1930s newspapers, one will come across references to the Secret Six. Who they were was rarely explained, because it didn't need to be. Everyone knew about the Secret Six.

From the crime pages in 1932 come these examples of Secret Six involvement in a range of small cases, often without any further description of the vigilantes:

- Illinois state police working under the "Secret Six" of Chicago held today four men accused of swindling $30,000 from merchants and banks in many Illinois cities through false checks. . . . Officer Hal Roberts of the Illinois State Police . . . was aided by Sergt. Roy Steffens and Charley A. Touzinsky of the "Secret Six."[48]
- It was disclosed yesterday that the information on which four youthful bank bandits were arrested Saturday was given police by the Secret Six. The youths have confessed robbing the Beverly State Savings bank, 103d and Loomis Streets, of nearly $6,000 last Tuesday.[49]
- James Morrison . . . was held at the detective bureau last night for St. Paul, Minn., authorities as an alleged member of the bandit gang which two years ago shot two women and stole $142,000 in a robbery of a bank at Willmar, Minn. He was arrested Wednesday by Lieuts. Leo Carr and William Knowles of the "Secret Six," while attempting to sell some bonds.[50]
- Three men were under arrest (in Aurora, Illinois) tonight accused of attempting to extort $7500 from Matt Kersch, roadhouse owner, as the aftermath of an attempted kidnaping. They were Ed, Walter and Martin Pryzcyl, brothers, captured through a decoy package and the efforts of the "Secret Six" of Chicago.[51]

That last case was one of several the Secret Six worked against extortionists, occasionally going so far as to get the wrong man charged. But the vigilantes liked kidnappers even less, and they pulled out all the stops against the abduction epidemic of the early 1930s. They led multicity raids, issued astounding reports, and claimed to have uncovered evidence of nationwide kidnapping corporations that didn't, apparently, exist. One of their number disguised himself as a woman in a huge operation to save a kidnapped banker. And when torture was called for, they tortured.

19

The Secret Six Conjures a National Kidnapping Monopoly

BEGINNING WITH THEIR first successful case in March 1930, when the Secret Six brought down the kidnappers of Theodore Kopelman, kidnapping was a focus for the vigilantes.

"The first job we had was a kidnaping job," Secret Six chief Col. Randolph told the Associated Press in February 1932. "The victim came to us, afraid to go to anybody else. The kidnapers were apprehended within a week and in 90 days we had them in prison. Since then we have had a kidnaping case on our docket practically continuously."[1]

Kidnapping was big business during the Great Depression, an equal-opportunity racket that reaped vast rewards for its best practitioners. The formula was simple: pick someone known for their wealth—a doctor, a businessman, a banker, or maybe just another criminal; spend a few weeks studying them—where they worked, when they went out and came home, the cars they drove; then make the snatch, try not to kill them in the process, and hide them somewhere—the back seat of a car would do, but some of the more sophisticated operations maintained makeshift prisons where victims could be kept for weeks.

After that, get the money, a step that demanded considerable finesse, as it required communicating clearly with the victims' very distressed spouses and business associates about the ransom amount and where and how it should be dropped off; and finally, money in hand, get rid of the victim. Most abductees were let go, alive and mostly unharmed, but some were killed, either by design or otherwise. It is believed that Charles Lindbergh Jr., taken March 1, 1932, as the era's most famous kidnap victim, was dropped and killed as his abductor was bringing him down the ladder from the child's second-floor bedroom.

The going rate for ransoms was typically $50,000 but could run as high as $200,000,* the amount set for some high-profile victims, including the Lindbergh baby.

The Federal Kidnapping Law, and FBI Director J. Edgar Hoover's aggressive enforcement of the law through the use of sweeping manhunts and nationally distributed lists of ransom cash serial numbers, shut down the scourge by the mid-1930s. Until then, it was up to local cops and state police to investigate the cases, although they typically had to stop at the borders of their jurisdictions and didn't have the budget for national pursuits.

The Secret Six, although founded to fight Chicago crime, faced no jurisdictional limits and enjoyed a virtually unlimited budget in the early years, meaning that until the FBI stepped in, they were the closest thing to a national antikidnapping force America had ever seen.

The Secret Six went after individual kidnappers, invariably with their own style and their peculiar flair for mayhem, but they also studied the crime, ascending to national prominence as abduction experts as they conjured a kidnapping corporation out of thin air.

The Secret Six vs. Kidnapping, Inc.

If one establishes a well-funded, well-publicized vigilante organization, for whom good press is essential to keeping both the dollars and public support flowing, one could do worse than to frighten people.

Cracking cases is all well and good, and the Secret Six had that in spades after eighteen months in business. But it would not have hurt the group to demonstrate that it was as an authority on crime, on crime trends, and on the growth in certain kinds of crime, particularly on sinister, coordinated organizations working brilliantly to rob innocent Americans of their wealth and freedom. More specifically, if the Secret Six made frequent pronouncements about an efficient kidnapping company with a business plan focused on the snatching up of men, women and children en masse for profit, the newspapers would carry the stories under blazing headlines, and the Secret Six would grow in prestige and support.

---

* Worth almost $1 million and $4 million, respectively, in 2024.

So that's what the Secret Six did on at least five major occasions, issuing studies, identifying culprits and victims, alleging the existence of a major kidnapping ring, and once even staging a raid on the ring—a ring which proved to be nonexistent.

"A one-gang national monopoly on kidnapings," was announced by Secret Six head Col. Randolph on September 14, 1931, a claim immediately carried nationwide by the wire services. The story alleged that Los Angeles was now host to an important branch office of the gang, formerly based only in southern Illinois, and was headed up by "former Al Capone gangster" Ralph Shelton, aka Ralph Sheldon, called in the story a "'branch manager' genius".[2]

"The kidnapping racket" the Secret Six had discovered was described in the Associated Press story as a "new system of extorting money from wealthy business men." The Secret Six also warned that "the gangs had more than 150 killers among them."

As evidence of this national kidnapping consortium and its opening of a main branch in Los Angeles, the report pointed to a single kidnapping, that of A. L. (Zeke) Caress. Caress was a Long Beach, California, bookmaker who claimed he'd been kidnapped by Shelton in early January 1931 and ordered to sign ransom checks worth $50,000 (the checks were confiscated by police in a nonfatal shootout with the kidnappers and never cashed).

In November 1931, two months after their first warning about the kidnapping monopoly, the Secret Six seemed to prove their case with a series of major raids around the Midwest "against a kidnap ring which has abducted 100 men in the last year."[3]

According to one widely distributed wire story, "Investigators of the 'Secret Six' . . . brought about the arrest of 'Dago Lawrence' Mangano, Al Capone Lieutenant, as the 'brains' of the kidnap band. He was captured with five other men in raids ordered by Alexander Jamie, Chief Detective of the 'Secret Six.'"

According to a second wire story about the raids, "The battle between the kidnap gang and an aroused citizenry, led by Chicago's famous 'Secret Six,' centered in St. Louis and Chicago, with minor skirmishes in other nearby cities."[4]

Evidence that the Secret Six had broken up the national kidnapping monopoly was immediately forthcoming, the newspapers asserted, when the gang responded to the raids by disgorging its victims without ransom payments. But how many freed victims there were, and who they were, varied from one story to the next:

- One article spoke of "release within 24 hours of eight kidnap victims by the midwestern gang"[5]
- A second article named just two victims but pointed to more: "Police believed it significant that both (furrier Alexander) Berg and Ralph J. (Fuzzy) Pearce, Rockford, Ill., gambler, who had been held eight days, were released within 24 hours after Lawrence (Dago) Mangano and five other Chicago gangsters were arrested. Word drifted into the detective bureau here meanwhile that several other men also had been released by kidnapers since the arrest of Mangano and his pals."[6]
- Patrick Roche, who worked closely with the Secret Six in the raids as chief investigator for the Illinois state's attorney's office, identified four released victims, Burg (or Berg; it was spelled both ways in the papers) and Pearce, as well as Meyer Gordon, owner of a Chicago jewelry store, and Jackie Fields, "reputed millionaire malt manufacturer."[7]
- But other men were also let go by the harried kidnappers, Roche claimed in that story, "Four others whose names are known by the 'Secret Six' but whose identity was not revealed."

Among those arrested with Mangano was Louis Spenilli, who "admitted trying to negotiate with Berg's kidnapers," some newspapers reported.[8] Other versions of the story alleged that Spenilli hoped to serve as a "go-between" in the Berg kidnaping and came to Chicago to bargain for his release.[9]

For reasons not made clear in the articles about the raid, the Secret Six seized on Spenilli's involvement as proof of their kidnapping monopoly claims: "This fact alone was considered definite proof that one kidnaping ring was responsible for almost all of the Mid-West's recent abductions."[10]

More definite proof of a single kidnapping corporation, however, was difficult to come by due to victim reticence, as both Patrick Roche and Alexander Jamie acknowledged after the raids. "We know that at least 100 men had been kidnaped in this vicinity during the last year, but we are handicapped because the victims are afraid to sign complaints," Roche told the press.[11]

And Jamie "pointed out the chief difficulty authorities met in their investigation was the reluctance of victims to report abductions or discuss their negotiations with the kidnapers." Jamie explained that "Most of the victims were gamblers, wealthy business men, bankers, brewers or gangsters who were anxious to avoid publicity and in most cases paid huge ransoms rather than obtain police aid."[12]

But in the end, the raids and arrests proved all for naught.

The Secret Six had identified "a one-gang national monopoly" in September 1931, directed an anti-kidnapping drive in November 1931, pointed to various circumstantial evidence dredged up in the raids as proof of said monopoly and, a day after the raids, endured another of the humiliations the vigilantes were suffering with increasing regularity.

"Five kidnapping suspects were released today," read a November 12, 1931, wire story. "[Chicago] Chief of Detectives William Schoemaker announc[ed] he had no evidence to connect them with the abduction of Alexander Berg of St. Louis and Ralph J. Pearce of Rockford, Ill, both released last night by their captors."[13] The story recalled the Secret Six claims about Mangano and his associates, but this time as farce, noting that the arrests "had been hailed as the death blow of a huge syndicate that had kidnaped more than 100 men."

But the last paragraph of the story offered a consolation prize of sorts to the Secret Six, with Schoemaker promising that "the matter is still under investigation and we will keep these men under surveillance."

Remarkably, the failure of the raid seemed to have had no impact on the Secret Six. Two months later, the persistent vigilantes were back in the news again, saying the same things. "Underworld operatives of the Secret Six . . . today claimed discovery of a huge kidnapping syndicate with ransom as its object and torture the means of enforcing its demands," the Associated Press announced in late January 1932. Lead Investigator Alexander Jamie, cited as the source for the story, "declined to reveal anything specific about the ring's activities but said it operated like a well organized business concern."[14]

A few days later, the United Press sought to beat its rival wire service with a better story about the kidnapping ring, and the Secret Six seems to have made a bargain with UP reporter Robert T. Loughran: We'll give you the names of victims and some juicy new details about how this band operates, but you can't say it came from us. The provenance of the United Press articles is undoubtedly the Secret Six, however, as it is full of the vigilantes' signature claims of unified, prolific, and well-organized groups out to destroy America from within.

Referring only to an unnamed "informant" as its source, the United Press described a "band of seven super-criminals" who "have exacted from victims by torture and terrorism more than $1,000,000."[15]

The seven super-criminals "each made a name for himself in the underworld as a bank robber or a holdup killer," the article asserted, but "decided they could do better collecting ransom money" and were staying busy at it. "The kidnapings have averaged almost one a week" in a broad swath of the Midwest, from Missouri to Wisconsin.

The United Press "informant" named some of the victims of this kidnapping corporation, including Alex Berg, Nell Donnelly and James Hackett. But here's another place where things broke down in the vigilantes' story. A review of the listed abductions and their outcomes suggest not a single corporation, but more what kidnapping has always been, the hare-brained schemes of individuals or small, independent teams of crooks who committed one or maybe two kidnappings before the authorities caught up with them. With that in mind, here are the Secret Six's alleged victims of this kidnapping corporation, and the eventual, very noncorporate outcomes:

- Alex Berg, St. Louis, Missouri, furrier, was kidnapped in November 1931. Convicted the following April of the crime were Curtis Medlock, Charles Heuer, Edward Barcune, and George Peak, none of whom had any connection with a kidnapping consortium.[16]
- Nell Donnelly was snatched in December 1931, also by an independent team: Martin Depew, Walter Werner, and Charles Mele, convicted the next year.[17]
- Gamblers James Hackett and James J. (Jack) Lynch were both believed to have been kidnapped by the same group, the infamous College Kidnappers, but again—as reported to the press by police officials at the time—this was another team of self-directed freelancers, "connected in no way with the organized gangs of Chicago and Southern Illinois."[18]

The utter absence of a kidnapping corporation troubled the Secret Six not at all, however. In March 1932, five months after the failed raid, two months after their dubious second report, Alexander Jamie was back on the record with a set of wild new claims about the kidnapping corporation. "The man at the head of it," Jamie declared, "whose identity we haven't yet discovered, is evidently a highly capable business executive."[19]

This latest article, written and distributed to newspapers around the nation by the Newspaper Enterprise Association, treated these latest Secret Six claims as something entirely new. "Existence of the kidnapping ring has been discovered by operatives working for (the) 'Secret Six,'" the article stated. The piece also offered up a Secret Six take on the kidnappers' primary base of operations: three places, oddly, none of them California.

"Kidnapping," claimed the article, "has ceased to be the work of isolated criminals working on their own and has become the job of a highly organized syndicate of desperadoes with headquarters in Chicago, Detroit and St. Louis."

In March 1932, two more victims of this kidnapping company were proposed by the Secret Six: Dr. Max Gecht and his wife, Georgia, snatched in December 1931.[20] After chaining the couple to beds in separate rooms, Dr. Gecht was set free to round up the modest $2,000 ransom. It took him two days, during which one of the kidnappers, Gus Sanger, became smitten with the wife and proposed they meet for a date after her husband got her free. She agreed and the kidnapper showed up at the appointed time and place, but instead of finding Georgia Gecht, Sanger fell into the waiting arms of the cops. After several hours of interrogation, he led them to the rest of his gang and avoided prosecution by turning state's evidence. William "Big Bill" Thomas and John Pingera got life for the crime the following May.[21]

Were these the men in charge of that "one-gang national monopoly" cited by Col. Randolph? Was one of these two the "highly capable business executive" Alexander Jamie had described? No. Illinois attorney chief investigator Patrick Roche, who worked with Georgia Gecht to apprehend her abductors, admitted "they weren't the big shots of the gang."[22]

Further, while Roche estimated the gang to which Thomas and Pingera belonged had committed as many as twenty-five kidnappings, that was a small fraction of the hundreds carried out in Chicago alone in less than a year.[23]

And yet, the Secret Six stories of the illusory kidnapping corporation continued. In March 1932, Jamie wrote a widely-distributed, five-story summary of things the Secret Six had learned about mobsters and racketeers over their two-year history. He focused his third piece on kidnapping, describing the methods of the perpetrators and asserting that "most of the major kidnapings in the mid-west have been committed by a group of about 15 men."

A final round of Secret Six claims about kidnapping appeared in newspapers in May 1932 and were attributed to Roy Steffen, described as a "star investigator for Chicago's 'Secret Six.'"[24] While Steffen did not allege the existence of a kidnapping monopoly or a kidnapping CEO, he told a story of a wealthy gambler and his servant girl abducted by "seven kidnapers." A similar claim appeared in a second abduction story in the piece, which stated that John Lynch, part owner of the Central News Bureau, had been grabbed "by seven men from his million dollar home on beautiful Lake Geneva, Ill."

So there we have it. Roughly every two months between September 1931 and May 1932, the Secret Six was announcing a new version of its ever-shifting kidnapping blob, sometimes led by one man, sometimes by seven, sometimes by fifteen, and sometimes boasting a national network of 150 or so hired killers to keep things running smoothly. Their primary lair might be California, southern Illinois, Chicago, St. Louis, and/or Detroit. They might be nationwide, or focused on the Midwest. But when one looks over the Secret Six list of victims of this single corporation, one finds perpetrators who were consistently independent from each other, not part of a single entity led by a "highly capable business executive." And when the Secret Six led that November 1931 raid on the kidnapping corporation, they came up empty.

Truth wasn't the goal, it seems, so much as staying in the headlines. And that worked, with each new Secret Six claim being welcomed by America's Depression-era media with the same breathless credulity as the last one. And the papers can't really be blamed, operating in relative darkness seventy years before the advent of electronic newspaper indexing and storage. Maybe some reporters and editors looked at the latest Secret Six kidnapping claims and wondered if they hadn't seen something very similar a few months before. But unless the journalists could put their hands on the physical newspapers from that previous report, nothing could be proved. And why bother, anyway? True or not, kidnapping stories sold newspapers and earned bylines for ambitious reporters, while a story about the Secret Six's manipulation of the mass media would interest, quite possibly, no one. The kidnapping claims put out by the Secret Six, even if they changed from month to month to stay fresh, always offered drama, and always had the same ring of authority.

Indeed, so respected was the Secret Six's expertise on the topic that when Congress held hearings on kidnapping and extortion, Secret Six head Col. Robert Randolph was invited to speak. "Murder isn't to be compared with kidnapping, it is merciful by comparison," Randolph told the Congressional House Postoffice Committee in late February 1932. Always ready with the dramatic flourish, Randolph exhibited a piece of rope that he claimed had been sent to a distraught mother. If the mother didn't pay the ransom, she was told, her daughter would be strangled.[25]

Randolph had come to Washington in support of a federal antikidnapping law, which would make the transport of kidnap victims across state lines a federal crime, punishable by death. A week after his testimony, the Lindbergh baby was kidnapped, making passage of the law that summer all but inevitable. Thanks to the Federal Kidnapping Law, often called the "Lindbergh Law," and its aggressive enforcement by FBI Director J. Edgar Hoover, America's kidnapping epidemic waned significantly by the mid-1930s.

The FBI never turned up that "highly capable business executive" the Secret Six warned the nation of, nor was an organized kidnapping corporation ever uncovered. Instead, the kidnapping cases the FBI prosecuted were invariably committed by independent groups beholden to no one.

So too were the kidnappings solved by the Secret Six, and they did solve a few, employing a toolset ranging from the high tech to the barbarous.

20

The Secret Six vs. the Kidnappers

Technology and Torture

WHILE THE SECRET SIX spent considerable energy tracking down a national kidnapping monopoly that existed only in its own imaginings, the vigilantes also worked individual cases, and here their efforts bore impressive fruit. Unimpeded by jurisdictional boundaries, budgetary concerns, or legal niceties like getting warrants and not torturing suspects, the Secret Six played key roles in freeing victims and catching perpetrators.

The Case of the Prison Tip

A strange item about the Secret Six appeared in newspapers across the nation on March 16, 1931: The Chicago vigilantes were demanding that the chaplain at the state penitentiary in Joliet, Illinois, be fired.[1] The chaplain, Rev. George Whitmeyer, formerly an Episcopal priest at a church in Herrin, Illinois, was accused in the Associated Press wire story of a number of noncriminal but problem behaviors:

- "Fomenting disaffection," was a general offense that referred apparently to making the prisoners unhappy with their conditions.
- "Carrying letters to and from prisoners," which was a violation of prison policy.
- Telling a prisoner that "what this place needs is a damn good riot," after which a riot was held. In the "short-lived uprising," conducted by "1,100 rebellious prisoners" on March 14, "one convict was killed, another fatally wounded and two seriously hurt."

- Delivering a short story written by convict James Gentile to his wife, a work of fiction in which plans for an escape were "conveyed in code."

Rev. Whitmeyer, according to the story, agreed to leave prison service "of his own accord" and praised the warden for "his great work in improving conditions at the Penitentiary."

The mystery, then, is why the Secret Six got involved. They were formed to fight gangsters in Chicago, not do away with soft-hearted chaplains in prisons forty miles southwest of the Windy City. The answer came a few days later, in another widely distributed wire story, in which Chaplain Whitmeyer defended his actions at the prison and blamed the Secret Six for problems there. Whitmeyer attributed "further causes of unrest" to "investigations constantly being made in the prison by such outside organizations as the Chicago Association of Commerce's 'secret six' committee, in an effort to obtain 'inside' information."[2]

The *Chicago Tribune* corroborated Whitmeyer's accusation, stating that "the Secret Six . . . requested his removal on the ground that he advised prisoners not to talk to that investigating body's operatives."[3]

Whether or not these prison interviews were humane, they were effective, apparently. Two months later, on May 9, 1931, authorities staged a raid in East St. Louis, Illinois, capturing "a gang of six kidnapers and bank robbers," newspapers reported. "Proceeds (of the gang's crimes) were estimated by their accusers at $6,000,000, of which $1,000,000 was fixed as ransom money, in kidnapings."[4]

According to the wire reports, "The captures ended a nation-wide search and more than eight months of intensive investigation, initiated by the postal department, and aided by Chicago and state highway police and the 'Secret Six' anti-crime business men's organization, which is reported to have received tips from within the state prison at Joliet and the federal penitentiary at Leavenworth, Kan."

The capture of the suspects was also a Secret Six operations, although that wasn't made clear in the wire story, which included this line: "The raiders were directed by Sergeants Roy Steffen and Charles Jasinski, of the Chicago state's attorney's office."[5]

The article claimed that Steffen (whose first name was sometimes given as "Leroy" and whose last name was usually mistakenly spelled "Steffens" in the press) and Jasinski (whose last name was sometimes spelled Touzinsky by the papers) "were working in cooperation with the crime fighting committee of Chicago millionaires known as the 'secret six,'" but Steffen's association with the Secret Six was probably a little more direct than that. He was frequently mentioned in other stories as a Secret Six detective or as having been assigned to the group, and he was a central player in an odd story, described in a future chapter, of the Secret Six's recovery of millions of dollars' worth of stolen bonds.

The connection between Chicago's law enforcement officers and the Secret Six was often murky, quite possibly on purpose, an arrangement which the vigilantes would fall back on during William Kuhn's defamation trial in late 1932. But more on that later.

Whatever his role was in the East St. Louis, Illinois, raid, Steffen operated capably. "So well was the raid planned that there was no disorder," the newspapers reported. "How many of the gang were captured, Sergeant Steffen refused to say. He identified three of them, however, as Tom Connor, Jack Britt and Tom Hayes."

The Case of the Uncooperative Family

Gustav E. Miller, twenty-three, son of a wealthy family in Joliet, Illinois, was kidnapped the evening of April 29, 1932, just after dropping his fiancée off at her home.[6]

Gustav's distraught family attempted "at first to deal with the kidnapers directly," the United Press reported a week into the abduction, but "was flooded with telephone calls, letters and telegrams threatening to kill the youth unless the money was paid. Unable to determine which demands were from cranks or imposters, the elder Miller called in the Joliet police."[7]

The Secret Six were also brought into the case, either by the Millers, according to some press accounts, or by Joliet Chief of Police Nicholas Fornango, who wanted the vigilantes involved on the strength of their past success solving kidnappings.[8]

During the nine days that Miller was missing, speculation ran rampant, with the Secret Six returning to their habit of finding connections in unconnected kidnappings. According to the United Press story, Chief Fornango suspected that the kidnappers of Gustav Miller were "the same Detroit gang" wrongly believed at the time to have kidnapped Charles Lindbergh Jr., an opinion "shared by crack operatives of the Chicago 'Secret Six'."[9]

Despite various dead ends, the investigators quickly winnowed down the demands for ransom to the real one, $50,000 in cash, an amount Gustav's father Max Miller, "a wealthy Joliet wholesaler," was ready to pay.

The Secret Six soon thereafter claimed to have "discovered the identities of four of the six kidnapers," according to the *Daily Illini*. The vigilantes told the Millers they knew who was behind their son's abduction and worked with the family to set up a trap to catch them.[10] "An agreement was made whereby young Miller would be brought to a place near Chicago and the ransom paid," the *Chicago Tribune* reported. "An arrest was to be made at this time."[11]

That's when things went off the rails. In their next conversation with the kidnappers, someone in the family revealed that the Secret Six had uncovered their identities and the kidnappers, terrified of the Chicago crime busters, immediately made arrangements with the Millers to free their son for a ransom listed by the *Chicago Tribune* at $2,500.

Unbeknownst to the Secret Six, Gustav's brother, Martin Miller, "received an anonymous call from Chicago instructing him to go to a certain Chicago address which he was told not to disclose," according to the Associated Press. "There a note awaited him with further instructions to meet his brother at the State park."[12]

"The youth was released at the entrance of the Starved Rock State park late Friday night," the *Chicago Tribune* reported. He was picked up by his brother Martin and his mother, Fannie.

The Millers had their son back, but the Secret Six didn't have their kidnappers, and they were peeved, their discontent summed up in the *Tribune*'s May 8, 1932, headline:

Victim's Family Spoiled Kidnaping Trap;
Blamed by Secret 6 Men for Escape of Gang

The kidnappers "might have been captured had members of the family kept their promise to aid authorities," someone with the Secret Six told the *Tribune*.

The Millers, according to the article, "called the incident 'a closed book,' and said they had no desire to cooperate in any police investigation. They denied that any ransom was paid."

The exasperated Secret Six agreed that the case was finished, admitting, "Nothing would be accomplished by arresting the four hoodlums now . . . for there was no corpus delicti until the family admits paying a ransom and the kidnaped youth makes an identification." Gustav couldn't help with that because he claimed "he was blindfolded throughout his captivity and could make no identification," the *Chicago Tribune* reported, adding, "However, police said his eyes were not red and he did not seem to be affected by the light."

The Case of the Square-Mile Stakeout

Norman B. Collins, president of both Security Bank of Chicago and the Second Security Bank, needed to catch a train for a business trip on the morning of October 10, 1932. He and his wife, Alice, headed for the train station at about nine o'clock that morning from their home* in Wilmette, Illinois, a well-to-do village about fifteen miles north of Chicago. But kidnappers had other plans for the couple, parents of one young son.

As Alice Collins related the next day:

> We had only gone a few blocks when three men in another automobile pushed us into the curb.
>
> They forced my husband and me out of our car at pistol point, put adhesive tape over our eyes and mouths, put us in the tonneau† of their machine, and covered us with rugs.
>
> Then they drove around for hours. One man apparently followed along in our car.
>
> Finally they took us out of the automobile and brought us into some sort of room. My eyes were bandaged tightly and I couldn't see. But they did take the tape off our mouths and tell my husband that he would have to get $100,000 or be killed.
>
> He said he couldn't get that much and argued with the men for perhaps half an hour. They finally came down to $5,000.
>
> When that sum was agreed upon, they taped my mouth again and drove me around for a while. Then they put me back in my own car and left me. I pulled the tape off my eyes and saw I was in a place I'd never seen before. I was dazed. So I drove and drove until I saw a familiar street and went home.[13]

---

* The home, at 630 Elmwood Avenue, Wilmette, was built in 1919 and still stands. It was valued by Zillow at just over $2 million in August 2024.

† An open rear passenger compartment, common in cars of that era.

Once home, Mrs. Collins, according to a United News article distributed nationally, "described the kidnaping in a hysterical telephone conversation with Melvin A. Traylor, president of the First National Bank."[14]

In turn, Traylor brought in James B. Forgan, chairman of the board of both of Collins's banks. Forgan called the Secret Six. Alexander Jamie, who the story said, "is known throughout the Midwest for his success in foiling kidnap plots . . . hurried to the Collins' suburban home."

Once there, the wire story related, "Jamie had attempted to comfort Mrs. Collins by telling her the 'Secret Six' even then was on the trail of the kidnapers," and the woman, described as "one of the prettiest young society matrons in Wilmette," "recovered her composure."

Immediately, the *Chicago Tribune* reported, "a county-wide search for the missing banker was being conducted by the Secret Six, the police, and friends headed by Mr. Forgan." However, "no trace of the kidnapers was uncovered until shortly before 5 o'clock last night, when a letter of instructions was found slipped under the door of the Collins home."

According to the *Tribune*, "The letter carried a map of an area bounded by Irving Park boulevard and Western Belmont and Kedzie avenues, and directed Mrs. Collins to take the money there. She was to be at Irving Park boulevard and Western avenue at 6 o'clock and to drive around the square mile every hour. . . . Continue driving around this square mile until you are relieved of package."

A chance to meet the kidnappers face to face was too rich for the Secret Six, who arranged one of the most elaborate stakeouts in their history.

"A Secret Six operative attired himself in the clothes Mrs. Collins wore when she and her husband were abducted," read one wire story.[15]

The disguise impressed some of the headline writers. "Secret Six Operative Dons Skirts To Foil Kidnappers," reported Baltimore's *Evening Sun* in a frontpage article October 11, 1932. The *Chicago Tribune* identified the skirted operative as Secret Six detective Louis Nichols. Crouched in the back of the car were Lt. Leo Carr and Sgt. William Knowles, who'd worked together as well on the Marion Wright extortion case and the subsequent, wrongful arrest of William Kuhn.

Alexander Jamie, Alice Collins, and James Forgan followed in a second car.

"The men were heavily armed with machine guns and other weapons," the wire story noted. While Nichols followed the course mapped out by the kidnappers, "other Secret Six agents, disguised as clerks, conductors and street laborers, strolled around in the neighborhood, while still others cruised the streets in automobiles, ready to do battle with the kidnapers."

The elaborate ruse lasted for two hours, but the kidnappers never materialized. The stakeout was not a failure, however. When the kidnappers got wind of the Secret Six's involvement, apparently, they abandoned the plot without collecting their ransom. Just before eight at night, "none the worse for his eleven hours of captivity," the *Chicago Tribune* reported, Collins was set free.[16]

The kidnappers put him on a streetcar, Collins revealed later that evening, and "told him not to get off until it reached the Irving Park–Kedzie intersection."[17] Collins "jumped from the street car at the designated spot, dashed into the corner store, and immediately telephoned home." Secret Six operatives raced to the store and picked him up.

Mr. Collins, whose age was given as both thirty-nine and forty-six in news reports, told the *Chicago Tribune* it was three kidnappers who'd apprehended him, driving a "wreck of a car." Collins said he "was driven around for hours," by the kidnapers, who "treated me considerably at all times," although he "suffered somewhat from lack of food." They did offer to buy him a sandwich at one point, and "one man gave me some whisky to keep me warm."

Collins estimated the age of one kidnapper at forty years old, while the other two "appeared to be very young." He told the *Tribune* they "made no direct threats, but occasionally referred to the higher ups. They said at one time, 'We don't know what we'll do if we don't get the dough.'"

Police, according to the Associated Press story, "theorized the kidnapers were amateurs and had freed their victim and fled in fear that their hiding place had become known."[18]

Jamie, according to the AP, "has histories of most of the known kidnapers in this territory, but was not prepared to say which of the gangs he suspected in the Collins case."

Collins said that "an adhesive bandage placed over his eyes was removed several times," and that "he had opportunity to survey his surroundings and his three kidnapers, all of whom he said he could identify. His captors, he related, talked as if they were unemployed and without funds. He gave them his purse containing four dollars and his watch."

His kidnappers were never caught, however, the crime unsolved to this day. The Secret Six had better luck with the kidnapping of a Peoria doctor. The era's best technology helped. Torture played a role as well.

An Argument for Torture

In an article written for the *New York Herald Tribune Magazine,* Col. Robert Isham Randolph made his clearest published endorsement of the dark side of law enforcement.

The article, which began on the front page of the magazine's August 7, 1932, edition, offered up Randolph's opinion of what he called the "third degree," slang for police abuses during the interrogation of suspects and witnesses: "I do not believe in the doctrine that the end justifies the means," Randolph wrote, "though I have personal knowledge of occasions when extra-legal methods have been effective in bringing criminals to justice."

Randolph advised against "the fist, the rubber hose or any other weapon," but only because such an item was "too likely to leave its mark." He continued, in a passage oft-quoted among those writing Secret Six histories, "I have known of a telephone book being used very effectively as a weapon. In the hands of a strong man it can knock a victim silly and not leave any mark."

Randolph, as people often do when making a controversial argument, turned to an extreme example, in this instance the kidnapping of Charles Lindbergh Jr.: "What constitutional guarantees, code of ethics or principles of justice," Randolph asked, "would be violated if, by any method, a confession could be wrung from one or more of the kidnapers and murderers of the Lindbergh baby, and the rest of the loathsome mob brought to justice?"

Randolph offered numerous defenses of the third degree in the article, opining that such methods as practiced by contemporary American police departments surely didn't match the "inquisitorial horrors" of the Middle Ages and were "probably nowhere as cruel as the public imagination pictures it." He added, "I doubt very much that it ever amounts to more than a beating or continued questioning to wear down a physically and mentally tired victim to the point of non-resistance and confession of the truth or something sufficiently near it to satisfy the inquisitor."

At times in the piece, Randolph, appeared to be arguing with himself, stating at one point that "the use of violence of any kind in compelling a prisoner to confess to the commission of the crime of which he is accused (is) obviously wrong, ethically and legally."

But elsewhere, he offered an endorsement of roughly the same thing, asserting that "continued questioning by relays of inquisitors who keep the victim awake and permit him no rest may be regarded as a form of mental torture, but I cannot believe that an innocent man could not support such an ordeal or be made to confess to anything but the truth." And then:

> The purpose of the "third degree" is not primarily to compel the defendant to testify against himself, but to disclose the truth. If the Fifth Amendment is to be interpreted as prohibiting the questioning of the accused as to his whereabouts or his actions at the time of the crime it defeats the ends of justice, and I am sure that the fathers never intended that it should.
>
> No innocent man could properly object to telling all he knows about the crime of which he is accused, and any means that is available to test the truth of his testimony ought to be properly and legally admissible.

The key phrase here, "any means available," served as a veritable blank check to America's police in their pursuit of a confession. Even America's Founding Fathers would approve, Randolph implied, of whatever tortures were necessary to force from the accused a "telling of all he knows" and to "test the truth of his testimony."

Note too that in Randolph's morally ambiguous world, a principle argument against violent interrogations is not about their inhumanity but that they don't work. "Usually they are ineffective," Randolph wrote. "The most intelligent and experienced police offices I know have told me that 'third-degree' methods—i.e. the use of violence—rarely produce results and always have repercussions that are damaging to the case against the defendant."

Randolph wrote carefully for the magazine, giving the reader hypotheticals, shades of gray, a conditional morality in which the proper and improper applications of the third degree should be obvious to anyone who loved justice. He did, however, offer a few general details of one specific case in which, he strongly implied but did not state, torture was used effectively.

"In a recent kidnaping case," Randolph wrote, "the two ringleaders in the criminal conspiracy were apprehended after their guilt had been definitely established by their own conversation, heard over tapped telephone wires and a cleverly concealed Dictaphone in the room of the chief conspirator.

This information was not evidence, and it was necessary to get an admission from one or both of them to complete the case against them and arrest the other parties to the conspiracy."

So, Col. Randolph, were they given the third degree, or weren't they? Were they tortured? And if so, by whom? Randolph didn't say, oddly. But the presence of the case in a story about the third degree suggests it must have been used, as does what happened next in Randolph's narrative: "One of them finally broke down and confessed."

Armed with that confession, the unnamed investigators confronted the second suspect, "he admitted his part, and the two confessions aided in the apprehension and conviction of the rest of the gang. They were all given prison sentences ranging from eighteen months to twenty-five years, and kidnaping for ransom has been definitely discouraged in that community."

What case was it? Randolph never said. But it must have been the kidnapping of Dr. James H. Parker. All the details line up. It was a Secret Six case. It was a grand case, reported nationwide, and one of the vigilantes' biggest wins. High-tech methods were used, and some amusing low-tech ones as well. And there was a second indication, along with Randolph's quasi admission, of torture.

The Case of the Tortured Kidnappers

Dr. James W. Parker, physician and chief of the Illinois Tax Securities Corporation, left his home in Peoria, Illinois, at 7:30 p.m. March 14, 1932, to attend a bowling tournament sponsored by his club.

At eleven o'clock that night, a man called the Parker home, telling his wife, "Dr. Parker will not be home tonight, but you'll hear from him in the morning." The man, according to the United Press, also told her where she could find his car.[19] The next day, Dr. Parker's empty car was "found on a road marking the city limits" of Peoria, the Associated Press reported.[20]

"Dr. Parker, once reputedly wealthy, was said to have lost considerable money recently," the AP reported. But speculation Parker had killed himself was dismissed by Mrs. Parker and his friends, who instead suggested he might have been kidnapped.

There were no traces of violence or suicide discovered with the car. After a fruitless, 24-hour search for the 65-year-old Parker, the police were beginning to lean toward kidnapping as well and "awaited ransom demands."[21]

Some authorities had begun to speculate that Parker "was kidnaped by men who hid in [Parker's] garage," the *Chicago Tribune* reported.[22]

Contributing to that theory was the way Parker drove away from his home. Dr. Donna Parker (both husband and wife were doctors), the United Press reported, "noticed a delay in getting the car out, and later saw its lights turned off. Although Dr. Parker is an expert driver, tracks showed the car wheels jumped the curb in backing out of the drive."[23]

On the fifth day, Dr. Parker's absence took a devastating toll. "The wife of the missing doctor, Mrs. Donna Parker, also a physician, is confined to her bed recovering from a heart attack suffered Friday, when she collapsed," the *Chicago Tribune* reported. "She is being attended by her son, Dr. James W. Parker, Jr."

Not helping things, presumably, were the friends of the family who "expressed the opinion he may have been kidnaped by enemies and slain." Other theories aired by the *Tribune,* also not helpful, were that Parker "may have been seized by a patient with a fancied grievance" or "may have been spirited from his home to attend a wounded gangster or perform an illegal operation."[24]

A week later, the press reported, Dr. Parker was still missing, nothing had been heard from any abductors, and local police "announced that they have adopted a 'hands off' policy" in the investigation and would stop looking for Parker, "at least for several days, in the hope that this may lead to [the kidnappers'] direct communication with the missing man's son," James.[25]

Ten days after Parker's disappearance, Peoria Chief of Police Thomas McCann announced "new clews unearthed through contacts with authorities in towns near Peoria." McCann said his detectives were "trailing a gang said to operate near Peoria."[26] Three days after that—and two weeks after Dr. Parker had disappeared, a one-paragraph story appeared in the press stating that "Demands for an exorbitant ransom were reported today to be delaying the return of Dr. James W. Parker."[27]

The story was the tip of the iceberg. Unbeknownst to the press and most of the public, a ransom demand of $50,000 had arrived at the Parker home soon after Dr. Parker's disappearance. That sum, worth almost $2 million in 2024, could not be paid, the family made clear, and the amount was subsequently negotiated down to $5,000.[28]

Meanwhile, the Secret Six were on the case, their investigation moving into high gear a week after the kidnapping. On March 21, 1932, a local attorney named Joseph Pursifull reached out to Parker's son, James Jr., and claimed the kidnappers had asked him to serve as a go-between on ransom negotiations. The kidnappers were "killers," Pursifull warned the younger Parker, advising that the family might want to consider mortgaging their home to amass the ransom.[29]

Pursifull's story of working with the kidnappers was plausible. Lawyers are known for their discretion, their knowledge of law and procedure, their ability to handle delicate financial negotiations to the satisfaction of all parties. Pursifull might have been entirely innocent, selected at random by the kidnappers, just trying to help a family through a difficult time. But with that call to Dr. James Parker Jr., Pursifull became suspect number one to the Secret Six.

With a virtually unlimited budget, no jurisdictional concerns, and no need for warrants, the vigilantes swooped in on their unwitting prey, conducting—despite the criminal justice outrages soon to follow—some of the finest surveillance work in their three-year reign, and leading to some of their best publicity as well.

Sam Tucker, a newspaper columnist in Decatur, Illinois, described the operation in exacting detail, asserting that "within half an hour" of Pursifull's emergence as the kidnapping middleman, the Secret Six "had established themselves in the same building as that in which the lawyer's office was located."[30] Tucker continued: "Skillfully, with complete technical knowledge, they traced the maze of telephone wires entering the building and tapped the pair leading to the lawyer's office. To this set of wires, they attached two instruments. One was similar to an ordinary telephone, having a silencer switch to avoid tell-tale clicks, by means of which the detectives could listen to all conversations taking place over the lawyer's telephone. The other instrument translated into numerals the clicking sounds made by the lawyer's dial, when he called any number from his office. With this instrument, and a numerical directory, it was possible to learn instantly the location of any telephone that the suspected man should call."

Needing a way to monitor all conversations in the office, not just telephonic, the Secret Six waited for Pursifull to step out of his office, Tucker wrote, at which point "the technician of the detective staff quickly slipped into the room with a pass key" and installed a Dictaphone "behind a steam radiator close to the lawyer's desk, where the little electrical eaves-dropper was entirely out of sight, but in excellent position to pick up every word spoken." Wires from the Dictaphone "were threaded out through a corner of the window, and led to the room used by the detectives a floor or two above."

Secret Six detective Roy Steffen, one of those monitoring Pursifull's office, testified in a criminal trial that May that the eavesdropping technologies quickly paid off.[31] First was a call between Pursifull and Dr. James Parker Jr., desperately trying to rescue his father: "When will you definitely know about the money?" Pursifull demanded, according to Steffen. "Friday noon? . . . I have to know definitely about it or otherwise I will have to relieve myself of this responsibility."

Soon after, Pursifull spoke on the phone to a man the Secret Six identified as James W. Betson, who had recently run unsuccessfully for mayor of Peoria: "This is P. talking," Steffen recalled Pursifull as saying at the start of the call. "They're asking for more time. I was up there last night and talked to them about three hours. I talked to them about mortgaging their home. They sent wires to Mississippi and all over. They want until Friday noon. You get in touch with the fellows and see what they have to say."

The Secret Six team, Tucker wrote, considered Betson "not explainable as a likely personal or professional friend." With that and the sinister nature of the conversation, the Secret Six's work expanded: "Instantly, a technician rushed to the neighborhood of this man's house, and half an hour later detectives were keeping the same unseen watch upon him, and everything that he said."

By Thursday, March 31, 1932—the seventeenth day after Dr. Parker's disappearance—the Secret Six believed they had enough to take action against Pursifull and Betson, but not quite enough for formal charges, nor quite enough to apprehend the rest of the gang. So the vigilantes, with the tacit approval of local authorities, took both men into their own custody, confining them not in the local jail but in the attic of a home described as standing in a Peoria suburb.[32]

Betson suspected subterfuge in the room where he was placed with Pursifull, wrote Sam Tucker in his article about the Secret Six investigation. So he "put a finger to his lips upon entering, in signal to his confederate not to speak. Then he searched the room carefully for a Dictaphone that might betray him."[33] Continued Tucker:

> He did not find any suspicious instrument on the premises. He did not find it because it did not occur to him that the very ordinary radio standing in a corner, with the usual aerial and ground wires, was a highly perfected sort of eaves-dropping device, amplifying every sound for the benefit of a stenographer and witnesses in another room. It did not occur to the conspirators, either, that the glassy eye of a bull on a picture calendar hanging high on one wall was rather more natural than a painting. The eye, as a matter of fact, was that of a detective who stood on the opposite side of the wall and watched every gesture made.

Once the men believed they were unobserved, Tucker wrote, "the conspirators in rapid whisper informed one another what had befallen each since their last meeting, and concocted a story to be used in their defense. In doing this of course they wove about themselves a net from which no lawyer could extricate them."

Three sets of headphones in the basement of the home were attached to the Dictaphone, one over the ears of Edith Smith, a stenographer, the other two being listened in on by the Secret Six, whose team in the cellar included Alexander Jamie, his adult son, Wallace Jamie, and Secret Six detectives Roy Steffen and Lew Nichols.[34]

Further details of what transpired between the two suspects was provided by Peoria Police Sergeant William G. Lyons, who had carved that hole in the wall and whose eye was peering through that calendar bull's eye. Lyons testified in court a few months later that he "saw Pursifull place two fingers to his lips, then over his heart, and shake hands with Betson." Then, according to Lyons, Pursifull "proceeded to tell the story he gave police about how he became the go-between in trying to collect ransom."[35]

None of this was regular policing, it should be noted. No police department in America would today tolerate, much less assist in, the imprisonment by vigilantes of two kidnapping suspects in the bugged attic of a local home. That the Secret Six was allowed free reign in the case is a testament to the esteem with which the group was held in those days, as well as perhaps the growing panic over the safety of Dr. Parker, now missing for more than two weeks.

Involved in the Secret Six scheme, along with the Peoria police, was Illinois State's Attorney H. E. Pratt. He was not entirely comfortable with the arrangement, admitting later in court that he allowed Pursifull and Betson to be spied on "against his better judgment," but he said he decided using a Dictaphone and stenographer made it okay, and insisted the transcription of their attic conversions be allowed as evidence, a plea the courts granted.[36]

The Secret Six, then, had warrantlessly amassed an impressive array of evidence against Pursifull and Betson. But they didn't have Dr. Parker back, the man still languishing in the clutches of unknown perpetrators who at any moment might grow tired of the game, dispatch their victim, and leave his lifeless body in a ditch.

So it was time for the Secret Six to resort to extreme measures. Surely this case qualified, if any Secret Six case ever did, for the "third degree" Col. Randolph had written about in that *New York Herald Tribune Magazine.* Surely, the use of "any means available" was warranted to get Pursifull or Betson to tell "all he knows" and to "test the truth of his testimony," as Randolph had put it.

When he wrote about the kidnapping in that article, Randolph didn't name names, but he didn't need to, the case clearly Parker's. The magazine article, published five months after Parker's kidnapping, described a "recent kidnaping case" in which "the two ringleaders in the criminal conspiracy were apprehended after their guilt had been definitely established by their own conversation, heard over tapped telephone wires and a cleverly concealed Dictaphone in the room of the chief conspirator."

Randolph conceded that "This information was not evidence, and it was necessary to get an admission from one or both of them to complete the case against them and arrest the other parties to the conspiracy." Randolph doesn't say what the Secret Six did to the men, if they were given the "third degree," if a telephone book was used, but it is probable. Recall that he'd written earlier in that article, "I have known of a telephone book being used very effectively as a weapon. In the hands of a strong man it can knock a victim silly and not leave any mark."

Whatever was done to Joseph Pursifull and James Betson while they were in Secret Six custody, it worked. As Randolph noted in his article, "One of them finally broke down and confessed."

On April 2, 1932—nineteen days after Dr. Parker was kidnapped, two days after the Secret Six picked up Pursifull and Betson and started working them over—newspaper across America carried a double shot of good news, about the arrests of the men and Dr. Parker's release.

Typical of the headlines was this one, from the front page of the *Daily Chronicle* in DeKalb, Illinois:

Kidnaped Man Returns Home; Secret Six Is Given the Credit For the Solving of Case

The *Fresno (California) Bee* put it this way:

Secret Six Win Safe Return Of Peoria Physician

From the *Sentinel* in Winston-Salem, North Carolina:

Chicago Secret Six Scores Another Victory Over Crime

The *Annison (Alabama) Star:*

Chicago Secret Six Defeats Kidnapers

And the ledes under those headlines were equally laudatory. One widely published article began: "The Chicago secret six, unique organization of business men crime fighters, today scored another victory with the return to his home unharmed and without payment of ransom of Dr. James H. Parker, 65, wealthy physician kidnaped March 14.

"Coincident with the safe return of the physician two well-known Peoria men were taken into custody on orders of Alexander Jamie, secret six director who with several detectives has been working secretly on the case since the disappearance of Dr. Parker."[37]

The dark side to the story was mentioned in some of the articles, however, corroborating Col. Randolph's strong hints that torture had been used against the men. "Both looked rather wearied and haggard after their 72 hours grilling," reported the *Chicago Tribune,* on April 4.[38]

Continued the *Tribune:* "Newspaper men have been barred from interviewing the two men. Members of Chicago's Secret Six, the state highway department, county and city authorities have been questioning the men since early Thursday when they were taken into custody.

"In the meantime Peoria's police authorities were still in search for three others connected with the kidnaping.

Betson informed his lawyer that the officers had beaten him severely in an effort to obtain a confession from him. He accused Alexander Jamie and Sergt. Steffens, Chicago, as his assailants.

Betson sobbed continuously while questioned by authorities."

A more detailed complaint was published by the *Tribune* the next day: "Betson charged that after being taken into custody last Thursday evening, Alexander Jamie of the Chicago 'Secret Six' and other officers of the same organization beat and kicked him severely."[39]

The *Chicago Tribune* glossed over the nuances of the men's apprehension and interrogation, but it's important to our story. As established in the newspaper articles quoted above, the Secret Six took Pursifull and Betson into private custody on Thursday, March 31, 1932, forcing them to spend at least some of that time locked together in a makeshift, thoroughly surveilled attic cell in a private Peoria home. Once the Secret Six had wrung sufficient information from them, quite likely through beatings administered by Alexander Jamie and Roy Steffen, the vigilantes handed the two over on Saturday, April 2, to authorities, who filed formal kidnapping charge against them.

A second round of interrogation likely occurred once they were in official custody. There is no indication the men were further abused, but it's likely they were at least subjected to exhaustive questioning by regular law enforcement. Of course by then, Parker was safe.

The *Chicago Tribune* said Parker was "mysteriously released" the evening of Friday, April 1, without the payment of ransom. "His return was accomplished through the efforts of the 'Secret Six' of Chicago," the *Tribune* reported. "He was blindfolded and pushed from an automobile near Peoria."[40]

After Pursifull and Betson were picked up, newspapers speculated, "the kidnapers became alarmed, fearing too much was known regarding their identity, and 24 hours later Dr. Parker was freed, altho the ransom demand had not been met."[41]

"The men who seized me," Parker said in a weekend interview with the United Press, "treated me well at all times. I was given decent food and my health did not suffer."[42] Parker said he'd been blindfolded "during the entire time he was held captive," the article stated, and "he was unable to obtain a good look at his captors. He said he was held in complete darkness except for an occasional airing. Much of this time, he said, he was kept in a large canopied bed which screened his guards from his vision. He believed he was kept at a farm about 100 miles from here."

By mid-April 1932, and probably thanks to the revelations of Pursifull and/or Betson, authorities had rounded up eleven more suspected kidnap-gang members, nine men and two women.[43]

Charges against one woman were dropped, and in May 1932 the remaining suspects went to trial. At the start of the trial, newspapers reported, "Attorneys George Springer and Edward Hayes, counsel for Pursifull and Betson, entered into the record today a statement of the evidence they will offer to show that their clients were beaten and forced to make confessions."[44]

The third degree administered by the Secret Six had no bearing on the case, however. The jury found eight of the suspects guilty, recommending twenty-five years for James Betson and five for Joseph Pursifull, with twenty-five years for three other kidnappers, lesser terms for the rest. Freed were Jessie Stoops, the wife of convicted kidnapper Raymond Stoops, who got fifteen years. The jury also acquitted the couple's seventeen-year-old son Dean Stoops, and Edward Woodford, hired hand at the Stoop's farm.[45]

Throughout his kidnaping, prosecutors alleged during the trial, Parker had been held at the Stoop farm, at Spring Lake Bottoms in Tazewell County, Illinois, and anyone seen on the property while Parker was there had been charged. Most of the indicted had subsequently been persuaded by authorities to provide written statements regarding the kidnapping, and these were key to the prosecution. Defense counsel alleged that "third degree methods were used to obtain the statements" from every suspected kidnapper, not just Pursifull and Betson, but that argument got nowhere with the jury.[46]

Randolph's praise of the third degree and its documented and successful use on at least one occasion might shed a little light on that odd story from the Illinois state prison at Joliet, discussed earlier in this chapter, in which Joliet prison chaplain George Whitmeyer complained about "investigations constantly being made in the prison" by the Secret Six and other groups. Whitmeyer, whose humanitarian inclinations had been upset by conditions at the prison, had advised the inmates not to speak with the Secret Six. Their presence was one of the things that caused "unrest," he said. In turn, the Secret Six called for Whitmeyer's ouster. What it was in particular Whitmeyer didn't like about the Secret Six visits wasn't mentioned in the press. Maybe Whitmeyer opposed the interrogations on principle. Maybe the Secret Six were interfering with the men's prison roles, or their jobs, or schooling, or sleep. Or maybe the Secret Six brought phone books.

So, whither the third degree? Col. Randolph swore by it, implied its effective use in the Parker kidnapping case (as corroborated by two victims), a case which ended with eight convictions and prison sentences totaling some 150 years. So, it worked at least once. But is it still a regular aspect of police work? Does the spirit of the Secret Six live on in police stations around America, where "any means available"—including the punching and kicking favored by Alexander Jamie—are used on each suspect or witness with the aim of his (or her) "telling of all he knows" and to "test the truth of his testimony"?

It still happens, surely, but the trajectory of policing over the last century has bent away from the approach Randolph touted. In fact, in 1931, a year before Col. Randolph wrote his infamous essay, a major federal report condemned the third degree both on Constitutional grounds and for its self-defeating nature. The Wickersham Commission, headed up by former US Attorney General George Wickersham, concluded that "the practice of the third degree involves the violation of such fundamental rights as those of (1) personal liberty; (2) bail; (3) protection from personal assault and battery; (4) the presumption of innocence until conviction of guilt by due process of law; and (5) the right to employ counsel who shall have access to him at reasonable hours." Noted the commission: "Courts give no approval to any of these practices, and convictions of crime based upon confessions of guilt secured by such methods are very generally set aside."[47]

Since then, when suspects and witnesses have sued over their abuse at the hands of police, including the kinds of violence alleged by Pursifull and Betson, they have often prevailed, their charges voided and their convictions overturned.[48]

In 1966, the constitutional rights of the accused were formalized in Miranda v. Arizona. Thanks to that case, police departments throughout America routinely read at time of arrest what are known as Miranda rights, including the right to remain silent under questioning and to summon an attorney during interrogations.

In 1932, however, with case law far from settled, Randolph's third degree apologia received little pushback. But there were offended moralists here and there, among them one Rev. Jason M. Gillis, a Catholic priest writing for *The Brooklyn Tablet,* a newspaper dedicated to the doings of the Catholic church in the New York area.

"A very good citizen may be a very bad reasoner," Gillis wrote of Randolph and his *New York Herald-Tribune* essay. "I started counting the fallacious or dubious statements in that brief article but stopped after the twenty-first. There were too many."[49]

Declaring that "bad means must not be used to secure a good end," Father Gillis wrote directly to Randolph: "You say you don't believe in an immoral principle and in the next breath you equivalently justify an immoral method, based upon the immoral principle."

Continued Gillis, "You say 'by any method.' That is what's wrong . . . Those who use the 'third degree' are not always sure that they have the real criminal. They may be torturing the wrong man. If they have the right man and know they have the right man, they ought to be able to prove it without the man's confession.

"Ladies, too, have been tortured unjustly," Gillis wrote. "To name but one, there is Joan of Arc. One such example in history is enough. One is too much. . . . No one who regrets the inquisition should defend the third degree. It is unChristian, unlawful and, as Mr. Randolph's paper gives evidence, illogical.

"It is time," Gillis declared, "that man's inhumanity to men should be ended."

We can't interview Col. Randolph, Alexander Jamie, and the other leaders of the Secret Six about why they approached kidnapping the way they did, why they beat suspects, where they got their intel from, and why they kept issuing implausible kidnapping reports. But the Secret Six's war on kidnapping fit within a larger pattern in which the group was striving to build—with remarkable promise—a new, vigilante-driven model of American law enforcement, a model that could be directed across America from Chicago, by the Secret Six.

PART V

LORD OF THE VIGILANTES

"But there is something ominous in the various reports that business men of other cities may be compelled to follow Chicago's example."

—James McCarthy, June 12, 1932

21

A Brief History of Vigilantism

VIGILANTISM, in proportion to the degree to which it is revered, is the least practiced of all human endeavors.

Defined as acting without legal authority to prevent, investigate, or punish perceived offenses and crimes, the first act of vigilantism probably occurred a few days after the creation of the first legal authority. Some ancient human society became advanced enough to establish some form of order, due process, collective decision-making where justice was concerned, and some malcontent immediately saw flaws in the system and took matters into his or her own hands.

Today, vigilantism is the stuff of dreams, of fantasy, of the triumph of pure good over pure evil, thanks to the inspiring courage of a few noble underdogs.

The veneration of the vigilante is a global industry that rakes in billions of dollars a year. Batman, Superman, the Hulk, Spiderman, the Avengers, the Equalizer, the A-Team, Wonder Woman, the X-Men, and hundreds more superheroes in comic books, on TV, and in movies, deliver the dream of vigilantism in its perfect form. Robin Hood, Zorro and the Three Musketeers represent earlier versions of the character type, but the genre hasn't changed much. Then as now, the heroes are imbued with impossible powers, of flying, invincibility, immortality, aim, swordsmanship, or luck. Spiderman spins actual spider webs. The mortals among them, such as the A-Team and the Equalizer, possess military or martial arts skills so perfected and perfectly applied that they qualify as superhuman. The villains they confront are usually perfect villains, practicing evil with abandon, their wrongness beyond question.

Add movies about cops, detectives, government agents, and experts in special operations who are fighting evil with a minimum of governmental oversight (James Bond et al.), and the list of vigilantes roughly doubles. Also part of the community are the amateur detectives and sleuths, probably thousands of them created by authors through the last two centuries, including Sherlock Holmes and Hercule Poirot, working without police support, funding, or oversight to solve crimes. And then there is the high-noon, main-street showdown of the classic Western, where the lone, sod busting pioneer faces down one bad guy, or a gang of them.

Hollywood and comic books will sometimes offer up a more realistic picture of vigilantism. *Kick-Ass* comes to mind, the 2010 movie where an average young man creates a costume and a superhero name (Kick-Ass, of course), and who is stabbed and hit by a car on his first heroic outing, and is subdued and about to be killed by gang members on another mission until he is saved by an (improbable) father-daughter vigilante team with advanced powers.

Also instructive is Martin Scorsese's *Taxi Driver,* in which a mentally disturbed man decides to free a twelve-year-old prostitute, is shot and almost dies in the process of killing three men to liberate the girl, and remains troubled after he recovers. The movie inspired another troubled man, John Hinckley Jr., to attempt to assassinate Ronald Reagan in 1981.

Although the concept of vigilantism appeals to the universal longing for a world that is morally simple, with problems that can be simply solved, the world is not morally simple, and its problems are far too complex to be fixed with one person's mystery-solving logic or well-directed punch.

So vigilantism is rare, but it is not nonexistent. Wikipedia's vigilantism page is probably as good a place as any to find an accounting of vigilantes and vigilante programs, and the list includes dozens of groups and individuals who have fought their definition of lawlessness around the world through the ages, or are still doing so.* Some are paramilitary groups who picked sides in civil wars. Some were formed to beat or kill drug dealers and other criminals. Unofficial groups fought fascists in Great Britain, terrorists in Afghanistan,

---

* Interestingly, the Secret Six was not listed on the page in May 2024.

and insurgents in India. Some vigilantes were simply a rabble which rose up on one occasion to punish or kill a single known criminal or sexual abuser. In America during World War I, The American Protective League, the Boy Spies of America, and other groups were formed to root out and punish those who harbored German sympathies. The Guardian Angels, established in New York City in 1979, claims thousands of members in thirteen countries and more than one hundred cities. Its members patrol the streets and can make citizens' arrests but, importantly, are not armed.[1]

The federal investigation of the January 6, 2021, Capitol insurrection has also benefitted from vigilantes. The Sedition Hunters, as they call themselves, "proved invaluable to the FBI," *The Guardian* reported in October 2023, noting the agency was "reeling from the fallout of the riots and overwhelmed by the subsequent federal investigation, the largest in American history, as an initial estimate of 800 rioters entering the Capitol ballooned to more than 3,000." The article noted that, "While the FBI approached the task with antiquated technology, the Sedition Hunters had all the latest tools."[2]

On the darker side of vigilantism stand organizations like the Ku Klux Klan, which enjoyed modest respect in its early, post–Civil War days, but whose single-minded focus on the (imaginary) crimes of Black people, including the offense of trying to vote, tarred it as a racist and oppressive force. Spontaneous white uprisings against perceived Black crimes, such as the 1921 race riot in Tulsa, Oklahoma, and four thousand lynchings in the Jim Crow South, might also be added to the annals of vigilantism in America.

The estimated eighty-three million Americans who own guns constitute in some respects a mass but informal vigilante force. While the vast majority of gun owners say protection of self and home is their primary reason for owning a firearm, then–NRA chief Wayne LaPierre implied a vigilante purpose for gun ownership in December 2012, declaring that "the only thing that stops a bad guy with a gun, is a good guy with a gun."[3]

Gun owners have been known to make things more official on occasions, forming militias and little neighborhood battalions. Among recent examples, a group of armed citizens who called themselves the Self-Defense Brigade organized in spring 2024 to patrol the streets of Hartford, Connecticut.[4]

There is not, however, nor has there ever been a group like the Secret Six, backed by millions of dollars, formed not by rabble, racists, or militants but by a business association, allowed by local authorities to investigate crimes, make arrests, incarcerate and interrogate suspects, tap wires, and carry guns. Never before or since the three-year reign of the Secret Six has American media referred to any vigilante group repeatedly by name for its role in cracking cases, arresting perpetrators, defeating kingpins, testifying before Congress, or releasing authoritative reports on crime and punishment.

It was a perfect storm of conditions that made the Secret Six America's (or quite possibly the world's) greatest manifestation of vigilantism. The group was born ten years after the advent of Prohibition in 1920, which made the crooked beer barons of Chicago rich and powerful, and a few months after the Great Depression gripped the nation with historic levels of both hopelessness and ruthlessness. There was plenty of crime in America's second largest city, but plenty of money as well, and enough outrage to inspire the flow of those dollars to a private justice crusade.

But the Secret Six, exceptional as they were, found themselves beset by the same gremlins that haunt all such efforts, at least where such efforts include the right to use violence and make arrests. Vigilantism is rare because it seems to be impossible to do it right. We love vigilantism in our hearts, but the endeavor has suffered from inherent flaws in every real-world application where full police powers were assumed. And, as we will see in the coming chapters, most of the things that can go wrong with vigilantism went wrong for the Secret Six—dramatically, very publicly, and sometimes hilariously.

Before they faded from history on a cold day in January 1933, however, the Secret Six came closer than any other group of vigilantes in human history to conquering a nation.

22

A Modest Proposal

IN FEBRUARY 1932, two years after the Secret Six's founding, Col. Robert Randolph went to Pittsburgh to make a bold proclamation in his speech before that city's Chamber of Commerce: "Organization of a 'Secret Six' in Pittsburgh or any other large metropolis where crime is a major problem would sound the death knell of the gangster."[1]

Continued Randolph, "Virtually all large cities face the same problems we are solving in Chicago. . . . Organization of a secret committee of businessmen in Pittsburgh would have a wholesome effect on the crime situation."

It was a recurring theme in Randolph's interviews and speeches at that time. Under the headline "Branches in All Cities," in the *Chicago Evening Post* of September 15, 1931, Randolph claimed that "practically all of the crimes against business are being conducted by nationally organized gangs" while "the jurisdiction of a state ends at its boundaries, and unless there is created a greater co-operation between anti-crime bodies—official or lay—such as the Secret Six in Chicago, and similar ones in other centers, the uprooting of this type of crime will be almost impossible."

While Col. Randolph implied a loose association among these anticrime groups, he seems to have harbored higher ambitions: Chicago's Secret Six—and Randolph, as the head of that group—should be in charge of all the Secret Sixes in all the other cities.

But Randolph may have decided proposing himself as America's king of the vigilantes would generate pushback. So, it seems, he had his friend

Frank Loesch, nationally respected authority on crime, and president of the Chicago Crime Commission, put forth the idea. On February 4, 1932, two days after Randolph called for Secret Sixes in Pittsburgh and other US cities, Loesch proposed that an "interstate organization should be formed of citizens" with a leader who was an "experienced man, publicly known, who would give his whole time to the work."[2]

Who else but Col. Robert Isham Randolph would fit the bill?

Loesch's call, published in no less than *The New York Times,* proposed a level of secrecy for the group that qualified as both autocratic and sinister: "This organization must be as secret as the criminal organization tries to be," Loesch declared. "No one outside the membership need know who are the members." And this chief of the national citizens' group would be its only face, all its employees unidentifiable and unaccountable, Loesch proposed, adding, "All contact with paid employees must be through him alone."

While Loesch suggested that this new secret, national group "would have the suppression of kidnappings and the arrest and prosecution of kidnappers as its single object," it is not hard to imagine broader goals for the organization Loesch envisioned, especially since the Secret Six was announcing other national crime syndicates at this time. Their playbook for crowing about a nonexistent kidnapping corporation had proved effective, so they put it to use again, following the plan almost word for word in announcing a nonexistent national bank robbing company.

Bank Robbing, Inc.

In September 1931, the same month the Secret Six first began announcing their discovery of a nationwide kidnapping gang (see chapter 19), they revealed the existence of a "large country-wide body of super-criminals" committing so far an estimated 25 percent of "daylight robberies about the United States, particularly those . . . involving shootings and large thefts from financial institutions."[3]

There were eerie similarities between the kidnapping and bank robbing enterprises discovered by the Secret Six. Both were run like regular companies and led by an unknown but highly capable chief executive. Both kept about 150 henchmen on the payroll. Both maintained lots of headquarters. And neither could be brought down by anyone other than the Secret Six.

"Vast Gang Syndicate Bared by 'Secret 6'," the *New York Daily News* announced on September 14, 1931. The data about this gang was compiled by the Secret Six, Randolph explained vaguely, "in our work with the banks." The bank robbing company employed, Randolph said, "as many as 148 killers, located all over the United States."

Two months later, in November 1931, the Secret Six had more to say about this national bank robbing firm. This time, the vigilantes had specifics, but the details weakened their case. "The investigators found traces of international alliances among the bank robbers," newspapers announced, "and counted up a toll of around $5,000,000 taken in 25 major robberies since 1925 by these allies—the Burke-Winkler gangs, the Sheltons of southern Illinois, Fitzgerald of Minneapolis, and, more remotely related, the Fleagles of Colorado. Here and there, the investigators discerned traces of interrelations of these gangs, and blamed the famous Denver mint raid on one affiliated band."[4]

Instead of a single corporation, then, we have something more amorphous: "allies" with "traces of interrelations." However, with the passing of two more months, in January 1932, the Secret Six was back with their old claims of a single, well-organized bank robbing firm, and the Secret Six as the only entity able to fight it.

"Alexander Jamie revealed today some of the secret workings of a vast bank-robbing syndicate," the story announced, "and of the master crime-fighting organization which he said is slowly but surely putting its underworld enemy out of business. The syndicate is ruled by a "board of directors" and extend(s) throughout many states. So vast was this organization, he implied, that no force less powerful than the 'secret six' itself could combat it successfully."[5] Coverage of Jamie's announcement included these details:

> According to Jamie the syndicate is controlled "by a master mind, a socially prominent business man with connections for the disposal of all types of securities."
>
> According to members of the secret six, activities of the bank robbing syndicate are wide spread. Headquarters have been established in Chicago, New York, Kansas City, Omaha, Philadelphia, Brooklyn, Los Angeles and East S. Louis, Ill.
>
> The gang has its own fences for disposing of stolen securities and maintains a regular fund at various headquarter cities for bribing police, prosecutors and judges, authorities state.
>
> Jamie said today that the mysterious "master mind" of the organization would be captured by the secret six operatives and he promised further arrests.[6]

As they had with the alleged kidnapping corporation, the Secret Six maintained a steady drumbeat about the national bank robbing business, major announcements coming every two months. March 1932 saw another variation on the Secret Six warning about a bank robbing conglomerate—the headcount was similar, but the region was smaller.

"The 'Secret Six' has compiled the photos and police records of a well-organized group of from 150 to 175 men who prey on banks in the midwest," Alexander Jamie wrote in the third of a five-article series about crime distributed nationwide by the Newspaper Enterprise Association. "They all know each other, work together and exchange information that may be of benefit in bank robberies."[7]

While the March 1932 iteration of the group lacked the national reach of the Secret Six's earlier profiles, Jamie implied that a national presence was only a matter of time: "Organized crime is rapidly becoming more powerful and more nationalized in the United States," he wrote, continuing, "It no longer recognizes state lines. High-powered automobiles, airplanes, radio and other modern inventions are being used by gangsters as they broaden their field from the strictly local areas in which they formerly operated. Gangs in widely separated cities are now working together as the 'crime trust' expands."

In this version of the story, Jamie was also backing away from earlier claims of a single bank robbing CEO. "I have been asked many times if there is a 'master mind' that has supreme direction of all these organized underworld activities," he wrote. "Frankly, I do not know. Such evidence would be very difficult to obtain."

Between late 1931 and early 1932, then, a clear pattern emerges. The Chicago vigilantes were not trying to inform, collect, and disseminate facts, or serve as a national clearinghouse of valuable intelligence on American kidnapping and bank robbery.

The Secret Six were marketing.

The pronouncements landed like clockwork, every two or three months, and the messaging with regards to both kidnapping and bank robbery seems to have been created less to share truth and more for maximal psychological impact: These twin wars on the American way of life were run like efficient, profitable American companies, the Secret Six kept saying, two growing firms doing business around the nation and headed up by top-notch CEOs.

Why was the go-to headcount always about 150 killers or henchmen, operating from coast to coast? That number meant about three henchmen per each of the nation's 48 states. No matter where you lived, one of them might be living next door.

The details of these two enterprises would change from month to month, maybe intentionally, to keep things fresh; what mattered most was the big picture, painted by the Secret Six to be frightening, and to demand a response. And the Secret Six, with its vast budget and freedom from jurisdictional limits or governmental oversight, declared itself the only force qualified to provide that response.

"So far," Col. Randolph declared in a September 1931 report, "we have been successful in matching wits with forgers, robbers, business and labor racketeers, high jackers, payroll bandits, kidnapers, promoters of fake charities, short weight merchants and a score of other criminal specialists."[8] The Secret Six, according to that report, "has cleared the way for federal or state prosecution of 51 criminal groups, including Al Capone's, has investigated 21 other situations, and is now ready to push 34 cases against the 'crime ring' in court."

Was it true? If it was, then the vast majority of those fifty-one prosecutions and thirty-four pending matters never made it into the indexed newspapers, at least not as Secret Six cases. In the researching of this book, virtually every newspaper mention of the Secret Six was looked into, and fifty-one prosecutions and thirty-four more cases about to get filed overstates the available record by a factor of something close to five.

The press was good at crime coverage. The *Chicago Tribune* kept a close watch on police reports and the courts, and they and their rival papers seemed eager to mention any Secret Six angle that popped up. Virtually every case published where the Secret Six helped in any way is noted somewhere in these pages. There were a good number of cases, along with plenty of investigations that went nowhere. They looked into the Lindbergh kidnapping, for example, investigated the murder of a reporter, checked out a boat bombing, all without contributing to the closure of those cases. But a survey of the press of the day indicates the Secret Six worked nothing close to the number of cases Randolph was bragging about.

Could it be that dozens of Secret Six cases made their way through the police blotters and the courts without anyone bringing them up? And keep in mind that these weren't minor cases, for example, a widow afraid of her husband's ghost. These were, Randolph claimed, cases against one of those major national crime corporations the Secret Six was blaming for huge bodies of outrages. If those cases ever led to arrests or went to trial, the Secret Six would have asked for credit, and the newspapers would have given it, gladly. No, the safest conclusion here is that Col. Randolph was, once again, inflating the truth to serve his own ambitions.

Six months after Randolph issued his dubious call for credit, Alexander Jamie was making similar claims (but leaving out specific numbers) while trying to downplay the powers of investigation, incarceration, and interrogation the Secret Six had assumed for itself. "Our organization assists the duly constituted law enforcement agencies," he wrote, "such as the police department, the sheriff's office, the state's attorney's office, the various federal law enforcement bureaus—and helps in any way it can to co-ordinate their work to bring about the detection and punishment of organized criminals."

Added Jamie, subtly hinting at Chicago as a national model of vigilantism, "Through our investigators we have been very successful in getting evidence in a large number of cases that have led to the clearing up of crimes and convictions in the courts. We employ a staff of trained investigators, many of whom were formerly identified with federal and other law enforcing agencies."[9]

Waiting for the FBI

While there was a federal agency in place to fight the kinds of gangs alleged to exist by the Secret Six, its arrival as the powerhouse of national law enforcement was still a few years away, leaving a vacuum that the Chicago vigilantes were uniquely qualified, and quite eager, to fill.

In 1929, the Bureau of Investigation, as it was known at the time, "had 339 special agents and less than 600 total employees," according to the FBI's online history.[10]

At that time, with a total head count of less than 10 percent of the Chicago Police Department, and prior to passage of many of the laws, policies and budgetary outlays essential to its authority, the FBI was still struggling to get noticed, while the Secret Six was solving high-profile cases and proposing itself as America's only solution to a growing national crime problem.

The FBI turned the tide by the mid-1930s, winning the public's enduring admiration (and thoroughly supplanting any talk of a national vigilante group) with the successful pursuit of celebrity gangsters—John Dillinger, Bonnie Parker and Clyde Barrow, "Baby Face" Nelson, Alvin Karpis, the Barker brothers, many more.

"Using whatever federal laws it could hang its hat on, the Bureau turned its full attention to catching these gangsters," according to the Bureau's history, which continued, "By the end of 1934, most of these public enemies had been killed or captured. In just a few transformative years, thanks to the successful battle against gangsters, the once unknown Bureau and its 'G-men' became household names and icons of popular culture. Along the way, Congress had given it newfound powers, too, including the ability to carry guns and make arrests. In July 1935, as the capstone of its newfound identity, the organization was renamed the Federal Bureau of Investigation—the FBI."

As it rose to prominence, the FBI never found those kidnapping or bank robbing corporations, their talented chief executives, or their 150-odd henchmen the Secret Six insisted they'd uncovered. The gangsters the FBI killed or imprisoned were all bit players, self-directed thugs and murderers who occasionally teamed up with a half-dozen of the like-minded to pull a bank job or kidnapping. But in 1932, when the Bureau of Investigation was still an obscure and mostly powerless federal agency, the Secret Six were the closest thing to national law enforcement America had, and their ambitions to make it official were becoming increasingly transparent.

Birthing a National Vigilante Franchise

As part of his justification for proposing a nationwide force of vigilante groups, Col. Randolph pointed to the fact it was already happening in two cities, St. Louis and Kansas City.[11]

Here, Randolph was guilty of a vast understatement. There's a chance he didn't know how popular the Secret Six model had become in the rest of the nation, because he couldn't conduct the search of indexed newspapers made possible by modern technology. But today, a review of the records turns up a startling array of communities and civic leaders nationwide inspired by the Secret Six.

Randolph was well aware of one of the first emulators, however, in Kansas City, Missouri, where the March 1930 kidnapping of Mike Katz, millionaire drug store owner, prompted outrage.* In mid-April 1930, two months after

---

* Katz was freed unharmed after payment of a $100,000 ransom.

the founding of the Secret Six in Chicago, the Kansas City Chamber of Commerce "unanimously adopted a resolution providing for the appointment of a secret committee of five, whose powers and finances will be unlimited, to combat crime conditions."[12]

The *Kansas City Star* described it as being formed "after the fashion of the citizens' body named in Chicago." The group was intended to combat "intolerable" crime conditions in the city and was "empowered to obtain any aid it may need in the way of finances and helpers."

St. Louis, Missouri, hosted similar efforts, as did the village of Raytown, Missouri. "To combat nightly robberies and burglaries," the press reported, "this little Jackson county town organized its citizens as guards and in three weeks of operation, not even a chicken has been stolen. Patterned after Chicago's 'Secret Six' and the old-time vigilantes, the group has 90 men and three officers, but the personnel is not publicly known. Four men patrol the streets and nearby roads each night, working in two shifts."[13]

In Illinois, at least a half dozen cities adopted the Secret Six approach to crime, sometimes seriously, sometimes less so. From the newspapers:

- For the purpose of investigating and suppressing racketeering in Belleville, the executive board of the Belleville Chamber of Commerce has . . . organize(d) a Sanction Committee, known as the "Secret Six." . . . The personnel of the committee will be kept a secret, not even the office of the Chamber of Commerce knowing the identity of its members. Its function will be to consider the merit of advertising, charity and investment proposals in an effort to discourage those which do not seem to be fair or have value.[14]
- Organization of the Lake County Citizens league, a group described as the equivalent of the Secret Six committee in Chicago, was announced [October 2, 1930] by Eugene Armstrong, secretary of the Libertyville-Mundelein chamber of commerce. The league's membership will be kept secret, Mr. Armstrong said. Its object, he said, is to raise $100,000 within the next few months to prevent racketeers from gaining a foothold in Lake county . . .[15]
- The [Elgin, Illinois] post of the American Legion has organized a committee known as the "Secret Six" to specialize in "anti-red" activities.[16]

- Rogers Park, a suburb north of Chicago, "now has its own Secret Six," the *Chicago Tribune* reported in February 1931. The article interviewed one of the men behind the effort, a "Mr. X," who declined to provide the number of members or their names, explaining that if they were identified, "they would come in for a lot of good-natured razzing from their friends and neighbors [which] would gradually get on their nerves, and might break up the drive."[17]

Did the Secret Six play in Peoria, the proverbial barometer for American propriety and taste?

Yes they did. Twice.

First came an October 1930 incarnation. "Chicago has the secret six and Peoria is to have a 'secret one hundred,'" the papers announced. "The Peoria organization, being formed by the safety committee of the Association of Commerce, will have as its objective the curbing of speeding and traffic violations. They will carry cards on which to record the license number of cars violating traffic laws and turn them in to the police for action."[18]

Fourteen months later, Peoria went back to the well. As reported in the local press, "Peoria businessmen have united in a demand on the city administration to 'furnish adequate police protection and stop crime.' . . . Under the banner of the association of commerce, the business men have appointed a 'secret committee' of 'ten' patterned after the famous 'secret six' crime prevention committee of Chicago."[19]

In New York City, whose proud citizens were sometimes known to look down on the slightly smaller metropolis to the west, business-driven vigilantism was one idea they could believe in. The Secret Six model was adopted by at least one commercial group in the city, as well as in other places around the state. Even the group's endorsement of torture found support, from a leading New York criminologist, as well as a high school in Oceanside.

Some of the coverage:

- The New York "Secret Six" is being formed by the Board of Trade. . . . Several of its members have been selected and have signified their acceptance. [Board President W. J. L.] Bonham and his aids have been in communication with Col. Isham Randoph, head of the Chicago organization, and have obtained valuable ideas from him, it was said.[20]

- "Chicago and other cities have their secret sixes," announced the *Buffalo Courier Express* in June 1932. "Now this village has joined the ranks. Angola's secret six is working for an early distribution of funds now in the possession of the New York State banking department." At issue in Angola was the closure of the Bank of Angola, which shut down after losing much of its depositors' money. Angola's secret six, the paper said, "the members of which refuse to reveal their identity, are now negotiating with a Buffalo attorney . . . to hasten payment of the impounded money to the hundreds of hard pressed citizens."[21]
- "Buffalo now has a citizens' vigilance committee similar to Chicago's 'Secret Six,'" the *Buffalo News* announced in February 1932. The group, known informally as the Secret 16, went to work immediately, playing a role in raids on thirteen "vice resorts" and the arrest of thirty women. By the next month, however, vice charges had been dismissed against at least eight women because of insufficient evidence.[22]
- Brooklyn got into the act in September 1932, with the launch of a "new campaign . . . to encourage Brooklyn business men to make a stand against organized racketeers." District Attorney William Geoghan led the charge, noting that "The people of Chicago had much the same problem that we have here. . . . Gangsters grew bolder and bolder and more and more successful. . . . Then the citizens got together, the Secret Six was organized . . . and finally they were driven out."[23]

While some of these New York examples, particularly in Angola with its shuttered bank, compared but faintly with the armed vigilante model set by the Secret Six, other communities were on board with everything, including violence and torture.

In July 1932, when Hyman Stark and three of his career-criminal friends decided to violently rob the mother of a Nassau County police detective, fracturing her skull, the cops rounded up all four thugs and applied a heavy dose of the third degree, which reportedly included their being "beaten with rubber hoses and fists during their examination at police headquarters in Mineola." As three of the suspects were being walked around the station, they caught "fleeting glimpses . . . of Stark lying half naked in the shower room in the basement of headquarters, with the threatening figures of half a dozen policemen standing over him."[24]

Stark died at that station, under conditions that were without dispute the simple beating to death of a man who had gone after the wrong victim. No one claimed he died while trying to escape, or that he had gotten into a fight at the jail. A few weeks later, in late July 1932, thirteen cops were charged in the case, four with second-degree murder, seven more with second-degree assault, two more on lesser charges.

Two weeks after charges were filed, the citizens of Nassau County answered back, more than one thousand of them forming the Nassau County Anti-Crime League, with the goal of raising money and pledges "to defend the 13 Nassau County policemen and police officials indicted in connection with the third degree death of Hyman Stark."[25]

Thomas S. Rice, a respected criminologist and a member of the Crime Commission of New York State, hailed the news in his weekly Sunday column on crime and punishment, proposing that the formation of the League might "prove one of the most significant events in the history of the criminal law in the United States." It was the League's implicit support for police brutality that won Rice's endorsement, and he expressed the hope that the new body would "see that the archaic and artificial protection thrown around the suspect . . . are overcome."[26]

Rice, who had declared in August 1931 that "The answer" for crime in the Empire State was "the formation of a criminal justice association . . . a fighting organization similar to the Secret Six," mentioned Col. Randolph's endorsement of the third degree in his August 1932 column. Citing Randolph's just-published, "brilliant article" in the *New York Herald Tribune Magazine*, in which Randolph endorsed the use of torture during interrogations, Rice summed up his philosophy thusly: "Make the law strong enough and simple enough to inspire both respect and dread."[27]

The Secret Six, a 1931 movie inspired by the Chicago vigilantes, also turned New Yorkers to violence against crime, inspiring a group of high school boys at Oceanside High School to form "The Secret Seven." The group collared two fifteen-year-old suspected thieves, who were "summoned to the secret chambers in the basement" of the school. James Sparling Jr., one of the suspects, "said the youths tied his hands in front of him with rope, hoisted him by the arms (from a steam pipe) until his feet barely touched the floor. They then beat him with a tennis shoe." The Secret Seven were, according to news reports, "assisted in the operation by Walter S. Boardman, school principal, [who] said he saw nothing wrong with the punishment."[28]

Besides triggering major efforts in Missouri, Illinois and New York, the Secret Six inspired lesser action, or at least calls for them, in some half dozen other states:

Nebraska: In the wake of the December 1931 murder of Harry Lapidus, respected political and business leader in Omaha, Police Commissioner Roy Towl began "outlining plans of forming a secret six similar to Chicago's successful crime commission." According to the *Chicago Tribune*, "Towle demanded that the secret six be installed at once, saying that in the last year there have been five unsolved gang murders.[29]

A week after Lapidus was killed, Don L. Kooken, Secret Six assistant director, came to Omaha and "held lengthy conferences with police officials.... Kooken was brought here yesterday to delve into the Lapidus murder mystery and crime conditions.[30]

South Carolina: Under the headline "'Secret Six' to Aid City," a newspaper in the state's capital ran a story in September 1932 about "a group of Columbians, six in number, [who] have quietly joined together as 'The Secret Six' to select qualified members for an organization to be known as 'Men of the Hour.'" A statement issued by the group offered little by way of the group's purpose, other than to assert that "few realize the acuteness of the situation now confronting Columbia and all its better citizens."[31]

New Jersey: In Atlantic City in December 1932, the press reported that "A crime commission of six men, modeled after Chicago's Secret Six,' has been formed here, with Mayor Harry Bacharach as chairman. The commission has drawn up a list of 'public enemies,' known underworld characters, who will be arrested on suspicion."[32]

Ohio: "A war on hoodlums and racketeers," the *Akron Beacon Journal* announced in December 1932, "was being organized in Toledo with a body of vigilantes, modeled after Chicago's 'Secret Six,' expected to take the chief initiative. Formation of the vigilantes' organization was disclosed with information that its membership is growing rapidly by enlistment of reputable citizens willing to use their fists and even weapons if necessary to fight against the outlaw bands."[33]

Statewide in Ohio, similar plans were underway in December 1933, almost a year after the demise of the Secret Six: "H. C. Robinson, criminologist at the London Prison Farm, announced a plan wherein 21 experts would be appointed to work secretly in investigation of criminal conditions in Ohio. The plan was reminiscent of Chicago's 'secret six' who were active in offensives against gangsters in that city. Robinson's secret group would be composed of college officials, prosecutors and men identified with peace enforcement [and] all of their work would be entirely 'under cover.'"[34]

Colorado: The February 1933 kidnapping in Denver of thirty-two-year-old Charles Boettcher Jr., prompted talk of the "formation of a citizens' vigilante committee similar to the Secret Six in Chicago." According to the wire stories, "Suggestions such a committee be formed among the wealthy and prominent citizens of Denver to meet an apparent influx of gangsters and hoodlums were made to members of Boettcher's family today by influential friends, a family spokesman said."[35]

Louisiana: Louisiana Attorney General Percy Saint, in an address before the American Bar Association Convention in Chicago in August 1930, declared that "Every community in the country should organize a 'secret six' committee similar to the one formed by Chicago millionaire business men to combat gangland." In his speech, Saint proposed that vigilantes should do more than supplement the local police—they should replace them: "The Louisiana attorney general declared law enforcement was generally ineffective because citizens themselves showed no interest in suppressing and preventing crime, leaving enforcement to poorly paid officers working unaided."[36]

If history must first repeat itself as tragedy, and then as farce, several items suggest the Secret Six achieved that last historic stage multiple times, well after they'd disbanded. First, from Georgia, in November 1933: "Kidnaping charges have been placed against four men described by Sheriff C. C. Layfield, of Muscogee county, as members of a "secret six" organization formed to investigate murder cases here. Indictments have been returned against the quartet charging each with two counts of kidnaping in the alleged abduction of Alberta Barker and Alzadie Barker, negroes [who claimed] they were taken from their home in Cusseta, nearby, in an automobile by four men and a woman and questioned about the slaying of two persons here in April."[37]

And then, two little stories, the first from Kansas City, Missouri, in February 1933: "The Nancy Drew Detective club, composed of 10 and 11 year old school girls, put a quick stop to a campaign of dog poisoning in the neighborhood of their school. After 11 pets had been poisoned in one week the girls formed a sort of 'Secret Six' organization. 'Our club met every day, discussed all clues and I guess we scared the poisoner away,' said President Beatrice Peet."[38]

And from Alabama in January 1934:

> Formation of a "Secret Six" to curtail "cribbing" [academic cheating] at Howard College was announced recently in The Crimson, student publication. The secret group will work along lines of an organization by the same name which functioned effectively against crime in Chicago a few years ago. Members of the "Secret Six," all students, are known only to the editor of the publication. They will report instances of "cribbing" to the administration of the school. Each week the paper plans to carry a report of the number of "cribbers" and the punishment meted. The place, time and method of the offense will be listed. If the violations do not cease, the management of the paper threatened to print names of offenders.[39]

Coupled with the widespread creation of actual Secret Sixes across the nation was the growing sentiment, shared in crusading newspaper editorials and articles, that such vigilante efforts might make sense in cities everywhere. "The new method of fighting crime had definitely proved that organized crime can be beaten by business," wrote journalist Neil Clark in his summer 1932 study of the group.[40]

A few more examples from the press's editorial pages:

- Minnesota: As Chicago sets itself to drive out its gangsters, other cities must set themselves to repel invasions as well as to expel their home grown racketeers, if any. Chicago has found it necessary to do the dispersing by means of vigilantes, the "Secret Six." Why? Because the law as officered conventionally was not doing anything to protect the citizenry. Must other cities, then, have their Secret Sixes? Or will the law as such function? The presence and activity of the gangsters anywhere is an answer to that question.[41]
- California: For the *San Francisco Examiner* in May 1932, the formation of a Secret Six in that city might have been necessary, but only if the police and courts failed. "Chicago ignored its evil repute for ten years—then, TOO LATE organized the Secret Six," the paper declared in an unsigned editorial. "Chicago waited until the gangs

were ORGANIZED, WELL FINANCED AND POLITICALLY PROTECTED. . . . If 600,000 in San Francisco openly declare for law and order San Francisco will not need a Secret Six to rehabilitate its reputation."[42]

- The *Minneapolis Sunday Tribune* also took a more cautious approach to the formation of Secret Sixes, calling them in June 1932 a regrettable step, but one that might be necessary: "Naturally, the 'Secret Six' deserves all the applause it received. But there is something ominous in the various reports that business men of other cities may be compelled to follow Chicago's example. This may be a commendable sign of an aroused public wrath, but it is by no means a healthy social development. It suggests too clearly that the citizen is losing faith in the regular forces of law enforcement and crime prevention. It smacks of a Vigilantism that has no place in a civilized society."[43]

In summary, while Col. Robert Isham Randolph was calling for Secret Sixes across the country, and hinting through his friend Frank Loesch that he ought to lead them all, the nation seemed to agree. Secret Sixes were sprouting up everywhere, and efforts that didn't follow the Windy City's vigilante model (to address college cheating, for example, or traffic violations, or the assets of a shuttered bank) were appropriating the Secret Six name regardless. A state attorney general, a respected criminologist, and newspaper editorial boards were calling Secret Sixes a viable next step to the problem of crime. The term "secret six" was also being used as a synonym nationwide for effective vigilantism. In a January 1933 interview, Frank L. Campbell, who checked brands for a Texas cattle operation, recalled the history of cattle rustling in the state. "In 1877," Campbell told the *Marshall (Texas) Evening Messenger*, "a group of Texas ranchers formed a sort of 'Secret Six,' called the Texas & Southwestern Cattle Raisers' Association, to run the thieves out of the Southwest."[44] Col. Randolph could not have picked a better time to pursue American vigilantism's top throne.

Finally, one last example of the preeminence of the Secret Six nationally, and another way it might have taken over all of America's vigilante forces except for a humiliating denouement, was reported in Los Angeles in September 1931.

The Case of the Boyfriend Bodyguard

Los Angeles District Attorney Buron Fitts, growing concerned about the arrival of gangsters to his city, did not turn to state authorities for help, did not hire more investigators, did not call in the nascent FBI. Fitts instead reached out to the Secret Six, after which he traveled to Chicago and met with Col. Randolph who, the *Los Angeles Times* reported, "prepared and presented to Fitts . . . a file containing more than 500 photographs, identification marks and other information on all gangsters and their associates that have come under the observation of the Illinois crime committee."[45]

Fitts got more than pictures from Randolph. In September 1931, news broke that the Secret Six had loaned Fitts one of their investigators, whose mission was "gathering evidence on gangster mobs." The evidence, Fitts told local newspapers, "was gathered during a four-month vigil of the secret service operative whose name he refused to reveal."[46]

"This man's life would be in great danger were his identity made public," Fitts said. "However I will admit he was loaned to me by the 'Secret Six' of Chicago under arrangements made when I was last in that city." Fitts said the unknown investigator "has applied Chicago methods to ferreting out gangsters and their hangouts" and the evidence he'd uncovered "is of untold value to us."

What had this secret operative discovered? The summary provided by the *Los Angeles Times* bore a peculiar resemblance to many other Secret Six gang pronouncements—high on fright, menace, and movie-worthy drama, light on facts. "Nineteen known gangsters and racketeers are making their headquarters here and fifteen of them are at present residing in Los Angeles county," the *Times* declared.

Thanks to the work of the "secret agent, who is personally acquainted with the racketeers," the *Times* said, Fitts' office "has complete data on the nineteen, as well as much vital information on their present movements and plans."[47]

On the same day the story about the secret detective broke, some newspapers had already learned his identity: Edgar "Ed" Dudley. If his name sounds familiar, it should. In November 1930, Secret Six investigator Ed Dudley was assigned to find out who'd been sending creepy extortion letters to Marion Wright. In early December 1930, Dudley had settled on William Kuhn Jr., as the culprit, and had arrested him and imprisoned him in a Secret Six jail until he could be formally charged. And in January 1931, after none of the evidence dug up by Dudley and his team satisfactorily established Kuhn's guilt, Kuhn was exonerated. Days later, Kuhn sued several Secret Six officials, as well as Marion Wrights and her father, for $100,000.

Kuhn's defamation case would not go to trial until late 1932, but it seems the Secret Six had had enough of Ed Dudley well before then. He was not so much loaned by the Secret Six, according to some reports, as gotten rid of. "Dudley, it was revealed in Chicago today," the *Los Angeles Evening Post-Record* announced in September 1931, "was 'let out' by the "Secret Six.' . . . Later, Fitts hired him and brought him to Los Angeles."[48]

So the nature of Dudley's Los Angeles assignation was in some dispute. He was either sent by the Secret Six to colonize the western city in furtherance of plans for a national organization, or he was fired by the Secret Six and hired out west through other machinations. Or maybe it was a little of both, Col. Randolph providing a glowing endorsement of Dudley's work in order to get him as far from Chicago as possible.

Randolph, unfortunately, misjudged the distance required between Chicago and Ed Dudley.

In late September, a few days after Dudley's name and shocking gangland findings were published, a second role for the detective was revealed in the press: bodyguard for Mildred "Billie" Rohrback. On May 20, 1931, Rohrback had been working as a photographer's assistant in a Hollywood office building when, a few doors away, two men were shot to death by David Clark, a former deputy district attorney and a candidate for a local judgeship.

The victims, described as a shady politician named Charles Crawford, and a similarly shady journalist named Herbert Spencer, were killed either in self-defense, or as part of a gang war, or in a political spat of some kind.[49]

Miss Rohrback had heard the gunshots, stepped out of the photographer's studio to see what was going on, and saw Clark fleeing the scene, making her an important witness in the case.

Prosecutors couldn't get Clark convicted in the first trial, held that August and ending with a hung jury, so a second trial was held, in late September 1931. Dudley, in addition to his gang investigation work, somehow ended up assigned to protect Miss Rohrback during both proceedings. And Dudley, although still reportedly married to a woman in Chicago, took up residence with the witness, a divorcee often described by the press of the day as young and very attractive.[50]

Within days of being outed as the source of that thrilling gangland report, former Secret Six detective Ed Dudley found himself in the middle of a swirl of embarrassing rumors. "Rohrback Girl Denies Wedding Ex-Investigator," read a September 30, 1931, headline in the *Los Angeles Times*.

In the article, both Rohrback and her mother denied Mildred had recently married Dudley, while "Dudley, from his apartment, refused either to deny or confirm the report." In the same story, Dudley "announced he has resigned his position with the office of the District Attorney."[51]

Dudley declined to discuss his departure from the office (later reports said he'd been fired and that he was vengefully bitter about it), but he was more direct about assertions in the local press that "Hollywood police and deputy sheriffs said many complaints had been made to them of disturbances at [Miss Rohrback's] home."[52]

"I want to correct this report of wild parties," Dudley told the *Los Angeles Times*, "and deny that such took place. I am positive there has been some error in the address where these so-called midnight orgies took place."[53] Despite his protestations, Dudley's shenanigans cost him at least two jobs. Along with leaving the attorney's office, he was also dismissed as Rohrback's bodyguard, and "Miss Jerry Six was assigned to watch the girl, who was taken to a downtown hotel."[54]

The relationship between Rohrback and Dudley proved to be an issue at David Clark's second murder trial, with Clark's defense lawyers harping on it to make the case that Dudley, as an employee of prosecutor Fitts while he was also both guarding and allegedly romancing Rohrback, might have exercised undue influence over her and her testimony. "The personal affairs of Mildred Rohrback, pretty state's witness, during the time she was guarded by a male investigator, overshadowed the charge of murder against David H. Clark at his trial today," the *Long Beach Sun* reported. "Miss Rohrback, twisting her gloves and casting her eyes toward the floor, testified that she had spent two days at a mountain resort with Ed Dudley, her guard."[55]

"The defense has scored a telling blow," reported the *Burbank Daily Evening Review*, "when it drew from Miss Rohrback's unwilling lips the admission that Ed Dudley, investigator for the District Attorney's office, had lived with her, her mother and brother, since the close of Clark's first trial, when he was assigned to guard the girl."[56] Continued the *Review,* "Dudley, she added, had paid the rent and grocery bills out of his own pocket. . . . Miss Rohrback, it developed yesterday, has just secured her final decree of divorce from Ivan L. Angle."

Clark got a hung jury in August 1931, but the jury all agreed on his innocence that October. He was acquitted and the murder charges were dropped.[57] Dudley would come back to Chicago in December 1932 to testify in William Kuhn's disastrous defamation trial, but he wasn't finished appearing in the press in Southern California. Some of the coverage was sad, some of it simply bizarre.

On July 15, 1932, both Dudley and Mildred, now described in the press as "Dudley's pretty wife" (and confirming the earlier rumors) testified about an assault on Dudley in which "[Frank] Clasby hit him over the head with a monkey wrench in his apartment at 4848 La Mirador, supposedly at the behest of political enemies." Clasby's defense attorney, oddly, was none other than David H. Clark, the man acquitted of murder the previous year.[58]

A year later, in August 1933, Dudley announced that he was prepared to reveal, before a Los Angeles grand jury, significant corruption in the offices of District Attorney Buron Fitts. "I'll tell them plenty," he warned, with press reports suggesting his falling out with Fitts dated to his firing by Fitts after his romance with Rohrback was discovered.[59]

A year after that, in September 1934, Dudley swallowed poison in a failed suicide attempt triggered when a new romantic partner left him. After six hours in the hospital, Dudley was arrested and charged with impersonating a federal officer and contributing to the delinquency of a minor.[60] The minor in question, his missing paramour, was identified as sixteen-year-old Ramona (or Barbara, in some reports) Winegar Alexander, whom the fifty-two-year-old Dudley had brought from West Virginia.[61]

Dudley disappeared after he was released on bond, but the missing girl surfaced and "made a lengthy statement to the district attorney's office in which she charged that Dudley had brought her to Los Angeles to aid in 'framing' Fitts, Blayney Matthews, Fitts' chief investigator, and Federal Judge George Cosgrave."[62]

Three years later, in August 1936, this unsurprising item appeared in the *Los Angeles Times:* "Mrs. Mildred Rohrback Dudley . . . obtained a divorce from Edgar Dudley, one-time investigator in the District Attorney's office.

Nurtured and blossomed while Dudley was assigned to guard the former Miss Rohrback, the romance withered and died, so she told the court yesterday, when Dudley deserted her on August 10, 1933.

"'Before he left me,' the young woman testified, 'he told me he didn't want to be married any more. He said he wanted to be free. We had no quarrel, he just left.' The couple married at Tijuana, Mex., on October 2, 1931."[63]

That wedding date, incidentally, put their nuptials smack in the middle of David Clark's second trial. The presumably quickie wedding happened on the same day, in fact, that Mildred was answering questions about her questionable relationship with Dudley.

Dudley botched the William Kuhn investigation to a degree that would prove to be historic. His unprofessional stint in witness protection derailed a double murder trial in Los Angeles. The man not only seduced the woman he was protecting, but he also apparently threw "midnight orgies" with her, and then blamed the neighbors. Finally, while still married to one woman, he lured an underage girl from West Virgina, romanced her, and set her up to bring down his various Los Angeles enemies. And the fact that he was a former Secret Six agent, mentioned often in reports of his escapades, surely dealt a blow to Col. Robert Randolph's fading dreams of franchising his vigilante model across America.

And Edgar Dudley wasn't even the Secret Six's worst hire. But terrible hiring decisions weren't the Secret Six's biggest problem. The whole enterprise was founded on unworkable premises, a house of cards waiting to spin down.

Even their name was a lie.

23

The Secret Six Were Neither

IN OCTOBER 1931, some twenty months after the birth of the Secret Six, founder Col. Robert Isham Randolph said something odd in a speech to the Rochester, New York, Chamber of Commerce: "No one knows who our operatives are and the operators themselves do not know each other."[1]

It was classic Randolph—dramatic, pulp-fiction worthy, and completely untrue.

If any of those secret Secret Six operatives got curious about who else was on the team, they need look no further than the nearest newspaper. In tens of thousands of articles published across the nation between 1930 and early 1933, the exploits of the Secret Six, as well as those carrying out the exploits, were published for all to read. This book itself includes hundreds of newspaper citations in which the Secret Six detectives, arresting officers, and undercover cops were identified.

A partial list, by no means exhaustive, of Secret Six employees listed in the newspapers would include Paul B. Shoop, C. A. Harned, Hal Roberts, Donald Kooken, O. W. "Buck" Kempster, Roy Steffen (often spelled Steffens), Charley A. Touzinsky, Charles Jasinski (Touzinsky and Jasinski may have been the same person, the name getting misspelled by some newspapers), Tommy Crawford, Wallace Jamie (Alexander Jamie's son, sometimes called Alexander Jamie Jr. in the press), Edward Farr, George "Chief" Redston, Walter Walker, Edward G. Wright, Marshall Solberg, William Knowles, Leo Carr, Edgar "Ed" Dudley, James B. Kerr, Louis Nichols, Joseph Altmeier, Michael Ahern, and others.

These names were not revealed by some enterprising reporter, or uncovered with the opening of a secret file cabinet. They were listed as a matter of course in crime coverage, no one making any effort to keep their names out of the press. In fact, the opposite seemed to have been the order of the day. One of countless newspaper stories, noteworthy both because of its "local boy makes good" tone as well as the detailed itinerary, began: "State Highway Officer Hal Roberts of this city and Sergeant Oliver Kempster of Sterling, both of whom are on special duty with the Secret Six organization for Chicago, went to Clinton this morning when word of the robbery was received here. They had returned home early this morning from Chicago and were assigned to assist the Iowa officers in the apprehension of the bank bandits."[2]

Also noteworthy was the coverage of the Secret Six in the *Chicago Commerce,* the weekly publication of the Chicago Association of Commerce. As head of the Association of Commerce, Col. Randolph presumably called the shots on all *Commerce* content. And so it must have been with his blessing that the formation of the secret body was front page news in the publication on February 15, 1930, a week after the organization had voted it into existence. And on page nineteen of its February 22, 1930, edition, the Association lauded the extensive coverage of the vigilantes.

"The crime campaign is receiving big headlines all over the country," the article proudly crowed. "Newspaper clippings by thousands from all over the United States . . . and telegrams and telephone calls have poured into the Association offices."

And so it went, from the first weeks of the Secret Six onward. Alexander Jamie released regular reports about imaginary national kidnapping and bank robbing companies, and he wrote a widely distributed, five-article newspaper series under his own name. Col. Randolph wrote for local and national publications regularly, granted interviews ad nauseam, made speeches all over America boasting of the Secret Six's success, and testified before Congress.

No, the Secret Six were not secret, *because they didn't want to be.*

But what about the Six part of the Secret Six? Who were these six brave men who, as Eliot Ness described them in *The Untouchables,* were "gambling with their lives, unarmed, to accomplish what three thousand police and three hundred prohibition agents had failed miserably to accomplish"?[3]

The answer: No one. They didn't exist. There was no six.

That doesn't mean people haven't spent the last ninety years trying to uncover them. The most popular suspects, appearing in various places,

Among the secrets the Secret Six failed to keep was the location of their headquarters, at 172 West Adams Street in downtown Chicago. The building is now a W Hotel. / Kevin Meredith

including on the Secret Six Wikipedia page (accessed in late 2024), were: Julius Rosenwald, president of Sears, Roebuck and Company, Frank J. Loesch, head of the Chicago Crime Commission (and the one who'd hinted Randolph should lead all of America's vigilante groups), utilities magnate Samuel Insull, accounting firm head Edward E. Gore, Chicago politician George A. Paddock (elected to Congress in the 1940s), and Harrison Barnard, head of the H. B. Barnard construction firm. (It was the shooting of Barnard employee Philip Meagher that led to the formation of the Secret Six.)

None of these men are still alive, and we can't ask them if they were the ones. But if we were able to talk to them, our next question would have to be: And what, exactly, did you do as one of the Secret Six? Did you go to prisons and interrogate inmates? Did you punch and kick kidnapping suspects? Did you

The opulent interior of the building at 172 West Adams, through which the Secret Six passed to get to their headquarters offices and fight with, among others, the purveyors of illegal alcohol. The lobby is now, ironically, a hotel bar. / Kevin Meredith

haunt alleys in the dead of night to catch extortionists, or order drinks at illegal speakeasies to chat up the denizens who might know something? Did you tap telephone lines, put your eyes up to peepholes, listen in on Dictaphones? Did you put on a woman's dress in a mile-square kidnapping stakeout?

No, it's safe to venture that none of these rich and powerful men ever did any of those things, because they didn't need to. The Secret Six had plenty of real cops on the payroll, almost two dozen of them turning up on one occasion, to catch an extortionist* who had demanded cash from four wealthy Chicagoans, including investment broker H. L. Nichols. "Twenty 'Secret Six' detectives had been marshalled for Saturday night," the Associated Press reported in January 1932, "when Nichols was to have paid."[4]

---

* Arrested as the extortionist was seventeen-year-old Donald Imhoff, best friend to Herbert Nichols, son of one of the extortion targets. Nichols confronted Imhoff in jail and asked him why he did it. "Gosh, Herb, I must have been in a daze," Imhoff replied.

Real cops, further, are not known for seeking help on real cop work—surveilling, gathering evidence, arresting suspects, interrogating them, risking life and limb on occasion—from rich businessmen with zero policing experience. The "millionaires' war on crime" was another of Col. Randolph's myths, a romantic invention the newspapers were only too glad to promote, because Secret Six sounded much better than Secret Police.

There was mentioned in the press, at least once, a hint of actual law enforcement work being done by some of members of the secret force, but it was an exception that proved the rule. In September 1930, Randolph was quoted thusly in an interview with the *Chicago Tribune*: "Some of the six, he stated, have been assigned to look after the prosecution of racketeers."[5]

But in the next sentence, Randolph seemed to put even this vague task in more capable hands: "The commerce association has employed an attorney, Marshall Solberg, whom State's Attorney Swanson has appointed as an assistant prosecutor, and Attorney Solberg is accumulating evidence."

It's not that the six men listed as the Secret Six did nothing. Most likely, they were doing the same thing many other members of Chicago's Association of Commerce were doing: giving money. And maybe they gave more than anyone else. Maybe they had better than average connections, meaning they called in the occasional tip on a grafting politician or a businessman who seemed crooked. But the idea that they were, to quote Eliot Ness again, "gambling with their lives, unarmed," is fiction.

The six men most often named as the Secret Six were all well known in Chicago, raising another challenge to the popular myth. In the extremely unlikely event millionaires Samuel Insull or Julius Rosenwald were to show up at a stakeout, interrogate a suspect, or gather evidence from a workplace, they'd be recognized, their cover would be blown and (per Eliot Ness's logic) they'd be marked for death.

Hollywood screenwriter Frances Marion struggled with the question herself in writing a screenplay for *The Secret Six* movie. Inspired by an article about the vigilantes in the August 1930 *Saturday Evening Post,* she fabricated a plot that had virtually nothing to do with the group, or even Chicago. Instead, the fictitious Central was the city where things took place, and the Secret Six were portrayed by six unnamed, well-dressed, middle-aged men.[6]

"This tribunal," declared a prosecutor early in the film, "known only as the Secret Six, represents the greatest force for law and order in the United

States. These men have gathered together to fight and destroy the vicious power of the gangster."

In the second of two brief scenes where they appeared, the six served as the movie's *deus ex machina,* accomplishing through means left completely unexplained what no one else could do, bringing down murderous mobster Louis Scorpio and his gang.

"I'm ready, here are warrants from the Department of Justice for all of them!" announced one of the six.

"What are they charged with?" someone asked.

"Fraudulent income tax returns!" he replied.

"I've got them on arson!" another of the six announced, waving his warrants.

"And here are deportation warrants for half of them!" announced a third.

A fourth member of the movie's Secret Six, identifying himself as a "representative of the Bar Association of America," promised that Scorpio's crooked lawyer, Richard Newton, would be disbarred.

By what conceit did the six conceal their presumably well-known identities? Frances Marion had them all put on the same kind of black masks the Lone Ranger wore in the 1950s television show. The 1931 flick, as campy as anything else of the era, served up a double dose of fiction, making up nonsensical things about six men who were themselves nonexistent.

Julius Rosenwald died in January 1932, and Col. Randolph was asked to deliver a eulogy at his funeral. Here then, with Rosenwald firmly beyond the reach of Chicago's vengeful gangsters, was Randolph's chance to tell all, to detail the brave Sears & Roebuck head's anticrime work: the stakeouts he manned, the warrants he procured, the wires he tapped, the many times he risked his life apprehending Chicago's hoodlums.

Randolph did no such thing, of course, because it never happened. What did Rosenwald do for the Secret Six? He gave money. "I wanted his support for the work of the secret six," Randolph recalled during his eulogy. Rosenwald's response according to Randolph: "I have given a great deal of money for the suppression of crime in the last few years [and] I am going to give you [a considerable sum]† and if I like the way you spend it you may come back for more."[7]

---

† The amount wasn't mentioned in the article.

A lot of people gave the Secret Six money. Well over six people, surely. There was no six.

But let's give Alexander Jamie himself, lead detective of the Secret Six, the final say. "The name Secret Six is really a misnomer," he wrote in early 1932 in one of his syndicated articles. Continued Jamie, "When the committee of business men was formed to combat crime, Colonel Randolph was asked how many members the committee would contain. Careful, then as now, not to reveal secrets of the organization, Colonel Randolph replied: "That is hard to say; maybe 150 members, maybe only six members." For the lack of a better name, the newspaper reporters termed our organization 'The Secret Six.'"[8]

So why did Col. Randolph, in the first days of the Secret Six, keep claiming there was a specific six, and he had named them? For example, in the April 1930 interview Randolph granted to journalist Roy Greenaway, two months after the formation of the vigilante group, Greenaway asked, "Who chose the Secret Six committee of the association commerce?"

Instead of explaining, as Jamie did two years later, that it was all a big misunderstanding, Randolph replied tersely, "I did the choosing."[9] Which was, we may now say with ninety years of hindsight, just another example of Col. Randolph being Col. Randolph.

While Randolph built a stable of swooning journalists, so enamored of the concept of the brave and secretive millionaire half dozen they could never bring themselves to ask the obvious questions, not everyone was so impressed.

In April 1930, the same month Greenaway wrote his fawning piece on Randolph and the Secret Six, a little item popped up on the *Chicago Tribune's* editorial page. "Of course, we don't know who the Secret Six is," some unnamed wag on the paper's staff had written. "It's a secret; but we are on tiptoe for developments. The very name, 'Secret Six,' thrills us to the marrow of our bones."[10]

The *Chicago Tribune* stands out for its balanced coverage of the vigilantes, reporting both the good and the bad, rarely succumbing to the sensational or the servile. One gets the impression the newspaper was just biding its time, waiting for the Secret Six's inevitable self-destruction.

PART VI

THE SECRET SIX AND THE CASES OF INFAMY

"When digging in the mud you use mud-digging tools."

—Col. Robert Isham Randolph, September 1, 1932

Swanson brought a gale of laughter from the crowd when he said that anyone who listened to a children's detective story over the radio and sent in three coupons from an oatmeal box would get a "Secret Six" star.

—Chicago Tribune, November 3, 1932

Introduction

What follows in the next chapters are the occasionally terrible, occasionally hilarious things that happen when private citizens decide to take the law into their own hands, amass millions of dollars, arm themselves, assume the powers of investigation, arrest, and incarceration with the collusion of the constituted authorities, and manage to convince the press, the people, and even Hollywood that they are the answer to American lawlessness.

The core problem with vigilantism is its inherent instability. The same things that make it strong make it weak. The vigilantes aren't elected, appointed, hired, or vetted; they choose themselves. They don't answer to any other authority. They don't have to follow the rules of due process. Jurisdiction is irrelevant. They can get confessions by whatever means necessary. There is no need for the inconveniences of judges and juries. They don't have to explain, justify, or apologize.

Inevitably, the people the Secret Six was supposed to protect and work with became its victims. Without oversight, they made terrible decisions in various matters, including hiring. Dreams of ruling a nationwide franchise of Secret Sixes clouded their judgment so severely that even their hometown ended up laughing at them.

If there is a patron saint of vigilantes, he has a wicked sense of humor. He let the Secret Six become heroes before he stood back and let them stagger to their humiliating demise, an ignominious end that arrived—on a cold day in mid-January 1933—with a whimper.

The true, unvarnished history of the Secret Six serves as Exhibit A in the case against vigilantism, the inherent problems of the practice writ large—larger than ever before or since, most likely.

The myth of the vigilante is strong enough to hide the inherent flaws, but those flaws do surface, eventually. For the Secret Six, a full accounting of all the ways things went wrong for the Windy City anticrime businessmen took more than ninety years.

The chapters to come include two remarkable attacks on the wrong targets, a shocking betrayal, and a case about a bomb that the Secret Six botched, after which they tried to redeem themselves with, of all things, another bomb.

But first, a Secret Six deal with the devil, a bargain so bad the Governor of Nebraska called it "one of the blackest pages in the state's history." In that case, the Secret Six's clumsy attempt at redemption was not a bomb, but more standard fare for the vigilantes: a lie.

24

The Case of the Deal with the Devil

The Gus Winkler Bargain

AT TEN O'CLOCK in the morning on September 17, 1930, a large Buick pulled up to the curb next to the front doors of the Lincoln National Bank, at the corner of O and Twelfth streets in Lincoln, Nebraska.

"Five men got out, not hurriedly, but leisurely," the *Kansas City Star* reported. "The sixth, the driver, stayed in his place at the wheel of the car. Its engine did not stop, but purred idly while he lighted a cigarette as he waited."[1]

Thus began one of the most remarkable crimes in American history. Continued the *Star*, "None of the six men was masked. One of the five who got out of the car carried in the crook of his left arm a queer looking weapon, the like of which had never been seen before in Lincoln. In that quiet, law-abiding capital city of Nebraska there had never been a bank robbery, or a daylight robbery of any kind. The machine gun he carried was probably the first ever brought into Lincoln."

The man with the machine gun lowered the weapon, lining it up inconspicuously with his left leg, according to the *Star*, and took up a position on the corner where he could keep an eye on all traffic, pedestrian or vehicular, approaching the bank. The other five men went inside, and "each drew a large automatic pistol."

The leader advanced into the lobby, shouting "Down! Down, everybody! Face down on the floor. This is a holdup. Down on your faces and you won't be harmed."

The leader then "moved about," the *Star* reported, "jabbing the muzzle of his pistol into the ribs of men and women who were slow and commanding: 'Face down on the floor or I'll kill you.'"

The first violence of the robbery occurred when cashier Phil Hall, "who had been a colonel in the World War, leapt to his feet and . . . drew back his fist. . . . The bandit swung his heavy pistol, brought it down on Hall's head. . . . Thereafter Hall was as docile as a kitten."

Bank employee Edith Hult was next to suffer violence, struck between the shoulders with a gun when she looked up from the floor.

Outside, two students at the state university in Lincoln spotted the man with the machine gun. "This looks like Chicago," one of then quipped. "The bandit grinned back at them," and they continued on their way, thinking the armed man a bank guard. Lincoln police office Elmer Beals noticed the robbery from across the street and decided the same thing, that the man was guarding a transfer of cash.

Others passing through what the *Star* called "the busiest corner in the city" also concluded it must be official business. If they paused to chat, the man with the machine gun would tell them to "Move on please," and so they would.

But when those who had business with the bank entered the building, they were quickly added to the collection of those lying prone on the bank floor. And when a young boy paused to peer into the bank, "saw the men with pistols inside and gave a startled exclamation," the man with the machine gun told him, "You're wanted inside."

"No, I'm not," the boy pleaded.

"Oh, yes, you are, get in there!" the man replied, and he used his machine gun to shove the lad into the building.

The same fate befell W. W. Hill, who paused to look into the bank window and was told to get inside. When Hill demurred, the robber told him, "Get in there or I'll blow a hole through you!"

A total of from ten to twenty people entered or were forced into the bank during the robbery, the *Star* reported. Among them was W. E. Barkley, president of the Lincoln Joint Stock Land Bank, who was knocked unconscious by a pistol to the head when he didn't lie down quickly enough.

Eventually, the people still outside the building started to realize the bank was being robbed, but calls to the police station didn't make that clear.

Eventually, two patrolmen pulled up to the bank to investigate, but when they were threatened by the man with the machinegun, they concluded that trying to apprehend him would be suicide and they headed back to the station.

Meanwhile, bank employee Florence Zeiser was forced at gunpoint to open the smaller of the bank's vaults, where the thieves found "a king's ransom in Liberty bonds and other securities, more than 2 ½ million dollars' worth," an amount approaching fifty million in 2024 dollars. The robbers grabbed the papers "in double handfuls" and "tossed them onto a blanket."

The money at each teller's station was swept into a canvas sack by other robbers, the total cash stolen $24,726, or close to half a million in 2024 dollars.[2]

With the job completed at 10:07 a.m., the robbers picked their way over the thirty or so bank customers lying on the floor, exited the bank, and scrambled to the Buick. "They had been in the bank only five minutes," the *Star* reported. There were no fatalities, no bullets fired, just a few head wounds.

The criminals had planned the robbery to an exacting degree, even equipping their getaway car with a siren like the one used by the Lincoln Police Department. "Everyone in Lincoln knew the sound of that police siren and what its wailing cry meant," the *Star* reported: "Stop all traffic and clear the way for us."

Among those clearing the way was a former city policeman, directing traffic around road construction. The man heard the siren and "waved other cars out of the street, making a clear passage for the bandits, and as they shot past him he waved a hand at them."

Ten miles east of Lincoln, a curious farmer watched as the Buick pulled up behind "a huge covered moving van," according to the *Star*. After the car had been driven into the van, the six men climbed inside, and a seventh took the wheel of the van and drove off. "The use of a van in which to escape was another innovation in daylight robbery," the *Star* reported. "They say no other bandits ever used one."

The impact of the heist, described by the *Star* as "the biggest of all bank robberies, the most daring, spectacular and unusual, and in some ways, the most amusing," was quick.

A week after the heist, and as a direct result of it and the impact it had on local perceptions of Lincoln National, the bank was shut down and sold to the Continental National Bank, which guaranteed all its cash deposits.[3] Lincoln wasn't the only one threatened with dissolution. "The bandits," the United Press reported, "took not only the Lincoln bank's funds but the securities of six smaller banks who had deposited them in Lincoln for safe keeping. The Lincoln National failed immediately after the robbery, and one of the smaller banks closed its doors shortly."[4]

Nine days after the robbery, Lincoln Mayor Don Love demanded and received the resignation of Peter Johnstone, who had been chief of police there for eleven years. On the same day, the Lincoln City Council wrested control of the police department from member William Foster and put the mayor in charge.[5]

Less than five months after the robbery, by early February 1931, the Lincoln police force had bought "machine guns, . . . riot guns, long range tear gas cannon and devices for laying down heavy smoke screens," as well as an armored car.

"Lincoln Police Armed to Teeth," announced one newspaper headline.[6]

The investigation of the crime would be aggressive as well. "Within a week after the robbery," the *Star* reported, "detectives representing insurance companies and associations of bankers swarmed into Lincoln (and) twenty-five detectives were there at one time."

There were no leads. "A strange feature of this robbery," the *Star* recalled, is that, although the bandits wore no masks and were seen by many persons, the descriptions of them are worthless because they all disagree."

Continued the *Star*, "For example, the bandit with the machine gun, who stood on guard, was described by one person as wearing dark clothes. Another said he wore a 'reddish' suit. A third declared he had on a dark blue suit. One said he had a complexion 'like a dope fiend' and another said he had a 'red face.'"

Several alert Lincolnites noted the Buick's Iowa license plate number, 97–13557. It was traced back to a car stolen from Sioux City two days before the heist.[7]

Officials kept digging. They wanted to collar not only the perpetrators of the crime, but to restore the bonds as well. While cash deposits were covered when Continental acquired Lincoln, the bonds represented a wealth that was not so easily made up. Without the actual documents, worth more than a million dollars, holders of those stolen bonds could not redeem them, and neither could the bonds be reissued. Bond holders, who included elderly folk and widows, according to newspaper coverage at the time, had nothing to show for their investments.

Despite the lack of evidence, the historic haul and brazen nature of the crime ensured that the police would keep at it. And so too would the Secret Six, drawn inexorably by the high-profile nature of the crime and its relative proximity to Chicago.

Bagging the Bank Robbers

In early May 1931, four mysterious law enforcement agents were a month into a stakeout at an apartment in East St. Louis, Illinois, on suspicion the men who frequented that dwelling had been involved in various crimes, including the Valentine's Day Massacre, the December 17, 1930, robbery of the First State Bank of Plano, in Plano, Illinois, and possibly other crimes, including the Lincoln National Bank robbery.

The four, working with official law enforcement agencies in Illinois and Nebraska, had gotten wind of the presence of the criminals about a month earlier, and had been watching the apartment off and on since then, the *Lincoln (Nebraska) Star* reported.[8]

On the night of May 8, 1931, the mysterious agents had spotted six suspects entering the apartment. However, "the officers held off making the arrest waiting for other men who were badly wanted," the *Lincoln Star* claimed, but when the two last criminals didn't show, the agents decided to settle for the six they had. "The gangsters were taken by surprise when officers pounced on them with drawn guns and held them until officers of the county sheriff arrived a few moments later."

Much of the information about the arrests came from one of those mysterious cops, a man identified by the *Lincoln Star* as "Sergeant Roy Steffen of the Cook county state's attorney's staff."[9]

This was an odd way to describe the man, who could only be the Secret Six's Roy Steffen. Sometimes called Leroy Steffen, or Steffens, or Steffan, Steffen was identified routinely in the newspapers of the day as a Secret Six detective, or sometimes as a sergeant, and at least once as a "star investigator" for the vigilante group, a man whose name popped up regularly in relation to Secret Six cases (including many detailed in this book), and whose involvement with Lincoln's stolen bonds would soon hit the press.

Who joined Steffen in making the bust? The *Lincoln Star* named Charles Touzinsky, Oliver W. Kempster, and Hal Roberts. So this was a Secret Six raid, start to finish. Like Steffen, these three were regularly named in the press as Secret Six operatives. But here too, the Secret Six connections were hidden. Touzinsky was listed, like Steffen, as an employee of the state's attorney's office, and Kempster and Roberts were described as employees of the Illinois state police.

Some papers mentioned the Secret Six, but only obliquely. Stories distributed by the United Press said the "raiders were directed by Sgts. Roy Steffen and Charles Jasinski [they must have meant Touzinsky] of the Chicago state's attorney's office, working in cooperation with the crime-fighting committee of Chicago millionaires known as the 'Secret Six.'"[10]

The *Lincoln Star* added that "East St. Louis police knew nothing of the raid or plans for it." Not the first or last time the Secret Six would keep local law enforcement out of the loop in a crime investigation.

In speaking to the press, Steffen was evasive on other matters as well, particularly about two of the men they'd arrested, who were suspected of involvement in the Lincoln National Bank robbery. "He merely stated that two men had been identified but refused to name the pair," the *Lincoln Star* reported, adding that Steffen said "he was acting under orders" but "did not say whose orders."

The press quickly uncovered the suspects' names from other sources: two career criminals named Thomas "Pat" O'Connor and Howard "Pops" Lee. Both were immediately charged in the Lincoln National Bank robbery.

O'Connor was the first to go to trial, in late September 1931, and mentions of the Secret Six were muted then as well.

Both Steffen and Hal Roberts took the stand, the first identified by the *Lincoln (Nebraska) State Journal* as a Chicago police officer, the second a member of the Illinois state police.[11] They'd both been asked to testify about a .38-caliber revolver they'd claimed to have found on O'Connor when they arrested him. The gun was incriminating beyond its mere existence, per the testimony of Steffen and Roberts. Most of the identification numbers on it had been ground off, and a cross had been cut into the tips of the bullets found in the gun, an alteration meant to ensure the rounds would shatter and do maximum damage when they struck a body. O'Connor, predictably, "swore on the witness stand that he did not have a revolver on him when arrested."

In the midst of his testimony, Steffen was asked "who paid him for his investigations in the Lincoln bank robbery case and other cases he was investigating."

"The Chamber of commerce of Chicago," Steffen replied.

The answer was odd. Either the reporter for the *Journal* misheard Steffen's answer, or Steffen misspoke. There was no Chamber of Commerce of Chicago in 1931. Search the pages of the 1931 *Chicago Tribune* and you'll find frequent references to the South Chicago Chamber of Commerce, and the East Side, South End and Waukegan-North Chicago Chambers of Commerce. What Steffen should have said was that his work was funded by the famous Secret Six, an organization founded by the Chicago Association of Commerce. But according to the *Journal*'s coverage of the trial, Steffen committed the error twice. "The chamber of commerce is paying me while I am in Lincoln and in a response to a telegram from your own governor asking that I co-operate with the authorities here," Steffen testified.

Only when he was provoked did he drop a vague reference to his real sponsors.

"Is Al Capone a member of that chamber?" defense attorney Don Gallagher asked Steffen.

"No, sir, but Charles Dawes (former US vice president and winner of the Nobel Peace Prize) and Rufus Dawes (Charles's brother and a prominent Chicago businessman), Isham Randolph and Alexander Jamie, head of the secret six committee in Chicago are."

Desperate to discredit Steffen and his associates to save his client, Gallagher next conducted the following, increasingly peculiar exchange with Steffen:

> Gallagher: Always a police officer in city of Chicago, Mr. Steffen?
> Steffen: For the past fourteen years.
> Gallagher: Any special work?
> Steffen: General police work.
> Gallagher: You work for the city of Chicago?
> Steffen: Yes.
> Gallagher: Do you know Al Capone?
> Steffen: I know what he is reputed to do.
> *The witness testified that he had seen Capone but had never conversed with him.*
> Gallagher: Do you know a fellow by the name of Sergeant Kempster?

Steffen: Yes, sir.
Gallagher: What does he do?
Steffen: He's a sergeant in the state police.
Gallagher: He was with you when the defendant was arrested?
Steffen: Yes.
Gallagher: You know it to be a fact that Kempster was indicted with Ted Newberry for running alcohol.
Steffen: I don't know that he was indicted with Newberry. I do understand he was indicted for conspiracy.
Gallagher: Aren't you one of the four horsemen?
Steffen: We were called that but it's not a self-styled name.

A few months before O'Connor's Lincoln National Bank robbery trial, the *Chicago Tribune* identified Kempster as a "highway policeman of Sterling, Ill." and listed him among twenty-three people indicted by a federal grand jury in Peoria May 7, 1931, "in connection with a huge alcohol distillery near Carbon Cliff in Rock Island County, Illinois." The alleged ringleader of the operation was Teddy Newberry, identified by the *Tribune* as a "Capone gangster and public enemy in charge of booze and beer on Chicago's north side."[12]

The date of Kempster's indictment is interesting. The day after it was issued, he joined three other Secret Six agents in those East St. Louis arrests. There's a chance the indictments remained sealed for a time, and he didn't know yet he'd been indicted as he stormed that gangster hideout; the *Tribune* didn't report on the indictments until mid-July.

Was a Secret Six man in cahoots with the gang of Secret Six archenemy Al Capone? Maybe not. In December, a jury acquitted Newberry, Kempster and nine others, and convicted fourteen.[13] Toward the end of Steffen's testimony in the O'Connor trial, defense attorney Gallagher attempted to land one more blow against the agent's credibility.

"You're a Chicago police officer," Gallagher said, "What were you doing in East St. Louis?"

Steffen's answer spoke of the kind of sweeping, multi-state investigation only the Secret Six could conduct. But once again, he forgot to mention the vigilantes: "Well, for your information Mr. Gallagher," Steffen replied, "we had a list of men we were searching for in connection with kidnaping, bank robberies and the Valentine massacre and we had warrants for them and we were going to East St. Louis. The state men got in touch with us and asked us to co-operate with them in the arrest of some of these men in connection with the Lincoln robbery so we went together."[14]

In the end, the jury was not swayed by the scandals or unanswered questions pertaining to the arresting agents. They convicted O'Connor in the Lincoln National Bank robbery, and he got a prison sentence of twenty-five years.

Neither Steffen nor anyone else from the Secret Six testified at the next trial, in late October 1931, of Howard "Pops" Lee, most likely because no one was claiming Lee had a gun on him when he was arrested. Instead, the prosecution found almost a dozen witnesses eager to confirm that it was Lee they saw at the bank, and the jury convicted him as well.[15] Like O'Connor, Lee was given twenty-five years in prison, and like O'Connor, he professed his innocence and promised to appeal.[16]

Jack Britt, a third man arrested in that May 1931 raid by the Secret Six, was tried twice for the Lincoln National Bank robbery, prosecutors failing to get a conviction either time, and charges were dropped.[17]

With three trials complete, two loose ends remained—the whereabouts and identities of the rest of the seven members of the bank holdup gang, and the whereabouts of those missing bonds.

A Fortuitous Car Wreck

Around noon on August 5, 1931, Michigan State Trooper Myron Gillette was patrolling in New Buffalo when he spotted two men in a new coupe, one of them loading a revolver. "He gave chase but was outdistanced," the *South Bend Tribune* reported.[18]

The men were heading north on US 12. They had driven some ten miles and were three miles south of Bridgman, Michigan, when driver John R. "Babe" Moran got careless. Maybe he was still trying to outdistance Gillette.[19] "They were traveling at a fast rate of speed when they attempted to swing around a large sedan going north," reported the *Herald-Press* newspaper of St. Joseph, Michigan. "A motor truck was approaching from the south. Moran cut in front of the sedan too short, and clipped the front bumper of the sedan. This threw the small coupe into the ditch. Witnesses reported that it turned over several times. Both men were severely injured."

The men were taken to a doctor in Bridgman, and from there to Mercy Hospital in Benton Harbor, Michigan. Moran, thirty, suffered a concussion and fractures of the shoulder and jaw. The other man, bearing a pilot's license that identified him as Jerry Kral, thirty-two, of Chicago, had a broken shoulder and "suffered a fractured skull and his face and arms were badly cut. There was a deep gash over his right eye, which severed a nerve and caused him to lose the sight of that eye."

Gillette, still in pursuit, was one of the first officers to arrive at the accident scene and, recognizing the suspicious car, joined other cops in searching the men's belongings, where they found "several quarts of whiskey and two large automatic revolvers."

Gillette called the state police headquarters and Lt. Lyle Hutson was assigned to investigate. Hutson showed up at Mercy Hospital early the next morning, August 6, to take a look at the men. "Hutson found Kral with a badly shattered head," the *Niles Daily Star* reported, "much like the shell of an egg that had been dropped, but still conscious and able to talk. Hutson studied his features. A vague picture formed in Hutson's mind. He had seen a picture of the man somewhere."[20] Jerry Kral, Hutson concluded, was someone else: Renowned gangster Gus Winkler. Hutson had the man's fingerprints taken and confronted him, and Winkler "admitted his correct identity, but denied he was connected with the score or more of bank robberies charged against him," reported the *Herald-Press*. "After Winkler's identity was established, the guard at the hospital was reinforced by another squad of state troopers."

Winkler had been a member of the infamous gang run by Fred "Killer" Burke, until Burke was tracked down in March 1931 and given a life sentence later that year for the killing of police officer Charles Skelly. Burke, generally believed to have been one of the gunmen involved in the St. Valentine's Day Massacre, was never convicted of that crime, but many other murders and bank robberies were blamed on him and his associates, including Winkler.

Among the crimes where Winkler was a suspect at the time of his arrest:[21]

- A $7,000 gem robbery in Detroit March 11, 1924
- The 1925 robbery of a mail truck in Toledo, Ohio, in which a police officer was killed; the crime netted $200,000
- The April 11, 1930, robbery of Citizens National Bank and Trust in Piqua, Ohio, during which a bystander was killed by indiscriminate machine gun fire[22]

- The robbery of the First State Bank of Plano, in Plano, Illinois, December 17, 1930
- The August 3, 1931, kidnapping at Beaver Dam, Wisconsin, of New York diamond salesman Julius Dreyfus, in which $200,000 of stones were taken
- Also on August 3, the robbery of $6,000 from the Bank of Dwight, Illinois, by a lone gunman driving a coupe similar to the one Winkler wrecked in[23]
- The St. Valentine's Day Massacre, in which Winkler was alleged to have been one of the killers, wearing a police uniform[24]
- The Lincoln National Bank robbery

"Every approach to Mercy hospital—and the injured bandits' hotel room—is guarded," local paper the *Herald-Press* reported a few days after the gangsters' wreck. "Out on the lawn a state trooper or two stroll about, shotguns in hand, long .45's dangling at their belts. On the front steps of the hospital more armed guards loaf away the hours. Upstairs in the long corridor that leads past the operating room and the doors of peaceful patients, strapping six footers with belted pistols dangling at their hips pace endlessly and quietly up and down—never but a few feet from the door where Winkler and Moran toss and moan on their cots."[25]

Law enforcement officials from around the Midwest swarmed the hospital in Benton Harbor to interview Winkler. Max Towle, district attorney in Lincoln, Nebraska, brought four witnesses along to see if they could connect Winkler with their historic bank robbery. "I believe we have a tight case against Winkler there," Towle told the *South Bend Tribune* three days after Winkler's capture.

Winkler wasn't in a confessing mood while he was in Michigan, however. Newspaper coverage described him as completely coherent despite his injuries, but he was silent, sulky, and evasive when questioned by the cops, as well as the reporters who were allowed into his hospital room. "I haven't pulled a job with Fred Burke for more than 12 years," Winkler lamented to one journalist. "Every time they gave Burke a write-up in the newspapers, I came in for my share of it. I tell you, you've got me pegged wrong on a lot of these jobs."[26]

Eyewitness visits to Winkler's bedside were mostly inconclusive, as the man was "so gravely injured," the *Herald-Press* reported, "holdup victims have been unable to make positive identification."[27] Nevertheless, law enforcement officials in three states—Wisconsin, Illinois, and Nebraska—wanted Winkler brought to their state first to be put on trial.[28]

In the end, Max Towle's witnesses, and the staggering loss his jurisdiction had suffered, helped him win the tug of war over who was going to get Winkler first. Nebraska extradition papers were drawn up, Winkler fought them and lost, doctors declared him well enough to travel, and on September 16, 1931—six weeks after he'd wrecked in Michigan—Winkler was brought to Lincoln to face trial for the Lincoln National Bank robbery.[29]

Winkler arrived by train, under heavy guard. Two of the men escorting him, according to the *Evening State Journal* of Lincoln, were "Sgt. Roy Steffens of Chicago" and "Hal Roberts of the Illinois state police force."

The Secret Six.

The Secret Six and the Lincoln Bonds

The Secret Six's Roy Steffen had been present from the start, summoned by the news of Winkler's accident and capture and appearing at Winkler's hospital bed by the morning of August 8—three days after the wreck. In one version of the story, the sheriff there, F. J. Cutler, learned of Winkler's identity, "rushed to the hospital and handcuffed Winkler to the bed. Then he got in touch with Alexander Jamie, the Secret Six investigator in Chicago."[30]

True to form, Steffen wasn't admitting his role with the vigilantes, telling the *South Bend Tribune* he was at the Michigan hospital as an "operative of the Illinois Bankers' Protective association." The *Herald-Press* called him "Sergeant Roy Steffen, of the Chicago police department" and said he was in charge of the "showup," an important event where victims of various crimes would have a look at Winkler.[31]

As would be revealed later, Steffen was there primarily in service to the Secret Six's long-running but ultimately futile quest to get a murder charge pinned on Al Capone. Maybe Winkler would admit his role, or know who'd done the killing, Steffen presumably thought, and somehow the trail would lead back to Capone.

Steffen and Winkler talked for hours, according to later newspaper reports, but Steffen didn't get the murder confession he wanted. Instead, he apparently badgered the gangster into offering him a consolation prize: The stolen Lincoln National Bank bonds. But the price for the bonds was dear indeed: Steffen had to get the bank robbery charges against Winkler dropped, and see that the gangster went free of all his other criminal entanglements.

According to press reports, Winkler had one more card to play in the negotiations, but it was a desperate one. He promised Steffen he "would die by his own hand first" before going to trial for the Lincoln heist.[32] It was a deal with the devil, but a bargain the Secret Six simply couldn't walk away from. If the bonds were returned, five or six flagging banks would be saved, thousands of bond holders would be restored to their savings, and the Secret Six would be heroes, once again, and a little closer to their dream of leading a national vigilante franchise.

Word of the bond deal began leaking within a week of the gangster's car wreck, but without any mention of the Secret Six. According to the Associated Press, someone with the sheriff's department in Benton Harbor had overheard Lincoln District Attorney Max Towle talking about the bank robbery and the missing bonds with Winkler. "Sheriff's officials here said they understood Winkler had denied participation in the robbery," the AP reported, adding however that "They said Winkler admitted to Towle that he 'knew where the bonds went'."[33]

Towle declined to confirm the details of his conversation with Winkler to the AP, but "indicated he would return to St. Joseph tomorrow after conferring with officials of the Bankers' Protective association in Chicago."

Recall that Secret Six detective Roy Steffen had claimed he was in Benton Harbor as an operative for the Bankers' Protective Association. Now Towle was saying he had to talk to them as part of deciding what to do about Winkler and those stolen bonds.

So who was the Bankers' Protective Association? Almost nothing appears about them in the indexed press of Illinois, and there's just one reference to them in the *Chicago Tribune* between 1930 and 1932, in relation to a bank robbery in Mazon, Illinois, in October 1930. They may have been a legitimate group, albeit small and mostly unmentioned in the press. So why would Towle need to confer with them, an obscure Chicago banking group, about a suspect in a Nebraska bank robbery, and the bonds stolen there? Because the Bankers' Protective Association wasn't who they said they were. It seems that briefly, in 1931 at least, the Secret Six had assumed the body's name for their own purposes.

Talk of the missing bank bonds faded for a few months after those first mentions in August 1931. Winkler was taken to Nebraska as soon as he was well enough to travel, in mid-September, and his lawyers asked that he be bonded out. Winkler's bond was set at an unprecedented $100,000, so he sent a telegram asking for help from Phil d'Andrea, described by the Associated Press as "the gun-bearing body servant of 'Scarface Al' (Capone)." Another several weeks passed, but by mid-October 1931, "d'Andrea had arranged $100,000 cash bond for the release of 'Gus.'"[34] This was no small sum, close to $2 million in 2024 dollars, described in local newspapers as the "largest ever received in the state of Nebraska."[35]

So why did Capone want Winkler out so badly? Stories at the time suggested Capone had chosen Winkler to run things while the kingpin served his federal tax evasion sentence. Winkler was an accomplished pilot, reportedly, and had been "in charge of Al Capone's aerial rum fleet."[36]

Winkler's freedom was short-lived, however. Released from prison October 15, 1931, newspapers reported, "Sheriff Claude Hensel immediately rearrested him on an order from Plano, Ill., where the St. Louis man is wanted in connection with a bank robbery last December, and back to the prison went Winkler."[37]

But four days later, on October 19, Winkler was truly a free man when Illinois officials decided to give up, at least temporarily, their claim to Winkler. They were swayed by the argument that sending Winkler to Illinois would delay his Nebraska prosecution, perhaps forever. Winkler walked out of the courthouse a little after one o'clock that day.[38]

The charges in the Plano bank robbery were dropped as well, after Thomas Slattery, described as Winkler's "double," was implicated in the crime.[39]

Meanwhile, the trials of O'Connor, Lee, and Britt in the Lincoln National Bank robbery continued, and while Winkler waited for his day in court for the crime, the first two were convicted and sentenced, the third went free. None of them, Winkler insisted, should have been charged. "The three men arrested for the robbery are innocent," Winkler had allegedly told Towle in August, a few days after his auto wreck. "I didn't figure in the job, but I know who did and I know where the bonds were taken."[40] But when Towle asked Winkler who the real robbers were, Winkler demurred. "You wouldn't believe me if I did tell you."

Winkler claimed numerous times between August and October 1931 that he could recover the Lincoln bank bonds, and the statements were duly reported by the newspapers, but some skepticism attended his words. Maybe Winkler was lying for his own reasons, or maybe his head injury had him imagining things.

But on November 8 of that year, the Secret Six finally, publicly attached themselves to the Winkler case and the missing bond angle, and the story grew legs. Hundreds of newspapers across America ran reports of the bargain, described by the United Press as "gangland's reported offer to swap $600,000 worth of stolen bonds for the freedom of August (Gus) Winkler."[41]

"Dispatches from Chicago," the *Omaha Bee-News* reported, "said negotiations for recovery of the bonds and securities have been carried on through the offices of the 'Secret Six,' who have been chiefly responsible for directing a relentless fight against Al Capone and his firmly entrenched underworld organization. . . . The names of the six men, with vast sums of money at their command, never have been made public."[42]

The final decision rested in the hands of Lincoln prosecutor Max Towle, and he was under considerable pressure to accept the deal. Among those pushing for its acceptance, the United Press related, were "the attorney general of Illinois, the Nebraska attorney general," and "a representative of Chicago's Secret Six."

This was a dilemma for Towle of the first order, which left him "deeply concerned," the *Omaha Bee-News* reported:

> (T)he county attorney knows the evidence against Winkler is not as strong as against the others and there is more than a bare possibility he might not be able to get a conviction. In that event . . . Towle would be placed in the uncomfortable position of having lost the $600,000 for its rightful owners without having accomplished anything. On the other hand . . . if he consents to dismiss the charges and the bonds are returned, he would take the risk of bitter criticism by the public on the theory he prosecuted the "small fry" but let the "big shot" with the money go free.

Towle's decision on how to proceed led to one of the most remarkable episodes in American gangster history: The Secret Six, sworn enemy of Capone and his gang, labored mightily with the prosecutor from Lincoln to clear the name of a Capone henchman.

Winkler insisted he was at a hotel in Buffalo, New York, when the Lincoln National Bank was robbed, so Towle and Roy Steffen themselves headed over to upstate New York in mid-November. There, they found what they were looking for:

> Alexander G. Jamie, chief of the "Secret Six" crime prevention committee, said last night that Gus Winkler's claim that he was in Buffalo, N. Y., the day of the $2,500,000 robbery of a Lincoln, Neb., bank, was substantiated by evidence gathered by Sergt. Roy Steffens, an agent of the organization, and Max Towle, county attorney from Lincoln. Handwriting experts, Jamie said, were already at work comparing Winkler's writing with that found on a Buffalo hotel register. . . . Steffens and Towle, he added, gathered other evidence, including statements from witnesses, which indicated that Winkler was in the eastern city the day in question.[43]

Catherine Keeler, a Chicago handwriting expert associated with Northwestern University, was one of those who looked at Winkler's registration at the Statler Hotel in Buffalo. Although Winkler had registered under the name Hugh H. Parker, Keeler confirmed that Parker and Winkler were the same man.[44]

The discovery, however, was not the victory Towle might have been hoping for. After his trip to Buffalo, interest in the case "has been revived to a white heat," in Lincoln, the *Omaha World-Herald* reported, and "the majority of opinion favors the prosecution of Winkler and forcing him to prove his alibi before a jury, regardless of whether the loot is recovered."[45]

The debate over the ethics of the situation, the *World-Herald* reported, "is almost the single topic of discussion in the homes, at women's bridge parties, around the luncheon table, in business offices and on the streets." Daily, both Towle and Nebraska Governor Charles Bryan were receiving "scores of letters" from "citizens throughout the state," as well as the rest of the country, "particularly from eastern states."

Towle, the *World-Herald* reported, "was visibly worried and irritable" upon his return from Buffalo, caught between "demands that he go ahead with the prosecution of Winkler, while Roy Steffens, Chicago Secret Six operative, and Emory Smith, attorney for the looted bank, and influential business men and politicians of Lincoln, hammer away on the other for dismissal of the charges."

Towle was also being squeezed between two of Nebraska's top elected officials. Attorney General C. A. Sorensen favored the deal with Winkler. Governor Bryan did not. "If the alibi is sustained, the charges should be dropped," Sorensen said. "The return of the bonds should not be sneered at. . . . Six banks had placed their entire capital stock in the Lincoln National Bank. . . . One has failed and others may fail if the securities are not returned."[46] Sorensen noted that "Some of these bonds represent the life savings of widows and old people."

Governor Bryan, on the other hand, remained certain that Winkler was guilty of the Lincoln National Bank and strongly opposed the deal, arguing that "the state has been humiliated by the overtures to permit the headman of the robbery gang to escape punishment by returning part of the loot."

At one point that November, Alexander Jamie lost his patience with the governor. "Chicago's 'Secret Six' today stepped out as intermediary between Gus Winkler, gangster aviator, and the state of Nebraska," the *Omaha World-Herald* reported, "after charging Nebraska officials with having made a 'political football' of the negotiations."[47]

"You may state that we have definitely washed our hands of the entire affair," Jamie told the *World-Herald,* which described Jamie as "considerably irked" by "Governor Bryan's denunciation of the offer as 'humiliating.'"

Alexander's pique was temporary, more theater than anything else, and the negotiations concluded on December 12, 1931, when Towle dropped the charges against Winkler. "I am dismissing the case against Gus Winkler because there is not only insufficient evidence to convict," Towle wrote in a lengthy statement published that day in the *Lincoln Journal Star,* "but I am satisfied in my own mind beyond any question of a doubt that he is innocent of the Lincoln National Bank & Trust company robbery."[48]

Towle offered extensive evidence of Winkler's innocence in the statement, including not just the Buffalo hotel records but the testimony of a Buffalo area dentist who had treated Winkler around the time of the robbery, the uncertain testimony of other witnesses, and some information he described as too sensitive to share. Winkler's exoneration, Towle insisted, was based only on the man's innocence and had nothing to do with his claim that "he had a good idea of where the securities could be located and he was willing to help us secure the return thereof."

Towle praised "the help coming from the Secret Six of Chicago and especially their investigator Roy Steffens." Towle also thanked "Alexander James and Ishan Randolph" for their help with the case. "It should be remembered that it was thru their efforts that the original solving of this robbery came about," Towle added, no doubt referring to the Secret Six's arrest of O'Connor and Lee, both quickly convicted of the crime.

Had a deal with the devil been proposed? Had anyone suggested Towle free Winkler in exchange for the bonds, regardless of Winkler's guilt? Yes, Towle said plainly, and clearly implicating the Secret Six: "I was called to Chicago to attend a conference and there was prevailed upon by some ten or twelve persons to enter into an agreement with Mr. Winkler that his case would be dismissed if he could go out and secure a return of the securities. Strong arguments were advanced why this should be done irrespective of Mr. Winkler's guilt."

Towle anticipated the unpopularity of his decision. "I realize that a great many people want Mr. Winkler prosecuted irrespective of his guilt or innocence, strange as it may seem," he wrote, countering that "if I was to prosecute and bring to trial a man whom I knew to be innocent I would be deserving of the severest kind of condemnation."

Despite his protestations, Towle's decision not to prosecute earned him that condemnation, and it was sweeping:

- "Did you ever before hear of a prosecuting attorney going half way across the country to get evidence to establish the innocence of an accused man, and that after several witnesses had identified him as one of the Lincoln bank robbers?" one aggrieved citizen asked on the front page of the *Lincoln Herald*.[49]
- "Winkler says he knows where the $600,000 stolen bonds are but doesn't have to tell," noted the *Superior Weekly Journal* of Nebraska. . . . The 'Secret Six'—who are they? It is all too plain that it was an 'inside' bank robbery—that the bonds were used to secure a gigantic business deal."[50]
- "Winkler has a guilty knowledge of that robbery, even though he may not have actively participated therein," argued the *Hastings (Nebraska) Democrat,* adding that the bond deal "proves his connection, near or remote, with the robbery. The insistence of some men that the Winkler offer be accepted is proof that there are men willing to condone crime for a consideration." Concluded the *Democrat,* after hinting that Nebraska Governor Bryan might consider summarily removing Towle from office for being "derelict in his duty": "There is a mighty putrid odor about the whole deal."[51]

- A men's Sunday school class at First Christian Church took a vote on the Winkler deal, reported the *Lincoln Evening Journal.*[52] "Members of the class voted almost 3 to 1," the paper reported, "that County Attorney Towle is to be criticized for dropping the case against Winkler."
- Even Towle's alma mater, the University of Nebraska, got their licks in. As quarterback there for the 1912–1913 season, Towle carried the Cornhuskers to an undefeated season. Dr. Louise Pound, chair of the school's English department, started her comments with that memory: "Our county attorney (Max Towle) is an ex-University of Nebraska football player, and has had his character expensively developed by football." Pound summoned irony in her next passage: "No doubt we should place extra confidence in his judgment," she wrote, before concluding darkly, "our county attorney protects the innocence of gangsters."[53]
- The Secret Six was also drubbed regularly by the press over the deal, the vigilantes earning among other criticism a cartoon in the *Federation News,* a publication of the Chicago Federation of Labor. Under a drawing of six masked musicians, one of them with his hat out requesting "Funds Please," the *News* wrote: "The spectacle made by the 'Secret Six' in bending all its efforts to save a Capone gangster from going to prison in Nebraska has been enlightening to those who believe this creature of the Chicago Association of Commerce is merely another business men's racket."[54]

But in the end, it was Max Towle's decision that exonerated Winkler, and we must imagine that the weeks following his December 12 release of the career criminal, with the bonds still missing and nothing to show for his widely maligned act of justice, were the longest of his life.

The wait lasted twenty-four days. On January 5, 1932, Winkler delivered. Some one thousand newspapers across America covered the story: "Gus Winkler Keeps Pledge to Return Bonds," announced the front-page headline in that day's *St. Louis Post-Dispatch.*

"In the offices of the 'secret six,'" the story read, "Sergeant Roy Steffens, assigned to the case since the first inkling that a cache of the loot existed somewhere near Chicago, handed the negotiable securities to W. E. Barkley, liquidating officer of the (Lincoln National) bank."

The *Chicago Tribune* set the value of the recovered bonds at $583,000 in a front-page story. Proof had also been provided that $2,217,000 in bonds had been destroyed, meaning they could be reissued, and reducing the total losses in the September 1930 robbery to about $15,000, "which is more than covered by insurance of $60,000."[55]

"Winkler kept his word," Roy Steffen told the *Tribune.*

The recovery proved essential to the thousands of individual bond holders "who lost securities that represented most of their savings," said E. H. Luikart, who'd been an officer of the Lincoln National Bank on the day it was robbed. "One woman had her whole fortune of $6,000 stolen. Now it will be brought back and she will be made happy."[56]

The recovery of the bonds would also help six "small Nebraska banks, several of which have been endangered thru their losses in the robbery," newspapers reported. A total of up to $90,000 would be returned to the six banks.[57]

And yet, the criticism of the deal persisted, most notably from the governor of Nebraska, whose denunciation was reported by the Associated Press and carried by at least a dozen papers in the state and dozens more nationwide:

> Declaring the Winkler case is "one of the blackest pages in the state's history," Governor Bryan today said the return of the Lincoln National Bank Bonds "has shocked the sensibilities of the people of Nebraska. . . . There is no other way to separate the return of these bonds by bank robbers from the dismissal of charges against the chief gangster who was returned here as the head of the gang that looted the bank with machine guns and strong-arm methods. If county attorneys throughout the state have the authority to cancel all charges and dismiss bank robbers at will in return for private negotiations to return loot after their capture, such legal officers have entirely too much authority. I sincerely hope the procedure in other criminal investigations . . . will not bring added humiliation to our state."[58]

So this was a partial win for the Secret Six. They'd recovered the bonds. They'd put two bank robbers in prison. But their eagerness to deal with a Capone mobster left them with a tattered reputation.

The solution?

Lie. Lie big, with a big elaborate story. And get Steffen to quit saying things like "Winkler kept his word."

As reported by the United Press the day after the bonds were recovered, "Both [Alexander] Jamie and [Max] Towle denied the recovery was facilitated by Gus Winkler, Capone gangster and friend of Fred Burke, notorious bank robber.[59] "Winkler had nothing to do with the return of the bonds," Jamie insisted to the United Press.

After months of newspaper reports from Steffen and the Secret Six that Steffen was negotiating a trade of the bonds for Winkler's freedom, Jamie simply denied everything. The deal never happened, he said. Instead, Steffen seems to have been coached into a new version of the tale—an outrageous fabrication. Instead of the calm handing over of stolen bonds as the second half of a deal with the devil, there were guns, and a whole family fearing for its collective life.

The 2:00 a.m. Phone Call

"The story of the recovery of the securities," the United Press reported January 6, 1932, "more reminiscent of a Sherlock Holmes yarn than routine police work, was told by Investigator Roy Steffens."[60]

The United Press story, which described Steffen as "part of Chicago's mysterious 'Secret Six,' super crime-fighting organization of business men," reported without pushback his new account of the bond recovery.

Steffen told the wire service that he and other detectives "had traveled 80,000 miles through 40 states on the trail of the bank raiders," continuing, "We were close behind them. A West Side Chicago apartment was located as their hideaway and we were about to raid the place."

Somehow, Steffen said, the criminals knew of the impending raid. And they did something odd. Instead of moving to another apartment, which gangsters typically did with impressive regularity in those days, they drove over to Steffen's house. And then they called him.

"Yesterday at 2 A. M. I was awakened by a phone call," Steffen told the United Press. "A voice said 'Call off that raid or you'll be killed. We're bringing the stuff over to the corner by your house right now.'"

Steffen swung into action, he recalled: "I was afraid they meant to kill me and my wife and children," he said. "I called Detective Charles Touzinsky and Hal Roberts and asked them to come over. Then my wife and I barricaded a room and hid the children there. She watched at a window while I got out my sub-machine gun."

"When the officers arrived," the United Press story recounted, "they went to the corner and found a suitcase standing under a lamppost. In it were the securities."

Several versions of Steffen's story made the rounds in early January 1932, all ending with the finding of the suitcase, but with important details differing.

In the *Chicago World Herald* version carried by a few newspapers, Steffen said they'd been surveilling "two places where we suspected the bonds were hidden. Night before last, we had about made up our minds that the time was opportune for a raid."[61] In this version of the tale, the caller didn't threaten Steffen's life, just told him that if he would "go immediately to the corner of Armitage and Newcastle avenues, you will find what you have been looking for."

Steffen said in that version he went with Touzinsky and Roberts to retrieve the suitcase, protected by "a good supply of machine guns trained on the corner by officers hidden about." He described the corner of Armitage and Newcastle avenues as "500 feet from my home, in what you might call a wild and wooly suburb of Chicago."

The suitcase holding the documents was cheap, newspapers reported, but weighing in at one hundred pounds under the burden of its contents.

While the United Press story noted the persistent rumors that the bonds had reappeared entirely thanks to Winkler, it included more denial from Alexander Jamie and ended with this unsourced speculation: "Apparently the criminals felt they had no chance to escape with the loot and gave it up rather than allow it to be taken in the raid."

Asserted Steffen to the United Press, "We were so close on the bandits' trail, they hadn't had a chance to clip a coupon from the bonds. It was the largest amount of loot ever returned voluntarily by thieves."

The reporter for the *Chicago World Herald* may have been struggling with the new account of things, writing that Steffen was "asked politely": "What part did Gus Winkler play in the return of these bonds?"

Replied Steffen cautiously, and perhaps mindful of the Secret Six officials attending his answer, "I can only say this. I had a hell of a lot of help from the underworld." But then Steffen added, "gingerly," as the *Herald* put it, "There has absolutely been no compromise with crime in the return of these bonds. And don't let [Max Towle] take any bum raps about it. He absolutely made no compromise with Winkler or anybody else."

In November 1931, Steffen and the Secret Six had been crowing about the deal with Winkler and how it would go down, boasting repeatedly of their imminent success in interviews with various newspapers and wire services. A few examples:

- "Winkler, at liberty here on $100,000 bonds, has assured Police Sergt. Roy Steffens that he will turn over the bonds within a few hours after charges are dropped."[62]
- "Sergeant Roy Steffens, assigned to the office of Chicago's 'secret six', [stated] that he 'sold' Winkler on the idea of obtaining the stolen bonds and securities for the Lincoln bank while the latter lay apparently near death."[63]
- "Sergeant Roy Steffens of the secret six spent hours with [Winkler] in the hospital . . . Steffen convinced him if he could get the bonds back he might . . . save 18,000 to 20,000 Nebraska bank depositors and redeem himself in the eyes of the state. County Attorney Towle, Steffens said, approved his bargaining with Winkler."[64]

But never mind. Instead of the deal Roy Steffen and the Secret Six had been promising to close on for months, the deal Steffen went to that hotel in Buffalo for, the deal that set Gus Winkler free, the Secret Six was two months later suddenly asking the public to swallow a completely different story, devoid of bargains with devils and instead featuring an apartment full of cornered criminals, staring fearfully down at one hundred pounds of stolen bank bonds they couldn't for the life of them figure out how to get rid of. Maybe there were no fireplaces or garbage cans near their apartment?

Steffen's story makes little in the way of sense, for that and other reasons. What criminals, upon realizing they're being watched, are too dumb to run away with the goods but instead decide to take the goods to the cops? Further, after that alleged 2:00 a.m. call, it took Steffen about an hour to assemble his forces for the visit to the lamppost in a "wild and wooly" section of Chicago. What if someone else had happened along and picked up the suitcase? Did the crooks drop it off and leave, or did they stay and wait, increasing the chances of being spotted and arrested or shot at?

And then, what about that impending raid? The Secret Six had obviously found the right place, since (according to Steffen, at least) the crooks told Steffen not to raid it. So after the bonds were dropped off at the corner, the

Secret Six wouldn't find the bonds in that apartment anymore, but maybe they'd find more of those Lincoln National Bank robbers they kept saying they really wanted. So was there a raid? If the bad guys considered their secret hideout so important they'd kill a cop for raiding it, shouldn't that have made the Secret Six want to raid it even more? The next day? But no, there was no Secret Six raid, at least not one discoverable in the indexed newspapers of Chicago, or anywhere else, in the next few days or weeks. And it would have been big news, of course.

The Secret Six did not appear to be remotely embarrassed about their new lies, neither did they blush when they used the incident to return to the older tale about a (also likely fictitious) national bank robbing firm. "Alexander Jamie, chief investigator for the secret six, retold today the story published last November," the Associated Press reported. "He told of an organized bank robbery gang of some 150 men operating in many states, lending 'brains' for one job or another, always under the domination of some master criminal."[65]

"This shows the scope of the gang," Jamie said of the return of the bonds.

While there were no more arrests in the Lincoln National Bank robbery by anyone, ever, or any more publicized raids by the Secret Six of major bank robber gangs, it wasn't for want of at least thinking about it, according to the AP. "Steffens promised that the 'secret six' would continue rounding up members of the robber gang. He also said Eddie La Rue, wanted by officers for the robbery, narrowly escaped capture last week in Chicago, but the secret six expects his arrest soon."

The Secret Six would never find Edward Doll, a man of nearly a dozen aliases, including Eddie La Rue, Edward or Eddie Foley, and the Burlington Kid. Instead, it was the FBI who caught the career criminal at his chicken farm near St. Petersburg, Florida, in February 1934. The FBI went after Doll not for a bank robbery, but because they suspected his involvement in the January 1934 kidnapping in St. Paul, Minnesota, of Edward Bremer.[66]

Doll knew nothing of Bremer's abduction but, in a desperate (and successful) bid to keep his wife and brother out of jail, he spent days confessing to many other crimes, including car thefts, kidnappings, bank robberies, and the Lincoln National Bank heist.[67]

Who teamed up with Doll to rob Lincoln National? Doll, who would go on to serve decades in prison for car theft and a 1933 bank robbery in Massachusetts, named six other men as accomplices: Big Homer Wilson, Edward

Bentz, Gus Stone, and three criminals he would identify only by their nicknames: Big Slim, Old Charlie and One Shorty, a.k.a. Shorty.

What about Thomas "Pat" O'Connor and Howard "Pops" Lee, arrested by the Secret Six, quickly convicted of the Lincoln robbery, and sentenced to twenty-five years?

They weren't there, Doll insisted. Doll, according to a lengthy FBI report about his interrogation, "stated that no one, with the exception of those he has named, participated in any way in the robbery and that those serving time and those suspected outside of the above named were innocent."

Doll's confession included considerable financial details about the return of the bonds to Max Towle and the Secret Six (Towle and an unnamed investigator for the Secret Six each got $10,000 for their trouble, Doll alleged), but Doll was never charged with the crime, and his confession never made it back to Lincoln court officials, apparently, or to the press of the day.

O'Connor and Lee continued to insist on their innocence, and in one bid for freedom, filed within days of the return of the bonds, the men submitted a motion in which they "asserted that agents of the Chicago 'secret six' know the identity of the bank robbers and know that O'Connor and Lee are innocent."[68] Regardless, they both went on to serve ten years in prison.[69]

In conclusion, some questions:

Did the Secret Six, led by detective Roy Steffen, propose freedom for a man everyone believed had robbed Lincoln National Bank, in exchange for a small fortune in bonds? Most likely, if months of newspaper coverage is to be believed.

Did the Secret Six, embarrassed about the terrible optics of negotiating with a man like Gus Winkler, ultimately disavow the bargain with a nonsensical dime store novel fabrication? Probably.

Did the Secret Six arrest the wrong men? Good chance of it.

But at least O'Connor and Lee were known hoodlums who had probably gotten away with other things. In their last year, the Secret Six would go after scores of apparently innocent people, including Chicago police officers and—like Frankenstein's monster—the man who'd created them.

25

The Case of the Crooked Cops

"A POLICE CAPTAIN is the most powerful man in his district," declared municipal court Judge John J. Lyle in August 1930. "He has the men, the guns and the legal power behind him to bring in or run out the hoodlums of his territory. There is, therefore, little excuse for crime waves in any district. It simply means that somebody is not on the job."[1]

Continued the article, published in Chicago's *Southtown Economist,* "His statement follows on the heels of a similar threat voiced by Col. Isham Randolph, president of the Chicago Association of Commerce, in his activities with the Secret Six."

It was an ongoing theme in Chicago crime news, and a concern harped upon frequently by the Secret Six. Chicago's rampant crime problem must be at least partly the result of corrupt cops. The math alone made perfect sense: At the time of the Secret Six's founding, Chicago employees hadn't been paid for months. Meanwhile, the lords of liquor and vice were raking in millions, with honest cops the only thing standing between them and their lucre. And even most honest cops had a price.

By November 1930, the Secret Six effort against dirty cops had picked up considerable steam, with action directed through official channels. "The 'secret six' of the Association of Commerce is actively sponsoring the grand jury investigation now underway," the International News Service reported in a nationally distributed story. "Evidence has been collected by this group which, it was said, is sufficient to cause the indictment of at least twelve police captains and innumerable subordinates, sergeants and patrolmen."[2]

There were no arrests immediately, but two months later, in January 1931, Col. Randolph and the Secret Six were in court again to prosecute police corruption. The event, a grand jury investigation into law enforcement collusion with criminals, was launched by John McGoorty, chief justice of the criminal court covering all of Cook County. It was, in not so many words, a put-up-or-shut-up moment for those alleging police corruption, particularly Chicago's famous vigilantes.

"A general call will be sent out for the heads of the various organizations which have from time to time attacked the police department," the *Chicago Tribune* reported, "and they will be asked to produce the evidence on which they based public statements. Among those to be summoned, it is reported, will be Col. Robert Isham Randolph."[3]

Randolph gave it his best shot. The Secret Six hired C. A. Harned to investigate speakeasies, what might be called Chicago's lowest hanging fruit for those interested in crime in the city. And Harned hit paydirt, testifying before McGoorty's grand jury that "he found 260 speakeasies in Chicago's loop, and believed there were 200–300 speakeasies there he could not find."[4]

Simple as the illegal drinking establishments were to uncover, proof they were there thanks to official corruption was harder to deliver. So Harned turned to inference. "Harned said he had found no actual evidence of collusion between police and those operating liquor places, gambling houses or vice resorts," the Associated Press reported, "but that the general aspect of the situation appeared to indicate that there were 'powers' behind the scenes. He demanded to know how, otherwise, the huge number of speakeasies could flourish without secrecy in the heart of the city and in the very neighborhood of the city hall."[5]

A valid question, perhaps, but in the end, Randolph could not put up, so he was forced to shut up. "Col. Robert Isham Randolph," the *Chicago Tribune* reported the next month, "president of the Chicago Association of Commerce and founder of the 'Secret Six' committee, told the jury that the committee, with its investigators, had no evidence of police corruption."[6]

So Chicago turned its hopeful eyes to Shirley Kub, and Ms. Kub did not disappoint, at least in terms of good press, delivering one of the oddest performances in the history of police corruption probes.

Shirley Kub, Police Corruption Crusader

"Tells Jury of Police Bribes," announced the all-caps front-page headline at the top of the January 20, 1931, *Chicago Tribune*. Shirley Kub, the *Tribune* reported, had parlayed her deep connections to the underworld into a highly sensitive job rooting out corruption in the Chicago Police Department. Among her projects was uncovering the bribing system that kept police attention away from brothels and gambling houses.

"Mrs. Kub," the *Tribune* reported, "as a secret investigator for Acting [Police] Commissioner [John] Alcock, unearthed considerable [evidence] on the subject of protected vice and tolerated gambling, the jurors were told.... For months, Mrs. Kub worked with two sergeants who had been removed from the Warren avenue district, supposedly to the traffic section, but in reality to investigate police captains, she told the jury."

In her campaign to entrap the city's compromised cops, a state's attorney's official alleged, "Mrs. Kub had 'engineered' many bribes while working as an undercover agent and . . . had knowledge which was 'most important' to the investigation."[7]

Before she'd accepted the $300* per month job working for Alcock, the *Chicago Tribune* said, she'd done work for John "Jack" Zuta, a top-ranking Chicago criminal who was killed in a gang hit in August 1930.

Kub was no longer working for the police at the time of her testimony, having been terminated under questionable circumstances. But she spoke confidentially to the grand jury that day, the Associated Press reported in a nationally distributed story, offering "testimony which was so important that it would be kept secret until it could be followed up."[8]

While Col. Randolph and his vigilante force didn't have the connections necessary to get at the roots of Chicago's police–racketeer partnership, the Secret Six was still playing at least a financial role in the vital work of the special grand jury. In mid-January 1931, county officials were dithering on a $50,000 appropriation request from the jury, so Randolph stepped up,

---

* Worth more than $5,000 in 2024.

promising to produce the full amount, worth close to $2 million in 2024. "It is the duty of the county board to raise the money," Randolph told the Chicago Tribune. "But if the board does not do its duty the investigation will not lack funds."[9]

Kub would get to continue her testimony, Randolph promised, despite the obstacles. And there were many. Not surprisingly, Kub had earned her share of enemies in her work for the city, among them Bernice Shaw, the jilted former girlfriend of Chicago Police Sergeant Jack Herdegen.

As told by the *Chicago Tribune,* Shaw informed the grand jury that, 1). Herdegen was taking bribes from the city's vice lords, 2). Zuta had paid the $1,500 in bribes required to get Herdegen promoted to sergeant, and 3). Kub was protecting Herdegen and other crooked cops while persecuting officials she didn't like. In fact, Shaw alleged, Kub had threatened to kill her if she spilled the beans on Herdegen.[10]

"Miss Shaw charged that Mrs. Kub was not averse to 'framing' a policeman, public official or private citizen whenever it would serve her individual purpose," the *Tribune* said. Kub, according to Shaw, could get cops plum assignments or "move them to the sticks." Some favored officers received a special privilege: "Others who wished to use her home for love trysts were accommodated," Shaw claimed.

Rumors, perhaps raised by other enemies of the woman, had surfaced that Kub had married a Black man, a scandal in itself in a day when the races, even in America's North, didn't mix at the altar. Kub slapped the story away, the *Tribune* reported, admitting that "she was married to a negro but said she had left him soon after their marriage 10 years ago."

Although Shaw and Kub were enemies, the *Tribune* described their stories as "dovetailing" and together "led to the tracing of graft money to many other policemen . . . some of them of high rank."

After a day of inquiry, the prosecutors and the special grand jury had their work cut out for them. The jury wanted to let Sergeant Herdegen tell his side of the story, and they wanted Acting Commissioner Alcock to appear, so he could address concerns that Kub's enemies had prevailed, getting her fired. "He will be asked if it is true that she recently was discharged, and why," the *Tribune* reported.

The grand jury also wanted to keep hearing from Shirley Kub. In her first day of testimony, Kub offered just a glimpse into official Chicago crookedness. The grand jury called her back to testify the next day, January 21, 1931.

But Shirley Kub didn't show up. She had disappeared. "Woman Detective, Foe of Gangs, Missing," blared one of dozens of headlines over a nationally distributed United Press story that week. "Mrs. Shirley Kub Fails to Appear in Chicago," the sub headline read, adding ominously, "May Be Slain."[11]

The story's lede hinted further at Kub's fate, considered a common one for those who presumed to take on Chicago gangdom or its corrupt police force: "Mrs. Shirley Kub, a former detective who boasted that she 'had something on almost every policeman in Chicago,' was mysteriously missing today and it was feared she had been kidnaped."

Although a contempt of court warrant was issued against Kub, given she had so far revealed "only half her story" and was "considered the most important witness" called by the special grand jury, officials speculated that she had not vanished willingly. "She may have been kidnaped or killed by someone who did not want her to testify—and indications are there were many," said Assistant State's Attorney Charles J. Meuller. "Or she may have fled because of fear of punishment by criminals or bribe taking policemen."

In the first days of Kub's disappearance, however, a more complex portrait of the woman had begun to emerge. Alcock denied that Kub had been assigned to work with two other undercover officers, described her role with the force as merely a "piperizer" or observer of individual policemen, and "said he had discharged her last month because her work was unsatisfactory."

The grand jury also received testimony from an unnamed Black newspaper reporter who was "seized at the Kub home, 744 North Pine avenue."

Why was he at the Kub property? And did his presence there have anything to do with the Black husband Kub said she'd parted ways with years before? "His story," the *Chicago Tribune* reported, "was that he went there at the [request] of Ned Ragland, a Negro who is said to be married to Mrs. Kub, but whom she has said was her chauffer. Ragland asked him to go there and take out the dog and canary, the Negro newspaper man said."[12]

Efforts to find Kub continued. Kub friend Harriet Borneck was arrested and held overnight, but she refused to say anything about the missing witness, explaining, "I'm a stand up baby and I'll tell you nothing."[13] Another Kub crony, Grace Bock, was threatened with perjury charges when she claimed not to know anything of Kub's dealings.[14]

But Kub nemesis Bernice Shaw, perhaps hoping to land another blow against her enemy, "has been driving around with detectives to places where Mrs. Kub might be found." Finding the woman, prosecutors insisted, was "vital to the exposure of graft conditions."[15]

More than a month passed before Kub was caught in Indiana, her capture provoking another round of blaring headlines over stories that grew increasingly more bizarre. The Illinois state's attorney's police force found Kub in Indianapolis on Saturday night, February 28, 1931, the *Chicago Tribune* reported. Sergeant Michael Ahern of the force said she had $17,000 in cash in her possession, a remarkable amount of money—worth close to $350,000 in 2024—whose existence no one could explain.[16]

Officials decided Kub had disappeared of her own volition, and not because she'd been kidnapped or frightened away, but for less valid reasons. She was released on bond but scheduled to be sentenced for contempt of court the following week. Court officials, still eager to hear the rest of her testimony about police corruption, brought her before the grand jury that Tuesday, March 3.

Kub refused to testify and was arrested again, and she spent an hour in jail before her lawyers could post bond, the *Chicago Tribune* reported. "I am no squawker," she said to the waiting media upon her release.

Ten days later, on Friday, March 13, Kub was sentenced to four months in jail by Criminal Court Chief Justice John McGoorty. The sentence was imposed for her refusal to testify March 3. Another sentence was to be imposed the following week for her January flight.[17]

"Ordinarily I would give a sentence of six months under such circumstances," McGoorty said, "but because of this defendant's sex I believe four months will satisfy the law."

McGoorty, the *Chicago Tribune* reported, "refused to listen to any plea for leniency and ordered Mrs. Kub taken to jail."

"The grand jury," he said, "is an institution entitled to respect."

On the day she began her first sentence, and with another sentence in the offing for Kub's earlier flight to Indiana, Kub lawyer Harold Levy said the woman had no choice but to run on January 19. But it wasn't the fear of gang reprisals or police retribution that provoked her departure, he said. As reported by the *Chicago Tribune,* "The attorney attempted to excuse Mrs. Kub's action by saying that she fled because the jurors and prosecutors were responsible for 'adverse publicity given to her' and because jurors seemed more interested in her colored husband than in evidence relating to the police department."

Another Kub attorney, Michael Ahern (not the same Michael Ahern who supervised the arrest of Kub in Indianapolis), complained that prosecutors "subjected Mrs. Kub to unfavorable publicity and photographs."

"Whose business was it if the defendant married a Negro?" Ahern asked. "Because of that publicity she felt she had to leave town."[18]

Were she to receive another four-month sentence for fleeing, Kub was looking at spending the better part of a year in the county jail. So by the end of her first day in lockup, she had seen the light. "It was reported last night," the *Chicago Tribune* revealed, "that after a few hours in jail Mrs. Kub communicated with jail officials and asked what Prosecutors Charles J. Mueller and Charles Lonsbury wanted her to do to 'square herself.'"[19]

Mueller and Lonsbury had this to say back, according to the *Tribune:* "They will not listen to Mrs. Kub until she is ready to tell the whole truth about all her connections, in and out of the police department. They said that a few days in jail may loosen her tongue and that they might then consider asking some mitigation in her behalf."

Kub spent a week in Cook County detention before she was brought back to the grand jury room. On March 20, 1931, two months after her first turn on the stand, she at last delivered a second day of testimony.

"The most sensational exposure of police political graft in Chicago history was threatened today," announced the United Press in another of its nationally distributed wire stories about the affair, "after Mrs. Shirley Kub, former police spy, had made good her promise to 'tell all' rather than remain in jail for contempt of court." Kub, the United Press story noted, "once was quoted as boasting she knew enough about graft 'to blast half the politicians and policemen in the city out of their jobs.'"[20]

She arrived from jail to the courthouse at ten o'clock in the morning that day, finishing her testimony fifteen hours later, at one o'clock the next morning. The hearing, as portrayed by the press in attendance, was as chaotic as one might expect.

"The only times she left the jury room," the United Press reported, "were during brief periods when Ned Ragland, a negro, who is said to be her husband, and George Miller, her chauffeur, were on the stand. While they testified, she went to her home and returned with large stacks of records."

The *Chicago Tribune,* two days after Kub's appearance in court, offered up a strange and more convoluted story of how the documents reached the grand jury: It was Miller who drove Kub—along with her secret reports—to Indiana when she fled the grand jury in January, the *Tribune* reported. Once she'd reached the Hoosier state, Kub had given Miller the reports and told him to give them to Ragland, who in turn gave them to a relative.[21]

On the day Kub was brought before the grand jury for her second day of testimony, Miller went to the state's attorney's office to tell what he knew of Kub's secret reports, said to be carbon copies of reports she had given Acting Police Commissioner Alcock.

Miller's motivation for betraying Mrs. Kub, his former employer? Romance. The *Chicago Tribune* mentioned a "jealousy existing between Ned Ragland, her colored husband, and George Miller" and said Miller had grown "tired of Ragland's attentions to Mrs. Kub."

The documents were retrieved from the relative's home, leaving Kub with "nothing to do but admit authorship and tell all she knew."

After she finished her fifteen-hour grilling by the grand jury, the *Tribune* reported, "Mrs. Kub stood outside the [jury room] door, and remarked 'Now I want to go home.'"[†] The jury foreman, Joseph Farmar, replied, "We would like to let you go home, Mrs. Kub, but we can't now. All we can do is to report to the court Monday what you have done to help us."[22]

But the jury showed pity on their star witness. "Mrs. Kub was shielded from interviewers and photographers by the grand jurors, who formed a cordon about her, and escorted her to the county jail. This was considered unusual, and evidenced, it was said, her importance to the grand jury."

"Utmost secrecy covered her testimony," the *Tribune* reported March 21, but a day later, its reporters were able to discover the general details of Kub's testimony and her cache of secret reports. The decidedly underwhelming findings, many of them leaked by an unnamed juror, included these allegations:

- The police captain assigned to Chicago's Loop District spent little time there.
- "Various policemen assigned to patrol the business district spent their time in some of the hundreds of speakeasies or gambling places which flourished in the district."

[†] The United Press reports said she was "almost crying" when she spoke these words.

- A "certain police official desiring promotion" paid $800 (worth about $15,000 today) to a city attorney "to assure him the desired job" but didn't get promoted and complained to Kub.

The *Tribune* also noted that "Each secret report rendered by Mrs. Kub to the acting police commissioner contained at the bottom of the sheet the name of the person supplying her with the information." The grand jury found the "names of these informers" to be of "vast importance," the *Tribune* said, because they would allow each one to be called for questioning by the jury. Not mentioned by the newspaper was any speculation about how the informers might feel about things, given the willy-nilly storing and transporting of highly confidential reports featuring their names.

Kub spent the weekend "in seclusion," the *Chicago Tribune* reported, "in a remote part of the county jail so that no efforts can be made to intimidate her before her return to the jury room."

Monday morning, she was back before the grand jury to finish her testimony, alleging—depending on which newspaper report you read—that Al Capone was in charge of the Chicago Police Department, or that he had delegated control to two of his proxies, Chicago city attorney James Breen and city sealer Daniel Serritella.[‡]

Breen declined to discuss the accusations, and Serritella blamed politics, as city elections were coming up in November.[23] Daniel Gilbert and Willard Malone, two Chicago police captains named by Kub as special targets of Breen's and Serritella's corruption campaign, also issued blanket denials to the *Chicago Tribune*. "Capt. Malone said that in five months his men had raided 113 gambling places and 72 vice resorts. He said that he has made more arrests in the first district than any captain in the last 10 years."

Kub, it should be noted, didn't accuse Malone of having "submitted to the dictates of political bosses," the *Chicago Tribune* reported. Her allegation was far vaguer, that he'd "jumped the traces," a metaphor from the horse and buggy days that referred to a horse running off the path.

One day after the completion of Kub's grand jury testimony, the state's attorney's office conducted sweeping raids of vice in the city. Fifty cops on

---

‡ The same Daniel Serritella discussed earlier in the book as the subject of a short-weighting sting conducted by the Secret Six.

the attorney's force were "divided into twelve swiftly moving squads," the *Chicago Tribune* reported. The officers "raided 37 places on the west side, made more than 100 arrests, and seized records believed to have a bearing on the police corruption investigation for which Mrs. Shirley Kub has been furnishing the special grand jury information for several days." The raids hit "gambling, vice, and liquor resorts." Arrested on disorderly conduct charges were thirty-five women and seventy-five men, among them Charles "Monkey Face" Genker, "who has a record as a keeper of vice resorts that dates back nearly 25 years."[24]

The day after the raids, Shirley Kub was freed after twelve days in custody. Her bond was set at $3,000, and she was warned that she'd better keep cooperating with the grand jury. Meanwhile prosecutors were poring over the seized documents to develop new leads.[25]

But the Kub investigation, launched with such fanfare in January 1931, had clearly stalled. Newspapers had promised "The most sensational exposure of police political graft in Chicago history," an expose expected to "blast half the politicians and policemen in the city out of their jobs." Instead, they got nothing but the usual raids and the usual suspects, and more empty promises.

In April 1931, in a last-ditch effort to get something—anything—out of Kub's time on the witness stand, State's Attorney John Swanson launched a sweeping financial probe of the Chicago Police Department. On the assumption that dirty cops would have lots of dirty money, Swanson started with the banks, sending subpoenas to two hundred Chicago banks for the records of any cops who kept deposits there.

First called before the grand jury were Loop Captain Willard Malone, Capt. Marcy Mullen of the Desplaines Street district, and Sgt. Owen Mangle, whose beat covered the Austin precinct. "Fifteen other police captains," newspapers reported, "have been called before the jurors." All those called on the first day were "said to have been implicated by the testimony of Mrs. Shirley Kub. Eventually, all 70 captains on the force will be examined about their deposits."[26]

By the end of the first day, the *Tribune* reported, the grand jury had the bank records of six police captains, including one captain who kept his money in two banks, and "at least two of the captains (who) had 'substantial' bank balances." The investigation would continue with an examination of wives' bank accounts, a search of safe deposit boxes, and a search of "outlying banks."[27]

Faint praise characterized the first day's findings.

"We developed information worthy of further analysis," grand jury foreman Joseph Farmar told the *Tribune*. "We found much that looks interesting."

"It looks as if we were on the right trail," agreed Prosecutor Charles Mueller, adding that "if there is any corruption the bank records should disclose it."

But Shirley Kub's testimony took a drubbing in the *Tribune* piece. "Capt. Malone failed to corroborate statements Mrs. Kub said he would verify," the paper reported. "Owen Mangle of the Austin station, also named by Mrs. Kub as one who could prove the truth of some of her assertions, also contradicted her testimony."

In the End, Nothing

Newspapers report the news. They do not report on the absence of news. So there was never a headline announcing that the investigation of police corruption in early 1930s Chicago wound down quietly with no further investigation. But the absence of news was perhaps the most newsworthy item of the whole affair. The investigation of something rotten in Chicago law enforcement—instigated by the Secret Six, continued by Shirley Kub—had proved a complete fiasco. Over the next few months, the stories about the investigation simply dwindled to nothing. There were no further grand juries. There were no arrests of crooked cops or the politicians covering for them. There were no mass layoffs of compromised officers and patrolmen. The Chicago police department was, it seems, essentially clean.

The Secret Six had done their best to uncover police crookedness, but after making some dramatic accusations, they gave up. So Shirley Kub took up the baton, but after a three-month snipe hunt punctuated by even grander accusations, a flight to Indiana prompted most likely by her inability to back up her claims, and the discovery—thanks to her jealous chauffeur—of a stack of confidential reports, her campaign fizzled as well.

And then, nothing.

Ironically, one of the few cops let go after the grand jury investigation was someone Kub was trying to save, Sergeant Jack Herdegen. And it wasn't collusion with racketeers that brought him down. "The basis of Herdegen's discharge," the *Chicago Tribune* reported, "was testimony that he had lived with Miss [Bernice] Shaw for two years while he was married to another woman."[28]

Kub's failure to make good on her promises was not just a single hiccup in an otherwise stellar career of corruption fighting. No, her chaotic foundering was par for the course, the woman inherently corrupt herself, a polygamous liar, a cheat, a thief, and a vindictive antisocial.

But she was good at hype, and that drew the Secret Six to her, like a moth to the flame.

26

The Secret Six vs. Swanson

A NUMBER OF FACTORS converged in early 1930 to birth the Secret Six, including months of crime and chaos, the shooting of construction superintendent Philip Meagher, and the demands of his employer, Harrison Barnard, that something be done.

But in September 1930, seven months after the group's founding, leader Col. Robert Isham Randolph was giving all the credit to John A. Swanson, the former judge elected in 1928 to serve as state's attorney for Cook County. "State's Attorney Swanson suggested we organize a real secret service," Randolph recalled. "He explained that while he has a staff of investigators attached to his office, all of the operatives are known and cannot, as a result, work with the secrecy that they need. Their effectiveness is limited because of that fact. So at his suggestion, we organized our 'secret six.'"[1]

The Secret Six worked closely with Swanson's office. When Swanson set up an office in Chicago's Loop district in October 1930, for example, the Secret Six was there. Secret Six detectives assigned to the office included, according to the *Chicago Tribune*, Roy Steffen and Charles Touzinsky.[2]

"Citizens having complaints about racketeers are to be invited to come to this office," the *Tribune* reported.

When Alexander Jamie was hired as the Secret Six's top detective in October 1930, he was described by the press as a "sort of law enforcement dictator," with Swanson among those "carrying out Jamie's orders."[3]

In early 1932, the now-seasoned vigilantes were still working closely with Swanson.

"Prosecution of Chicago racketeers has been handled by a special division of the state's attorney's office," read an Associated Press story run by papers nationwide, "with undercover work done by the Secret Six crime-fighting organization of Chicago business men."[4]

Thanks to the partnership, the AP reported, proceeds of graft in the city had been reduced by some 30 percent, or about $1 million, in the previous year.

Two years after the founding of the Secret Six, in March 1932, Randolph retold the story with more drama of Swanson's essential contribution in a speech before 1,100 Chicagoans: "The state's attorney did have a constructive suggestion. 'I have investigators whose duty it is to collect evidence' the attorney said, 'but they are paid on the public payroll. . . . They are all known and it is difficult for them to get evidence. . . . I suggest you organize a real secret service where the operators would not be known or know each other. Supply them with money to run with the wolf pack and buy information from the jackals. With evidence we can get conviction in any court. Without it we cannot."[5]

By September of that year, however, the partnership, the mutual respect, and the trust would be broken irrevocably, in a most peculiar way.

The Secret Six kept its main offices in the Midland Building at 172 West Adams Street, a location well known to the public, according to a September 1, 1932, story in the *Chicago Tribune*. In order to work more discreetly, the vigilantes would sometimes open up secret offices, and at some point they did so in the State Bank building at 120 South La Salle Street.[6]

As the Secret Six conducted operations from that location, something seemed off about the phones, according to a man identified in the *Tribune* story only as Alexander Jamie's son, but who must have been Wallace Jamie.

"A few days ago we became suspicious that the wires were tapped," the younger Jamie said. "The telephone company investigated and confirmed our suspicions. Sergt. [Michael] Ahern and others were sent to trap the wire tappers. They found Frank ["Cockeyed"] Carroll, a well known wire tapper, and Gordon White, who said he was an investigator for the state's attorney, in the room. They were taken into custody. Carroll had credentials showing he was employed by the James H. McQueeney Detective agency, so McQueeney was taken into custody, too."

Odd as the story already was, it only got stranger. "They were released when they proved they were sent there by the state's attorney's office,"

120 South La Salle Street, where the Secret Six set up a secret satellite office, and where their phones were tapped by the state's attorney. / Kevin Meredith

Wallace Jamie said, adding, "which we had been investigating intensively for the last 18 months."

Why was the Secret Six investigating the offices of John Swanson, the man credited with creating the vigilante group? Alexander Jamie, reached by the *Chicago Tribune*, confirmed his son's report and elaborated, vaguely, "I have been investigating the state's attorney's office for the last eighteen months. . . . I have made satisfactory progress and have found that a political-criminal cabal exists."

Swanson was surprised by Alexander's claim when questioned by the *Tribune*. "As to the existence of a political-criminal cabal, it's a secret to me," Swanson said. "I welcome any investigation of my office and will give Jamie every assistance if he cares to go through it."

But more surprised was Col. Randolph himself, head of the Secret Six. "Mr. Randolph said his own relations with State's Attorney Swanson were most cordial," the *Tribune* reported. "He could not guess the motive for an attack on the prosecutor."

"This is a joke—that the state's attorney and the Secret six are investigating each other," Randolph told the *Tribune*. "State's Attorney John A. Swanson originated the Secret Six. He formed it for his extra legal activities. He is its father. It was supposed to be working for him."

The *Tribune* offered up verbatim the most remarkable portions of their interview with Randolph:

> Q.—Did you assign (Alexander) Jamie to investigate Swanson?
> A.—No, he runs his office with a free hand. He can investigate the President if he wants to.
> Q.—Have you seen any need of an investigation of Swanson?
> A.—No, I do not know of any reason why Swanson should be investigated.
> Q.—Do you know of the existence of what Jamie calls a cabal?
> A.—No, that's news to me.
> Q.—Do you know what (Alexander Jamie) has been doing lately?
> A.—O, he investigates lots of things that never lead anywhere. Many a wild goose is chased.

Bewildered as he was by the investigation of Swanson, Randolph promised to support it. The Associated Press reported the next day that Randolph had "conferred with Jamie and said he would not interfere in the controversy."[7]

As for the state's attorney's wiretapping project, Swanson told the *Tribune* he didn't know he was spying on the Secret Six. "We were informed that a blackmail ring was in process of formation," Swanson said. "We located an office in the State Bank building, 120 South La Salle street, in which the ring was supposed to be operating, and we tapped the wires."

The members of the suspected blackmail ring may have known they were at risk of being watched, by someone, Swanson hinted. "Conversations overheard were in code," he explained. But two names kept popping up: Alexander Jamie, And Shirley Kub.

"Swanson declared his wire-tappers had heard the name of Mrs. Shirley Kub, formerly a police investigator, mentioned over the telephone several times," read the widely published Associated Press account of things. "This he said, has caused his men to be suspicious, as her activities have several times been the subject of investigation. When informed that Mrs. Kub was in the employ of the secret six he expressed surprise."[8]

Newspapers had a heyday with the item. Hundreds of publications across the nation ran the story, often on the front page, with headline writers working overtime to come up with the best short-form take on the oddity of things.

"Spier Spying Upon Spiers," announced the *Biddeford (Maine) Daily Journal.*

"Spies In Secret Office of Secret Six! Woman Too!" exclaimed the very surprised *Fresno (California) Bee.*

The front page of the *Maryville (Missouri) Daily Forum* went with ridicule or, in modern parlance, snark: "Detectives Trail One Another to Keep in Practice."

Not to be outwagged, the *Chicago Tribune* offered this sentence in their front-page story, under the whimsical headline "Secret 6 and Swanson Go A-Spying": "Mr. Swanson's office has wire tappers eavesdropping on secret conversations over a secret wire to a secret office of the Secret Six, where Mrs. Shirley Kub, a secret agent of the Six, is in command."

The story was full of strange revelations. Swanson told the *Tribune* he was surprised that Michael Ahern was working for the Secret Six. Swanson had thought that Ahern, after spending three years working for Swanson's office, had returned to service with the Chicago police.

It was Ahern, recall, who while working for Swanson led the team that found Kub in Indianapolis and dragged her back to Chicago (Ahern and Kub presumably agreed to let bygones be bygones when they passed each other in the halls of their secret office).

Col. Randolph had some strange news to ponder as well. "Also a mystery to Randolph was the employment of Mrs. Kub," the *Tribune* reported. "He said he was unacquainted with her past, which included the enforced giving of testimony regarding police graft and her associations with the late Jack Zuta, vice monger, her brief incarceration in the county jail for defying the grand jury, and a 30-day house of correction sentence imposed on her last year on a larceny charge."

Randolph's plea of ignorance regarding Kub defies logic, of course. The grand jury investigation was front page news for months in early 1931, and after the Secret Six stepped aside because they had no proof of police corruption, Shirley Kub became the star witness, her escapades reported not just thoroughly in Chicago, but nationwide. And Randolph was more than familiar with the grand jury's work. He had offered at one point $50,000 to keep it going.

Kub's larceny conviction, less than a year after the grand jury hearings, was also covered in the *Chicago Tribune*. "Sent to Jail," read the brief caption under Kub's picture, featured on page twenty-four of the *Tribune*'s December 30, 1931, edition. "Shirley Kub, police spy, sentenced for thirty days for failing to pay jeweler."

The value of the purloined jewelry, other papers said, was $35, or about $600 in 2024 dollars. She was also fined for the theft, to the tune of at least $200 (some papers said $300), or a little under $4,000 in modern currency.[9]

So the story also spoke to Kub's criminal incompetence. Recall that she was caught with an eye-watering $17,000 in cash in March 1931. Later that same year, she had been reduced to stealing $35 worth of baubles.

Did Randolph just not see her picture in that December 1931 *Chicago Tribune*? Did no one with a Secret Six connection notice the item about the conviction and sentencing of one of Chicago's most famous antipolice corruption crusaders? They hired her and put her in charge of one of their offices without so much as a check of the local press?

But once Col. Randolph was apprised of his agent's sketchy history by the *Chicago Tribune,* he doubled down: "Her employment, however, was explained by Mr. Randolph with the words: 'When digging in the mud you use mud-digging tools.'"

More would be heard from Shirley Kub in the months to come, much more. And the surprising little tiff between the Secret Six and John Swanson would soon blossom into all out war. But for now, one last story bears repeating: the time Shirley Kub destroyed a candy company.

Among the scuttlebutt that emerged while Kub was testifying to the grand jury in March 1931 was that she "promoted some enterprises for herself while acting as a police investigator," the *Chicago Tribune* reported. "As the story goes," the *Tribune* said, "Mrs. Kub interested officials of a candy company in a proposition whereby she guaranteed to double their output by distributing punch boards to be used as sales bait."[10]

Punch boards were a simple gambling system, typically consisting of a wooden board into which holes had been drilled. Each hole was stuffed with a rolled up piece of paper with a prize printed on it. Pay your money, pick a hole, see what you won. The prize might be candy, or it might be something more substantial. Cash, for example. Because humanity is liberally sprinkled with suckers, the operators of punch boards in 1930s Chicago could make a lot of money. The only obstacle to the scheme was the law, which frowned on punch boards. But Kub had a plan. She had during her time as a police spy of some sort wriggled her way far enough up the Windy City's power rungs that she met with a "prominent politician" and he "secured an injunction restraining police from interference with the punch boards."

What happened next, true or false, sounds enough like Kub's work that it might be real: "When the sales peak was reached the woman, reaping the profits of her scheme, sold her stock [in the candy company] to a purchaser who was eager to pay the high price he believed the profits warranted. Thereupon, it is said, the politician intervened to have the injunction dissolved. The police renewed their activity, the punch boards were withdrawn, and the business collapsed."

Regardless her checkered past, once Shirley Kub was outed as a Secret Six detective, Swanson's wire-tapping of her and her office ended.

But the Secret Six's misbegotten project to destroy their creator carried on, with the brazen hubris and laughable incompetence that had become their signature MO.

The Case of the $100 Bribe

In early September 1932, the Secret Six promised to continue their year-and-a-half investigation of the state's attorney's office, and continue they did. Less than two months later, they had the goods on John Swanson and his "political-criminal cabal."

The vigilantes had sent their detectives to the Great Northern Hotel, where men surnamed Warnecke and Nenning were collecting contributions for Swanson's reelection campaign. One detective "posed as a speakeasy owner and paid $25 to Warnecke," the *Chicago Tribune* reported. "Another investigator said he paid $20 to a man named Nenning."[11]

The timing of things was quite strange, however. The two checks had been made out seven months earlier, around March 1932, but the Secret Six had waited until two weeks before the November elections to accuse Swanson of being friendly with the purveyors of illegal liquor.

The allegations, further, came one day after the Secret Six did something they promised at the time of their founding they wouldn't: they got into politics. On October 25, 1932, they endorsed Thomas Courtney for state's attorney of Cook County. In their announcement, they took a swipe at Swanson that was both sweeping and puzzling, considering the closeness with him they'd publicly reiterated since their founding. Said Randolph when he announced the endorsement, "After more than two years of work in the investigation of criminal cases for prosecution by the office of State's Attorney Swanson we are convinced that his conduct does not warrant his re-election."[12]

Swanson responded to the accusations with a furious denunciation. "These charges are utterly false," he told the *Tribune*. "This is a studied effort by Randolph to vilify me."

Swanson accused Randolph and his fellow vigilantes of being nothing more than "reform racketeers," alleging that "the Secret Six started out along the lines suggested by me, which at first were effective. Then it fell under the malign influence of Mrs. Shirley Kub."

Swanson dismissed Alexander Jamie as "a former prohibition agent," but he saved his fiercest vitriol for his erstwhile partner in crime-fighting.

"Randolph has a pleasing personality," Swanson said, "but coupled with his desire of self advertising is apparently a lust for money." After dredging up old stories about engineering work Randolph was paid to do for corrupt Chicago officials in the 1920s, Swanson continued, "It seems passing strange, to say the least, that Mrs. Kub, Jamie and Randolph said nothing for seven months about these so-called charges against me. . . . I never heard of the people mentioned in the Kub-Jamie-Randolph statement."

Perhaps Swanson's rebuttal was more vigorous than the Secret Six had expected, so the next day they lobbed a more powerful charge at the prosecutor. Now the bribe amount was $100, paid by Secret Six detectives to a corrupt member of Swanson's staff for secret documents about a murder.[13]

On the day that accusation was leveled against Swanson, Col. Randolph was delivering a speech in Kansas City, Missouri. After touching on Prohibition and Al Capone, Randolph directed his ire against the state's attorney. "We are opposed to Swanson because everything in his office is for sale," Randolph said. "We know that, because we went into his office and bought what we wanted."[14]

Swanson's response to the latest Secret Six accusations arrived in three parts.

First, he noted that the secret document the Secret Six had been bandying about wasn't secret at all, was just "a copy of a statement in an arson murder case [which] previously had been made public in a Felony court hearing."[15]

Second, Swanson offered another round of outraged criticism against the Secret Six and its leader, Col. Randolph. "When I suggested that the Secret Six be organized I intended it to be a legitimate agency for the detection of crime," Swanson recalled, lamenting that the group had "degenerated into nothing other than a front for a political organization." He also issued an additional round of criticism against Randolph's lucrative consulting work for local government.

Third, and most effective, Swanson decided to give the Secret Six the opportunity to make good on their claims. "If any one has any evidence of corruption on the part of any employee of this office, I want that employee indicted and prosecuted at once," Swanson thundered within a day of the Secret Six's $100 bribery accusation.

"At a newspaper conference this morning," the Associated Press reported October 26, 1932, "Swanson called in two of his aides and before the reporters gave orders for issuance of subpoenas for Randolph, Jamie and Shirley Kub, woman investigator for the Secret Six. 'The business of these fellows claiming they bribed someone,' Swanson declared, 'ought to be aired out before the grand jury.'"[16]

Swanson was no doubt well aware of the Secret Six's habit of making dramatic, unsubstantiated claims about crime, both national and local. He'd seen it firsthand the previous winter in the grand jury room, when first Col. Randolph and then Shirley Kub could come up with nothing solid about the sweeping police corruption they'd alleged.

With elections less than two weeks away and his job on the line, Swanson's office moved quickly, serving Alexander Jamie with a subpoena at his home that evening, ordering him to appear before the grand jury the next morning.

As for the head of the vigilantes, the *Chicago Tribune* reported, "Randolph was served with his subpoena as he alighted from a plane at the Chicago airport on his return from Kansas City where he made a speech on Chicago crime conditions. Detectives Arnold Bloom and William Brady handed the summons to Randolph as he stepped from the plane. They said he appeared surprised."

Shirley Kub, however, could not be found, so state's attorney's officials gave Alexander her subpoena while others continued searching for her. And here, as one might expect, another Secret Six story veered from merely odd to surreal:

> Mrs. Kub's former husbands were being sought by the state's attorney's investigators for a clew to her present whereabouts. The investigators recalled that Mrs. Kub had hidden from a special grand jury investigating police conditions and that later she testified that during this period of hiding she had married a George Miller. She married Miller, she said, after she was told her previous marriage to another man was illegal. Detectives said that Miller is now in a federal penitentiary for interstate shipment of a stolen automobile. . . . According to the police, Mrs. Kub first attracted public notice in 1922 when one of her husbands shot a youth who had followed her to Chicago from California.

There's a lot to unpack here. We'll get to the multiple husbands in a bit, but first let's look at the story of that 1922 shooting, which was national news at the time, and bore all the hallmarks of a life perpetually mired in chaos, poor judgment, and antisocial inclinations.

The Case of the Lovestruck Teenager

In 1922, Shirley Kub, 32, was living in San Diego with her husband, "wealthy commission merchant" William Kub, and her three children when she met nineteen-year-old Stanley White, the son of prominent physician J. Francis White. Dr. White was serving as physician to Kub's children and sometimes brought his son to the visits. When Mrs. Kub learned the teen sold automobiles, she decided to buy a car from him. Soon, the teen fell in love with the woman, described as "handsome" in press reports of the day, and Mrs. Kub returned his affection to an unknown degree. Stanley was a welcome change from her husband, she claimed, who was the second man she'd married and very abusive, sometimes beating her multiple times per day.

After Stanley fell in love with her, Kub and her husband returned to Chicago, the boy followed her (or possibly drove her there, accounts varied), and William Kub grew suspicious, going so far as to tap the telephone lines of their home. On September 1, 1922, William assaulted Shirley again over her affair with Stanley ("I slapped her," he admitted), so she called Stanley to ask for protection and he raced over to the Kub home. There, a struggle ensued, William Kub retrieved his gun, and shot Stanley in the head, either in self-defense (William's claim) or in "cold blood" (Shirley's claim).[17]

Newspapers nationwide ran with the story. In an article about the shooting published in a Buffalo, New York newspaper, Shirley Kub waxed philosophical about the tragedy: "Love? What is love? I married William after my first marriage that was a nightmare. And I thought for several years that I could love the man although he beat me unmercifully when ever he felt like it. . . . I stayed only because of the children. I think that's the way most marriages turn out."

Continued Kub about the injured boy:

> The kid fell in love with me, I guess, just because I was older and sort of understood him. . . . I wasn't in love with the kid—he's only 19 . . . but he was attentive and thoughtful and I was glad of some one's being kind. . . . And then the fool had to take himself seriously and had to interfere with William. He meant well, of course, but it was so darned melodramatic. I'd been beaten before—I could have stood another. I don't forgive my husband for shooting him . . . but I think Stanley was wrong too. The whole thing was wrong. No, I won't go to Stanley. What's the use? He can go back to his father when he's better.

William Kub was arrested when it seemed Stanley might die, but a few days after the shooting, the youth was recovering, Mr. and Mrs. Kub had reconciled, and no further news of the shooting appeared in the indexed press.

Ten years later, with new husbands in her life and a shaky career as a police reform crusader underway, it was time for Shirley Kub and her bosses, Alexander Jamie, and Col. William Randolph, to defend their accusations against John Swanson's office. Their appearances before the jury went about as well as Kub's affair with young Stanley. But at least no one was shot this time.

A Grand Jury Fiasco

Randolph was first to show up for the hearing, on October 28, 1932. Prior to being called into the grand jury room, the *Chicago Tribune* reported, "He appeared nervous, pacing back and forth and talking in jerky sentences."[18]

The press swarmed around the man, asking him why undercover bribes and illicit payments made in March weren't aired until October, just two weeks before the elections. "We had some loose ends to pull in," Randolph explained, adding vaguely, "We are not through yet and the tapped wire stories will explain everything."

Randolph spent more than a half hour before the grand jury. In the meantime, Jamie and Kub showed up. Apparently, the woman who couldn't be found the night before had been produced, either through the efforts of Jamie or one or more of her husbands. "Jamie seemed confident when he arrived with Mrs. Kub," the *Chicago Tribune* reported, adding this odd detail: "Observers noted he sometimes lit two cigarets at a time—one for himself and one for Mrs. Kub."

With Randolph testifying behind closed doors, the press descended on the Secret Six's top detectives. "A conversation was carried on with reporters," the Tribune recalled, "but Mrs. Kub did most of the talking, always speaking of 'we.'"

When Randolph appeared, exiting the jury room, the reporters turned their attention back to him. "I have no statement to make," Randolph told the throng. The *Chicago Tribune* said he "hurried away, even from Mrs. Kub and Jamie, who had jumped from their seats to greet him."

The hearings were closed to the press, but the *Tribune* uncovered the nature of everyone's testimony soon enough, from unnamed sources.

Asked during the hearing why he'd waited so long to present evidence of bribery, Randolph "finally said he had not heard of the case until about a week ago." He also admitted, when asked about his differences with Swanson, that Swanson's office had always cooperated with the Secret Six. "I have no complaint," he told the grand jury.

Kub, the second Secret Six witness called into the grand jury room, was described by the *Tribune* as "barely four feet tall and stout," wearing "a blue knit dress, trimmed with white collars and cuffs, and a fur piece across her shoulders."

Like Randolph, the *Tribune* reported, she testified for about half an hour. She said virtually nothing. "It was reported that she gave the jury no information, always falling back on the contention that she was working for the government and could not give information. 'Shit,* I can't say a word. It is all government stuff,' Mrs. Kub said time and again." The low point of the Kub's testimony, as reported by the *Tribune,* was summed up this way: "It

* "Sh—" was how the *Chicago Tribune* captured Kub's curse.

was said she aroused the jurors when she said she knew the charges must be true. Pressed for an explanation she finally said her knowledge was 'because of a woman's intuition.'"

Jamie went last, and spent almost two hours before the grand jury. According to the *Chicago Tribune's* anonymous insider, Jamie admitted "he had no direct knowledge of the bribe payment." In summary, Jamie revealed that the Secret Six had botched their sting on Swanson's office. "He sent an investigator with two 'cover men' to make the payment," the *Tribune* reported. "The 'cover men,' he said, failed to cover because they stayed in the automobile while the briber went in and made the payment. The case, therefore, is the word of one man against another, he admitted."

Things went from bad to worse for Jamie. The grand jury asked him who the investigator was who had delivered the alleged bribe. "He did not remember the first name," the *Tribune* revealed, "but said he knew the last name and thought he could produce the man if given permission by the government. He could not explain, it was reported, what the government had to do with bringing in the witness."

Jamie was asked if he had any other allegations he cared to make against Swanson's office, besides the bribing case. He said he had one other case, but after "he was given some instructions on fundamental principles of law (he) admitted that in the other case he was wrong and had no complaint." The grand jury concluded the meeting with Jamie by demanding testimony from the mysterious Secret Six briber himself, telling Jamie, "Bring him in tomorrow morning, government or no government."

The *Chicago Tribune* was there for Jamie's exit from the jury room: "He was nervous when he came out, and apparently anxious to evade an interview. As he stood surrounded by reporters, who were firing questions at him, Mrs. Kub hurried to his side from the seat on which she had waited for the two hours. She reached up to the six foot former prohibition agent and took his hand. 'Don't say anything, don't make any statements,' she said. Jamie took her advice."

So it had come to this for the renowned Secret Six, archnemesis of Chicago gangsterdom, the force credited with bringing down Al Capone, now emerging as the dismantler of corruption at the highest levels of Chicago law enforcement: Around March 1931, the vigilantes had begun their investigation of Cook County State's Attorney John Swanson. Eighteen months later, in early September 1932, Alexander Jamie accused Swanson of operating a "criminal-political cabal" out of his office. But the only evidence he could come up with—presented two months later, just before the November elections—were hazy memories of payments no one else could corroborate, and Shirley Kub's "women's intuition."

The Secret Six had one last chance to save face. Bring the undercover briber himself to the jury room. Per the *Chicago Tribune:* "They must produce the witness or stand the consequences of disseminating a story which cannot be proved, investigators indicated."

But the vigilantes had one last card to play, the *Tribune* noted: "The three Secret Six representatives said they would have to get permission from the federal authorities to give out the name." So the enterprising *Tribune,* which covered with equal enthusiasm both the Secret Six's dramatic accusations and their inevitable, ignominious collapses, reached out to First Assistant United States Attorney William J. Froelich, "who has been besieged by Randolph, Jamie and Mrs. Kub for the last few days."

Froelich was unable to help his Secret Six friends, telling the *Tribune* that "the government had nothing to do with any case now being investigated by the state authorities. He refused to disclose the reasons for the Secret Six visits to his office." The *Tribune* continued to press Froelich: "The federal prosecutor was later asked if he had at any time prevented Jamie from giving the county grand jury the name of the investigator supposed to have paid the bribe."

Replied Froelich: "Randolph, Jamie or any one else has my permission at any time to tell the grand jury about such a man, if they know of one." So Jamie, in a follow up appearance before the grand jury a few days later, finally remembered both the name and address of the man they'd sent to Swanson's office to pay that $100 bribe: Lester McKeon, of 718 North Lotus Street in Chicago. Jamie remembered other things about McKeon, too. He was out of town the previous night but might have returned. He'd quit working for the vigilante force a month before. And the records he'd bought with that bribe concerned not just the murder case but four others—an assault and three robberies.[19]

A secret six investigator and several policemen, either with the state's attorney's office or the Chicago force, headed over to that address, and quickly confirmed that it did not exist. There is a North Lotus Avenue in Chicago, but no North Lotus *Street* in the city. And on North Lotus Avenue, there are houses numbered 716 and 720, both built in 1904 according to Zillow, but no 718 between them, neither is there room available between them to have built a home or even a shed.

"Police said there was no building at the address Jamie gave them for McKeon's residence," the Associated Press reported, and "no one in the neighborhood could be found who knew of him."[20] If Lester McKeon was a real person, he apparently never was found, no indexed paper recording his much-anticipated appearance before the grand jury, or even his existence.

At this point, one must start searching for concepts from the field of mental pathology to capture what the Secret Six had done. John Swanson had helped create the Secret Six and was praised regularly as a valuable partner of the vigilantes. But then they turned on him, launching an eighteen-month investigation which turned up nothing more than two vague acts of official corruption, neither of which they could substantiate.

Instead of admitting they didn't have anything on Swanson, however, they kept the charade going, ensuring that when their case eventually fell apart, they would not only look like clowns, but like perjurious clowns. And the man against whom they'd committed that perjury was John Swanson, Chicago's most powerful law enforcement official.

And Swanson was furious, both professionally and personally. The Secret Six had wasted precious grand jury time while they generated headlines calling Swanson's integrity into question. So Swanson, on October 28, 1932, came out swinging. "As a result of the admissions made to the grand jury by Shirley Kub and the former prohibition agent, Alexander Jamie," Swanson said in a statement issued that day, "I am proceeding with a view of taking both criminal and civil action against the Kub woman, Jamie and I-Sham† Randolph and those associated with them."[21]

Continued Swanson in his statement, "Such political blackmail cannot and will not be tolerated." Swanson warned that he would go after the "character assassins" using "criminal libel and conspiracy laws and possibly the bigamy statute." For the latter charge, Swanson dredged up another Kub scandal, rumors that had apparently crystalized during Kub's and Jamie's testimony before the grand jury.

† Col. Randolph's middle name, Isham, was often corrupted to "I-Sham" by Swanson during his fight with the vigilantes.

The Case of the Threatened Parole Officer

First, a little background from earlier in this book: A man identified in the press as George Miller had driven Shirley Kub to Indianapolis in January 1932 to help her escape another day of testifying to the grand jury about police corruption. Miller had reportedly been competing for Kub's affections with her husband, Ned Ragland, a Black man whose race was invariably mentioned when his name came up in the papers. While in Indianapolis, Kub had married Miller under the belief, or so she said, that her marriage to Ragland was invalid. Ragland however continued to pursue the woman he believed to be his wife, so Miller, perhaps hoping to get Ragland in trouble with the law, had told authorities that Kub's secret police reports had been placed with Ragland's relatives. And then Miller got sent to federal prison for stealing a car.

George Miller was almost certainly the same man as George Mueller; the press was just spelling his name wrong when they called him Miller. George Mueller first shows up in the indexed press in February 1932, when his conviction and sentencing for car theft appeared in a few newspapers. The man, "said to be the husband of the police investigator known as Shirley Kub," got two years in Leavenworth for the interstate transport of a stolen car, which was a federal crime.[22]

So the year had started off busily for Mueller. In January 1932, he helped Shirley Kub flee to Indiana, and then married her there. In February, he was sentenced for car theft. In March, he was still free and played a leading role in his wife's grand jury testimony.

At some point after that, he reported to Leavenworth to begin his sentence, but Shirley Kub wouldn't have it. She'd started the year with two husbands, now she had none. She wanted Mueller out of Leavenworth, and she had no compunctions about using the Secret Six to spring him. Nor did the Secret Six, apparently, have any qualms about being used.

As detailed in Swanson's statement and reported by the *Chicago Tribune*, Kub told Alexander Jamie that Mueller's conviction was a "bum rap." Jamie believed her, admitting to the grand jury that "Mrs. Kub's word is law."[23] Their plan was to get George Mueller out on parole, which required the cooperation of federal parole agent William McGrath. So Jamie and Kub met with McGrath. Jamie required no introduction, and he introduced Kub as merely Mueller's bereft wife and "a respectable woman," without any reference to her thirty-day sentence for jewelry theft or her other brushes with the law. Jamie and Kub asked McGrath to parole Mueller, but McGrath "refused to be intimidated into recommending a parole."

At that point, the Secret Six descended to the level of the official corruption they claimed all year to have been fighting: "Jamie confessed [to the grand jury] that after Agent McGrath refused to act," the *Chicago Tribune* reported, "he, the Kub woman and an agent for the Secret Six, together with police officers, tried to get affidavits making charges against the parole agent in an effort to have him discharged from the federal service."

The affidavit failed, apparently, Mueller still in prison while his wife worked at other things. The *Tribune* article offered two guesses at why the Secret Six had turned on Swanson, neither a credit to the vigilantes. "When the Secret Six came under the domination of Shirley Kub," Swanson wrote after the grand jury fiasco, "it abandoned the field of legitimate investigations and turned its attention to politics and began to get money to continue its work by securing rewards for the recovery of stolen property. It was necessary for them to have a friendly state's attorney who would agree to drop prosecution as requested from time to time by the Kub woman and Jamie. This is something that I could not do."

Or maybe the Secret Six's antagonism against Swanson had to do with Samuel Insull, the *Chicago Tribune* theorized. Insull, based in Chicago, had grown fabulously wealthy as the pioneering founder of multiple utility companies, and he was still riding high in February 1930, the month of the Secret Six's founding. At the annual shareholders meeting of the Peoples Gas, Light and Coke Company on February 25, 1930, Insull announced a 70 percent growth in the firm's revenues from the time he took over the business in 1919. His grateful investors offered a "resolution of appreciation" for his steady hand and elected his son, Samuel Insull Jr., to the company's board of directors.[24]

Insull, long rumored to have been one of the (fictitious) six anonymous men who ran the Secret Six, probably was one of the many people (hundreds? thousands?) who gave the group money. In fact, some were speculating that Insull had given the vigilantes 10 percent of their funds, a suspicion repeated by the *Chicago Tribune* in their 1932 article. With a total Secret Six budget reported to be anywhere from a million to five million dollars, this would have been no small commitment, even though Col. Randolph admitted in the 1940s that the Secret Six had collected and spent a far more modest $350,000 (although still respectable, at almost $7 million in 2024 dollars). Insull, who'd promised 10 percent of the vigilantes' budget, eventually gave $35,000, Randolph said.[25]

Two and a half years after the Secret Six was launched, Insull's dissolution arrived with a vengeance. It was the Great Depression that took him down. Although he managed to keep himself afloat with the help of loans for a few years, by July 1932 he was being described as "penniless" by the press, with not even enough cash on hand to afford a place to live.[26]

Losses to Insull's concerns were estimated at two billion dollars (close to $40 billion in 2024 dollars) at the time, with the number of devastated investors numbering in the hundreds of thousands. And in early October of 1932, just a few weeks before the Secret Six aired their ill-fated bribe allegations against John Swanson, Swanson charged Samuel Insull and his brother Martin with larceny and embezzlement.[27]

Swanson called for the arrest and extradition of both men, and Martin was quickly apprehended in Canada, while Samuel was reportedly shuttling all over Europe—England, Portugal, France, Greece. "I assure you," Swanson announced, "that the people of Cook county will never permit two men who are charged with having swindled thousands of persons out of many millions of dollars to escape."[‡]

Was Swanson's pursuit of an early Secret Six supporter behind the vigilantes' fumbling attacks on the prosecutor? Swanson's grand jury may have suspected as much, the *Chicago Tribune* reported, and reportedly planned to ask Col. Randolph how much Insull had contributed to their cause.[28]

Regardless the motivations of the Secret Six in their campaign against Swanson, the true failure of the vigilantes to damage the attorney's reputation was evidenced by the man himself, at a campaign event described by the *Chicago Tribune* as well attended, with "packed houses" at two theaters and loud speakers for "overflow crowds lining the curbs."[29]

After promising that his fight against crime would continue, Swanson took special aim at the Secret Six and its leaders. "They charge that some one in my office got a bribe," Swanson said. "All they claim is that somebody saw somebody who heard that someone else got a $100 bribe. When they

[‡] The men were eventually tried and found innocent.

were called before the grand jury and finally gave us a name and address, it turned out to be a vacant lot and nobody around there had ever heard of the man. They said that this happened in July. Now they bring out the story ten days before election."

The *Tribune* added that "Swanson brought a gale of laughter from the crowd when he said that anyone who listened to a children's detective story over the radio and sent in three coupons from an oatmeal box would get a 'Secret Six' star." Two months later, the Secret Six would cease to exist. But Col. Randolph didn't know that yet, and his manic determination to land a solid blow against Swanson proceeded with a vigilantic self-certainty that might better be described as raw madness.

The Case of the Corrupt Brother

On November 3, 1932—five days before the election—Randolph was back in court again, this time as a "private citizen," but there to make very public charges against John Swanson.

Speaking before Chief Justice John Prystalski of the Criminal Court, Randolph alleged that John Swanson's brother Al Swanson, who worked for Swanson in the state's attorney's tax collection department, had been accepting weekly payments from convicted tax scofflaw Herman J. Goldberg in exchange for lowering Goldberg's taxes.[30]

Randolph, who presented copies of the checks to the judge, would not reveal the source of his convoluted charges, and presented his account under "information and belief," a phrase meaning he had no other evidence for his claims. On the day Randolph made his accusation, John Swanson called them "damned lies" when contacted by the *Chicago Tribune*. Swanson continued, "Any crook can bring a baseless charge in this matter and avoid the responsibility for what he says. Randolph knows that if he testified positively to the statements made by him today he would be liable to imprisonment for perjury.

"These keyhole artists gave a vacant lot as the address of their supposed investigator," Swanson noted, adding that Randolph's "lack of confidence in his baseless charges . . . is so completely demonstrated that a child can understand it."

Swanson wasn't finished. On November 4, 1932, one day after Randolph had leveled his charges, Swanson got permission to address the court, and there he delivered a retort for the ages, his statement so vivid Judge Prystalski had to repeatedly order him to stop. He began by referring to Randolph as "a long eared, tow headed jackass whose heart is as black and foul as the hinges of hell."[31] Prystalski protested, but Swanson barely paused before he forged on, next describing Randolph as a "slippery eel, coward and yellow cur."

After another warning from the judge, Swanson continued, with an indictment of all three Secret Six officials: "Shirley Kub, she of many husbands, Alexander Jamie, the former prohibition agent, who is under her complete domination . . . these buzzards, vultures—"

At that point, Judge Prystalski's patience exhausted, he interrupted for the last time. "I must ask you to desist reading from that statement any more," he said. Swanson left the courtroom to finish his delivery. The next words after "vultures," the *Chicago Tribune* revealed, were some of Swanson's most poetic, and one can sympathize with the prosecutor for wanting them aired: "and carrion birds, were called from their foul nest, in which nest there has been a saturnalia of passion and voluptuousness."

Two days later, the Secret Six accusations against Swanson's brother were dismissed with a formal and slightly less colorful rebuke from the grand jury. The jury's written statement, while not naming Randolph or the Secret Six, seemed to be referring to all of them with phrasing that bore an eerie resemblance to the Secret Six's founding documents issued three years before: "There appears to be ever evident connivances and conspiracy to seize the agencies of justice in Cook county so that law enforcement agencies may become the tool of corruption and crime."[32]

The grand jury gave Randolph a fair hearing, it must be said, calling in Northwestern University handwriting expert Catherine Keeler[§] to examine the checks Randolph presented as evidence against Al Swanson. Keeler told the jury the checks were clearly forged by Goldberg, who was apparently a regular creator of forged documents.

That same day, Randolph's courtroom performance was also condemned unanimously by more than three hundred Chicago attorneys meeting for

[§] Catherine Keeler, recall, also examined the Buffalo, New York, hotel registration card filled out by Gus Winkler at the time of the Lincoln National Bank robbery—a key exhibit in Winkler's controversial exoneration.

lunch at the Hamilton Club. A leader of the resolution drive was, significantly, Edwin Sims, identified by the *Chicago Tribune* as director of the Chicago Crime Commission, also a creation of the Association of Commerce and, in better days, a close ally of the Secret Six in the war on Windy City crime. Sims called Randolph's courtroom diatribe "one of the most vicious and outrageous attacks ever attempted on a public official."[33]

Swanson, who stated that Randolph would never utter his accusations under oath, "invited Randolph to repeat his charges to the grand jury," the *Chicago Tribune* reported. Randolph showed up, the *Tribune* wrote, and "created a new sensation when he admitted to the jury that he knew nothing of the truth of the charges, but merely had made them at the request of Judge Harry M. Fisher, a member of the party supporting Mr. Courtney" against Swanson.[34]

While Judge Fisher also suffered disapprobation for his role in the scandal, Swanson aimed most of his fury at the Secret Six in subsequent grand jury proceedings. He quickly found one very disillusioned former employee of the vigilante group, whose testimony was reported thusly by the *Chicago Tribune*:

> George Redston, a cigar store employe at 946 Belmont avenue, who formerly worked for the Secret Six . . . charged that Mrs. Kub had him arrested and held in a police station for 36 hours because he discovered her real identity and had a photograph of her and (her Black husband Ned) Ragland. Redston charged that the organization operated smoothly until the advent of Mrs. Kub. She promptly took charge, he said, and was responsible for the plan to try to entrap employees of Prosecutor Swanson. Redston said he heard Jamie protest against her plans, but that she replied: "We will have to play the game any way we can."[35]

Swanson also did a little more digging into Shirley Kub's matrimonial affairs, turning up a marriage annulment document filed against George Mueller by one S. Elizabeth Mueller—Shirley Kub. "In the suit," the *Chicago Tribune* reported, "Mrs. Kub said she was married to Mueller in Indianapolis on February 27, 1931. She said that at the time she was married to Ned Ragland, a Negro, but believed her marriage to him was void. On learning, subsequently, that it was still in force, she started action to obtain annulment of her marriage to Mueller."[36] And all this while she was on the run from that Cook County grand jury.

In 1932, Kub would file an annulment petition against Ned Ragland, and he would countersue, in another messy chapter from the life of Shirley Kub.

The Case of the Inconvenient Husband

Ned Ragland was born October 18, 1891, presumably in Illinois, maybe in or near Joliet. A Ned Ragland graduated the eighth grade and qualified for high school in Joliet, Illinois, in June 1907, when our Ned Ragland would have been fifteen. Six years later, in September 1913, when the Ned of our book would have been a month shy of his twenty-second birthday, a Ned Ragland was arrested for "acting in a suspicious manner" around the Union train station in Joliet. He was released after a night in jail.[37]

Shirley Kub married Ragland in Aurora, Illinois, in the summer of 1924, two years after that unfortunate incident, described a few pages back, involving the teenaged lover who took a bullet to the head while trying to defend Mrs. Kub from a previous husband. Interracial marriages in the 1920s, particularly between Black and white people, were vanishingly rare, even in the northern states where they were legal. One study put the number of such marriages at one one-hundredth of a percent.[38] But for seven years, Kub and Ragland made a go of it, buying a home at 1816 Maypole Avenue in Chicago and living there as husband and wife.[39]

But in 1932, Kub filed paperwork in which she attempted to cast doubt on the marriage, claiming "she married Ragland after they had spent an afternoon at various places of amusement 'drinking intoxicating liquors.'" All that drinking, she said, made her "so intoxicated as to deprive me of my reason." Afterwards, her sobriety returned, Kub "repented of her act," and she and Ragland "did not live together as man and wife."

Ragland fought back, not against the annulment itself—the marriage was by now irretrievably broken, one must imagine—but against some of the terms Kub was laying out. Ragland, in a filing submitted to the courts November 1, 1932, claimed that Kub's annulment filing was intended to divest him of his share of the Maypole Avenue property, which he helped to purchase.

Ragland's suit claimed that Kub deserted him on January 28, 1931, a date that coincided roughly with her flight from the grand jury and, a few weeks later, her marriage to George Mueller. "Ragland's suit," the *Chicago Tribune* reported, "charges that Mrs. Kub, as a 'result of a conspiracy with a Fred

Anderson . . . and three other men, intimidated him by force, threats and misrepresentations to submit to the annulment suit." Ragland said the men drove him to Aurora "where he was forced to allow an attorney to act for him and to submit to the severing of his marital contract."

Observed F. L. Barnet, Ragland's attorney, "It is strange that it took Mrs. Kub six and one-half years to decide that her marriage to my client was illegal." Ragland also complained that he was physically banished from his home: "His suit says he was forced to leave the premises by some of Mrs. Kub's Secret Six employees."

The story about Ragland's suit ended with this nugget, irrelevant except that it also spoke to the strange dealings of the Secret Six in its waning days, an organization whose operatives kept turning up to do things that had nothing to do with law enforcement, after which some of them vanished into the mist: "State's attorney's detectives yesterday obtained a trace of Lester McKeon, the man who Jamie said paid the $100 bribe. . . . They found the home of his mother, who is ill, and hope to apprehend him shortly." Nothing more came of that revelation, however.

Ned Ragland would file another lawsuit, in January 1933, alleging false arrest. Named as defendants in the suit were state's attorney John Swanson, several of his deputies, and Michael Ahern, listed as a state's attorney's policeman, but who also worked at times for the Secret Six.[40] It's not clear from the story when the arrest happened, possibly in early 1931, when those closest to Shirley Kub were getting picked up, jailed, and forced to testify before the grand jury about the woman's whereabouts.

After that, Ned Ragland faded from the pages of the indexed newspapers, the outcomes of his lawsuits not appearing in searches. But he seems to have been able to keep the home at 1816 Maypole Avenue that he and Kub bought together, because it was listed as his final address when, in April 1935, at the age of forty-three, he "died in the county hospital . . . from an internal disorder."[41]

The Rest of the Story

John Swanson lost his reelection bid, but the Secret Six and Col. Randolph probably had nothing to do with it. From the top of the ticket, where Franklin D. Roosevelt defeated incumbent President Herbert Hoover soundly, to the rest of the races around the nation, Democrats swept out Republicans, the latter party taking most of the blame for the Great Depression. Republican Swanson was just another victim of the surge.

Swanson, now a lame duck, seems to have given up prosecuting his enemies at the Secret Six for perjury, for bigamy, for wasting everyone's time with vendettas and false claims that weren't even trying to look like crime fighting anymore. Lester McKeon was never found, if the indexed press of the day is to be believed. And in two months, Shirley Kub would serve as the final cause, the last straw, in the dissolution of the Secret Six. But Shirley Kub couldn't stop being Shirley Kub. A few more sad chapters from a toxic life full of them:

- In September 1933, Kub sued to get more money from the estate of her uncle, William McLean Young. The man had left $100,000 (worth almost $2 million in 2024) to charities and his other kin, including Kub's three sisters, but Shirley got just $500.[42]
- In March 1938 a parked car belonging to Chicago firefighter Daniel Curtin was struck by another vehicle, which then sped off. The license plate was traced to Kub, and a warrant was issued for her arrest. In the *Chicago Tribune* piece about the accident, her résumé had been oddly upgraded. No longer a jewel thief, bigamist, or police reform imposter, she was described as "a special investigator for John H. Alcock when he was acting commissioner of police."[43]
- Legal notices posted in the Woodstock, Illinois newspaper in 1936 and 1939 listed Shirley E. Kub and others in foreclosure actions by, respectively, Allied Lumber Company and Home Federal Savings and Loan Association.[44]
- In 1962, Kub failed to file a federal tax return, claiming she hadn't made enough money and, anyway, she was blind. In 1974, Kub was found liable for the taxes from that earlier year. In its final ruling, the federal tax court declared that she had "utterly failed to offer any evidence to establish that she was blind within such definition." Kub, the court noted, met with IRS agents to discuss her case "in restaurants, a bus depot, and other places in downtown Chicago. Mrs. Kub always went to such meetings alone by means of public transportation."[45]

People get into trouble all the time for not paying their taxes, but most don't try to make it all go away with an easily disproven claim of blindness. And in the tax court ruling filed in Kub's case, her dealings with engineer Robert V. Mehaffey were presented in enough detail for us to see the same Shirley Kub who made herself famous in the 1920s and 1930s.

Kub was somehow able to win engineering contracts for Mehaffey with the Illinois Department of Public Works and Buildings, but in return, she wanted $500 per month, in cash. As Mehaffey's business with the state increased between early 1964 and late 1966, Mehaffey told IRS investigators that Kub "'never stopped bothering him' as she persistently requested greater amounts of money than she had been receiving."

Their business relationship ended with a "final argument" in December 1966, and Mehaffey reported he was "glad to be rid of her."

In their investigation of Kub, the IRS had also been looking into the income Kub had made selling antiques. Had Mehaffey ever bought anything from her? the IRS asked him. "He stated that he had never bought any pieces from Mrs. Kub's collection of antiques since 'he would be afraid the item would be either broken or overpriced.'"

On January 18, 1933, however, despite personal and professional failings already well established in the Chicago press, Shirley Kub was still an employee in good standing of the Secret Six, and when a tavern got bombed, she was sent to investigate it. Her appearance at the crime scene spelled doom for the vigilantes, but she was not the only one to blame. December 1932 and January 1933 were disastrous months for the Secret Six, for reasons that had nothing to do with Shirley Kub. The Secret Six answered a bombing extortionist with another bomb, making everything worse. And the wrongly arrested and nationally maligned William Kuhn would at last get his day in court.

27

The Secret Six on Trial

FIRST, A RECAP: In late 1930, eighteen-year-old Chicago socialite Marion Wright received a series of typewritten extortion letters signed "Lester McKay" and warning that if she didn't cough up $25,000 pronto, "Lester" would fatally dispatch her or someone in her family using, among other methods, a "deadly dart" with a range of three thousand feet.

Marion's father, wealthy steel magnate William Van Doren Wright, hired a bodyguard for his daughter and called in the Secret Six. Less than a year since their founding, the vigilantes had already made a name for themselves in their fight against kidnappers and extortionists, and Mr. Wright was not the only crime victim who turned first to them for help.

After a quick and thoroughly incompetent investigation led by Edgar Dudley, the Secret Six settled on William Kuhn as the extortionist. The young stock clerk had been on a few dates with Marion, the last ending with him pawing drunkenly at her in the back of a taxicab. Kuhn was known to talk to his drinks at speakeasies, sometimes worked late, and had access to typewriters at his job. In the hotel room where he lived, detectives found two detective novels, which contributed in their minds to the profile of Kuhn as an extortionist.

So the Secret Six arrested him and placed him in their own jail at the St. Clair Hotel, locking him up with a Secret Six plant who tried to get the boy to confess. After several days and nights there and what some newspapers described as a grueling interrogation, the Secret Six convinced Marion to sign a charging document, Kuhn was formally arraigned in Chicago's criminal court, and the story of his alleged crime, complete with his picture, was published in newspapers coast to coast.

A month later, in January 1931, the charges were dropped on various grounds, including that Kuhn was in Boston when some of the letters were mailed, that Kuhn's employer's typewriter didn't match the machine used to type the extortion letters, and that neither his small collection of detective novels nor his peculiar drinking habits established a criminal mindset.

Immediately upon his exoneration, Kuhn filed a $100,000 lawsuit for false arrest and malicious prosecution against Marion and William Wright, Edgar Dudley, Alexander Jamie, and criminologist Ferdinand Watzek.

Kuhn couldn't sue the Secret Six itself. Although the group was internationally known and revered, emulated across America, the basis of a Hollywood movie, and so forth, the Secret Six wasn't incorporated and thus couldn't be named as a defendant.

The Kuhn trial began on November 15, 1932. Where had the young man been in the two years since the Secret Six arrested him? A ranch in Wyoming, possibly the only place where he could find gainful employment after the whole nation was informed of the charges against him.[1]

The first order of business at the trial was testimony from Kuhn, who had to endure a grilling by the defense about his drinking and his drunken last date with Marion. "On the cab on the way home did you try to kiss her?" he was asked.

"Yes, I did," he confessed.

"Don't you know that a man should never ask a girl for a kiss?"

Kuhn was spared the burden of answer, as the court sustained an objection to that question.[2]

The defense focused on William Kuhn's unsavory qualities, and perhaps they struck a blow or two in the minds of the jury. But the elephant in the courtroom was Kuhn's innocence, easily established in January 1931 with a wealth of exculpatory evidence after the Secret Six had subjected the young man to a pillory of nationwide, career-ending proportions.

Kuhn's defamation trial was important enough that even Dudley, who'd been spending his time of late humiliating himself in Los Angeles, showed up for it. "Dudley's whereabouts had been something of a mystery since the start of the suit," the *Chicago Tribune* reported under the headline "Missing

Sleuth Surprises Court in Kuhn Suit." Dudley revealed his new home as Hollywood, California.[3]

Once Dudley got to the stand, the bulk of his testimony was simply to confirm the basis on which he'd decided Kuhn must be guilty. "Young Kuhn was taken into custody as a result of deductions by Dudley," reported the *Chicago Tribune*, which treated its subscribers to steady coverage of the two-week trial. "The latter admitted in his testimony at the present trial that he considered it suspicious that Kuhn was regarded as eccentric by speakeasy proprietors. Other circumstances which inclined him to a belief in Kuhn's guilt, he testified, were: Kuhn, a broker's clerk, worked late in his office at about the time the letters were written and, when questioned, mentioned the Wicker Park postoffice, where all the blackmail letters (one had actually been sent from the Loop) were mailed."[4]

Dudley, however, backtracked from his earlier contention that detective novels found in Kuhn's room helped establish his guilt, denying under oath "that such books convinced him that Kuhn had written the extortion letters."[5]

The trial was not without its light moments, one of them provided by Dudley. Kuhn lawyer Frederic Burnham was concerned that Dudley might have been coached on his testimony by defense attorney Edward Everett. "Were you in Attorney Everett's office after court the other night?" Burnham asked.

"Yes, I was," replied Dudley.

"And you didn't talk about this case?" Burnham persisted.

"If you want to know, I'll tell you," Dudley replied. "I went there to find out where I could get a bottle of decent bourbon."

Ferdinand Watzek, the crime expert from Vienna, Austria, who'd wrongly declared that one of the typewriters at Kuhn's workplace was the same as Lester McKay's, didn't show up for the trial but had given a deposition a year before that more or less admitted his error. The differences between the machines were so obvious, in fact, that Kuhn's attorney argued anyone could spot them without resorting to so much as a magnifying glass. So Watzek chose a mea culpa so contorted the *Chicago Tribune* simply reported it without any attempt to elucidate: "As for Watzek, he gave an opinion to Dudley that the samples of typewriting taken from a machine in the brokerage office where Kuhn worked were identical with those in the extortion letter submitted to him. He meant that opinion to be official and the Secret Six accepted it as such. It was not until he was leaving for Vienna, a year later, and made a deposition, that Watzek stated he told Dudley the opinion was not to be regarded as official."[6]

Also testifying unhelpfully for the Secret Six were the vigilante group's detectives, Lt. Leo Carr and Sgt. William Knowles. Carr admitted that "none of the evidence which tended to clear (Kuhn) with writing extortion notes . . . had been presented to the state's attorney's office before the youth was arraigned in the Felony court."[7]

The *Chicago Tribune* offered up a verbatim of the damning exchange:

> (Kuhn attorney Frederic) Burnham asked if any one had explained to the prosecutor the differences between the typewritten extortion letters and the sample of typewriting taken from the brokerage office of Winthrop, Mitchel & Co., where Kuhn had been employed.
>
> "I don't remember that anyone did," the policeman replied.
>
> "Did any one tell Brooks that the whole brokerage force had worked in the office of Winthrop-Mitchell on the nights when you had believed Kuhn had gone there alone?" asked Attorney Burnham.
>
> "I don't believe so," was the answer.
>
> "Or did anyone one tell the state's attorney's man that one of the extortion notes had been written and mailed in Chicago on a day when William Kuhn was in Boston?" Attorney Burnham asked.
>
> "No," Carr answered.

But Carr was not a defendant in Kuhn's lawsuit, and the Secret Six may have thought they had an ace up their sleeve thanks to him. Two aces, really.

First, as reported by the *Chicago Tribune,* "Carr said he, not the Secret Six or the Wrights, was responsible for Kuhn's arrest."

"Police Officer Takes Blame for Kuhn's Arrest," the *Chicago Tribune* declared in a November 23 headline. According to the *Tribune,* Carr testified "that he alone was responsible for the arrest of Kuhn on charges of having written extortion letters."[8]

Carr, the *Chicago Tribune* reported in another story, "testified that he actually took Kuhn into custody, without a warrant . . . because he believed he had sufficient evidence. Carr not being a defendant, the plaintiff was then required to show that the officer acted at the direction of the defendants—which Carr denied."[9]

The Secret Six's second ace was Carr's contention that he barely had anything to do with the Secret Six. Stated the *Tribune*, "Lieut. Carr's testimony yesterday apparently removed the blame from the Secret Six, since Carr explained that he was connected with that group 'only indirectly.' He 'represented the police department' as a contact man with the Secret Six, he said."[10]

The upshot of Carr's testimony, just a footnote in the Kuhn case, should not be ignored, because it speaks volumes about what the Secret Six had become in less than three years. Search "Carr" and "Secret Six" in the indexed press and one turns up a solid handful of high-profile crimes, cases where the vigilantes succeeded and Carr was lauded as one of their own, a member in good standing of the vigilante force, doing his part for justice. As noted earlier in this book, Carr was named explicitly as working for the Secret Six when a gas station was bombed because the ghost of a dead Indian chief wanted his home back, when someone offered an illegal tax-fixing scheme to the Story & Clark Piano Company, when Norman Collins was kidnapped, and when James Morrison, involved in a $142,000 bank robbery in Willmar, Minnesota, was arrested.

But now that a Secret Six case had gone south, Carr was content to portray himself—no doubt with the Secret Six's grateful approval—as a shape-shifting apparition of Chicago law enforcement, a gendarme without portfolio, a cop beholden to no one as he made whatever arrests suited his whims on any given day.

Vigilantes do not stand for elections, do not get their funds or their authority from elected leaders, and thus do not have to worry about offending the people. They can take credit for the nationwide shredding of a young man's reputation and then, when that young man is found to be blameless, deny they had anything to do with it. The Secret Six had become little different from the gangsters they swore to shut down, destroying an innocent person with impunity.

And the Secret Six might have gotten away with it except that twelve more people—the jurors at Kuhn's wrongful arrest trial, specifically—at last got to sit in judgment of the vigilantes. And the vigilantes were no better prepared to face the Kuhn jury than they'd been to convince several grand juries of law enforcement corruption in 1931 and 1932. While Carr had his story straight, Sgt. William T. Knowles hadn't gotten the memo. Knowles' name frequently appeared next to Carr's in newspaper stories about Secret Six adventures, and on the witness stand he admitted he "was acting as an investigator for the Secret Six" in the Kuhn case and "originally signed the complaint on which Kuhn was arraigned" before "Miss Wright substituted her signature when Judge John Lyle refused to accept that of Knowles."[11]

As for Alexander Jamie, often identified in the press as the head of the Secret Six, the jury was treated to a mishmash of conflicting claims. At one point while he was testifying, Jamie "entered a categorical denial of any responsibility for the arrest of Kuhn" but also "admitted that he had worked on the Kuhn case personally." Other testimony revealed that Jamie was one of several Secret Six personnel who escorted Kuhn to the Felony Court on the day of his arraignment.[12]

Marion Wright took the stand briefly in her own defense. No longer a teen, the twenty-year-old Miss Wright had journeyed back from Paris to appear at the trial. The *Chicago Tribune* described her as "clad in black" and speaking in a "soft voice" as she told the jury she'd been frightened by the extortion letters and was an "unsophisticated debutante" who had no idea what she was signing when Kuhn's arraignment paperwork was set before her.[13]

But surely the most sympathetic witness was Marion's father, William Van Doren Wright, whose call to the Secret Six two years before had ended in disaster. Marion had been attacked in a taxicab by her drunken companion, successfully fought him off, and decided she no longer wished to have anything to do with him. But because her father had called the Secret Six, she'd ended up having to go to court to defend herself from him once again.

Mr. Wright, one of the last witnesses called to the stand, spent two and a half hours testifying. Asked about the identity of Lester McKay, the elusive extortionist, Wright proved combative. "Have you any idea or knowledge as to the identity of the writer?" he was asked. "No, but I have a firm conviction," he retorted. Did he glare at Kuhn as he said the words? The *Chicago Tribune* didn't say.[14]

Wright made clear however that he didn't want to stir up trouble and "was specific on the point that at no time had he heard the word 'arrest' used in connection with young Kuhn."

By the time he was done testifying, another villain had emerged. "At the end of the long session," the *Chicago Tribune* reported, "the voice of the witness was a weary mumble, trailing off into a reiteration of his protests at various points of the proceedings, that 'I wasn't trying to frame anybody; I don't know anything about laws and courts; I was just led around.'"[15]

What Wright implied, the *Tribune's* headline writer stated explicitly:

Father Accused in $100,000 Suit Blames Secret 6

In his closing arguments, defense attorney Edward Everett returned to the theme that William Kuhn was a shady character, a drinker, and a "fortune hunter" whose arrest had been entirely logical, even if he was ultimately exonerated.

> He was anxious to know rich girls, like plenty of other young men who'd rather marry a fortune than get themselves a job to support them. This is the fellow who asked a girl to go to the Bal Tabarin, and took her instead to a speakeasy when she'd never been in one before, and urged her to drink. I ask you if this isn't the sort of man who'd write these extortion letters? All that is necessary in this case is that you decide there was probable cause for these defendants to have believed Kuhn guilty of the crime charged.[16]

Kuhn attorney Frederic Burnham wasted little time defending his client from Everett's attacks, instead using his closing arguments to revisit the shoddy detective work that led to Kuhn's false arrest. "I called attention to the discrepancies in those typewriting samples that could be seen plainly with the naked eye," Burnham recalled. "Did these defendants heed that warning? They did not. These mighty sleuths of the Secret Six refused to believe that it meant anything when a letter was mailed from Boston by Kuhn, on the same day that one of these extortion letters was mailed here in Chicago."

Burnham then turned to attack Dudley's character: "Edgar Dudley placed plenty of emphasis on the fact that two detective stories were found in Kuhn's room—among thirty other books—and he harped on that until we made him look so ridiculous he decided to strike it out of the picture himself. Dudley's testimony was full of venom, spite, and malice. It was his business to get a big case—he'd been waiting a month in the office of the Secret Six for one to show up, and he wouldn't take heed of any of the points in Kuhn's favor".

Before the trial's presiding judge, Peter Schwaba, sent the jury back to render their verdict, he told them, "you must decide that the person or persons who caused his arrest did not have a preponderance of evidence against him on which to base such an arrest." The jury began deliberating about 11:15 a.m. December 2, 1932. Their decision was reached on the evening of the same day and announced the next day across the top of the Chicago Tribune's front page:

Kuhn Wins Over Secret Six

Damages were reduced by the jury from the $100,000 Kuhn had originally demanded to $30,000, still a hefty sum though, worth about half a million in 2024 dollars. The jury blamed four men for false arrest and malicious prosecution: William Wright, Ferdinand Watzek, and the two Secret Sixers, Edgar Dudley and Alexander Jamie. Marion Wright was absolved.[17]

Jury Foreman Alfred A. Mertsky, speaking to the *Chicago Tribune* after their ruling was announced, said the twelve members were swayed by the "preponderance of the evidence," and from the start "were unanimous in voting to find the Secret Six men and Dr. Watzek guilty." Most of the jurors agreed to exclude Marion Wright from the first ballot, and several wavered on her father's guilt, but after "six or seven ballots," all were in agreement about all four men's culpability.

"The highest award we considered was $50,000," Mertsky said, "based on the expense young Kuhn was put to due to his arrest, the defamation of his character and subsequent humiliation."

Although the Secret Six said Kuhn had failed a lie detector test about the extortion letters, Mertsky dismissed the technology as "a mechanical device that cannot be trusted to read a man's mind." But then Mertsky turned to John O'Connor, one of the defense attorneys, and quipped, "Brother, I'd certainly have liked to use that lie detector on about fifteen of your witnesses."

By the time the verdict was read that evening, O'Connor was one of the few people involved in the suit still hovering around the courthouse. He promised to appeal the verdict, and a hearing was set for December 17 to begin that process. "He is confident," the *Chicago Tribune* reported, "that the verdict will not hold in a higher court, and that 'no money will ever be paid.'"

But no matter how the case wound up, real damage had been done, the press of the day suggesting that two respected families had been upended by the Secret Six's bungling. "Miss Wright and her father were believed

END OF SECRET SIX SEEN IN POLITICAL CHANGES

Left to right: Col. Robert Isham Randolph, Shirley Kub, and Alexander Jamie, as featured under a headline foretelling doom for the group in the December 5, 1932, *Chicago Tribune*. / Chicago Tribune/TCA

last night to be on their way to New York, preparatory to sailing again for France," the *Tribune* reported, "where they may remain permanently."

Kuhn was hitting the road as well, returning to the ranch in Pitchfork, Wyoming, he'd fled to after his arrest and exoneration. "I know my brother will be delighted to hear this," his older brother Wendell said of the jury's decision. "The important part of the verdict is that it vindicates him completely."

Significant damage was also done to the Secret Six. "End of Secret 6 Seen; Setbacks Hit Spy Service," the *Chicago Tribune* announced in a December 5, 1932, headline.[18]

Prophesies of Doom for the Vigilantes

While the $30,000 Kuhn verdict was seen as a potentially fatal blow against the vigilantes, a variety of issues at that time had newspapers across the nation prophesying the group's final days. In a widely distributed Associated Press article, the chief issue was funding, with Alexander Jamie noting that "times have changed" since the days when "we had all the money we needed."[19]

The same article, however, said, "There is enough money for another year." The source of the statement seemed to be Col. Randolph, but that wasn't made clear in the article. If true, of course, there wasn't really a funding crisis, was there? But it was probably another of Randolph's lies. The *Chicago Tribune's* story noted that the Secret Six had "met with a series of reverses in the last few months which has pointed (to) the need for the official and not private investigation of crime."

Among those setbacks:

- "The departure of Samuel Insull . . . reported to have been one of the leading contributors."
- The "mud slinging . . . in which Randolph and Jamie attacked State's Attorney Swanson . . . but in each case [were] unable to substantiate the charges when summoned before the grand jury."
- The employment for eighteen months of Shirley Kub, "a fat, grotesque little woman . . . bride of a Negro* . . . jailed for contempt of court . . . an intimate of Jack Zuta, a gangster . . . and a defendant in a larceny case in which she was sentenced to the Bridewell."[20]

But it was the Kuhn case that did the most to prompt the Secret Six's final reckoning in the press. The city's business leaders, the *Chicago Tribune* suggested, were reluctant "to contribute further to the Secret Six, in view of recent disclosures of its practices. The fact that Mr. Wright finds himself assessed with damages in the Kuhn case as a result of his seeking the aid of the organization is not expected to loosen any purse strings."

The *Tribune* did not mention the Secret Six's devolvement from heroic anticrime crusaders to bumbling laughingstocks, but an exchange during the Kuhn trial hinted at that downfall as well. Kuhn attorney Frederic Burnham, as he questioned witnesses, repeatedly referred to the "Secret Six."

* The worst elements of the *Chicago Tribune*'s vitriol against Kub were left out of earlier drafts of this book, but are included here, after some reflection, as regrettable but illuminating cultural artifacts.

Edward Everett, representing the defendants, took umbrage, the *Chicago Tribune* noted, declaring "that Burnham had 'sought to stigmatize' the Secret Six by referring to the organization by that name."[21]

How did Everett want Burnham to refer to the group, if not by the moniker once both emulated and uttered reverently nationwide as shorthand for a band of courageous antigangster vigilantes? Reported the *Chicago Tribune*: "The real title of the group, he declared, is the crime prevention and punishment committee of the Chicago Association of Commerce."

Everett's proposal quickly broke down for sheer unwieldiness: "Some mild hilarity was occasioned in the courtroom by Everett's efforts to avoid reference to the Secret Six as such and substitute the formal title he had mentioned. He was finally advised by the chuckling Burnham to stick to the shorter phrase."

Along with the humor, however, was insight, including in an editorial published in the *Jacksonville (Illinois) Daily Journal*. "Hastily Accused," read the headline, which pointed to the Kuhn verdict as an indictment of the whole vigilante enterprise:

> It is unfortunate that this committee which had its inception in an uprising of citizens to stop the crime wave, should have become involved in scandal. Being secret, the organization has been carrying on pretty much as it pleased, and no doubt some of those in the inner circle were carried away by this taste of unusual power. They have made some grievous mistakes in their eagerness to prove that they could get the criminal, whether or not they got the right one. The best solution for the crime problem lies in a centralized police system, manned by officers who serve by merit alone, and who regard their responsibility of law enforcement as a sacred duty.[22]

The *Chicago Tribune*, in its article about what it believed to be the impending collapse of the Secret Six, cited one additional matter: the vigilantes' outrageous behavior in the Solomon Smith case. It was one of the last crimes investigated by the Secret Six, a case involving not one but two bombs, the second condemned by local officials as an "infernal machine."

An infernal machine, it should be noted, that was entirely the handiwork of the Secret Six.

28

The Case of the Two Bombs

ON NOVEMBER 9, 1932, a package postmarked in LaGrange, Illinois, arrived in the mail to the Chicago home of Solomon Smith, president of the Northern Trust Company. His wife, Frederika Shumway Smith, thinking it might be a present for her four-day-old granddaughter, set upon it eagerly, but "as she started to open it, she became suspicious on noticing the plaster of paris," the *Chicago Tribune* reported in early December 1932. Her fears came too late—the box exploded before she could set it down, and "the force of the explosion threw her against a wall." The woman suffered no injuries however, or only minor ones; the press wasn't clear on that.[1]

The explosion ripped through the front of the box, leaving the box lid—and the sinister message written on the lid's underside—unscathed. "This is just a warning," it said. "Wait. Say nothing. Do nothing."[2]

Despite the warning, Solomon Smith notified the Secret Six, and the agents headed over to his apartment in the stately, twenty-story building that still stands at 1242 North Lake Shore Drive.

The vigilantes decided to work the case alone and keep it secret, perhaps because at this point they believed that everyone in Chicago law enforcement who wasn't the Secret Six was hopelessly, albeit improvably, corrupt. It would be almost a month after that package had blown up in Ms. Smith's hands before the constituted authorities were notified and the press was given the story.

"The box was carefully patched together by agents of the Secret Six," the *Chicago Tribune* reported on December 2, when the story finally broke.

In November 1932, a small bomb was mailed to the apartment of Solomon and Frederika Smith at 1242 North Lake Shore Drive (building on right). The blast blew Frederika against the wall. / Kevin Meredith

Within the remains of the small box, made of imitation leather, typically used to store index cards, the agents reassembled a fiendishly clever design: "It contained an aspirin bottle filled with the powder, wadding and bird shot of about six shotgun shells. Imbedded in plaster of paris was the battery of a small flashlight. Slender copper wires connected the battery and the powder in such a manner that the explosion would occur when the lid of the box was opened or when a piece of adhesive tape across its top was removed. Either action would lift a piece of cardboard that separated two wires and they would then touch, the connection then established acting as the detonating agent."[3]

"Expert opinion," the *Chicago Tribune* continued, "was that the bomb was intended only to maim, that its force would have been unlikely to cause death."

On November 19, ten days after the bombing, a letter arrived for Mr. Smith. "How did you like our little present?" the note began, going on to demand $4,000 (worth about $75,000 in 2024). "There's more where that came from," the letter writer warned, signing the note "J. F."

The letter instructed Smith to place an ad in the *Chicago Tribune* personals column reading "Everything OK, addressing J. F. and signing it SS."

Once the ad was placed, the missive said, further instructions would follow. "Your life will be the penalty for failure to comply with our demands, attempts to capture us or notification of police. You can see that we have means of enforcing our demands and if you don't want any bloodshed you will follow further instructions closely. We are in a position to watch your moves and you had better keep quiet."

While still hiding the crime from authorities and the press, the Secret Six brought the letter and the exploding box to the Northwestern University crime lab, where "handwriting experts" determined that the same person had written both messages, a person who was "used to writing a foreign language."

The letter writer may have been a woman, according to an Associated Press story about the crime. "Authorities . . . believed the bomb apparently failed to function with as deadly a force as its makers intended."[4]

As he'd been instructed, Mr. Smith placed ads in the newspaper on November 27, 28, and 29, "but no further word was received. Mr. Smith and the Secret Six were of the opinion the bomb and extortion letters were not the work of any organized gang, but possibly of a crank."

And that was it, or so it would seem. Case closed.

But no, the mystery of who almost blew up Frederika Smith was far from over. "The constituted authorities of Chicago, state and federal," the *Chicago Tribune* reported on December 5, 1932, were "angered last week when they discovered that the Secret Six had known for four weeks that a bomb had been sent through the mails to Mrs. Solomon A. Smith, wife of the banker, without giving the police, state's attorney or postoffice inspectors any information so the culprits might be sought while the trail was still warm."

Stung perhaps by the criticism, the Secret Six resumed their investigation into the case, this time with federal authorities.

"Working on secret clues," read a wire story that appeared in newspapers December 9, "post office inspectors and 'secret six' operatives are pushing their hunt for the terrorist who mailed the bomb. . . . News of the bomb outrage was kept secret for 21 days."[5]

Solomon Smith himself was also not ready to drop the case. "I have started the most determined investigation within my power," he told the press in early December.[6]

Not wanting to be blamed for investigative delays, apparently, Mr. Smith had his lawyer speak on his behalf to the *Chicago Tribune:* "Paul E. Lavery, attorney for Mr. Smith, said he and Mr. Smith thought the Secret Six a super-organization and they had no doubt notification would be given to the properly constituted authority, as the law demands."[7]

Some of the coverage of the bombing noted that Smith, besides heading up one of Chicago's largest banks, was a director at two utility companies founded by Samuel Insull, long reputed to be one of the Secret Six.*

After the rush of coverage the first nine days of December 1932, the investigation into the Solomon Smith extortion proceeded more quietly thenceforward, at least where the press was concerned. But that didn't mean things weren't happening. "The extortionists have never ceased their attempts to obtain money from the Smiths," the Associated Press reported in January 1933. "The terrorists are understood to have written Mr. Smith eight notes, demanding $8,000."[8]

The extortionist, "J. F.," was apparently struggling to come up with a good way for Mr. Smith to pay the $8,000 (which was double the initial demand and worth about $150,000 in 2024 dollars). Meanwhile, the Secret Six was coming up with new plans for J. F.'s capture.

After Smith was told to drop off the cash at a certain address, the Secret Six decided to "have one of its operatives walk around and around the same block," the *Chicago Tribune* reported, "dropping a package of money. If it was not gone when he made his next trip past the spot, he was to pick it up, carry it along, and drop it again."[9]

The *Chicago Tribune,* which detailed the Secret Six's machinations with doses of both ridicule and hyperbole, described what happened next under a section head reading "Ouch, My Poor 'Dogs.'": "The drop the handkerchief

---

* See the chapter entitled "The Secret Six Was Neither" for more detail.

ritual was followed all one night, with watchers posted about the block. The only result was that the operative who dropped and picked up the decoy package had to consult a chiropodist the next day. He estimated that he had traveled 22 miles."

After that plan failed, the *Tribune* continued, the Secret Six turned to Northwestern University's crime laboratory to concoct a new plan. "An extortion note to Mr. Smith had directed that the money be placed at another spot near Riverside. Instead of watching the spot, (Alexander) Jamie and his assistants, it is said, placed about the place some specially prepared earth concocted in the crime detection laboratory, with the objective of getting an accurate footprint of their quarry."

That plan failed as well, the *Tribune* reported: "The place was left unwatched. The next morning the absence of the package showed that the extortionist had been there. But so, apparently, had a troop of Boy Scouts. The Secret Six found enough footprint evidence for a dozen extortion cases."

The Secret Six were getting desperate. They'd been criticized for neglecting to pull in the authorities after Smith brought them into the bombing case. Other very unpleasant things were happening to them in December 1932, including the Kuhn verdict and a funding shortage. If only the Secret Six could catch the man who mailed that bomb to Mrs. Smith, they could redeem themselves, reestablish their value to Chicago, and maybe even resume talk of running a national franchise.

Communications with the extortionist continued, and a new agreement was worked out: The $8,000 in cash would be left in a hollow tree stump on December 30, in a location detailed by the *Chicago Tribune* as a "forest preserve, near Riverside, between Forbes road and the Des Plaines river, and not far from the Riverside Brookfield High school."[10]

It was a trap, of course. As the *Tribune* explained in a particularly mocking passage:

> The Secret Six executives, because of the wariness shown by the letter writer in avoiding their earlier traps, decided that super-detective methods would be necessary, and accordingly consulted the officials of the crime detection laboratory of Northwestern university. The supertrap was laid. . . . A decoy package was stuffed into the stump. Attached to the other end of the string was the "trigger" of the mousetrap. Under the spring of the trap was an

> explosive cap. When the package was lifted the string sprung the mousetrap. Its spring set off the cap. The cap exploded a large can of flashlight powder. The explosion of the flashlight powder lighted a short fuse attached to a couple of sticks of dynamite.

The explosives sat there for more than a day while agents of the Secret Six waited in a shed a few hundred yards away. The trap was finally sprung on New Year's Eve, but by the time the vigilantes reached the stump, the extortionist had recovered from the shock of two sticks of detonating dynamite and fled back to his car, which quickly sped away.

While at least poetic justice had been meted out by the Secret Six, who nearly blew up someone who had nearly blown up Frederika Smith, local authorities were less inclined to admire the poetry of the situation. Uproar, in short, ensued. "That bomb was a dastardly and dangerous thing!" thundered George Miller, a member of the Cook County Board of Commissioners. "Great danger attended all those who visited the Riverside forest preserve on the week-end, and I feel that State's Attorney Courtney should investigate the circumstances to determine whether criminal action shall be taken against the Secret Six."[11]

Commissioner Marie Plumb echoed Miller's sentiments at the body's January 10 meeting. "There was a hideous thing hanging over the forest preserve when that trap was set," she said. "By what right did they go into the forest preserve? . . . This is just another example of the invisible government which carries on regardless of, and in many cases in spite of, the constituted authorities."

"The ire of the commissioners was aroused," the *Chicago Tribune* reported, "by the fact that the bomb . . . was placed only a few hundred yards from the Riverside-Brookfield High school, and that the guards watching it were too far away to warn any children who might have tampered with it out of curiosity during the thirty-six hours before the suspect arrived on the scene."

The commissioners adopted a resolution declaring that "this unguarded infernal machine . . . might easily have been the cause of death or serious injury to some innocent child or respectable citizen, or . . . might well have been the cause of a forest fire."

The Secret Six would have to consult with officials of the forest preserve before planting any further explosives there, the resolution declared, adding that before any more explosive traps were laid, the Secret Six needed to establish its ability to pay for damage caused by "the carelessness or foolhardiness of its agents."

The commissioners also urged further investigation of the blast. "I suggest that we call in representatives of the Secret Six for an explanation of the affair," said Commissioner Peter M. Kelly.

Three days later, on January 13, 1933, the commission got that meeting. Alexander Jamie himself showed up. Perhaps the commissioners expected contrition, a promise of better behavior going forward, but what they got was unapologetic flippancy.

"Why did you put this bomb in the forest preserve, just 100 feet from the Riverside-Brookfield High school?" demanded Commissioner Frank J. Kasper. "You should have protected the children. You should have put up a bond for injury to persons or property."

Replied Jamie, "It was just a Fourth of July salute. I don't really consider that there was a bomb placed in the forest preserve. In fact, there was none."[12]

Jamie continued with a justification of the trap, recounting the original explosive attack on Mrs. Smith, and asserting that the string-triggered explosives was the best way to catch the extortionist.

"And supposed some small boy had pulled that string?" Commissioner Kasper asked. "It could have injured his eyesight."

"Well," Jamie replied, "we had the thread of the trap concealed under a leaf."

Kasper, unpersuaded, moved to "have a complete report of the matter submitted to the board by the superintendent of the forest preserve."

The point was moot. In five days, the Secret Six would be all but dead.

29

The End of the Secret Six

IN THE WEE HOURS of January 16, 1933, South Chicago's Jeffery Tavern was bombed, the explosion going off in the doorway of the popular roadhouse. The blast occurred just after closing time, so the only occupant of the establishment was the janitor. No one was hurt, and the explosion did no more than $150 in damage (a little under $3,000 in 2024), but "windows were broken and plaster shattered in buildings nearby," the Associated Press reported. "Residents of the neighborhood reported they were thrown from their beds by the force of the blast."[1] A motive for the attack remained elusive, but the tavern owners claimed not to serve booze, so that policy emerged as a cause. "Police said they believed gangsters disgruntled by refusals of the proprietors to purchase liquor might have been responsible."

The attack caught the attention of the Secret Six, and Alexander Jamie decided it needed looking into, so he sent Shirley Kub to the bomb site. Rumors of the group's impending demise had been swirling for more than a month, ever since that $30,000 verdict in the Kuhn case. Within a few days of the embarrassing loss in court, however, the Chicago Association of Commerce met to discuss the group's fate, and they announced a plan to persevere.[2]

It wasn't looking good, however. A vigilante effort can't rely on regularly collected, legally mandated tax revenues, so it must count on belief, confidence, faith, and all of those had taken devastating hits in recent months. Behind the scenes, things were getting desperate for the vigilantes. By early January 1933, someone within the group had proposed a merger with the

Chicago Crime Commission, also a creation of the Association of Commerce, but a body that eschewed cloak and dagger tactics in favor of gathering and disseminating information. It was the Commission's "Public Enemies" list, for example, that served the police as a guide in going after Chicago's worst gangsters and racketeers.

The Commission's response to merger talks were, to put it generously, less than positive. "The directors of the commission unanimously refused to even negotiate on such a proposition," the *Chicago Tribune* reported beneath a headline that summed up how bad things had gotten: "Crime Board Scorns Secret 6 Plea for Merger; Extra Legal Groups Hard Pressed for Funds."[3]

The commission did make a counteroffer, but it served only to suggest more scorn, if not active contempt. It "agreed to have one of its members, Charles R. Holden, a former president, meet with representatives of the other organization from time to time to informally exchange views on accomplishments." The *Tribune* story implied, however, that even that meager offer was on shaky legs: "Mr. Holden went to California soon after."

Despite the funding crisis, the battered reputation, the terrible press, it was full speed ahead for Alexander Jamie. Maybe he was holding out hope for one more solid win, a case that would rehabilitate the Secret Six, get the money flowing again, and restore the group's standing.

Sending Shirley Kub to the bomb-damaged Jeffery Tavern was exactly the wrong idea, however, a gambit so ill-advised it brought the hammer down for good. New Chicago Mayor Anton J. Cermak, who had defeated "Big Bill" Thompson for the city's top job in November, delivered the Secret Six's death blow. "The mayor became incensed, it was learned, when Mrs. Kub was sent by the 'Secret Six' Monday to investigate the bombing of the Jeffery Tavern, south side night club," read one of several versions of the story picked up by newspapers around the country.[4] "I'm tired of hearing that she is intruding on police investigations," Cermak declared. "From now on I want no policeman to talk to her or give her any information. Furthermore, I don't want her around the city hall."[5]

Alexander Jamie was described as "astounded" by the mayor's actions. "It's part of our job to investigate such crimes," he protested.[6] "I sent her there because I believed her to be the best qualified investigator in Chicago," he told the *Chicago Tribune*. "For some reason the mayor objected to our investigation. Mrs. Kub did not interfere with the police and I am unable to understand the mayor's objection."

Added Jamie weakly in an interview with the Associated Press, "As for our investigators not being fit associates for Chicago policemen, well, I could say something about that if I wanted to."[7]

But Cermak went a devastating step further than freezing out Shirley Kub, ordering the withdrawal of Chicago police officers assigned to the vigilantes. Among those returned to regular duty were Lt. Leo Carr and Sgt. William Knowles, and four more detectives left unnamed by the *Chicago Tribune*. The storied vigilante partnership of Carr and Knowles was done, the two no longer working together to catch bombers, extortionists, and unhappy Native American ghosts. Carr went to the Grand Crossing police station, Knowles to West North Avenue.[8]

"Without police aid, the body cannot function," noted the *Daily Times-Press* of Streator, Illinois. In a last-ditch effort to save the Secret Six, Col. Robert Randolph fired Shirley Kub. "Randolph expressed the hope that his move might cause the mayor to reconsider."[9]

Cermak didn't reconsider, but the mortally wounded Secret Six did not completely die that day, limping along for a few more months, the vigilantic version of a dead man walking. "We do not want to operate without the aid of police and other authorities," Randolph admitted a week after Cermak's decision. But they would try to keep things going, he told a reporter for the Consolidated Press Association, promising "that the group he heads would continue to function just as long as possible without official help."[10]

The last Secret Six case discoverable in the indexed press was, appropriately enough, another scare involving wealthy bank president Solomon Smith. Now the criminals were demanding $5,000. "For God's sake, Solomon, we need money and we need it bad," one of them wrote in a letter received at the Smith home January 25. "We already have sent you a package that your wife got. . . . If you double cross us and set detectives on our trail, as you did before, you will never live to see the sun set tomorrow."[11]

Two unnamed Secret Six operatives joined a contingent of Lake Forest police to protect the Smith home that night, the *Chicago Tribune* reported, but nothing more came of the threats. A month later, in a tacit nod to the group's dissolution, Alexander Jamie incorporated the Secret Six name. "It's just a precaution," Jamie told the *Chicago Tribune*. "The popular name, the Secret Six, has been widely advertised and I didn't want any one stepping in to appropriate it." Jamie denied that the Secret Six would become a private detective agency.[12]

But on March 16, 1933, the Chicago Association of Commerce formally ended its association with the Secret Six and announced it would no longer fund the group. Undeterred by earlier promises, or reality, Alexander Jamie said the group would go on as a not-for-profit detective agency, and revealed that Col. Randolph was no longer the group's chief.[13]

While the most significant event in the death of the Secret Six was their loss of Chicago support in January 1933, the absolute end is unknown, the moment Alexander Jamie walked away with the sad realization he would never be able to reassemble the shattered pieces.

Col. Randolph Dreams On

Col. Randolph did not simply fade away at that point. Thanks in large part to his Secret Six work, he was given two titles during the Chicago Century of Progress Exposition—director of operations and maintenance and chief of police. The event, informally known as the World's Fair, drew millions of visitors to the Windy City between May 1933 and October 1934.[14]

Randolph was still speaking of his work with the Secret Six years after the group faded into ignominy. If anything, Randolph's boasts grew more outlandish and more detached from reality as time passed. Randolph, who once seemed to be posturing for a role as head of a national vigilante enterprise, had since the fall of the Secret Six turned his ambitions to global proportions. During a 1939 visit to New York City, for example, Randolph assured that the Secret Six was the best answer to shutting down the regimes of Adolf Hitler and Benito Mussolini. Both fascist governments, he said, "could be smashed by the same type of well-financed undercover work with which his organization undermined the rule of Al Capone."[15]

"Of course, Germany and Italy are gangster governments," Randolph told the *New York Times*. "It would be more risky organizing an anti-government group than it was to head an anti-crime organization, but I believe it would work."

Randolph's years-old dreams of leveraging his Chicago work into something nationwide were also persisting, the *Times* story indicated. "If we ever had a dictatorship in this country," he said, "I would want very strongly to head such a secret movement to restore democracy."

The *Times* refrained from asking Randolph why, if the Secret Six was such a good idea, it had lasted less than three years and had not been successfully emulated in any other city. And the newspaper let him claim, as publications universally have from that day forward, that the Secret Six brought down Capone: "Colonel Randolph recalled how the Secret Six . . . spent $350,000 in undercover activities—many of which he admitted were 'not exactly legal'—that led to the breaking of the gangster's grip on Cook County, Ill."

Randolph ran unsuccessfully for Congress as a Republican in 1938, and returned to the Army during World War II, rising to the rank of full colonel as a transportation officer at the Seattle Port of Embarkation. But in 1943, a decade after the fall of the vigilante force, he was still talking about the Secret Six, still recalling the time he met with Al Capone, still taking credit for bringing him down. And in a *Seattle Post-Intelligencer* article about Randolph's return to active duty, he was claiming a new achievement, saying the Secret Six "once saw to it that a ten-ton truck was driven through the front door of a brewery."[16]

Fourteen years later (see chapter 16), Eliot Ness would describe just such a truck in *The Untouchables*, the 1957 book he cowrote with Oscar Fraley. Although Ness gave much credit to the Secret Six for the founding of his federal anticrime team, the G-man made clear his many brewery raids were inspired by his team's intelligence alone. While it's possible the Secret Six provided the coordinates for at least one such raid, it's also quite possible the story of the ten-ton truck was another of Randolph's many embellishments.

And yet, after its demise, the spirit of the Secret Six reappeared now and then in actual crimefighting. In 1935, Alexander Jamie showed up in St. Paul, Minnesota. No longer claiming any Secret Six affiliation, he finally found the official corruption he'd spent years trying to uncover in Chicago. "St. Paul Police Ousted on Graft Charges," announced the headline at the top of the *Minneapolis Journal*'s front page on June 24, 1935. "Chief Among 3 Suspended; 4 Dismissed."

Allegations listed by the newspaper included "police ownership of slot machines," and nefarious connections among police officials, prostitutes, gamblers, and criminal lawyers. Among the findings, "a system whereby police officers tipped off gamblers and prostitutes of forthcoming raids."[17] The corruption had been uncovered over the previous year by Police Commissioner Ned Warren, using the era's highest crimefighting technology: Telephone lines had been tapped, and "conversations recorded on more than 400 phonograph records through the use of Dictaphones." Key to the voluminous evidence were "panograph machines, which make aluminum records of telephone conversations."

Who directed the investigation? Alexander Jamie, described in the article as "former chief of Chicago's 'Secret Six.'" And among Jamie's staff was at least one other former Secret Sixer, his son, Wallace Jamie. Fascinating as it might be, a complete accounting of all the things the Secret Six operatives, arrestees, and victims went on to do is beyond the scope of this book. A few of the more interesting denouements are worth mentioning, however.

Some Final Loose Ends

In late January 1933, a month after the guilty verdict and the $30,000 settlement in the William Kuhn false arrest case, the defendants filed a two-hundred-page appeal in which they asked for a new trial. The award was excessive, the brief declared, adding that "The court also erred . . . in not allowing the defense 'to show the general character of Kuhn in reference to his propensity for intoxicating liquors.'"[18]

A month later, Judge Peter Schwaba rejected the request for a new trial but proposed a reduction of the award to $20,000. Kuhn, surely motivated in part by a reluctance to suffer more hits to his reputation from the witness stand, agreed through his attorneys to the reduced amount, but that was still too much for the four guilty men, and they promised further appeals.[19]

The last entry in the case discoverable in the indexed press appeared in the *Chicago Tribune* on January 16, 1934, when an appellate court tossed out Kuhn's award altogether, absolved William Wright of any guilt, and proposed a new trial for Alexander Jamie and Edgar Dudley. (Watzek wasn't mentioned.) Most likely, Kuhn gave up at that point, the moral victory he'd scored against the disbanded vigilantes perhaps good enough.[20]

The self-exiles of William Kuhn and Marion Wright lasted no more than a year or two, after which both found love, albeit unevenly in Marion's case. Marion Wright returned to the United States from France, and in February 1936, got married to William Holabird Towne of Southern Pines, North Carolina. The ceremony was held in Summit, New Jersey.[21]

In November of that same year, William Kuhn was apparently done with the Wyoming dude ranch and married Carolyn Potter, daughter of a Connecticut banker. The ceremony, conducted in San Francisco, was presided over by California Superior Court Judge Sylvain Lazarus.[22]

Four years later, Marion Towne was living with her husband in Pasadena, California, according to the 1940 US Census. She had no children and reported three years of high school. She enlisted during World War II, serving in the Women's Army Corps as a medic. She and William divorced toward the end of the war, and soon after, while Marion was serving at Fort Oglethorpe in Georgia, William climbed to the top of Hollywood's tallest building to end his life with notable drama: "Hollywood Blvd. and Vine St. was chosen yesterday by William H. Towne, 37, former aircraft worker . . . as a scene for a suicide. Leaping from the roof of a 12-story building at the intersection, Towne plunged to his death on the roof of a one-story structure at the rear of the corner office building. On his person, police found a note . . . in which Towne stated that he had been contemplating his act for some time."[23]

Marion got married again, to James Walker, had two children, and died of cancer in Massachusetts in 1965. She was fifty-two.[24]

After 1933, nothing more appeared in the searchable press about her brush with the extortionist "Lester McKay," the Secret Six, or the "queer" but wrongly arrested paramour who sued her.

Did she keep one or two clippings from the hundreds published nationwide about her extortion and all that followed? Did she tell her children of the scandal or laugh over it when she got together with family and friends? Given the bitter way it ended, probably not. And with the difficulty in those days of uncovering news more than a day or two old, or from more than a city or two away, she and William Kuhn (who also died young, in his fifties) probably never knew the critical parts they played in a much bigger story, about a gang of decent men who succumbed to vigilantism, men whose fear, power, and money drove them mad.

Epilogue

Balance Sheet of the Secret Six

THIS BOOK is full of bad guys and would-be heroes who fell. But the true villain here is vigilantism, a beloved concept that in practice leads to disaster. "Nearly all men can stand adversity," goes the aphorism often misattributed to Abraham Lincoln. "To truly test a man's character, give him power."

No man, or woman either, probably, can survive the power that vigilantism bestows. Unanswerable to anything but one's own conscience, unconstrained by due process, jurisdictional boundaries, the law, or the Constitution itself, and fighting enemies who have been reduced—as everyone's enemies invariably are—to caricatures of simple and irredeemable evil, the question for every vigilantic endeavor is not if it will fail, but when.

But let us not reduce the Secret Six themselves to caricature. As indicated by the many accounts that live on, most of them were sincere, good people who wanted to improve Chicago. And often, they succeeded. A summary of what they got right is in order.

First and historically most important was their support of Eliot Ness and his Untouchables. In his book of the same name, Eliot Ness was having coffee with the Secret Six's Alexander Jamie when he came up with the idea for a band of unbribable, "untouchable" federal lawmen.[1]

"Suppose the Prohibition Bureau picked a small, select squad," Ness proposed with growing excitement. The dozen or so men would be "given a free hand" to crack down on Al Capone's liquor and vice empire and dry up the money he used to bribe cops and other officials.

Jamie, a former Prohibition agent himself before the Secret Six hired him as their top investigator, loved the idea. And he needed to be on board if it was going to see the light of day because, as Ness tells it in his book *The Untouchables*, only the Secret Six had the power to get Ness's plan off the ground.

"It sounds good, real good," said Jamie, whose wife was Ness's big sister. "I think I can get the Secret Six to back the idea. And if they do, it's as good as in the works."

As they finished their coffee in the quiet corner of a Chicago restaurant, Jamie promised to see if he could get Secret Six head Robert Randolph to support the plan. Several uncertain weeks passed before Ness was called into the office of George Emmerson Q. Johnson, United States Attorney for the Chicago area.

"I understand you're the one who came up with this plan for closing down Capone's breweries," Johnson said, "which has been brought to my attention by Robert Isham Randolph." So Randolph had also bought into the idea of a team of uncorruptible raiders and sold it to the feds. But who would lead it? Ness wondered.

"Frankly, I had several men in mind," Johnson told Ness, "but you were recommended highly to me by the Secret Six and also by your brother-in-law Alexander Jamie." Ness immediately accepted, of course, and became a legitimate American hero.

Adding to the good the Secret Six did are the individual cases where the vigilantes played a major role, and sometimes the only role:

- Theodore Kopelman kidnapping case (chapter 4)
- Congressman Oscar De Priest extortion case (chapter 8)
- Police shakedowns of Verner Daniels, the Black still owner (chapter 17)
- Plumbers Union corruption (chapter 17)
- The arrest of Montgomery Ward embezzler Edward Andell (chapter 17)
- The theft of gems from Lawrence F. Stern (chapter 17)
- The Daniel Serritella short-weighting scandal (chapter 18)
- Merchandise thefts from trucks (chapter 18)
- The "Indian ghost" gas station bombing (chapter 18)

- Story & Clark Piano Company tax fixing scheme (chapter 18)
- Jacob K. Karchmer milk fund charity scheme (chapter 18)
- $30,000 false check scheme (chapter 18)
- Beverly State Savings bank robbery (chapter 18)
- Arrest of bank robber James Morrison (chapter 18)
- Matt Kersch extortion (chapter 18)
- Roundup of the East St. Louis, Illinois kidnapping and robbing gang (chapter 20)
- Gustav Miller kidnapping (chapter 20)
- Norman Collins kidnapping (chapter 20)

Not all of these eighteen cases resulted in arrests, and some of the prison sentences were overturned, but in each case the Secret Six did solid detective work that the regular police couldn't or wouldn't do. Kidnapping victims were freed unharmed, further thefts were stopped, and perpetrators were in many cases at least called to account temporarily.

The Secret Six did not do nearly as much to bring down Al Capone as the legends report, but the vigilantes at least provided a distraction while the federal government did the real work of smashing Capone's empire and putting him in prison. Did they really put that critical witness on a South American cruise? The verdict that comes to us from the press of the day: maybe, but maybe not.

The Secret Six should also be praised as a progressive force. When a Black Congressman came to them for help with an extortion threat, they leapt to the job. When the Black operator of an illegal still complained of police shakedowns, they were on that case too. They never should have hired Shirley Kub, and her termination was at least a year late, but her marriage to a Black man—considered a disgrace in 1930s America—did not trouble the Secret Six at all. And Kub was not the only woman they hired. Recall that it was a woman detective, Florence Johnson, keeping meticulous financial records on Louis Karchmer's milk scheme—a demanding role, and not without its risks—and it was she who turned up as the star witness at his federal fraud trial.

Undoubtedly, there were other cases worked by the duly constituted authorities that wouldn't have happened without Secret Six involvement. They reported at one time that they were receiving tips by the bushelful, and some of those must have been passed on to the cops, leading to crackdowns and arrests without any mention of the Secret Six.

Overall, then, Chicago benefitted in many ways from the presence of the Secret Six. But the bigger a vigilante project is, the bigger are its foibles and mistakes, and the Secret Six racked them up:

- Taking false credit within months of their founding for the capture and sentencing of eight bombers. The offense here was creating the impression not just that the Secret Six was succeeding where it was not, but that the officially constituted authorities were failing where they were not.
- Claiming repeatedly to have found national kidnapping and bank robbing corporations, without evidence and without any corroboration from real law enforcement agencies. Spreading disinformation about crime helps no one but the criminals.
- Pointing repeatedly to nonexistent Chicago Police corruption, and corruption in State's Attorney John Swanson's office.
- The bungled Marion Wright extortion case and the resulting lawsuit by a justifiably aggrieved young man serve as a textbook example of how not to investigate a crime. They picked a possible suspect, ignored a wealth of exonerating evidence, and got hit with a $30,000 settlement. No money was ever paid, but the PR proved disastrous.
- The Lincoln National Bank bond deal with Gus Winkler is what happens when you decide to work in the gray areas of law enforcement. They got the bonds back, restored the savings of widows and the elderly, and kept several banks afloat, but cozying up to a gangster who obviously knew who the robbers were did such damage to the Secret Six's reputation that the vigilantes were forced to refute stories of the deal with a ridiculous lie.
- When Solomon Smith's wife opened an exploding package, he called the Secret Six. The Secret Six should have called the local police and the postal authorities, but the vigilantes kept the officials in the dark for weeks. That was their first mistake. The second was planting explosives in a public forest to catch the extorter. The third was not catching the extorter.
- At least once, they tortured a suspect to get the names of his fellow conspirators in the kidnapping of Dr. James Parker. Yes, their victim had essentially confessed to the crime, but what if they had

> less evidence next time? What if they had to turn their attention to potentially innocent people who *might* know something? What if every city decided to use that approach? Where would it have ended?

And then, where should the November 1930 pinochle raid fall (chapter 9)? Good or bad? Some of both, probably. The Secret Six had learned of the plan to rob the patrons of a West Loop café during pinochle night, and they told the cops. Unfortunately, according to press reports, the cops waited until the robbery was underway to break it up, shooting ensued, and Leonard Sanor was killed in the crossfire. Why did the cops wait? Did the Secret Six tell them to? Was this another Secret Six fiasco?

Of course, three thugs were put away, a fourth was seriously wounded, and their days of terrorizing Chicago's innocents were probably over. Like the Secret Six, then, the case of the pinochle raid was mixed, some good and some bad. But one of the marks of civilization has been steady, incremental refinements to the art and science of living together, keeping the good and winnowing away what isn't good. Vigilantism faded away because the good it can do comes at a price civilized people aren't willing to pay.

And so it went for the Secret Six. Hatched in the chaotic, gangster-infested nest of 1930s Chicago, cheered nationwide by those who saw hope in its model, the Secret Six took less than three years to destroy itself.

Today, the Windy City vigilantes live on as an odd paradox, remembered as heroes while no one proposes their resurrection. Civilization has, it seems, moved on.

ACKNOWLEDGMENTS

AS I BEGAN researching the Secret Six in earnest in 2023, the newspapers of the early 1930s became my current events. I would follow a particular story from start to finish, opening the ancient papers for the next chapter in the saga, as though it were all happening today. Over and over again, I would find myself stunned by the stories, the twists and turns of Shirley Kub's sordid life, Edgar Dudley's blundering in Chicago and Los Angeles, an Col. Randolph's inexorable descent info madness. Part of the delight in consuming outrageous news is discussing it around the water cooler, sharing the latest tidbits with family and friends, and waiting together for the next news drop, but those joys weren't available as I studied the Secret Six. Fresh news to me meant nothing to anyone else.

But I had to tell someone. So my wife, Michelle Andra, became my sole sounding board, the only person who understood my project well enough to appreciate my daily reports of the latest Shirley Kub indiscretion, the latest development in the campaign to launch a nationwide Secret Six, Edgar Dudley's apparent seduction of a sixteen-year-old girl. Michelle, holder of a PhD in psychology, did more than listen. The story of the Secret Six is, ultimately, a story about human psychology, and her insights into human nature were vital to this effort. She was perhaps not as surprised as I by some of the foibles I uncovered, given that they sprang from pathologies psychologists study thoroughly. Asked to evaluate Shirley Kub, she offered an unofficial diagnosis: antisocial.

So thank you, Michelle, for making the solitary job of writing historic nonfiction a little less lonely.

Also, a word of thanks to the librarians of the Chicago History Museum, particularly the staff of the Abakanowicz Research Center, where special collections are kept. I had set aside two days in September 2023 to go through Col. Robert Randolph's voluminous files at the Center, viewing a long reel of microfilm page by page, scanning what I needed, and saving it to a thumb drive. When my drive failed on my first day there, they loaned me one of their own drives and followed up by emailing me my files, both courtesies above and beyond their job description.

NOTES

Introduction

1. "Capone Ready to Give Up Racketeering. . . . Gives Credit to Secret Six for Stopping Crime Wave," *Orlando (FL) Evening Star,* July 30, 1931, 1.

Chapter 1: The Case of the Extorted Debutante

1. "Debutante to Help Investigators of Letters Threatening Life and Demanding $25,000," *Cincinnati (OH) Enquirer,* December 12, 1930, 1, 6.
2. "Debutante to Help Investigators of Letters Threatening Life and Demanding $25,000," *Cincinnati (OH)Enquirer,* December 12, 1930, 1, 6.
3. "Debutante to Help Investigators of Letters Threatening Life and Demanding $25,000," *Cincinnati (OH) Enquirer,* December 12, 1930, 1, 6; second source, with more accurate spelling and punctuation: "Delay Extortion Hearing as Girl Makes Her Debut," *Chicago Tribune,* December 11, 1930, 9.
4. "Debutante to Help Investigators of Letters Threatening Life and Demanding $25,000," *Cincinnati (OH) Enquirer,* December 12, 1930, 1, 6.
5. "Tells Secret 6 Clews in Suit for $100,000," *Chicago Tribune,* November 17, 1932, 1, 6.
6. "Blackmail Note of Boy, 13, Gives Cops a Surprise," *Chicago Tribune,* November 16, 1932, 1.
7. "Home Bombed in Kidnap Case," *South Bend (IN) Tribune,* December 21, 1931, 2.
8. "Bombing Seen in Old Scheme; Blast That Damages Mansion May Be Move of Kidnaping 'Gang,'" *Newark (OH) Advocate,* December 21, 1931, 2.
9. "Mailed Bomb Perils Wife of Solomon Smith," *Chicago Tribune,* December 2, 1932, 1.

10. "Decision Near in Kuhn Suit; Girl Testifies," *Chicago Tribune,* December 1, 1931, 1, 8.

11. "Decision Near in Kuhn Suit; Girl Testifies," *Chicago Tribune,* December 1, 1932, 1, 8.

Chapter 2: A City on Fire

1. "No Federal Mop for Chicago's Crime Wave," *The Literary Digest,* March 20, 1926, 7, 8.

2. "Row Gets into Senate; Crowe Strikes Back," *Chicago Tribune,* February 28, 1926, 1.

3. "Chicago Murder Rate Cut; Other Cities Show Rise," *Chicago Tribune,* December 2, 1932, 18.

4. Jeffrey A. Miron and Jeffrey Zweibel, "Alcohol Consumption During Prohibition," Working Paper No. 3675, (National Bureau of Economic Research, April 1991).

5. See for example: "What is Al Capone's Net Worth?," *Market Realist,* September 2023, https://marketrealist.com/what-is-al-capones-net-worth/.

6. See for example: "Prohibition Profits Transformed the Mob," *Prohibition: An Interactive History, Mob Museum,* September 2023, https://prohibition.themobmuseum.org/the-history/the-rise-of-organized-crime/the-mob-during-prohibition/.

7. "Says Capone's $150,000 Is Backing Thompson; Judge Kyle Puts at $50,000 the Gangster's Contribution in Fight of 1927," *New York Times,* February 17, 1931, 4.

8. "Slay Doctor in Massacre," *Chicago Tribune,* February 15, 1929, 1, 2.

Chapter 3: The Tenth Man

1. "Tenth Man is Shot in Chicago Streets," *Miami (FL) Herald.* February 6, 1930, 3.

2. "U. of C. Shooting Puts Business on Gangs' Trail," *Chicago Tribune,* February 6, 1930, 3.

3. Forrest Crissey, "Business Fights Crime in Chicago," *Saturday Evening Post,* August 16, 1930, 12.

4. "Reward in C. A. C. Crime Wave," *Chicago Daily News,* February 7, 1930, 1.

5. "Raids by Police To Harass Gangs Out of Chicago," *Chicago Tribune,* February 8, 1930, 4.

6. "Business to Start War on Gangs Today," *Chicago Daily News,* February 7, 1930, 1.

7. "Chicago Crime War Is Revived; Business Men Start Campaign Of Their Own To Stop Killings," *Arizona Daily Star,* February 8, 1930, 4.

8. "Resolution Adopted by Executive Committee Offering $5,000 Reward in One Case; Committee of Six Appointed by Col. Randolph to Make Study of

Problem," *Chicago Commerce* (a publication of the Chicago Association of Commerce), February 15, 1930, 1.

9. "Raids by Police to Harass Gangs Out of Chicago," *Chicago Tribune*, February 8, 1930, 4.

10. "Catch Suspect in Shooting on U. of. C. Campus," *Chicago Tribune*, February 9, 1930, 10.

11. "Police Snatch Suspects from Boxing Bouts," *Chicago Tribune*, February 8, 1930, 1.

12. "Chicago Sweeps 915 Into Jail; Police Speed on Haunts of Underworld," *Minneapolis Tribune*, February 10, 1930, 1.

13. "Hail Gang Who's Who as Crime-War Guide," *Chicago Daily News*, February 8, 1930, 1.

14. As reported here: "Chicago Turns on Gunmen; Threaten Vigilante Action; Daily Paper Prints Names and Addresses of Gangsters," *Sault (Sault Ste. Marie, Ontario) Star.* March 13, 1930, 2.

15. "Gun Toters Up to Swanson; 917 Are Seized in Crime Raids: Records on 271; Grand Jury Action to be Demanded," *Chicago Tribune*, February 10, 1930, 1.

16. "917 Are Seized in Crime Raids; Records on 271; Grand Jury Action To Be Demanded," *Chicago Tribune*, February 10, 1930, 1, 2.

17. "Chicago Sweeps 915 Into Jail; Police Speed on Haunts of Underworld," *Minneapolis (MN) Tribune*, February 10, 1930, 1.

18. "1,100 More Jailed in Chicago; War Against Gunmen Cuts Holdup Wave," *Minneapolis (MN) Tribune*, February 17, 1930, 1.

19. "Police Snatch Suspects from Boxing Bouts," *Chicago Tribune*, February 8, 1930, 1.

20. "Gun Toters Up to Swanson; 917 Are Seized in Crime Raids: Records on 271; Grand Jury Action to be Demanded," *Chicago Tribune*, February 10, 1930, 1.

21. "All Cells Filled by Chicago Raids," *Reading (PA) Times*, February 17, 1930, 7.

22. "1,100 More Jailed in Chicago; War Against Gunmen Cuts Holdup Wave," *Minneapolis (MN) Tribune*, February 17, 1930, 1.

23. "Harried Gangsters Employ Lawyers in War against Court," *Bismarck (ND) Tribune*, February 12, 1930.

24. "Chicago Sweeps 915 Into Jail; Police Speed on Haunts of Underworld," *Minneapolis (MN) Tribune*, February 10, 1930, 1.

25. "Tells of Chicago Racketeer System; Chief of Vigilantes Amazed at Gangsters' Grip on Business World; City Politics Involved; Two More Bombings Bring Year's Total to 13 As Police Continue Theatrical Round-Up," *Baltimore (MD) Sun*, February 13, 1930, 1.

26. "1,100 More Jailed in Chicago; War against Gunmen Cuts Holdup Wave," *Minneapolis (MN) Tribune*, February 17, 1930, 1.

27. “Chicago Citizens Open War on Crime; Business Group Assails Officials and Begins Drive To End Reign of Violence” *New York Times*, February 8, 1930, 32.

28. Vigilance Committee Is Likely Development in City of Chicago; Business Men Feel They Should Organize Among The Same Lines as The Gangsters If They Expect To Clean Up City,” *Richmond (IN) Item*, February 11, 1930, 4.

29. “Editorials: Direct Action,” *Herald and Review* (Decatur, IL), February 10, 1930.

30. “Secrecy to Mark Crime Fight Thru C. A. C. Committee; Col. Randolph Chooses 6 ‘Men of Courage’ to Conduct Move,” *Chicago Evening Post*, February 8, 1930, 1.

31. “Secrecy to Mark Crime Fight Thru C. A. C. Committee; Col. Randolph Chooses 6 ‘Men of Courage’ to Conduct Move,” *Chicago Evening Post*, February 8, 1930, 1.

32. “Vigilante Band Aims To Curb Chicago Crime; Association of Commerce Adopts Frontier Enforcement Tactics; Leaders Described as Secret Sextet,” *Baltimore (MD) Sun*, February 9, 1930, 1.

33. “‘Secret Six’ Open Warfare on Rackets as Crime Cure,” *Chicago Tribune*, February 22, 1930, p. 2.

34. “‘Secret 6’ Opens War on Rackets as Crime Cure,” *Kansas City (MO) American*, February 27, 1930, 3.

35. “Secrecy to Mark Crime Fight Thru C. A. C. Committee; Col. Randolph Chooses 6 ‘Men of Courage’ to Conduct Move,” *Chicago Evening Post*, February 8, 1930, 1.

36. “‘Secret Six’ Speed War on Crime,” *Chicago American*, February 8, 1930, 1, 2.

37. “Raids by Police to Harass Gangs Out of Chicago,” *Chicago Tribune*. February 8, 1930, 4.

38. “Reward in C. A. C. Crime Wave,” *Chicago Daily News*, February 7, 1930, 1.

Chapter 4: A Burning City Sparks a Nation’s Hope

1. “Col. R. I. Randolph, Retired Engineer” (obituary), *New York Times*, October 25, 1951.

2. Clem Lane, “Col. Randolph Right Man for Difficult Job; Fitted by Training to Head Secret Committee to War on Crime,” *Chicago Daily News*, February 10, 1930, 1.

3. Lane, “Col. Randolph Right Man for Difficult Job,” 1.

4. “Vigilantes Determined to Rid Chicago of Crime, Says Leader,” *Baltimore Sun*, February 11, 1930, 1.

5. Lane, “Col. Randolph Right Man for Difficult Job,” 1.

6. “Chicago Plans Gigantic Drive Against Crime; Form ‘Secret Six’ Committee to Employ Investigators in Same Manner as Army Espionage,” *Journal and Courier* (LaFayette, IN), February 20, 1930, 1.

7. W. A. S Douglas, "Tribute Money is Diverted to War on Crime," *Baltimore Sun*, February 21, 1930, 1.

8. "'Secret 6' Opens War on Rackets As Crime Cure," *Kansas City American*, February 27, 1930, 3.

9. "Vigilantes Determined to Rid Chicago of Crime, Says Leader," *Baltimore Sun*, February 11, 1930, 1.

10. "Tells of Chicago Racketeer System; Chief of Vigilantes Amazed at Gangsters' Grip on Business World; City Politics Involved; Two More Bombings Bring Year's Total to 13 as Police Continue Theatrical Round-Up," *Baltimore Sun*, February 13, 1930, 1.

11. Douglas, "Tribute Money is Diverted to War on Crime," 1.

12. See, for example, "Group Ready for Crime War; 'Secret Six' Favors Equal Treatment for 'Higher-Up' and Thugs," *Courier-Journal (Louisville, KY)*, February 22, 1930, 1–2.

13. See, for example, "'Millions for Prosecution; Not One Cent for Tribute,' Declares Chicago Business to Gangsters," *Fort Collins Coloradoan*, February 21, 1930, 1.

14. "Racketeers Cost $45 Per Citizen, Chicagoan Says; Secret Six Committee to Submit Plan Today to Free City of Menace," *Minneapolis Tribune*, February 21, 1930, 13.

15. Chicago Police Department, "Annual Report, 1930," 10, 12.

16. Oscar Hewitt, "Keep Payrollers; Fire Cops; Aldermen Get Auto Cash, But Police Must Go," *Chicago Tribune*, December 21, 1929, 1–2.

17. "Millionaires War on Crime," *Knoxville (Kentucky) Journal*, February 21, 1930, 1.

18. "Would Purge Chicago of Crime in 6 Months; Secret Committee Head Fixes This Objective of His Group; Big Fund Available," *Omaha World-Herald*, February 28, 1930, 4.

19. Douglas, "Tribute Money is Diverted to War on Crime," 1.

20. "Racketeers Cost $45 Per Citizen, Chicagoan Says; Secret Six Committee to Submit Plan Today to Free City of Menace," *Minneapolis Tribune*, February 21, 1930, 13.

21. "'Secret Six' Open Warfare on Rackets as Crime Cure," *Chicago Tribune*, February 22, 1930, 2.

22. "Citizen Corps for Crime War Nearly Ready; Randolph Due to Name His Board of 100 Tomorrow," *Chicago Tribune*, February 23, 1930, 6.

23. See, for example, "'Crimeless Chicago in Six Months,' Cry of Law Committee," *Selma (AL) Times-Journal*, February 28, 1930, 3.

24. "Racketeers Cost $45 Per Citizen, Chicagoan Says; Secret Six Committee to Submit Plan Today to Free City of Menace," *Minneapolis Tribune*, February 21, 1930, 13.

25. "Citizen Corps for Crime War Nearly Ready; Randolph Due to Name His Board of 100 Tomorrow," *Chicago Tribune*, February 23, 1930, 6.

26. See, for example, "Millions for Prosecution of Chicago Gangs; 'But Not a Cent for Tribute' City's Answer to Racketeer Encroachment," *Lewiston Evening Journal*, February 21, 1930, 1.

27. "Chicago Police Now Hunt Higher-Ups in Gangland," *Baltimore Sun*, February 21, 1930, 1.

28. "Citizen Corps for Crime War Nearly Ready; Randolph Due to Name His Board of 100 Tomorrow," *Chicago Tribune*, February 23, 1930, 6.

29. "Chicago Plans Gigantic Drive Against Crime," 1.

30. See, for example, "Group Ready for Crime War," 1–2.

31. "Citizens Declare Big Battle on Chicago Gangland," *Evening Times* (Sayre, Pennsylvania), March 10, 1930, 5.

32. See, for example, "'Crimeless Chicago in Six Months," 3.

33. "Thousands of Items Printed Throughout Country Telling of Association Stand for Clearing Out Gangsters," *Chicago Commerce* (publication of the Chicago Association of Commerce), February 22, 1930.

34. Pierre John Huss, International News Service. "'Secret Six' Starts War on Chicago Underworld," *New Castle (PA) News*, March 10, 1930, 1.

35. "Prosecute Gunmen Under Law Against Concealed Weapons," *Chicago Herald and Examiner*, February 11, 1930.

36. See, for example, "The Secret Six," *Montana Standard*, March 8, 1930, 6.

37. See, for example, "Private War on Crime," *Daily Inter-Lake (Kalispell, MT)*, March 5, 1930, 4.

38. See, for example, *Kokomo (IN) Tribune*, March 5, 1930, 4.

39. "Civil War," *Anaheim (CA) Bulletin*, March 29, 1930, 4.

40. See, for example, "Head of 'Secret Six' Denies Vigilante Aim," *Miami News-Record*, March 5, 1930, 1.

41. "Girl Confesses Kidnappings; Women and 5 Men Are Indicted as Extortionists; Secret Six Act; Blonde's Story Starts 5 on Way to Chair," *Chicago Herald and Examiner*, March 11, 1930, 1.

42. "Kidnaper and 585 Other Prisoners Seeking Paroles," *Chicago Tribune*, September 23, 1939, 9.

43. "Woman Bares $28,000 'Jobs' of Kidnap Ring; Swanson Promises a Speedy Trial for 5 Men and Feminine Aid," *Chicago Daily News*, March 11, 1930.

44. See, for example, "Chicago 'Secret Six' Breaks Up Crime Ring," *Montreal Star*, March 11, 1930, 9.

45. "Make Ransom an 'Andsome' Racket," *Daily News* (New York), March 11, 1930, 194.

46. "Woman Bares $28,000 'Jobs' of Kidnap Ring."

47. "Women Clash as 5 are Indicted for Kidnaping," *Chicago Tribune*, March 11, 1930, 5.

48. "Women Clash as 5 are Indicted for Kidnaping," 5.

Chapter 5: Early Impact (and a Little Lying)

1. See, for example, "Defense fund Believed Under Way to Fight Work of 'Secret Six,'" *Newark Advocate*, March 25, 1930, 1.

2. "Kidnap Gang Gets 20 Years," *Chicago Herald and Examiner*, June 6, 1930, 1.

3. "Tell of Queer 'Kidnap' Plot," *Vidette-Messenger of Porter County*, June 7, 1930, 4.

4. C. Roy Greenaway, "Businessmen Organize Vigilance Committee to End Terror Reign . . . Has Already Sent Seven to Prison and Struck Terror to Other Thugs," *The Toronto Star*, April 10, 1930, 1.

5. "Head of Chicago's 'Secret Six' Tells of Progress Being Made in Suppression of Crime; Says Gangsters Are Losing Grip," *Des Moines (IA) Tribune*, March 27, 1930, 36.

6. "'Secret Six' Fights Rackets in Chicago," *Reading (PA) Times*, April 3, 1930, 3.

7. Edwin Balmer, "Drama Goal of Gangster," *Los Angeles Times*, June 16, 1930, 1.

8. "Trapped As He Sets Bomb; Police Seize Dynamiter at Door of Café," *Chicago Tribune*, May 19, 1930, 1.

9. "Speedy Trial Sents Bomber to Penitentiary," *Chicago Tribune*, May 23, 1930, 21.

10. "Labor Trouble Suspected in Factory Bomb," *Chicago Tribune*, December 28, 1930, 7.

11. Owen L. Scott, Consolidated Press Association, "New Psychology in Crime Battle," *Altoona (PA) Mirror*, April 4, 1930, 29.

12. "Head of Chicago's 'Secret Six' Tells of Progress Being Made in Suppression of Crime; Says Gangsters Are Losing Grip," *Des Moines (IA) Tribune*, March 27, 1930, 36.

Chapter 6: The Truth of the Secret Six

1. Roy C. Greenaway, "'Secret Six' Wars on Chicago Gangsters," *The Toronto Daily Star*, April 10, 1930, 1, 2.

2. "Big Bill Files $1,000,000 Suit in Radio Ban," *Baltimore (MD) Sun*, December 23, 1930, 1.

3. Edwin Balmer, "Killers Aim at Drama" *Los Angeles Times*, June 16, 1930, 1, 2.

4. "Gang Foe Describes Chicago's Warfare; How 'Secret Six' Started Own Bootleg 'Joint' to Trap Capone Related in Tokyo," *Japan Advertiser*, March 3, 1934.

5. Norton Rosengarten, "Colonel's Committee Ran a Speakeasy as Bait To Trap Chicago's Gangsters," *Memphis (TN) Press-Scimitar,* date uncertain, probably mid-1930s.

6. "Judge Issues Dry Law Writs Against 51 Places," *Chicago Tribune,* June 21, 1932, 11; "Dry Agents Seize Liquor in Raids on Two Cafes," *Chicago Tribune,* December 15, 1930, 8.

Chapter 7: Shooting in the Dark

1. "Find Third Victim of Gang Shooting in Washington Square," *Chicago Tribune,* June 2, 1930, 2.

2. Frederick C. Othman, "Chicago Gangs Slaughter Six More . . . Outbreak Thought Result of City's Effort to Oust Racketeers," *Birmingham (AL) Post-Herald,* June 2, 1930, 1, 2.

3. "War over Rural Beer; Kill 3," *Chicago Tribune,* June 2, 1930, 1, 2.

4. "Offers New Theory for Lingle Killing," *New York Times,* July 7, 1930, 4.

5. Diana Dretske, "Gangsters Bring Prohibition Violence to Fox Lake," Dunn Museum online article, accessed February 24, 2024, https://lakecountyhistory.blogspot.com/2011/10/.

6. "Crime Board Asks Exile of Gang Leaders," *Chicago Tribune,* April 24, 1930, 1, 8.

7. "Names of 28 Are Given to Police," *Hamilton (Canada) Spectator,* April 24, 1930, 17.

8. "Al Capone Murder Hazard of Tom Thumb Racketeers," *Daily News* (New York), September 1, 1930, 293.

9. "Racketeer Bait Hooks Business, Employers Told," *Chicago Tribune,* September 3, 1930, 8.

10. "Swanson Acts on M'Goorty's Call to Battle; All Agencies To Join to Protect Public," *Chicago Tribune,* September 10, 1930, 1.

Chapter 8: The Case of the Extorted Congressman

1. Biographical Directory of US Congress, s.v. "Oscar Stanton De Priest," accessed March 2024, https://bioguideretro.congress.gov/Home/MemberDetails?memIndex=D000263.

2. "City Goes Republican," *Suburbanite Economist (Chicago),* April 9, 1915, 1.

3. Encyclopedia of Chicago, s.v. "Oscar DePriest" by Charles Branham, "Oscar DePriest," accessed March 2024, http://www.encyclopedia.chicagohistory.org/pages/2402.html.

4. "Chicago Elected Negro to Congress; Oscar DePriest Chosen in Martin B. Madden's Old District," *Edwardsville (IL) Intelligencer,* November 9, 1938, 10.

5. Annette B. Dunlap, "Tea and Equality; The Hoover Administration and the DePriest Incident." *Prologue*, Summer 2015, 16.

6. "Trap $10,000 De Priest Extortionists; Two Captured As Police Trail Plot Collector," *Chicago Tribune*, September 14, 1930, 1, 2.

7. "Forger Sought as Brains of De Priest Plot; Police Suspect Moshiek in Extortion Attempt," *Chicago Tribune*, September 15, 1930, 3.

8. "Trap $10,000 De Priest Extortionists; Two Captured as Police Trail Plot Collector," *Chicago Tribune*, September 14, 1930, 1, 2.

9. "De Priest Extortionist Gets Off Light," *Birmingham (AL) Reporter*, June 20, 1931, 1, 4.

10. "Pleads Guilty to Conspiracy Today," *Dixon (IL) Evening Telegraph*, June 11, 1931, 1.

11. "Chicago's 'Secret Six' Fights Fire with Fire, Says Colonel Randolph," *Rochester (NY) Democrat and Chronicle*, October 15, 1931, 20.

12. Biographical Directory of US Congress, s.v. "Oscar Stanton De Priest," accessed March 2024, https://bioguideretro.congress.gov/Home/MemberDetails?memIndex=D000263.

13. "Secret Six Seizes Two as Plotters," *Chicago Herald and Examiner*, October 24, 1930.

Chapter 9: The New Top Cop, and the Case of the Pinochle Shootout

1. "U. S. To Help Smash Chicago Gangs; Federal Men Concentrate in Chicago," *Belvidere (IL) Daily Republican*, November 20, 1930, 1.

2. "Jamie Named to Aid 'Secret Six' in Crime Drive," *Chicago Tribune*, October 31, 1930, 3.

3. "Law Enforcement Units in Chicago Area Plan to Join; Vollmer, Police Expert, Tells Officials Crime Now Is Problem of Districts," *Minneapolis (MN) Journal*, November 20, 1930, 17.

4. "U. S. Dry Agent Is New Investigator for 'Secret Six'," *Belleville (IL) News-Democrat*, October 31, 1930, 2.

5. Lemuel F. Parton, "Who's News Today." *Rock Island (IL) Argus*, January 8, 1932, 10.

6. "Capone's Brother among 18 Indicted," *Democrat and Chronicle* (Rochester, NY), December 13, 1930, 4.

7. W. F. Peterson, "New Leader in Chicago's War on Crime," *Journal Gazette (Mattoon, IL)*, November 1, 1930, 1.

8. "Customer Caught in Crossfire of Bullets, Slain," *Minneapolis (MN) Journal*, November 30, 1930, 4.

9. "1 Slain in Bandit Battle; Seize Four," *Chicago Tribune*, November 30, 1930, 1, 2.

10. "Seizes 2 Killers in Café Holdup; Wins Hero Prize; Policeman Tyrrell Gets $100 Tribune Award," *Chicago Tribune*, December 21, 1930, 6.

Chapter 10: The Case of the Queer Actor

1. "Girl's Father Takes Stand in $100,000 Suit: Wright Defends His Acts in Kuhn Case," November 30, 1932, *Chicago Tribune*, 5.

2. Kathleen McLaughlin, "Father Accused in $100,000 Suit Blames Secret 6: Steel Magnate Tells Story of Extortion Arrest," *Chicago Tribune*, November 18, 1932, 3.

3. "Police Officer Takes Blame for Kuhn's Arrest: Lieutenant is Witness in $100,000 Suit," *Chicago Tribune*, November 23, 1932, 7.

4. "Delay Extortion Hearing as Girl Makes Her Debut: Signs Complaint Against Kuhn, Goes to Party," *Chicago Tribune*, December 11, 1930, 9.

5. "Rich Youth is Accused: Wealthy Young Chicago Man Faces Lyle on Serious Charge," *Daily Chronicle* (DeKalb, IL), December 10, 1930, 1, 8.

6. "Girl and Dad Fight Youth's $100,000 Suit," *Chicago Tribune*, November 16, 1932, 1.

7. "Decision Near in Kuhn Suit; Girl Testifies," *Chicago Tribune*, December 1, 1932, 1, 8.

8. "Kuhn Suit Near Decision; Girl Tells Her Story; Marion Wright Is Final Defense Witness," *Chicago Tribune*, December 10, 1930, December 1, 1932, 8.

9. "Kuhn Suit Near Decision; Girl Tells Her Story; Marion Wright Is Final Defense Witness," *Chicago Tribune*, December 10, 1932, December 1, 1932, 8.

10. "Girl and Dad Fight Youth's $100,000 Suit," *Chicago Tribune*, November 16, 1932, 1.

11. "Rich Youth is Accused: Wealthy Young Chicago Man Faces Lyle on Serious Charge," *Daily Chronicle* (DeKalb, IL), December 10, 1930, 1, 8.

12. "Missing Sleuth Surprises Court in Kuhn Suit: Defendant Dudley Appears to Testify," *Chicago Tribune*, November 29, 1932, 7.

13. "Rich Youth is Accused: Wealthy Young Chicago Man Faces Lyle on Serious Charge," *The Daily Chronicle* (DeKalb, IL), December 10, 1930, 1, 8.

14. Kathleen McLaughlin, "Father Accused in $100,000 Suit Blames Secret 6: Steel Magnate Tells Story of Extortion Arrest," *Chicago Tribune*, November 18, 1932, 3.

15. "Gets Verdict of $30,000 Damages on False Arrest: Man Sues Steel Magnate and Members of Chicago Secret Six When Their Case Fails," *Belleville (IL) Daily Advocate*, December 3, 1932, 3.

16. "Rich Youth is Accused: Wealthy Young Chicago Man Faces Lyle on Serious Charge," *The Daily Chronicle* (DeKalb, IL), December 10, 1930, 1, 8.

17. "Missing Sleuth Surprises Court in Kuhn Suit: Defendant Dudley Appears to Testify," *Chicago Tribune*, November 29, 1932, 7.

18. "Decision Near in Kuhn Suit; Girl Testifies," *Chicago Tribune,* December 1, 1932, 1, 8.

19. "Seize Youth in Society Extortion Plot: Death Threats to Debutante Ask $25,000," *Chicago Tribune,* December 10, 1930, 1.

20. "Tells Secret 6 Clews in Suite for $100,000," *Chicago Tribune,* November 17, 1932, 1, 6.

21. "Debutante To Help Investigators; Of Letters Threatening Life and Demanding $25,000. Chicago Broker's Assistant Trapped by Typewriter Identity—Poison Darts Conan Doyle Idea." *Cincinnati (OH) Enquirer,* December 12, 1930, 1, 6.

22. "Girl and Dad Fight Youth's $100,000 Suit," *Chicago Tribune,* November 16, 1932, 1.

23. "Capitalist's Son Falsely Held 2 Months; William Kuhn Seeks $100,000 Redress for Arrest in Threats Against Chicago Debutante," *San Francisco Examiner,* February 7, 1931, 17.

24. "Expert Tells of Lie Detector Test on Kuhn: Ex-Prosecutor a Witness for Defense in Suit," *Chicago Tribune,* November 22, 1932, 8.

25. "'Lie Detector' Test to Combat False Arrest Claims," *Herald and Review* (Decatur, Illinois), November 22, 1932, 1.

26. Katheen McLaughlin, "Father Accused in $100,000 Suit Blames Secret 6: Steel Magnate Tells Story of Extortion Arrest," *Chicago Tribune,* November 18, 1932, 3.

Chapter 11: The Passion of William Speer Kuhn Jr.

1. "Police Officer Takes Blame for Kuhn's Arrest: Lieutenant is Witness in $100,000 Suit," *Chicago Tribune,* November 23, 1932, 7.

2. "Story of Kuhn Evidence Told by Policeman: Quizzed by Lawyer in $100,000 Suit," *Chicago Tribune,* November 24, 1932, 27.

3. Brooks campaign ad, *Champaign and Urbana Citizen,* March 18, 1932, 4.

4. Kathleen McLaughlin, "Father Accused in $100,000 Suit Blames Secret 6: Steel Magnate Tells Story of Extortion Arrest," *Chicago Tribune,* November 18, 1932, 3.

5. "Decision Near in Kuhn Suit; Girl Testifies," *Chicago Tribune,* December 1, 1932, 1, 8.

6. Kathleen McLaughlin, "Father Accused in $100,000 Suit Blames Secret 6: Steel Magnate Tells Story of Extortion Arrest," *Chicago Tribune,* November 18, 1932, 3.

7. "Expert Tells of Lie Detector Test on Kuhn: Ex-Prosecutor a Witness for Defense in Suit," *Chicago Tribune,* November 22, 1932, 8.

8. "Decision Near in Kuhn Suit; Girl Testifies," *Chicago Tribune,* December 1, 1932, 1, 8.

9. "Delay Extortion Hearing as Girl Makes Her Debut: Signs Complaint Against Kuhn, Goes to Party," *Chicago Tribune,* December 11, 1930, 9.

10. "Rich Youth is Accused: Wealthy Young Chicago Man Faces Lyle on Serious Charge," *Daily Chronicle* (DeKalb, IL), December 10, 1930, 1, 8.

11. See, for example, "Deb in Blackmail Plot," *The Sandusky (OH) Register*, December 12, 1930, 14.

12. "Kuhn Hearing in Threat Case Set for Jan. 14," *Chicago Tribune*, December 12, 1930, 6.

13. "Debutante To Help Investigators; Of Letters Threatening Life and Demanding $25,000. Chicago Broker's Assistant Trapped by Typewriter Identity—Poison Darts Conan Doyle Idea," *Cincinnati (OH) Enquirer*, December 12, 1930, 1, 6.

14. "Bare Extortion Plot Against Society Girl; Attempt to Obtain $25,000 From Debutante Daughter of Steel Company Official Savors of Oriental Mystery Thriller," *Tacoma (WA) Daily Leger*, December 10, 1930, 1.

Chapter 12: Nolle Prossed

1. "Extortion Suspect in Love, Judge Thinks," *Los Angeles Times*, January 13, 1931, 18.

2. "Youth Accused of Society Plot May Get Probation," *Chicago Tribune*, January 15, 1931, 6.

3. "Freed in Society Plot; Sues Girl and Secret Six: Kuhn Demands $100,000 for False Arrest," *Chicago Tribune*, January 22, 1931, 7.

4. "'Poison Dart' Suspect Freed: William Kuhn Says He Will Sue Girl and Father for Charging Extortion Plot," *Charlotte (NC) News*, January 22, 1931, 13.

5. "Tells Secret 6 Clews in Suite for $100,000," *Chicago Tribune*, November 17, 1932, 1, 6.

6. "Freed in Society Plot; Sues Girl and Secret Six: Kuhn Demands $100,000 for False Arrest," *Chicago Tribune*, January 22, 1931, 7.

7. "End of Secret 6 Seen; Setbacks Hit Spy Service," *Chicago Tribune*, December 5, 1932, 3.

8. "Freed in Society Plot; Sues Girl and Secret Six: Kuhn Demands $100,000 for False Arrest," *Chicago Tribune*, January 22, 1931, 7.

9. W. A. S. Douglas, "Three of Chicago's Secret Six Are Sued For $100,000 Damages," *Baltimore Sun*, January 22, 1931, 1.

10. "Capitalist's Son Falsely Held 2 Months; William Kuhn Seeks $100,000 Redress for Arrest in Threats against Chicago Debutante," *San Francisco Examiner*, February 7, 1931, 17.

11. "S. M. Boy Fights Chicago Big 6," *San Mateo (CA) Times*, February 7, 1931, 1.

Chapter 13: Al Capone Comes Home

1. Robert T. Loughman, "Capone Faces New Troubles upon Release; Once Profitable 'Rackets' No Longer Lucrative for Gang Leader; 'Secret Six' Will Watch Every Move; Federal Government Still Curious about Income Tax Payments," *Pittsburgh (PA) Press*, March 16, 1930, 2.

2. William Lawson, "Capone Speeds for Chicago; Warden Spirits Gangster Out; Causes Uproar," *Chicago Tribune*, March 18, 1930, 1.

3. Genevieve Forbes Herrick, "Capone's Story: By Himself; 'Just a Big Beer Man; The Best People Buy It. He Gives Self Up; Warned from City," *Chicago Tribune*, March 22, 1930, 1–2.

4. Robert Loughran, "Capone to Seek U.S. Protection While in Miami," *Miami (FL) News*, March 23, 1930, 1.

5. James Doherty, "Warned from Chicago," *Chicago Tribune*, March 22, 1930, 2.

6. "Capone Takes Stock among His Henchmen." *Miami (FL) Herald*, March 23, 1930, 8.

Chapter 14: Al Capone Goes South

1. Joe Hutchison, "Al Capone's $31 million Prohibition-era Miami Beach Mansion is Demolished Despite 26,000 People Signing a Petition To Save It." *Daily Mail (London, UK)*, August 15, 2023.

2. Casey Piket, "Villa 93 on Palm Island," Miami-History.com, September 16, 2021, http://www.miami-history.com/p/villa-93-on-palm-island.

3. "Al Capone's Florida Home Heads for Wrecking Ball!" TopTenRealEstateDeals.com, July 2023, http://toptenrealestatedeals.com/weekly-ten-best-home-deals/home/al-capones-florida-home-heads-for-wrecking-ball.

4. "Two Brothers of Al Capone Are Held Here; Arrests Follow Raid on Palm Island Residence; Liquor is Seized," *Miami (FL)Herald*, March 21, 1930, 1.

5. See, for example, "Capone and Three Pals are Nabbed," *Wichita (KS) Eagle*, May 9, 1930, 1.

6. "Ritter Tells Capone He May Come to Miami; U. S. Judge Issues Order Invalidating Carlton's Edict to Sheriffs," *Miami (FL) Herald*, March 23, 1930, 1, 8.

7. "Mailed Fist of Florida Law Closes in Upon 'Al' Capone As He Heads Toward Home," *Miami (FL) News*, March 19, 1930, 1.

8. "Ritter Tells Capone He May Come to Miami; U. S. Judge Issues Order Invalidating Carlton's Edict to Sheriffs," *Miami (FL) Herald*, March 23, 1930, 1, 8.

Chapter 15: Al Capone, Miami, and the "Chicago Plan"

1. "Mailed Fist Is Being Used To Squelch Chicago Gunmen, Say Custodians of McGurn; Windy City Detectives Declare Crime Element Is on Run," *Miami (FL) Daily News*, April 5, 1930, 1.

2. "Two Brothers of Al Capone Are Held Here; Arrests Follow Raid on Palm Island Residence; Liquor Is Seized," *Miami (FL) Herald*, March 21, 1930, 1.

3. "State Seeks Padlock on Capone Home; Estate Terms as Haven for Criminal Gang," *Miami (FL) News*, April 22, 1930, 1.

4. "Alleged Capone Aide Is Jailed at Miami; Jack McGurn, Believe Al's Right Hand Man, Arrested Playing Golf," *Palm Beach (FL) Post*, April 1, 1930, 12.

5. "Capone Brother Arrested Again," *Miami (FL) Herald*, April 12, 1930, 13.

6. "Caretaker for Capone Files $1,000 Appeal Bond," *Miami (FL) Herald*, April 24, 1930, 2.

7. "Leavitt Loses Job for Trips to Capone Home," *Miami (FL) News*, May 6, 1930, 2.

8. "Miami Police Arrest Pioneer Resident without Warrant; Frank Gallat Taken from Dinner Table in His Home to City Jail," *Miami (FL) Herald*, May 9, 1930, 1.

9. "Capone Seeks U. S. Court Order against Police; Wharton Given Warning to Leave after Attack," *Miami (FL) News*, May 9, 1930, 1, 4.

10. "Capone Freed As Arrest Is Held Illegal," *Miami (FL) Herald*, May 9, 1930, 1, 12.

11. "Coast Guard Sweeps Lake for Rum Ship," *Chicago Tribune*, May 14, 1930, 6, and "Capone Gives $100 Bond on Third Arrest," *Miami (FL) Herald*, May 20, 1930, 1, 2.

12. "Children Are Guests at Capone Residence," *Miami (FL) Herald*, May 18, 1930, 9.

13. "Police Patrol outside Capone Walls as Miami Guests Feted," *Miami (FL) News*, May 29, 1930, 1.

Chapter 16: Col. Randolph Meets the Kingpin

1. Owen L. Scott, "Capone-Moran Gunmen Renew Ancient Feuds," *Miami (FL) News*, June 3, 1930, 1.

2. "'Scarface Puts on a Party—and Zuta Is Riddled," *Everett (WA) Daily Herald*, August 2, 1930, 1.

3. "Beer Supply Is Cut Off," *Valdosta (GA) Daily Times*, June 13, 1930, 2.

4. "Lingle Murder Is Said Linked to Gang Graft," *Miami (FL) News*, June 22, 1930, 1, 2.

5. "Ralph Capone Draws 3 Years in Prison for Income Frauds," *Miami (FL) News*, January 16, 1930, 1.

6. "Hoodlum Gets Term in Jail; Jack Guzik, Member of Capone Gang, Sentenced to Five Years," *Greensboro (NC) Record*, December 31, 1930, 2.

7. "Capone Allies Seized by U. S.; Harry and Sam Guzik Held on Tax Charge," *Chicago Tribune*, September 26, 1930, 1.

8. "Al Capone's Business Manager Is Sought," *Evansville Press*, October 3, 1930, 28.

9. "Hunted by U.S.," *Chicago Tribune*, October 30, 1930, 1.

10. "Seize Frank Nitti, Capone Treasurer; Roche Traps Gang Leader Sought by U.S.," *Chicago Tribune*, October 31, 1930, 1.

11. "Nitti, Capone's Manager, Unable to Furnish Bail; Lodge in Cell Pending Plea for Writ," *Chicago Tribune*, November 1, 1930, 7.

12. "Story Book Detective, Just Fable, Sleuth Finds," *Buffalo (NY) Times*, February 16, 1931, 1–2.

13. Oliver Sherwood, "Secret Six of Chicago Nears End of Labors; Citizens' Committee Gives Report on Works; Tells of Routed Hoodlum Gangs," *Oakland (CA) Tribune*, November 22, 1931, 65.

14. "Capone Leader Pleads Guilty and Gets Term; Frank Nitti Admits Income Tax Evasion and Draws 18 Months," *Rock Island (IL) Argus*, December 20, 1930, 1.

15. "Chicago As Expected," *Los Angeles Times*, February 26, 1931, 22.

16. "Capone, Surrounded by Gunmen, to Face Federal Charges in Chicago," *San Bernardino County (CA) Sun*, Feb. 25, 1931, 1.

17. "Chicago Public Enemy No. 1 Now Convict 40886," *Chicago Tribune*, May 5, 1932, 8.

18. Harry T. Brundidge, "Head of Chicago's 'Secret Six' Here, Describes Dramatic Hotel Conference He Had with Capone," *St. Louis (MO) Times Star*, November 22, 1932.

19. Ted Tod, "'I'm Through! Secret Six Licked Me,' Says Al in Interview," *Chicago Herald and Examiner*, July 30, 1931.

20. "Court Warns Capone He Cannot 'Bargain' For Light Sentence," *Lancaster (PA) New Era*, July 30, 1931, 1, 4.

21. Neil M. Clark, "Mystery of the Secret Six," *Sacramento (CA) Union*, August 21, 1932, 17.

22. Eliot Ness, with Oscar Fraley, *The Untouchables*. (New York: Pocket Books, 1987), 73.

23. Eliot Ness, with Oscar Fraley, *The Untouchables*. (New York: Pocket Books, 1987), 135.

24. Eliot Ness, with Oscar Fraley, *The Untouchables*. (New York: Pocket Books, 1987), 222–223.

25. Eliot Ness, with Oscar Fraley, *The Untouchables*. (New York: Pocket Books, 1987), 112–114.

26. Eliot Ness, with Oscar Fraley, *The Untouchables*. (New York: Pocket Books, 1987), 195–200.

27. "Capone Has Turned Detective, Report," *Dixon (IL) Evening Telegraph*, April 10, 1931, 1.

28. "Body Of Missing Attorney Is Found," *Dixon (IL) Evening Telegraph*, April 27, 1931, 1.

29. "Chicago Won Respectability in Snagging the G. O. P. National Convention; Now Democrats May Meet There, Too," *Santa Cruz (CA) Evening News*, Dec. 30, 1931, 10.

30. "Assassins Get $200 for 'Job'," *Minneapolis (MN) Star*, September 25, 1931, 24.

31. "'Secret Six' Holds Secret Witness against Capone," *Oakland (CA) Tribune*, September 24, 1931, 13.

32. Neil M. Clark, "Mystery of the Secret Six" *Sacramento (CA) Union*, August 21, 1932, 17.

33. "Randolph Tells Secret Six Fight against Capone," *Chicago Tribune*, September 25, 1931, 15.

34. "Chicago Needs Cleanup," *Woodland (CA) Daily Democrat*, October 30, 1931, 8.

Chapter 17: The Best Cases of 1931

1. Owen L. Scott, "Noose Gradually Tightens About Throat of Chicago's Underworld As Public Sentiment Hits Crime," *San Bernadino (CA) County Sun*, December 6, 1930, 4.

2. "Foe of Chicago Gangs to Speak at Dinner Here," *Buffalo (NY) Times*, January 29, 1931, 16.

3. Kenneth G. Crawford, "Story Book Detective, Just Fable, Sleuth Finds," *Buffalo (NY) Times*, February 16, 1931, 1–2.

4. "Smashing the Power of the Gunmen and Gangsters; 'Secret Six' Aims to End Reign of Terror That Is Daily Menace to Life in City of Chicago," *Australian Worker: Official Journal of the Australian Worker's Union*, December 17, 1930, 17.

5. "Randolph Calls Water Meeting Mayor's Trick," *Chicago Tribune*, January 13, 1931, 10.

6. "Seize Two Cops, Hunt Six Others on Rum Charges; Still Operator Complains of Shakedowns," *Chicago Tribune*, January 6, 1931, 3.

7. "Racket Bureau Seizes Books of Plumbers' Union," *Chicago Tribune*, January 23, 1931, 2.

8. "Plumbers Act To Rid Union of Racketeers," *Chicago Tribune*, February 2, 1931, 1.

9. "Exit the Racketeer," *Chicago Tribune*, June 30, 1931, 12.

10. "Held in Embezzlement from His Firm," *Belleville New-Democrat*, August 11, 1931, 1, 2.

11. "Five Trapped in Luxurious Apartment; Their Arrest in Gary May Solve $104,000 Jewel Robbery in Chicago," *Gary (IN) Evening Times*, November 4, 1931, 1, 6.

12. "Jewel Robbery Link Seen in Arrest of 4," *Brooklyn (NY) Daily Eagle*, November 4, 1931, 3.

13. Oliver Sherwood, "Secret Six of Chicago Nears End of Labors; Citizens' Committee Gives Report on Works; Tells of Routed Hoodlum Gangs," *Oakland (CA) Tribune*, November 22, 1931, 65.

14. "Chicago Wins War on Crime," *Los Angeles Times*, December 21, 1931, 4.

Chapter 18: The Best Cases of 1932

1. John Boettiger, "Trial Discloses Secret 6 behind Serritella Quiz," *Chicago Tribune*, May 4, 1932, 5.

2. "Probe Records Seized in Office of Serritella; Jurors Hunt Evidence of Short Weight Plot," *Chicago Tribune*, April 2, 1931, 3.

3. "City Hall is Raided in Chicago, 28 Taken," *New York Times*, April 2, 1931, 1.

4. John Boettiger, "Trial Discloses Secret 6 behind Serritella Quiz," *Chicago Tribune*, May 4, 1932, 5.

5. "Serritella Sent to County Jail for Year's Term; Hochstein Also Is Given Cell Sentence," *Chicago Tribune*, May 21, 1932, 4.

6. John Boettiger, "Trial Discloses Secret 6 behind Serritella Quiz," *Chicago Tribune*, May 4, 1932, 5.

7. "Serritella Sent to County Jail for Year's Term; Hochstein Also Is Given Cell Sentence," *Chicago Tribune*, May 21, 1932, 4.

8. "Serritella's Conviction is Upset by Court," *Chicago Tribune*, November 7, 1933, 3.

9. "Dan Serritella Ruled Mentally Ill by Court," *Chicago Tribune*, April 17, 1953, 19.

10. "Shoe Thieves Are Convicted," *Jacksonville (IL) Daily Journal*, January 17, 1932, 1.

11. "Eight Sentenced to U. S. Prison for $9,000 Theft," *Chicago Tribune*, January 17, 1932, 8.

12. "Secret Six Stops Merchandise Theft," *Jacksonville (IL) Daily Journal*, February 18, 1932, 13.

13. "She's Related to Two Ghosts in Court Case," *Pantagraph* (Bloomington, Illinois), February 21, 1933, 1.

14. "Discontent of Indian's Ghosts Held To Be Motive for Bombing," *Courier-Journal* (Louisville, Kentucky), February 22, 1933, 14.

15. "Reveal Bomb Plot to Give Ghost Rest; Widow's Care of Indian 'Spirt' Blamed for Oil Station Blast," *Wisconsin State Journal*, February 26, 1932, 4.

16. "Juror Replaced in 'Ghost Trial'; Evidence Begins," *Chicago Tribune*, February 18, 1933, 8.

17. "Bare Strange Plot to Give Ghost a Home," *Chicago Tribune*, February 26, 1932, 1.

18. "Widow is Freed in Ghost Trial Over Bombing," *Chicago Tribune*, March 3, 1933, 1.

19. "She's Related to Two Ghosts in Court Case," *Pantagraph* (Bloomington, Illinois), February 21, 1933, 1.

20. "Discontent of Indian's Ghosts Held To Be Motive for Bombing," *Courier-Journal* (Louisville, Kentucky), February 22, 1933, 14.

21. "Bare Strange Plot to Give Ghost a Home," *Chicago Tribune*, February 26, 1932, 1.

22. "Business Blunder Causes Woman To Bomb Former Home," *Jacksonville (IL) Daily Journal*, February 27, 1932, 1.

23. "Double Crossed Hubby's 'Ghost,'" *Muncie (IN) Morning Star*, April 18, 1933, 5.

24. "Pick Bomb Trial Jury with Open Mind on Ghosts; Widow Tells of Mate's Deathbed Warning," *Chicago Tribune*, February 22, 1933, 2.

25. "Business Blunder Causes Woman To Bomb Former Home," *Jacksonville (IL) Daily Journal*, February 27, 1932, 1.

26. "Widow Is Freed in Ghost Trial over Bombing," *Chicago Tribune*, March 3, 1933, 1.

27. "Karchmer Ousted, Wonders If Legion Will Return Dues," *St. Louis (MO) Star and Times*, May 14, 1924, 7.

28. "Legion Expels Karchmer after Five-Hour Trial," *St. Louis (MO) Post-Dispatch*, May 14, 1924, 1.

29. "Karchmer Ousted, Wonders If Legion Will Return Dues," *St. Louis (MO) Star and Times*, May 14, 1924, 7.

30. "Police Seize Karchmer for Charity Fraud," *St. Louis (MO) Star and Times*, July 15, 1925, 3.

31. "Blind Entertainment Ticket Sales $2594," *St. Louis (MO) Globe-Democrat* July 24, 1935, 9.

32. "Warn Against a Blind Tie Salesman," *Record-American* (Mahanoy City, Pennsylvania), February 10, 1927, 2.

33. "Gives Up Trying to Get $470,000 Due for Neckties." *St. Louis (MO) Post-Dispatch*, January 10, 1928, 10.

34. "Newspapers Help Put Fraud Out of Business," *Bismarck (ND) Tribune*, September 21, 1927, 2.

35. "Gives Up Trying To Get $470,000 Due for Neckties," *St. Louis (MO) Post-Dispatch*, January 10, 1928, 10.

36. "Blind Tie Man in Trouble Again," *Mound City (MO) News-Independent*, November 21, 1929, 7.

37. "Pair Nabbed by U. S., Accused of Running a 'Charity Racket,'" *Chicago Tribune*, February 9, 1930, 12.

38. "Girl Exposes Charity Racket," *Decatur (IL) Daily Review*, March 11, 1932, 17.

39. "Girl Operative for Secret Six Gets Defrauder," *Times* (Streator, Illinois), March 10, 1932, 9.

40. "Jake Karchmer Given 2 Yrs. For Charity Racket," *Chicago Tribune*, March 13, 1932, 7.

41. "Jacob K. Karchmer's Conviction Reversed," *St. Louis (MO) Daily Globe-Democrat*, November 1, 1932, 20.

42. "New Racket in Selling Pictures of President," *Kirksville (MO) Daily Express and News*, August 20, 1933, 5.

43. "Business Men Charged with Failure to Register," *St. Louis (MO) Daily Globe Democrat*, August 11, 1934, 11.

44. "Jacob Karchmer Freed of Solicitation Charge," *St. Louis (MO) Star and Times*, Oct. 11, 1934, 3.

45. "Mrs. Jacob Karchmer Dies of Auto Injury," *St. Louis (MO) Post-Dispatch,* April 29, 1935, 11.

46. "Trap Employe of Assessor as Tax Fixer," *Chicago Tribune,* Oct. 6, 1932, 1.

47. "Two Trapped in Tax Fixing Plot Freed on Bonds," *Chicago Tribune,* October 7, 1932, 6.

48. "Dixon Officer Captures Four Big Swindlers," *Dixon (IL) Evening Telegraph,* March 22, 1932, 1.

49. "Arrest of 4 Bank Robbers Credited to Secret Six," *Chicago Tribune,* June 6, 1932, 3.

50. "Seller of Stolen Bonds Held as $142,000 Robber," *Chicago Tribune,* July 31, 1932, 14.

51. "Held for Extortion," *Pasadena (CA) Post,* March 20, 1932, 2.

Chapter 19: The Secret Six Conjures a National Kidnapping Monopoly

1. "Anti-Kidnaping Law Urged," *Evening Star* (Washington, DC), February 26, 1932, 5.

2. "Sheldon Names U. S. Kidnap Czar; Abductors of Caress Hold Monopoly, Says Secret Six," *Los Angeles Evening Express,* September 14, 1931, 3.

3. "'Secret Six' of Wealthy Fight Crime in Chicago," *Tulare (CA) Daily Times,* November 11, 1931, 1.

4. "Battle against Huge Kidnap Ring Pushed After Two Victims Freed; War Centers in St. Louis and Chicago," *San Bernardino County (CA) Sun,* November 12, 1931, 3.

5. "Attorney May Solve Series of Kidnapings," *Belleville (IL) News Democrat,* November 12, 1931, 12.

6. "Battle against Huge Kidnap Ring Pushed After Two Victims Freed; War Centers in St. Louis and Chicago," *San Bernardino County (CA) Sun,* November 12, 1931, 3.

7. "Attorney May Solve Series of Kidnapings," *Belleville (IL) News Democrat,* November 12, 1931, 12.

8. "Battle against Huge Kidnap Ring Pushed After Two Victims Freed; War Centers in St. Louis and Chicago," *San Bernardino County (CA) Sun,* November 12, 1931, 3.

9. "Kidnap Gang Frees Rich St. Louisan; Ransom Is Denied," *Kansas City (MO) Journal,* November 11, 1931, 1.

10. "Battle against Huge Kidnap Ring Pushed After Two Victims Freed; War Centers in St. Louis and Chicago," *San Bernardino County (CA) Sun,* November 12, 1931, 3.

11. "'Secret Six' of Wealthy Fight Crime in Chicago," *Tulare (CA) Daily Times,* November 11, 1931, 1.

12. "Attorney May Solve Series of Kidnapings," *Belleville (IL) News Democrat*, November 12, 1931, 12.

13. "Release Five Suspects for Kidnap Cases," *Jacksonville (IL) Daily Journal*, November 12, 1931, 9.

14. "Secret Six Reveals Big Kidnap Gang," *Lincoln (NE) Star*, January 25, 1932, 7.

15. Robert T. Loughman, "Super-Crime Gang Exposed; 7 Desperadoes Blamed in Scores of Kidnapings; Cleaned Up Million," *Pittsburgh (PA) Press*, January 27, 1932, 1.

16. "Berg Kidnaper's Plea for Parole Up Thursday," *St. Louis (MO) Star and Times*, November 1, 1937, 1.

17. "Louisville Case Recalls Kansas City Kidnapings," *Pittsburgh (PA) Press*, October 11, 1934, 6.

18. "Solution of Kidnaping of Nine is Near; Trio of Alleged Gang in Custody; Police Seeking Others," *Dixon (IL) Evening Telegraph*, November 9, 1933, 1.

19. Bruce Catton, "Kidnaping Is Most Vicious Racket of Organized Criminals," *Sheboygan (WI) Press*, March 5, 1932, 4.

20. Bruce Catton, "Chicago Pays Two Million Ransom; Ring, Born in Detroit, Murdered Boy Victim," *Greensboro (NC) Daily News and Record*, March 8, 1932, 4.

21. Fred Pasley, "Just Flirting Trapped One Kidnap Gang," *Daily News* (New York, NY), September 12, 1933, 16.

22. Bruce Catton, "'Harvest' of Chicago Kidnaping Ring Estimated at $2,000,000 in Two Years," *The Cincinnati (OH) Post*, March 8, 1932, 9.

23. Frederick Griffin, "Heyday of Kidnapping," *Toronto (Canada) Star Weekly*, August 19, 1933, 21.

24. Austin O'Malley, "First Full Facts about the Astounding Plague of Organized Kidnapings, America's Latest and Vilest Racket," *Minneapolis (MN) Star Tribune*, May 22, 1932, 51.

25. "Tales of Torture Told to House Group; Committee Likely To Make Extortion by Mail New Federal Crime," *Evening Sun* (Baltimore, MD), February 25, 1932, 3.

Chapter 20: The Secret Six vs. the Kidnappers

1. "Prison Chaplain Helped to Stir Disorder, Claim," *Evening Sun* (Baltimore, Maryland), March 16, 1931, 1.

2. Robert L. Loughran, "Pastor Reveals Prison Cruelty" *Buffalo (NY) Times*, March 22, 1931, 1.

3. "Bare Foiled Plot for an Outbreak at New Prison," *Chicago Tribune*, March 17, 1931, 9.

4. "Legal Battle Started for Custody of Trapped Gang." *Wausau (WI) Daily Herald*, May 9, 1931, 1.

5. "Police Arrest Burke's Thugs," *San Bernardino (CA) County Sun*, May 9, 1931, 1.

6. "Kidnapers Return Gustav E. Miller, Former Student; No Ransom Paid; 'Secret Six' Charge Parents With Refusal To Co-operate With Police," *The Daily Illini*, May 8, 1932, 1, 2.

7. "Kidnapers Sought by 'Secret Six,'" *Riverside (CA) Daily Press*, May 5, 1932, 1.

8. "Ask 'Secret Six' To Extend Help," *Imperial Valley Press* (El Centro, California), April 30, 1932, 1.

9. "Kidnapers Sought by 'Secret Six'" *Riverside (CA) Daily Press*, May 5, 1932, 1.

10. "Kidnapers Return Gustav E. Miller, Former Student; No Ransom Paid; 'Secret Six' Charge Parents with Refusal To Co-operate with Police," *The Daily Illini*, May 8, 1932, 1, 2.

11. "Charge Victim's Family Spoiled Kidnaping Trap; Blamed by Secret 6 Men for Escape of Gang," *Chicago Tribune*, May 8, 1932, 8.

12. "Kidnapers Release Youth, Lose Ransom," *Bristol (TN) Herald Courier*, May 8, 1932, 16.

13. "Banker Set Free after Kidnaping; Wife Released Early To Hunt for $5,000 Ransom Demanded," *Democrat and Chronicle* (Rochester, NY), October 11, 1932, 1, 4.

14. "Banker Set Free after Kidnaping; Wife Released Early To Hunt for $5,000 Ransom Demanded," *Democrat and Chronicle* (Rochester, NY), October 11, 1932, 1, 4.

15. "Kidnapers Foiled by Publicity; Chicago Banker Freed after Being Captive 12 Hours," *Journal Gazette* (Matoon, IL), October 11, 1932, 1.

16. "Kidnapers Free Banker, Elude Trap of Police," *Chicago Tribune*, October 11, 1932, 1.

17. "Kidnapers Free Chicago Banker; Release Collins Though Ransom Money Not Paid . . . Reaches Phone As Secret Six Is Waiting for Message," *Long Beach (CA) Sun*, October 11, 1932, 1, 6.

18. "Banker Set Free after Kidnaping; Wife Released Early To Hunt for $5,000 Ransom Demanded," *Democrat and Chronicle* (Rochester, NY), October 11, 1932, 1, 4.

19. "Peoria Man Believed to Be Held by Kidnapers," *Belleville (IL) News-Democrat*, March 15, 1932, 2.

20. "Peoria Doctor Missing; Auto Found on Road," *Evansville (IN) Journal*, March 15, 1932, 1.

21. "Doctor Kidnaped, Officers Think" *Argus-Leader* (Sioux Falls, SD). March 16, 1932, 1.

22. "New Clews Link Gang to Parker Kidnap Mystery," *Chicago Tribune*, March 24, 1932.

23. "Peoria Physician Believed Kidnaped," *Pantagraph* (Bloomington, IL). March 15, 1932, 1.

24. "Ransom Demand Is Awaited for Peoria Doctor," *Chicago Tribune*, March 22, 1932, 6.

25. “Police Drop Kidnap Probe,” *Dailly News-Times* (Neenah, WI), March 22, 1932, 1.

26. “New Clews Link Gang to Parker Kidnap Mystery,” *Chicago Tribune*, March 24, 1932.

27. “Exorbitant Ransom,” *Austin (TX) American*, March 27, 1932, 2.

28. “Chicago ‘Secret Six’ Restores Kidnaped Doctor to Society; Peoria Men Attempting to Act As Go-Betweens Arrested,” *Daily Independent* (Murphysboro, IL), April 4, 1932.

29. “Kidnapers Are Found Guilty,” *Daily Chronicle* (DeKalb, IL), June 1, 1932, 1, 7.

30. Sam Tucker, “As I View the Thing” *The Decatur (IL) Daily Review*, June 19, 1932, 6.

31. “Dictaphones Used To Get Kidnap Data,” *Journal Gazette* (Mattoon, IL), May 20, 1932, 8.

32. “Kidnapers Are Found Guilty.” *Daily Chronicle* (DeKalb, IL), June 1, 1932, 1, 7.

33. Sam Tucker, “As I View the Thing” *Decatur (IL) Daily Review*, June 19, 1932, 6.

34. “Dictaphone Evidence Admitted; Jury Hears Conversation of Pursifull and Betson,” *Journal Gazette* (Mattoon, IL), May 26, 1932, 8.

35. “Dictaphone Evidence Admitted; Jury Hears Conversation of Pursifull and Betson.” *Journal Gazette* (Mattoon, IL), May 26, 1932, 8.

36. “Dictaphone Evidence Admitted; Jury Hears Conversation of Pursifull and Betson,” *Journal Gazette* (Mattoon, IL), May 26, 1932, 8.

37. “Kidnaped Man Returns Home; Secret Six Is Given the Credit for The Solving of Case,” *Daily Chronicle* (DeKalb, IL) April 2, 1932, 1.

38. “Kidnap Charges Filed Against 2 Held at Peoria,” *Chicago Tribune*, April 4, 1932, 10.

39. “Kidnap Suspect Denied Bond Cut by Peoria Judge,” *Chicago Tribune*, April 5, 1932, 7.

40. “Physician Held 17 Days Freed by Kidnapers,” *Chicago Tribune*, April 2, 1932, 1.

41. “Kidnapers of Doctor Parker Were Bluffed,” *Urbana (IL) Daily Courier*, April 4, 1931, 1.

42. “Chicago ‘Secret Six’ Restores Kidnaped Doctor to Society; Peoria Men Attempting to Act As Go-Betweens Arrested,” *Daily Independent* (Murphysboro, IL), April 4, 1932.

43. “Twelve Held As Kidnapers; Peoria Abduction Gang Admits Part in Ransom Plot,” *Decatur (IL) Daily Review*, April 15, 1932, 1.

44. “Early End for State’s Case in Peoria is Seen; Many Motions Made by Defense in Kidnap Trial Denied,” *Dixon (IL) Evening Telegraph*, May 26, 1932, 2.

45. “Eight of Eleven in Peoria Kidnap Band Convicted,” *Dispatch* (Moline, IL), June 1, 1932, 1.

46. "State's Case on Kidnaping Charge Nearing Close," *Daily Independent* (Murphysboro, IL), May 19, 1932, 3.

47. National Commission on Law Observance and Enforcement, Wickersham, George W. (Chair) et al., "Report on Lawlessness in Law Enforcement," 1931, 4–5.

48. See, for example: Ashcraft v. State of Tennessee, 322 U.S. 143 (1944); Bram v. United States, 168 U.S. 532 (1897); Brown v. State of Mississippi, 56 S.Ct. 461 (1936); Brown v. Walker, 161 U.S. 591 (1896); Chambers v. State of Florida, 09 U.S. 227 (1940); Fisher v. State, 145 Miss. 116 (1926); Haynes v. State of Washington, 373 U.S. 503 (1963); Hopt v. Utah, 110 U.S. 574 (1884); Leyra v. Denno, 347 U.S. 556 (1954); Lynumn v. State of Illinois, 372 U.S. 528 (1963); Malinski v. People of the State of New York, 324 U.S. 401 (1945); Miranda v. Arizona, 384 U.S. 436 (1966); Moore v. Dempsey, 261 U.S. 86 (1923); Powell v. Alabama, 287 U.S. 45 (1932); Rhode Island v. Innis, 100 S.Ct. 1682 (1980); Townsend v. Sain, 372 U.S. 293 (1963); Ward v. State of Texas, 316 U.S. 547 (1941); White v. State of Texas, 310 U.S. 530 (1940); Williams v. United States, 341 U.S. 97 (1951); Wilson v. United States, 162 U.S. 613 (1896); Ziang Sung Wan v. United States, 266 U.S. 1 (1924); (Cases compiled by Abbie Ortman for her University of Oregon June 2016 master's thesis project, "Police Pressure: The History of U.S. Police Interrogations.")

49. Jason M. Gillis, "Curious Logic in Defense of the 'Third Degree,'" *Brooklyn (NY) Tablet,* August 27, 1932.

Chapter 21: A Brief History of Vigilantism

1. Per Guardian Angels website, "About," accessed May 2024, https://www.guardianangels.org/about.

2. Rich Tenorio, "Sedition Hunters: how ordinary Americans helped track down the Capitol rioters," *Guardian,* October 28, 2023.

3. "For Most U.S. Gun Owners, Protection Is the Main Reason They Own a Gun," Pew Research Center. August 16, 1923; Peter Overby, "NRA: 'Only Thing That Stops a Bad Guy with a Gun Is a Good Guy with a Gun,'" *All Things Considered, National Public Radio,* December 21, 2012.

4. Matt Austin, "Armed citizen patrols start in Hartford amid violence concerns," *NBC Connecticut,* March 19, 2024, http//www.nbcconnecticut.com/news/local/armed-citizen-patrols-start-in-hartford-amid-violence-concerns/3238606/.

Chapter 22: A Modest Proposal

1. "Chicago Crusader Urges Pittsburgh 'Secret Six,'" *Pittsburgh (PA) Press,* February 2, 1932, 27.

2. "Urges Secret Society to Fight Kidnappers; F. J. Loesch, Chicago Anti-Crime Leader, Calls for an Interstate Organization," *New York Times,* February 4, 1923, 42.

3. "'Secret Six' Unveil Fight on Big Crime; Has Cleared Way for Prosecution of 51 Crime Groups," *Kenosha (WI) News*, September 15, 1931, 19.

4. "Weird Trail Leads to Loot of Millions," *Alton (IL) Evening Telegraph*, November 10, 1931, 1.

5. "Crime Syndicate Ruled by 'Directors," *Daily News* (Los Angeles, CA), January 7, 1932, 10.

6. "Securities of Over Million to be Returned; 'Secret Six,' of Chicago, On Trail of Stolen Bonds," *Times* (Streator, IL), January 7, 1932, 9.

7. Alexander Jamie, "Vice Swells Gang War Chest As Crime Octopus Grips Nation," *Dixon (IL) Evening Telegraph*, March 22, 1932, 10.

8. "'Secret Six' Unveil Fight on Big Crime; Has Cleared Way for Prosecution of 51 Crime Groups," *Kenosha (WI) News*, September 15, 1931, 19.

9. Alexander Jamie, "Director Tells How Secret Six Makes War on Racketeers," *Ventura County (CA) Star*, March 24, 1932, 6.

10. "The FBI and the American Gangster, 1924–1938," Federal Bureau of Investigation website, accessed June 2024, https://www.fbi.gov/history/brief-history/the-fbi-and-the-american-gangster.

11. "'Secret Six' Unveil Fight on Big Crime; Has Cleared Way for Prosecution of 51 Crime Groups" *Kenosha (WI) News*, September 15, 1931, 19.

12. "Civic Crime Group; Chamber of Commerce Acts To End Terrorism, Kidnaping and Extortion Here," *Kansas City Star*, April 14, 1930, 1.

13. Neil M. Clark, "Mystery of the Secret Six," *Sacramento (CA) Union*. August 21, 1932, 17, and "Jackson's 'Secret 90' Rids Town of Crime," *Buffalo (NY) News*, November 17, 1932, 1.

14. "'Secret Six' Will Be Formed Here," *Belleville (IL) Daily Advocate*, Nov. 19, 1932, 1.

15. "Lake County to Organized Secret Crime Foe Group," *Chicago Tribune*, October 3, 1930, 2.

16. "Legion Form 'Secret Six.' Aim to Terrorize Militant Unemployed," *Daily Worker* (New York, NY), July 12, 1932, 1.

17. "Howard Street Vigilantes To Fight Hoodlums," *Chicago Tribune*, February 1, 1931, 83.

18. "'Secret 100' to Report Traffic Violators," *Journal Gazette* (Mattoon, IL), October 17, 1930, 5.

19. "Peoria Business Men Asking Protection," *Daily Dispatch* (Moline, IL) December 24, 1931, 8.

20. Tom Pettey, "Gotham Graft Battlers Seek to Oust Mayor," *Chicago Tribune*, March 13, 1931, 3.

21. "Angola Group Starts Fight for Distribution of Money; 'Secret six' Contemplates Mandamus Action To Loosen Funds Collected in Bank Liquidation," *Buffalo (NY) Courier Express*, June 21, 1932, 15.

22. "30 Arrested As Vice Crusade Opens; Raid Series Reveals Secret 16 Busy Here," *Buffalo (NY) News*, January 26, 1932, p. 1; "Secret Vice Drive Here Fails; Evidence Gathered Nullified by Court; Judge Keeler Frees Eight Women Arrested in Crusade Similar to Chicago's 'Secret Six' Campaign," *Buffalo (NY) News*, February 17, 1932, 1.

23. "Chicago's Secret Six Pattern Here in New War on Racketeers," *Brooklyn (NY) Daily Eagle*, September 19, 1932, 1.

24. "Indictments Found in '3d Degree' Death," *New York Times*, July 23, 1932, 1, 2.

25. "Anti-Crime League Formed in Nassau to Defend Police," *Brooklyn (NY) Times Union*, August 9, 1932, 7.

26. "Nassau County Anti-Crime League Formed to Obtain Legislation to Put Common Sense in Criminal Procedure and Break Silence of Prisoners," *Brooklyn (NY) Daily Eagle*, August 14, 1932, 12.

27. Thomas S. Rice, "Declares Secret Six Needed in New York; Criminologist Rice Urges Business Men to Model After Chicago Group That Fought Capone—Says Police Can't Do Real Undercover Work," *Brooklyn (NY) Daily Eagle*, August 4, 1931, 1.

28. "Secret Seven Takes School Law in Hand," *Cincinnati (OH) Post*, June 4, 1931, 13.

29. "Slaying Moves Omaha to Form Own Secret Six," *Chicago Tribune*, December 25, 1931, 30.

30. "Detective Starts on Omaha Slaying," *Minneapolis (MN) Tribune*, January 2, 1932, 4.

31. "'Secret Six' to Aid City," *Columbia (SC) Record*, September 29, 1932, 5.

32. "Six To War on City Crime," *Buffalo (NY) News*, December 2, 1932, 4.

33. "Toledo Vigilantes War on Gangsters; Citizens Volunteer, Plan Ouster of Outlaws from City," *Akron (OH) Beacon Journal*, December 10, 1932, 1.

34. "Experts Will Work on Crime Problem," *Galion (OH) Inquirer*, December 9, 1933, 6.

35. "Denver May Have Own Secret Six," *Brooklyn (NY) Daily Eagle*, February 16, 1933, 17.

36. "Need 'Secret Six' in All Communities," *The Edwardsville (IL) Intelligencer*, August 19, 1930, 1.

37. "Four Men Cited at Columbus for Kidnaping Trial; 'Secret Six' Organization Bared by Indictment of Alleged Members," *Atlanta (GA) Journal*, November 15, 1933, 25.

38. "Girls' Club Stopped Poisoning." *Clinton (IL) Journal and Public*, February 1, 1933, 2.

39. "Form 'Secret Six" to Curb Cheating; Group at Birmingham College to Fight 'Cribbing' by Students; Publicity is Threatened," *Cincinnati (OH) Post*, January 15, 1934, 16.

40. Neil M. Clark, "Mystery of the Secret Six," *Sacramento (CA) Union*, August 21, 1932, 17.

41. "Who's to Repel Boarders?" *Minneapolis (MN) Journal*, August 28, 1930, 10.

42. "Gang Rule Must Get No Foothold in This City," *San Francisco (CA) Examiner*, May 23, 1932, 12.

43. James B. McCarthy, "First Full Facts about the Astounding Plague of Organized Kidnapings, America's Latest and Vilest Racket," *Minneapolis (MN) Sunday Tribune*, June 12, 1932, 58.

44. "Cattle Thefts Kept Him Busy for 50 Years," *Marshall (TX) Evening Messenger*, January 9, 1933, 5.

45. "'Public Enemy' List Disclosed," *Los Angeles Times*, September 24, 1931, 19.

46. "Chicago Man Aiding Fitts in Gang War," *Long Beach (CA) Sun*, September 24, 1931, 1.

47. "'Public Enemy' List Disclosed," *Los Angeles Times*, September 24, 1931, 19.

48. "Fitts Gang Aide Questioned in Mystery Quiz; Ed Dudley, Ex-Chicago Sleuth, Is Closeted with Prosecutor." *Los Angeles Record*, September 25, 1931, 1.

49. "Crawford, Spencer 'Put on Spot,' Slain as Gangs Battle for L.A. Vice Power," *Los Angeles Evening Express*, May 21, 1931, 1.

50. "State Demand to Jail Clark Fails in Court," *Los Angeles Evening Express*, September 30, 1931, 1, 8.

51. "Rohrback Girl Denies Wedding Ex-Investigator," *Los Angeles Times*, September 30, 1931, 22.

52. "Girl Witness is Held in Custody; Police Hear Reports of Wild Parties at Home of Hollywood Girl," *Daily Facts* (Redlands, CA), September 26, 1931, 4.

53. "Clark Trial Jury Chosen," *Los Angeles Times*, September 30, 1931, 21, 22.

54. "Girl Witness is Held in Custody; Police Hear Reports of Wild Parties at Home of Hollywood Girl," *Daily Facts* (Redlands, CA), September 26, 1931, 4.

55. "Mountain Trip With D. A. Man Told by Girl; Clark Defense Tries To Show Undue Influence by Fitts Aide," *Long Beach (CA) Sun*, October 2, 1931.

56. "Girls' Testimony in Clark As Held as Defense Victory," *Burbank (CA) Daily Evening Review*, October 1, 1931, 6.

57. "Jury in David Clark Case Finds Defendant Not Guilty," *Lynwood (CA) Tribune*, October 23, 1931, 1.

58. "Clark Defends Frank Clasby; Principals of Famous Murder Trial Face Again," *Los Angeles Evening Post-Record*, July 15, 1932, 1.

59. "Graft Showup For L. A. Set As Dudley Up; Former Fitts Air Before Grand Jury in Crime Situation Quiz," *Los Angeles Evening Post-Record*, August 9, 1933, 2.

60. "Suicide Fails, Dudley Jailed; Ex-Investigator Held After Takes Poison Dose," *Los Angeles Times*, September 4, 1934, 23.

61. "Missing Fitts Ex-Aide Found, Subpoenaed in Jury's Probe," *Daily News* (Los Angeles), September 18, 1934, 3.

62. "Dudley Grand Jury Visit Believed Back of Probing Fitts' Use of Secret Fund," *Daily News* (Los Angeles), September 8, 1934, 3.

63. "Death Echo in Divorce; Witness in Clark's Murder Trial Granted Decree from Former Guard," *Los Angeles Times*, August 20, 1936, 22.

Chapter 23: The Secret Six Were Neither

1. "Chicago's 'Secret Six' Fights Fire with Fire, Says Colonel Randolph," *Rochester (NY) Democrat and Chronicle*, October 15, 1931, 20.

2. "Recover $100,000 in Clinton, IA., Bank Holdup; Four Taken into Custody Shortly after Bold Theft," *Dixon (IL) Evening Telegraph*, March 15, 1932, 1.

3. Eliot Ness, with Oscar Fraley, *The Untouchables.* (New York: Pocket Books, 1987), 11.

4. "Youth Confesses Writing Letters Demanding Cash," *Pantagraph* (Bloomington, IL) January 31, 1932, 1.

5. "Racketeer Bait Hooks Business, Employers Told," *Chicago Tribune*, September 3, 1930, 8.

6. Attached to Frances Marion's script for *The Secret Six* was an article by Col. Randolph that ran on page twelve of The *Saturday Evening Post*, dated August 16, 1930, under the headline "Business Fights Crime in Chicago." Source: Wilson Kreiner Wilson, "Frances Marion, *The Secret Six*, and the Evolving Heroine in 1930s Hollywood," *Historical Journal of Film, Radio and Television* 38, no. 2 (March 2017), 246–262, https://doi.org/10.1080/01439685.2017.1300003.

7. "Julius Rosenwald Backed Secret 6," *Jacksonville (IL) Daily Journal*, January 22, 1932, 2.

8. Alexander Jamie, "Director Tells How Secret Six Makes War on Racketeers," *Ventura County (CA) Star*, March 24, 1932, 6.

9. Roy C. Greenaway, "'Secret Six' Wars on Chicago Gangsters," *Toronto Daily Star*, April 10, 1930, 1, 2.

10. "And We Are Waiting . . . ," *Chicago Tribune*, April 21, 1930, 12.

Chapter 24: The Case of the Deal with the Devil

1. A. B. MacDonald, "'The Biggest Bank Robbery' Surpassed Others Also in Its Unusual and Comic Features," *Kansas City (MO) Star*, March 15, 1931, 39.

2. "Lincoln Loot over Million," *Omaha (NE) Bee-News*, December 18, 1930, 20.

3. "Continental Buys Lincoln National Bank," *Grand Island (NE) Daily Independent*, September 24, 1930, 1.

4. "Nebraska Will Get Winkler," *Evening State Journal* (Lincoln, NE), August 20, 1931, 2, 7.

5. "Johnstone Resigns as Chief," *Lincoln (NE) Star*, September 26, 1930, 1.

6. "Lincoln Police Armed to Teeth," *Hastings (NE) Daily Tribune*, February 5, 1931, 10.

7. "Bank Bandit Chase Futile," *Oklahoma World-Herald*, September 18, 1930, 1, 8.

8. Otho K. DeVilbiss, "Lincoln Suspects Identified; Two of Gangsters Taken in Roundup Are Wanted Here" *Lincoln (NE) Star*, May 10, 1931, 1.

9. Otho K. DeVilbiss, "Lincoln Suspects Identified; Two of Gangsters Taken in Roundup Are Wanted Here," *Lincoln (NE) Star*, May 10, 1931, 1.

10. "Rest of Burke's Gang Jailed in St. Louis Raid," *Austin (TX) American*, May 9, 1931, 1.

11. "Identify Gun as Property of Tom O'Connor," *Lincoln (NE) State Journal*, October 2, 1931, 19.

12. "Reveal Capone Ally Indicted by U. S. in Peoria," *Chicago Tribune*, July 17, 1931, 5.

13. "Newberry Held Guiltless; Ten More Acquitted; Peoria Jury Convicts 14 in Rum Trial," *Chicago Tribune*, December 12, 1931, 18.

14. "Identify Gun as Property of Tom O'Connor," *Lincoln (NE) State Journal*, October 2, 1931, 19.

15. "Nine Identify Lee as Lincoln Bank Robber," *Omaha (NE) Morning Bee-News*, October 22, 1931, 1.

16. "'Pop" Lee Given 25 Years," *Evening State Journal* (Lincoln, Nebraska), November 21, 1931, 1.

17. "Heavy Expense in Bank Robber Cases," *Rock County (NE) County Leader*, December 31, 1931, 2.

18. Everett Holles, "Winkler Calls His Dying Pal 'Whining Punk," *South Bend (IN) Tribune*, August 9, 1931, 1, 2.

19. Details from two articles are used in this account: "Hold Two Men Injured in Bridgman Crash; Gun, Bullets Found on Two Men in Crash," *Herald-Press* (St. Joseph, Michigan), August 5, 1931, 1; "Gangland Spotlight Turned on St. Joseph in 1931; Auto Crash Landed Gus Winkler Back of Jail Bars Here," *Herald-Press* (St. Joseph, Michigan), December 31, 1931, 22.

20. "Detective Hutson First to Find Out Winkler Identity; Former Niles Policeman, Now on State Force, Checked Records," *Niles (MI) Daily Star*, August 8, 1931, 1.

21. Unless otherwise noted, crimes listed are from "Police in Dark After Quizzing Hurt Gangster," *Herald-Press* (St. Joseph, Michigan), August 8, 1931, 3.

22. "Machine Guns Used in Piqua Bank Robbery. One Killed Four Are Shot," *Sidney (OH) Daily News*, April 11, 1930, 1.

23. "Bandit Gets $6,000 at Bank of Dwight," *Pantagraph* (Bloomington, IL). August 4, 1931, 2.

24. Everett Holles, "Winkler Calls His Dying Pal 'Whining Punk," *South Bend (IN) Tribune*, August 9, 1931, 1, 2.

25. "Day and Night Vigil Is Kept Over 2 Gunmen," *The Herald-Press* (St. Joseph, Michigan), August 8, 1931, 1.

26. Everett Holles, "Winkler Calls His Dying Pal 'Whining Punk," *South Bend (IN) Tribune*, August 9, 1931, 1, 2.

27. "Await Winkler's 'Tell All,'" *Herald-Press* (St. Joseph, Michigan), August 8, 1931, 1.

28. "Winkler May Be Cause of Fight Among 3 States," *Nebraska State Journal*, August 12, 1931, 1.

29. "Winkler Brought to Lincoln," *Evening State Journal* (Lincoln, NE), September 16, 1931, 1.

30. "How the 'Secret Six' Coaxed $3,000,000 Loot Home in a Suitcase," *Fresno (CA) Bee*, March 26, 1932, 25.

31. "Await Winkler's 'Tell All,'" *Herald-Press* (St. Joseph, Michigan), August 8, 1931, 1.

32. "Weird Trail Leads to Loot of Millions," *Alton (IL) Evening Telegraph*, November 10, 1931, 1.

33. "Think Winkler Knows Where Bonds Went," *Omaha World-Herald*, August 10, 1931, 2.

34. "Assert Capone Wants Winkler to Head Racket; Needs Leader While He Is Serving Term in Prison on Tax Violation," *Grand Island (NE) Independent*, November 10, 1931, 1.

35. "Winkler in New Legal Tangle," *Omaha (NE) Morning Bee-News*, October 15, 1931, 1.

36. "Assert Capone Wants Winkler To Head Racket," *Grand Island (NE) Independent*, November 10, 1931, 1, 2.

37. "Hearing of Winkler Case is Postponed; Robber Suspect Sent Back to Cell Despite His $100,000 Bond," *Norfolk (NE) Daily News*, October 15, 1931, 1.

38. "Free Winkler to Hold Him," *Hastings (NE) Daily Tribune*, October 22, 1931, 3.

39. "Gangland Spotlight Turned on St. Joseph in 1931; Auto Crash Landed Gus Winkler Back of Jail Bars Here," *The Herald-Press* (St. Joseph, Michigan), December 31, 1931, 22.

40. "Winkler Says Knew Trio Held at Pen," *Evening State Journal* (Lincoln, Nebraska), August 10, 1931, 2, 7.

41. "Gang May Swap Valued Loot for Aide's Freedom," *Fresno (CA) Bee*, November 9, 1931, 1.

42. "Return of Stolen $600,000 Bid for Winkler's Liberty. . . Dicker with Friends of Bandit Carried on by 'Secret Six,'" *Omaha (NE) Bee-News*, November 8, 1931, 1.

43. "Inquiry Proves Winkler's Alibi; 'Secret Six' Agent Finds Accused Man's Handwriting in Buffalo Hotel," *Tulsa (OK) World*, November 21, 1931, 11.

44. "Winkler and Britt Released," *Evening State Journal* (Lincoln, NE), December 12, 1931, 1.

45. "One Topic in Lincoln, the Gus Winkler Deal," *Omaha (NE) World-Herald*, November 21, 1931, 3.

46. "Gangland Offers to 'Trade' for Winkler Freedom; Authorities Puzzled at Overture to 'Swap' $600,000 Stolen Bonds for His Release," *Belleville (IL) Daily Advocate*, November 9, 1931, 1.

47. "'Secret Six' Quits Winkler Negotiations; Jamie, Irked, Sees 'Politics' as Offer Debated," *Omaha World Herald*, November 10, 1931, 4.

48. "Winkler and Britt Released," *Evening State Journal* (Lincoln, NE), December 12, 1931, 1.

49. "Alleged Bank Robers Liberated," *Lincoln (NE) Herald*, December 18, 1931, 1.

50. "Local and Personal," *Superior (NE) Weekly Journal*, December 17, 1931, 5.

51. "Protests Too Much," *Hastings (NE) Democrat*, December 17, 1931, 4.

52. "Believe Towle Is To Be Criticized," *Lincoln (NE) Evening Journal*, December 21, 1931, 13.

53. "The Sportolog: That Big Builder," *Omaha (NE) World-Herald*, December 21, 1931, 19.

54. "'Secret Six' Defends Capone Gangster," *Federation News*, December 5, 1931.

55. "Stolen Bonds Restored by Capone Ally," *Chicago Tribune*, January 6, 1932, 1.

56. "W. E. Barkley is Jubilant as He Arrives in City," *Lincoln (NE) State Journal*, January 7, 1932, 12.

57. "Six Nebraska Banks Profit by Bond Return," *Lincoln (NE) State Journal*, January 7, 1932, 12.

58. "Winkler Keeps Word, Returns Stolen Bonds," *Grand Island (NE) Independent*, January 6, 1932, 1, 2.

59. "Dixon Officer Aided in $575,000 Bond Recovery," *Dixon (IL) Evening Telegraph*, January 6, 1932, 1.

60. "Dixon Officer Aided in $575,000 Bond Recovery," *Dixon (IL) Evening Telegraph*, January 6, 1932, 1.

61. "Half Million of Loot Recovered," *Falls City (NE) Daily News*, January 7, 1932, 1, 3.

62. "'Secret Six" May Recover Bank Loot of $2,875,000," *Times* (Streator, IL), November 9, 1931, 7.

63. "Assert Capone Wants Winkler To Head Racket," *Grand Island (NE) Independent*, November 10, 1931, 1, 2.

64. "Bankers, Law Bargain with Gangster to Save Institution; Story of Hunt for $2,500,000 Loot from Nebraska Is Revealed through Dickering with Winkler," *Miami (FL) News*, November 10, 1931, 3.

65. "Winkler Keeps Word, Returns Stolen Bonds," *Grand Island (NE) Independent*, January 6, 1932, 1, 2.

66. "Agents Hurry to Florida in Bremer Case. 6 on Way from Washington to Question Suspects Held in Tampa; Couple Seized in S. Petersburg," *Miami (FL) Herald*, February 16, 1934, 1.

67. FBI report dated February 23, 1934, based on interviews with Doll conducted February 14–21, 1934, in Tampa, Florida by FBI agents H. E. Anderson, R. A. Alt, R. L. Shivers, and R. L. Main. (Available at https://vault.fbi.gov/barker-karpis-gang/bremer-kidnapping; part 15, p. 203).

68. "Two Make Another Try for Freedom," *Minneapolis (MN) Star*, January 8, 1932, 13.

69. Nebraska Supreme Court Briefs, Vol. 33, Gen. No. 28266, Thomas Pat O'Connor v. State of Nebraska, filed February 17, 1932, College of Law, University of Nebraska-Lincoln; Vol. 37, Gen. No. 28297, Howard Lee v. State of Nebraska, filed May 28, 1932; Descriptive Records of Inmates, Department of Correctional Services, State Penitentiary and State Reformatory, Vol. 6, 201, Thomas Pat O'Connor, No. 10929, September 10, 1941; and Vol. 6, 205, Howard Lee, No. 10958, September 10, 1941. RG 86, Nebraska State Historical Society.

Chapter 25: The Case of the Crooked Cops

1. "It May Be Police Heads Next: Lyle; Judge Warns Captains Might Yet Make Front Page Crime News," *Southtown Economist* (Chicago, IL), August 28, 1930, 1.

2. "U. S. To Help Smash Chicago Gangs; Federal Men Concentrate in Chicago," *Belvidere (IL) Daily Republican*, November 20, 1930, 1.

3. "Grand Jurors To Open Police Inquiry Today; Critics of Departments To Be Called," *Chicago Tribune*, January 7, 1931, 8.

4. "Lists 260 Saloons in Chicago's Loop; 'Secret Six' Investigator Tells Jury of Speakeasies," *Rock Island (IL) Argus*, January 14, 1931, 1.

5. "Cook Grand Jury Is Out of Money," *Jacksonville (IL) Daily Journal*, January 14, 1931, 9.

6. "Offers to Give Jury Evidence of Corruption," *Chicago Tribune*, February 10, 1931, 5.

7. "Chicago Woman Detective Gone, Fear Kidnaping," *Belleville (IL) Daily News-Democrat*, January 21, 1931, 6.

8. "Records Indicate Police Well Paid; Chicago Special Grand Jury Receives Starling Evidence in Its Inquiry of 'Protection' Funds," *Oneanta (NY) Daily Star*, January 20, 1931, 1.

9. "Head of Secret Six Responds to Jury Appeal," *Chicago Tribune*, January 14, 1931, 1.

10. "Records Indicate Police Well Paid; Chicago Special Grand Jury Receives Starling Evidence in Its Inquiry of 'Protection' Funds," *Oneanta (NY) Daily Star*, January 20, 1931, 1.

11. "Woman Detective, Foe of Gangs, Missing; Mrs. Shirley Kub Fails to Appear in Chicago; May Be Slain," *Lancaster (PA) New Era,* January 21, 1931, 3.

12. "Records Missing in Promotion of Sergt. Herdegen," *Chicago Tribune,* January 23, 1931, 6.

13. "3 Policemen Suspected in Vice Graft Quiz," *Chicago Tribune,* January 24, 1931, 2.

14. "Woman Witness Disappears in Police Inquiry," *Chicago Tribune,* January 21, 1931, 1.

15. "Records Missing in Promotion of Sergt. Herdegen," *Chicago Tribune,* January 23, 1931, 6.

16. "Woman Police Spy Jailed for Defying Jurors," *Chicago Tribune,* March 4, 1931, 3.

17. "Woman Police Spy Jailed for Defying Jurors; Report Mrs. Kub Ready to 'Talk,'" *Chicago Tribune,* March 14, 1931, 2.

18. "Vote Reprimand for Captain in Trial of Police," *Chicago Tribune,* March 10, 1931, 4.

19. "Woman Police Spy Jailed for Defying Jurors; Report Mrs. Kub Ready to 'Talk,'" *Chicago Tribune,* March 14, 1931, 2.

20. "Woman Spy for Police Reveals Chicago Graft," *Belleville (IL) Daily New-Democrat,* March 21, 1931, 2.

21. "Seclude Police Spy as Jurors Study Reports," *Chicago Tribune,* March 22, 1931, 3.

22. "Graft Bared by Woman Spy; Jury in Night Session Gets Police Records," *Chicago Tribune,* March 21, 1931, 1, 6.

23. "Breen Silent on Spy's Charges to Graft Jury; Politics Responsible, Is Seritella's Reply," *Chicago Tribune,* March 28, 1931, 6.

24. "Raid 37 Places, Arrest 110 in Hunt for Graft: 50 of Prosecutor's Police in Cleanup," *Chicago Tribune,* March 25, 1931, 1.

25. "Woman Police Spy Freed After Giving Testimony to Jury," *Chicago Tribune,* March 26, 1931, 12.

26. "Three Police Officials Go to Grand Jury," *Mt. Carmel (IL) Daily Republican-Register,* April 20, 1931, 6.

27. "Jurors Obtain Bank Records of Police Cash; Evidence 'Interesting,' Foreman Says," *Chicago Tribune,* April 21, 1931, 1.

28. "Order Sergt. Herdegen Ousted," *Chicago Tribune,* March 11, 1931, 11.

Chapter 26: The Secret Six vs. Swanson

1. Bruce Catton, (NEA Service Writer), *Oklahoma News,* September 10, 1930, 5.

2. "Swanson Opens Loop Office to Fight Rackets," *Chicago Tribune,* October 8, 1930, 2.

3. "U. S. Dry Agent Is New Investigator for 'Secret Six,'" *Belleville (IL) News-Democrat*, October 31, 1930, 2.

4. F. A. Resch, "Racketeering in Chicago Takes $1,000,000 'Rap' during Year," *Sacramento (CA) Bee*, March 18, 1932, 15.

5. "Law Disregard U. S. Menace—Randolph; 'Secret Six' World Is Told," *Pantagraph* (Bloomington, IL), March 18, 1932, 3, 14.

6. "Secret 6 and Swanson Go A-Spying; Sleuth on Each Other and Find Pair of Cabals," *Chicago Tribune*, September 1, 1932, 1, 4.

7. "War of Words Continues," *Enquirer* (Cincinnati, Ohio), September 2, 1932, 19.

8. "Spier Spying Upon Spiers; Woman Spills Secret as Chicago Authorities Watch Secret Six," *Biddeford (ME) Daily Journal*, September 1, 1932, 1.

9. "Woman Sleuth Jailed," *Rock Island (IL) Argus*, December 30, 1931, 1.

10. "Mrs. Kub Will Complete Story of Graft Today," *Chicago Tribune*, March 23, 1931, 5.

11. "Swanson Wars on 'Secret 6' as Reform Racket; Calls Randolph Charges Utterly False," *Chicago Tribune*, October 26, 1932, 3.

12. "'Secret Six' for Democrat; Swanson's Record Failes To Satisfy Chicago Agency," *Kansas City (MO) Star*, October 25, 1932, 1.

13. "Secret Six is Accused in Bribery; Prosecutor Probes Charge Investigators Bribed State's Attorney Employee," *Scranton (PA) Times*, October 27, 1932, 2.

14. "Bootlegging Easy Avenue for Criminals," *Chillicothe (MO) Constitution Tribune*, October 26, 1932, 1.

15. "Secret 6 Heads to Face Grand Jurors Today; Randolph and Jamie Get Subpoenas," *Chicago Tribune*, October 27, 1932, 1.

16. "Jury Quizzing for Secret Six Heads Ordered; Swanson Objects to Randolph's Charges and Prepares To Conduct Investigation," *Rock Island (IL) Argus*, October 26, 1932, 4.

17. Story compiled from the following sources: "Husband Accuses Mother of Three of Infidelity Then Shoots Youth" *Evansville (IN) Press*, September 1, 1922, 2. "Victim of Irate Husband Deserted; Woman Repudiates Boy Shot in Fight," *San Francisco Chronicle*, September 4, 1922, 5. "Rich Hubby Shoots Lad Over Wife," *Arlington (NE) Review-Herald*, September 7, 1922, 3; "Youth of 19-Years Shot by Husband of Woman He Loved; She Is His Senior by 13 Years," *Buffalo (NY) Evening Times*, September 8, 1922, 9.

18. "Jurors Order Showdown for Secret 6 Today; Quiz Randolph, Jamie and Shirley Kub," *Chicago Tribune*, October 28, 1932, 6.

19. "Investigator Names in Secret Six Probe," *Appleton (WI) Post-Crescent*, October 28, 1932, 1; and "Swanson Plans to Prosecute Secret 6 Trio; Police Fail to Find Office Briber," *Chicago Tribune*, October 29, 1932, 1.

20. "Plans Action Against Head of Secret 6." *Jacksonville (IL) Daily Journal*, October 29, 1932, 1.

21. "Swanson Plans to Prosecute Secret 6 Trio; Police Fail to Find Office Briber," *Chicago Tribune*, October 29, 1932, 1.

22. "George Mueller Gets Two Years," *Streator (IL) Daily Times-Press*, February 11, 1932, 1.

23. "Swanson Plans to Prosecute Secret 6 Trio; Police Fail to Find Office Briber," *Chicago Tribune*, October 29, 1932, 1.

24. O. A. Mather, "Business News Mixed; Future Still Uncertain," *Chicago Tribune*, February 26, 1930, 23, 26.

25. "'Secret Six' Described; Speaker Who Led Chicago Clean Up Talks Here," *Tacoma (WA) News-Tribune*, March 16, 1943.

26. N. D. Kannibelle, "Samuel Insull, Utility Prince, Now Penniless." *Chattanooga (TN) Times*, July 31, 1932, 28.

27. "Swanson Acts for Arrest of Samuel Insull," *Chicago Tribune*, October 7, 1932, 2.

28. "Swanson Plans to Prosecute Secret 6 Trio; Police Fail to Find Office Briber," *Chicago Tribune*, October 29, 1932, 1.

29. "Swanson Asks Re-Election as Foe of Crime; Wants to Prosecute Tim Crowe and Insull," *Chicago Tribune*, November 3, 1932, 4.

30. "Randolph and Swanson Clash on New Charges," *Chicago Tribune*, November 3, 1932, 1, 10.

31. "Swanson Rips Randolph," *Chicago Tribune*, November 4, 1932, 2.

32. "Grand Jury Indicts Swanson Accuser; Prosecutor's 2 Aids Absolved of Tax Fraud; Unproven Charges Are Condemned," *Chicago Tribune*, November 6, 1932, 1.

33. "300 Attorneys Criticize Fisher and Randolph; Pass Resolution Condemning Swanson Attack," *Chicago Tribune*, November 6, 1932, 8.

34. "End of Secret 6 Seen; Setbacks Hit Spy Service," *Chicago Tribune*, December 5, 1932, 3.

35. "Reveals $24,000 Fund Raised to Pay Randolph; Secret Six Head on Canal Pay Roll at Same Time," *Chicago Tribune*, November 4, 1932, 2.

36. "Swanson Scans Marital History of Shirley Kub; Suit Reveals Her Married to Two Men at Once," *Chicago Tribune*, November 1, 1932, 3.

37. Compiled from "Graduates from Eighth Grades; 203 Finish 8th Grade," *Herald News* (Joliet, Illinois), June 7, 1907, 13; "No Loiterers Wanted at Depot," *Herald News* (Joliet, Illinois), September 11, 1913. 2; Billiongraves.com, "Ned Ragland" entry, accessed May 2025, https://billiongraves.com/grave/Ned-Ragland/16900365.

38. Laura Walker, "Interracial Marriages in the US, 1850–2017," Tableau.com. December 4, 2019; https://medium.com/data-science/interracial-marriage-in-the-united-states-1850-2017-d6dfc3678e07, accessed June 2025.

39. "Former Husband of Shirley Kub Files Fraud Suit; Negro Seeks Accounting on Property," *Chicago Tribune*, November 2, 1932, 8.

40. "Negro Ex-Mate of Shirley Kub Sues for $60,000," *Chicago Tribune*, January 20, 1933, 7.

41. "Former Husband of Shirley Kub, Detective, Dies," *Chicago Tribune*, April 16, 1935, 23.

42. "Shirley Kub Files Suit Attacking Uncle's Will," *Chicago Tribune*, September 29, 1933, 6.

43. "Woman and 3 Men Jailed as Dougherty Leaves Safety Court," *Chicago Tribune*, March 5, 1938, 8.

44. "Legal Notices," *The Daily Sentinel* (Woodstock, Illinois), May 15, 1936, 2; *The Daily Sentinel* (Woodstock, Illinois), December 7, 1939, 3.

45. Shirley E. Kub v. Commissioner. United States Tax Court, 33 T.C.M. 1282 (1974). Filed October 24, 1974.

Chapter 27: The Secret Six on Trial

1. "Wants $100,000," *Herald and Review* (Decatur, IL), November 18, 1932, 22.

2. "Girl and Dad Fight Youth's $100,000 Suit," November 16, 1932, *Chicago Tribune*, 1.

3. "Missing Sleuth Surprises Court in Kuhn Suit: Defendant Dudley Appears to Testify," *Chicago Tribune*, November 29, 1932, 7.

4. "Decision Near in Kuhn Suit; Girl Testifies," *Chicago Tribune*, December 1, 1932, 1.

5. "Girl's Father Takes Stand in $100,000 Suit: Wright Defends His Acts in Kuhn Case," November 30, 1932, *Chicago Tribune*, 5.

6. Kathleen McLaughlin, "Kuhn's $100,000 Suit Due to Go to Jury Today: Argument to Be Wound Up This Morning," *Chicago Tribune*, December 2, 1932, 5.

7. "Story of Kuhn Evidence Told by Policeman: Quizzed by Lawyer in $100,000 Suit," *Chicago Tribune*, November 24, 1932, 27.

8. "Police Officer Takes Blame for Kuhn's Arrest: Lieutenant is Witness in $100,000 Suit," *Chicago Tribune*, November 23, 1932, 7.

9. Kathleen McLaughlin, "Kuhn Wins Over Secret Six: Youth is Given $30,000 by Jury in Arrest Suit: Debutante Cleared; 4 Ordered to Pay," *Chicago Tribune*, December 3, 1932, 1, 2.

10. "Police Officer Takes Blame for Kuhn's Arrest: Lieutenant is Witness in $100,000 Suit," *Chicago Tribune*, November 23, 1932, 7.

11. "Missing Sleuth Surprises Court in Kuhn Suit: Defendant Dudley Appears to Testify," *Chicago Tribune*, November 29, 1932, 7.

12. "Story of Kuhn Evidence Told by Policeman: Quizzed by Lawyer in $100,000 Suit," *Chicago Tribune*, November 24, 1932, 27.

13. “Decision Near in Kuhn Suit; Girl Testifies,” *Chicago Tribune*, December 1, 1932, 1, 8.

14. “Girl’s Father Takes Stand in $100,000 Suit: Wright Defends His Acts in Kuhn Case,” *Chicago Tribune*, November 30, 1932, 5.

15. Kathleen McLaughlin, “Father Accused in $100,000 Suit Blames Secret 6: Steel Magnate Tells Story of Extortion Arrest,” *Chicago Tribune*, November 18, 1932, 3.

16. Kathleen McLaughlin, “Kuhn’s $100,000 Suit Due to Go to Jury Today: Argument to Be Wound Up This Morning,” *Chicago Tribune*, December 2, 1932, 5.

17. Kathleen McLaughlin, “Kuhn Wins Over Secret Six: Youth is Given $30,000 by Jury in Arrest Suit: Debutante Cleared; 4 Ordered to Pay,” *Chicago Tribune*, December 3, 1932, 1, 2.

18. “End of Secret 6 Seen; Setbacks Hit Spy Service,” *Chicago Tribune*, December 5, 1932, 3.

19. “Secret Six Admits Financial Dilemma,” *Belleville (IL) Daily Advocate*, December 5, 1932, 12.

20. “End of Secret 6 Seen; Setbacks Hit Spy Service,” *Chicago Tribune*, December 5, 1932, 3.

21. “Police Officer Takes Blame for Kuhn’s Arrest: Lieutenant is Witness in $100,000 Suit,” *Chicago Tribune*, November 23, 1932, 7.

22. “Hastily Accused,” *Jacksonville (IL) Daily Journal*, December 4, 1932, 3.

Chapter 28: The Case of the Two Bombs

1. “Mailed Bomb Perils Wife of Solomon Smith,” *Chicago Tribune*, December 2, 1932, 1.

2. “Bomb Sent Through Mail Perils Mrs. Solomon A. Smith,” *Chicago Tribune*, December 2, 1932, 38.

3. “Mailed Bomb Perils Wife of Solomon Smith,” *Chicago Tribune*, December 2, 1932, 1.

4. “Attempt is Made on Life of Bank Head; Mrs. Solomon A. Smith Escapes Injury When She Opens Package Containing Bomb,” *Hinton (WV) Leader*, December 8, 1932, 6.

5. “Bomb and Intended Victim,” *Billings (MT) Gazette*, December 9, 1932, 8.

6. “Attempt is Made on Life of Bank Head; Mrs. Solomon A. Smith Escapes Injury When She Opens Package Containing Bomb,” *Hinton (WV) Leader*, December 8, 1932, 6.

7. “Police Advised a Month Late, Open Bomb Hunt,” *Chicago Tribune*, December 3, 1932, 1.

8. “Terrorist Flees Amid Bullets; Banker and Secret Six Try to Capture Extortionist,” *South Bend (IN) Tribune*, January 5, 1933, 2.

9. "The Secret Six Does a Flashy Piece of Work!!; Some Light Is Thrown on a Swell Crime Trap," *Chicago Tribune*, January 5, 1933, 5.

10. "The Secret Six Does a Flashy Piece of Work!!; Some Light Is Thrown on a Swell Crime Trap," *Chicago Tribune*, January 5, 1933, 5.

11. "County Orders Investigation of Secret Six Trap; Commissioners Denounce Planting of Bomb," *Chicago Tribune*, January 11, 1933, 4.

12. "Secret Six Trap Just a Salute, Jamie Explains; Defends His Bomb at County Meeting," *Chicago Tribune*, January 14, 1933, 7.

Chapter 29: The End of the Secret Six

1. "Bomb Explodes in Doorway of Chicago Roadhouse Today," *Daily Advocate* (Belleville, IL), 1.

2. "Secret Six Is to Continue Efforts," *Daily Republican* (Belvidere, IL), December 6, 1932, 8.

3. "Crime Board Scorns Secret 6 Plea for Merger; Extra Legal Groups Hard Pressed for Funds," *Chicago Tribune*, January 10, 1933, 3.

4. "Secret Six's Fate Hangs in Balance Today," *Daily Times-Press* (Streator, Illinois), January 18, 1933, 2.

5. "Cermak Withdraws Policemen from the Secret Six," *Decatur (IL) Herald*, January 18, 1933, 8.

6. "Mayor Cermak Recalls Police from Secret Six; Claims Woman Investigator Intruding on Police Investigations," *Jacksonville (IL) Daily Journal*, January 18, 1933, 1.

7. "Cermak Recalls 5 Police Assigned to 'Secret 6' as Woman Opens Probe," *Indianapolis (IN) Star*, January 18, 1933, 1.

8. "Transfer Police from Secret Six to Active Duty," *Chicago Tribune*, January 22, 1933, 8.

9. "Secret Six's Fate Hangs in Balance Today," *Daily Times-Press* (Streator, IL), January 18, 1933, 2.

10. Oliver Sherwood, "Secret Six Group Handicapped by Political Test," *La Crosse (WI) Tribune*, January 25, 1933, 5.

11. "Solomon Smith Receives a New Threat Letter," *Chicago Tribune*, January 27, 1933, 3.

12. "Jamie Applied for Secret Six Incorporation," *Chicago Tribune*, February 21, 1933, 3.

13. "Secret Six is Cut Off from Funds by A. of C.," *Chicago Tribune*, March 17, 1933, 7.

14. "'Secret 6' Head Named World Fair Official," *Evening Sun* (Baltimore, MD), April 22, 1932, 1; "Head of Secret Six Will Boss Police at Fair," *St. Cloud (MN) Times*, May 9, 1932, 5.

15. "'Secret Six' Tactics Could Smash Dictators, Says Head of Group That Undermined Capone," *New York Times*, April 27, 1939.

16. Paul O'Neil, "Army Promotes Man Who Led 'Secret Six,'" *Seattle (WA) Post-Intelligencer*, March 17, 1943.

17. "St. Paul Police Ousted on Graft Charges; Chief Among 3 Suspended; 4 Dismissed," *Minneapolis (MN) Journal*, June 24, 1935, 1.

18. "New Trial Motion in Secret 6 Damage Suit Is Continued," *Chicago Tribune*, January 14, 1933, 7.

19. "Damage Award in 'Secret Six' Trial Reduced," *Los Angeles Times*, February 20, 1933, 8.

20. "Court Reverses $30,000 Award in False Arrest," *Chicago Tribune*, January 16, 1934, 8.

21. "Marion Wright Weds Wm. H. Towne in East," *Chicago Tribune*, February 10, 1936, 11.

22. "Carolyn Potter is Bride: Connecticut Girl Married to W. S. Kuhn Jr. in California," *New York Times*, November 30, 1936, 18.

23. "Man Ends Life in Hollywood Roof Leap," *Los Angeles Times*, May 10, 1945, 6.

24. "Mrs. James E. Walker," *Springfield (MA) Union*, January 28, 1965, 17.

Epilogue

1. Eliot Ness, with Oscar Fraley, *The Untouchables* (New York: Pocket Books, 1987), 11–21.

BIBLIOGRAPHY

Burrough, Bryan. *Public Enemies: America's Greatest Crime Wave and the Birth of the FBI, 1933–1934*. New York: Penguin Press, 2004.

Hazelgrove, William Elliott. *Al Capone and the 1933 World's Fair: The End of the Gangster Era in Chicago*. Lanham, MD: Rowman & Littlefield, 2017.

Hoffman, Dennis E. *Scarface Al and the Crime Crusaders: Chicago's Private War Against Capone*. Carbondale, IL: Southern Illinois University Press, 1993.

Merriner, James L. *Grafters and Goo Goos: Corruption and Reform in Chicago, 1933–2003*. Carbondale, IL: Southern Illinois University, 2004.

Ness, Eliot, with Fraley, Oscar. *The Untouchables*. New York: Pocket Books, 1987.

Stout, David. *The Kidnap Years: The Astonishing True History of the Forgotten Kidnapping Epidemic that Shook Depression-Era America*. Naperville, IL: Sourcebooks, 2020.

INDEX

Kevin E. Meredith first covered crime in 1985 as a general reporter for the *News of Orange County* in Hillsborough, NC, a historic town with its fair share of armed robbery, hostage taking, and theft. As an award-winning reporter at the *Savannah News-Press,* he covered the military, local education, and election corruption. Since earning his MBA in 1994, he has focused his professional life on the sale of computer technologies but has continued to write on diverse topics, including evolutionary psychology, history, and crime.

For Indiana University Press

Sabrina Black, Editorial Assistant
Tony Brewer, Artist and Book Designer
Anna Francis, Assistant Acquisitions Editor
Anna Garnai, Production Coordinator
Katie Huggins, Production Manager
Gigi Lamm, Director of Sales and Marketing
Alyssa Nicole Lucas, Marketing and Publicity Manager
Darja Malcolm-Clarke, Project Manager/Editor
Annie L. Martin, Editorial Director
Dan Pyle, Online Publishing Manager
Michael Regoli, Director of Publishing Operations
Pamela Rude, Senior Artist and Book Designer